NOUS·SOMMES·PRETS

College
MENTAL HEALTH
Practice

College
MENTAL HEALTH
Practice

Edited by
Paul A. Grayson
Philip W. Meilman

Routledge
Taylor & Francis Group
New York   London

Routledge is an imprint of the
Taylor & Francis Group, an informa business

Routledge
Taylor & Francis Group
270 Madison Avenue
New York, NY 10016

Routledge
Taylor & Francis Group
2 Park Square
Milton Park, Abingdon
Oxon OX14 4RN

Printed in the United States of America on acid-free paper
10 9 8 7 6 5 4 3 2 1

International Standard Book Number-10: 0-415-95119-4 (Hardcover)
International Standard Book Number-13: 978-0-415-95119-7 (Hardcover)

Library of Congress Cataloging-in-Publication Data

Grayson, Paul A.
    College mental health practice / Paul A. Grayson, Philip W. Meilman.
        p. cm.
    Includes bibliographical references and index.
    ISBN 0-415-95119-4 (hardcover : alk. paper)
    1. College students--Mental health services.   I. Meilman, Philip W. II. Title.
    [DNLM: 1. Student Health Services. 2. Mental Health Services. 3.
Students--psychology. 4. Universities.   WA 353 G784c 2006]

RC451.4.S7G73 2006
616.8900835--dc22   2006008390

Visit the Taylor & Francis Web site at
http://www.taylorandfrancis.com

and the Routledge Web site at
http://www.routledgementalhealth.com

Contents

Introduction

PAUL A. GRAYSON AND PHILIP W. MEILMAN

This volume is patterned after an earlier endeavor, *College psychotherapy* (Grayson & Cauley, 1989), written almost two decades ago—a lost halcyon era, or so it sometimes seems. Like its predecessor, *College mental health practice* asks practicing college psychotherapists, a cross section of authorities in the field, to spell out how they do this highly specialized work. College mental health is a distinctive therapeutic specialty by virtue of students' particular developmental issues, the distinctive characteristics of students' experience at college, and the influence of the academic institution on the mental health service itself. Who better to explain these unique features than a panel of expert practitioners?

That a lot has changed since the earlier volume was written can be inferred from the change in terms. *College psychotherapy*— and, still more, *college counseling*—sound almost quaint at this point, conjuring up images of relaxed professionals helping students confront their normative developmental challenges in peaceful, contemplative 50-minute installments. Today developmental issues are still germane, but clinicians must also brace themselves for suicidal and self-cutting students, substance abusers, eating disorders, psychotic breaks, and the chronically mentally ill. For a host of reasons (see Chapter 1), acute crises and chronic disturbances have become commonplace. (Whether the earlier days were quite so tranquil as they're sometimes portrayed is another question; those of us with long tenures can recall plenty of tense situations back then.) *College Mental Health Practice* seems an apt title to encompass the wide range of activities in which contemporary practitioners engage to assist their more psychologically disturbed and behaviorally risky cases.

What's also changed over the years has been movement in the direction of what we might call forceful interventions, therapists acting both *in loco parentis* and in protection of the institutional well-being. Decades ago, college mental health clinicians, mirroring the stance of the institutions they served, were loath to interfere in students' lives. The thinking was that fostering the development of soon-to-be-adults required treating them as such, like adults. This thinking was no doubt influenced by an earlier cohort of students, who had fought against paternalistic authority on many fronts—the Vietnam War and military draft, racial segregation and discrimination, unequal treatment of women, cultural standards, and sexual mores. For college clinicians back then, many of whom had been students during the protests, it was a natural impulse to respect students' autonomy and eschew a decision-making role in their lives.

Gradually, however, college clinicians, again in concert with their sponsoring institutions and also with several court decisions, have swung back to a more directive stance, assuming a greater sense of responsibility for patients' behavior and the campus's welfare. The rising levels of psychological disturbance are one reason for the shift. (A nationwide shift toward conservatism may be another.) It seems unconscionable to leave students to their own devices when the choices they make may be not only self-destructive but also damaging to the community, and moreover when inaction may provoke a lawsuit charging negligence. It's also true that more students nowadays seem to want adult guidance, and many seem to flounder without it. These young people are accustomed to involved—if not overinvolved—parents, and they expect something similar from their therapists—not "Let me figure this out on my own," but "Tell me what I should do" or even "Do it for me."

Students who make risky and dangerous choices do warrant strong responses. Nevertheless, the trend toward forceful therapeutic interventions does give rise to tricky questions. Just how bad or risky do circumstances have to be to justify switching from what May (1988) once memorably described as the psychotherapeutic voice to the administrative voice? How does playing an administrative role affect the therapeutic alliance and the process of psychotherapy? At what point should clinicians violate students' right to confidentiality in the name of protecting them? At what point should clinicians take steps that their patients might oppose in the interest of protecting the larger student community? And when, if ever, should the university's reputation, and the university's expectations of the mental health service, enter into clinicians' therapeutic deliberations?

Diversity is another hallmark of the current era. Far more than in the past, students today differ in race, ethnicity, country of origin, gender (proportionately more women attend now), sexual orientation, socioeconomic class, and age. These differences bear on students' college adjustment and their needs and expectations in treatment. Differences also mean that the old developmental norms for separating from families and forging an identity no longer fit across the board. All students are developing, but they follow differing maturational pathways. Meanwhile, beyond the campus, a similar opening up of possibilities is taking place within society at large. Ours is a splintered age, where people watch different television programs, listen to different music, read different magazines or blogs, cultivate different pastimes. People work in jobs that not only are changing, but may never have existed before. Divorce, remarriage, blended families, same-sex parents, and cross-racial adoptions have transformed our notions about family. So much freedom and choice, such ferment and change, leave precious few consensual guideposts about how young persons should mature into adults.

We can discern other noteworthy trends as well. Computers, cell phones, and other devices have become dominant in students' lives. College careers no longer follow predictable trajectories of four consecutive years at the same institution. Alcohol and street drugs are still used and abused, but now students also use, and increasingly abuse, medications. The cost of college has skyrocketed, forcing many students to work long hours to finance their educations, and instilling in them and their families a consumerist, what-am-I-getting-for-my-money mentality.

All these themes affect students' adjustment, find their way into therapy sessions, and inform the pages of this book.

About This Volume

College Mental Health Practice is organized primarily around discrete problem areas: families, relationships, depression and anxiety, academics, eating disorders, and so on. We are aware that this plan imposes an artificial order on what in practice is anything but orderly. The problems of flesh-and-blood students don't fit into tidy content pigeonholes, nor do they docilely conform to diagnostic guidelines. Yet one has to start somewhere. The problem-focused chapters each describe a significant area of undergraduates' concern and, taken together, give a rounded idea of what ails students and how therapists can clinically respond.

There is in these pages no overarching theoretical or clinical point of view. A diversity of approaches is represented, often within the span of a single chapter, and with a few exceptions most chapters emphasize practice over theory. Partly this is by design, since we asked the authors to concentrate on what actually happens in sessions, and when possible to give practical tips and provide clinical examples. (All cases are disguised.) But we suspect that even without editorial prompting the chapters would have had a practice-based flavor, since the overall therapeutic profession is evolving from one-size-fits-all, sweeping approaches toward interventions that target specific disorders and symptoms—evidence-based interventions. Beyond this, working day-to-day with students discourages any tendency toward theoretical purity. To work effectively with these quick-moving patients, whose symptoms and problems come and go and whose attendance in treatment is spotty, one learns to react quickly, flexibly, and pragmatically.

To reflect the heterogeneity of the field, we have sought diversity among our contributors. They represent institutions that are public and private, from different regions of the country, of different sizes and missions, including historically black, Catholic, and Jewish universities. Most are or were until recently directors of college counseling services, a few are staff clinicians, and several have worked with students from their positions within academic departments. All are distinguished observers of the college mental health scene. Not that we personally agree with every last point our contributors make, nor would they always see eye to eye with one another, and for that matter they haven't always applauded our editorial input. The opinions expressed in these chapters are, as they say, the responsibility of each author. But we view their differing judgments and recommendations as an accurate reflection of the state of our field as we grapple with difficult-to-resolve tensions and sometimes difficult-to-reach patients. We agree with Robert May's observation (Chapter 3) that in the absence of clear-cut answers there is value in raising fundamental questions.

While we have set ourselves an ambitious agenda, by no means do we cover everything that college clinicians do. We have not emphasized group treatment, or focused at all on career counseling, outreach, workshops, psychological testing, supervision, self-help libraries, informational websites, online screening tools, research, university committees, disabilities testing and accommodations, staff development, orientation programs, training of peer helpers, or consultations with faculty and administrators. For excellent coverage of many of these topics, the reader is referred to Archer and Cooper (1998). Nor does this volume venture into the pros and cons of independent mental health services versus services subsumed within the health service, or the implications of being led or staffed by counseling psychologists, clinical psychologists, psychiatrists, or other disciplines. This book has primarily set its sights on the transactions between therapists and students in individual psychotherapy sessions. This topic has proved ample enough for one volume.

We would like to close by offering some expressions of gratitude. Thanks to our editors at Routledge, who have been encouraging and supportive from the outset of this project. We wish to thank our authors for contributing their expertise and for good-naturedly indulging our bouts of obsessiveness and mulishness. Thanks to our colleagues and supervisors—far too numerous to single out—at New York University (P.G.) and at Cornell and Georgetown (P.M.). Their support has been vital, and we continue to learn from our professional exchanges with them. We would be remiss if we didn't also express appreciation to college students. For all that college clinicians may harp on their patients' crises and psychopathology, we remain privileged to work with such rewarding and interesting patients, and at academic settings, no less.

On the home front, we particularly wish to thank Li Rong and Martha and remember Julie (P.G.), and thank Alice, Anna, and Laura (P.M.). Finally, if we may, this is our chance to publicly profess our appreciation for the opportunity to work with each other. This is the third book project we've shared, and not only are we still friends but we'd do it all over again.

References
Archer, J., Jr., & Cooper, S. (1998). *Counseling and mental health services on campus*. San Francisco: Jossey-Bass.
Grayson, P. A., & Cauley, K. (1989). *College psychotherapy*. New York: Guilford.
May, R. (1988). Boundaries and voices in college psychotherapy. In R. May (Ed.), *Psychoanalytic psychotherapy in a college context*. New York: Praeger.

1
Overview

PAUL A. GRAYSON

Any clinician who comes to work at a college clinic soon discovers that college mental health is a world unto itself. To understand students, you need to become acquainted with the developmental issues of their stage of life, and also the quite specific stresses of living and studying at college. You have to understand individuals who are remarkably diverse, and not only in culture, race, sexual orientation, and age, but also in their presenting concerns, psychological health, psychological mindedness, and readiness for treatment. Outsiders sometimes wonder if it gets repetitive listening to the same old student complaints all day long. The truth is, you never quite know what to expect when a new college patient enters the office.

Clinicians new to college services must also learn to practice in fresh and flexible ways. "Therapist" feels too narrow and pure to capture the scope of the work. In addition to their more conventional role as counselors or psychotherapists, college clinicians are variously called on to do triage; manage referrals; provide reassurance, feedback, and information; serve as long-term supports and patient advocates; conduct consultations; and handle crises. "Sometimes," one clinician wearily remarked after seeing a string of high-maintenance cases, "this feels more like case management than therapy."

As if all this weren't enough to absorb, would-be college clinicians also have to adjust to a very particular clinical setting. Treating a college student on campus is quite different from seeing the same student in a private practice or community clinic. College clinicians must handle tricky phone calls from parents and deans, balance patients' needs against the community welfare, and judge when to make exceptions to therapeutic neutrality and confidentiality. Political acumen is an asset when one works on campus. Clinicians must ally themselves with various constituencies who don't always understand their methods or share their goals.

This chapter takes a bird's-eye view of college students, aspects of treatment, and the college context. Here, in brief, are distinguishing themes of our ever more complicated clinical specialty.

Students

Development

The traditional starting point for understanding students is their stage of life. College students are at a pivotal transitional point, leaving behind adolescence (and childhood) on the tortuous road to adulthood. Their in-between status makes confusion and missteps inevitable. Each student must find his or her way based on the contradictory guidance of parental role models, peer influences, media messages, school teachings, online sources, inner promptings, and trial and error. Seen from this perspective, students' upsets are, in part, normal growing pains. Adjustment problems are what you get during times of rapid developmental change (Grayson & Cauley, 1989).

Although academic psychologists have churned out elaborate lists of specific developmental challenges for college students, three overlapping tasks have traditionally stood out in importance. The first is separating from family (Blos, 1979), the final stage of the separation-individuation struggles that originate in toddlerhood. Now in college, students must further pull away from parents to be autonomous and engage in campus life. When they're not ready to let go, or parents won't let them, the unhappy result is dependency, detachment from college, and a general posture of helplessness.

Does the traditional separation narrative still apply today? Certainly, many students still struggle to break away from parents and stand on their own two feet. But many others aren't struggling at all these days, proudly calling their parents "my best friends" and keeping in constant cell phone contact. Some observers worry that such close ties are creating an entitled, pampered "nation of wimps" (Marano, 2004). Yet it is also arguable that ongoing closeness with parents is for some students a benign developmental variant; indeed, in some cultures it is normative. At any rate, not everyone is so lucky or unlucky as to be tied to so-called helicopter parents. Many undergraduates have been raised by emotionally distant, narcissistic, abusive, or erratic caretakers, or handed off from one parent figure to another. For these damaged souls, the task of separating from parents is complicated because they've never been healthily attached. Some of these students are all too practiced at pushing others away. Others do reach out, but in a clinging or clumsy fashion, or perhaps by staging suicide attempts or starving themselves, forcing their oblivious parents to take notice at last.

The second traditional developmental challenge for both adolescents (Erikson, 1968) and college students (Arnstein, 1984) is identity formation. Forming an identity is an enormous and rather nebulous project, partly a matter of forging a confident, accepting, inclusive, cohesive, resilient, and accurate idea of self, and partly making choices and commitments in regard to academics, career, socializing, sex, political and religious values, and cultural affiliations. Plainly, all this is a tall order, today more so than ever. The difficulty of forming a coherent and confident sense of self seems magnified when society itself seems so unstable and unsure, fragmented by a bewilderment of lifestyle and value choices. Identity problems are easy to spot with students who are markedly indecisive or rigid, self-critical or self-aggrandizing, self-involved or self-effacing. To some extent, however, no undergraduate is immune. Scratch the surface of a bulimic or binge drinker or suicidal student—or any student—and the same gnawing insecurities tend to appear: "Am I good enough?" "Am I lovable?" "Am I normal?" "Where do I belong?"

The third traditional developmental task is intimacy—achieving mature and satisfying intimate relationships (Group for the Advancement of Psychiatry, 1990). As with separation and identity, these days there seems to be less agreement on what the goal is. Plenty of students still pair off romantically and sexually, and plenty more wish they could. Yet many others seem fine without a steady boyfriend or girlfriend, preferring group socializing and "hooking up" to the old mating rituals of dating and relationships, or simply putting love and sex on hold while they tend to their educations. It's hazardous to speculate about which path is healthiest without knowing the individual student's motives and experiences. Intimacy problems come in many forms: shyness and loneliness, inability to commit, sexual concerns, couples' problems, romantic breakups, stalking, obsessive relationships, and abusive relationships. Indeed, if we count friendships as well as love relationships, intimacy issues are implicated in most students' treatments, whether or not they're a presenting problem.

Developmental issues underlie students' adjustment problems and inform our understanding of them. When we listen to students' accounts, it helps to remember that so much in their thinking is still new and tentative, and their relationships with parents and peers and their sense of themselves are still in flux. Developmental issues also inevitably affect students' reactions within the therapeutic relationship. Some college students are wary of starting treatment because it threatens their fledgling autonomy. Others are afraid to terminate, feeling emotionally unequipped to go it alone. Some dependently lean on therapists for all the answers, while others counterdependently reject everything they hear, as if the slightest agreement would compromise their autonomy. Students also may use sessions for identity building and relationship-testing purposes—trying out new ideas for size, showing off their vocabularies, asking for reassurance and feedback, or experimenting with assertive or angry or flirtatious or trusting manners of relating.

As for therapists' best response in light of students' developmental needs, there's no foolproof way to react to persons who are partly still adolescents, partly young adults. When possible it's therapeutic to treat them like adults, and so reinforce their autonomy. But not every student is developmentally ready (or culturally appropriate) for such treatment. Sometimes one has to be a guidance-giving, nurturing, limit-setting parent. One sign of progress is when a patient who formerly was pulled by parental responses begins inviting a more egalitarian therapy relationship.

The College Experience

In addition to the challenges their stage of life poses, students are also exposed to immediate stressors from the college experience. In certain respects undergraduate conditions may foster psychological development, in others they may postpone adult responsibilities, but either way the daily hassles of being a student are another source of our patients' distress.

Academics   When students perform badly in their studies, family conflicts and psychological insecurities are often to blame. Thus, poor grades may be a mute protest against intrusive parents' interference, an academic collapse during senior year may stem from anxiety about graduating, and procrastination may be linked to perfectionism or low self-esteem.

But not all academic problems are psychological conflicts in disguise (Grayson & Cauley, 1989). The volume of work and level of competition at a given college may simply be too much for some students to handle. And just as emotional problems can sabotage studies, study problems can roil the emotions. Resolving a student's emotional crisis sometimes calls for an academic intervention—reducing the course load, getting an extension, or transferring to a less competitive institution where it's possible to be a "big fish in a little pond" (Marsh & Hau, 2003).

Social Life   With the possible exception of themselves, no subject fascinates students more than other students. From a developmental and educational standpoint, this is as it should be. Students arguably learn more about themselves and the world from peer interactions than from all their courses.

But campus social conditions are not always benign. For residential students, it can be torture to share a cell-like dormitory room with a noisy, bullying, or drug-taking roommate, and even good roommate relationships can feel suffocating. The situation is especially oppressive for those who don't fit in socially or who feel economically or culturally out of place, the surrounding laughter and activity constantly reminding them of their outsider status. Commuting students, too, often feel excluded, shortchanged on the full college experience. Students who study abroad face not only the usual undergraduate pressures but also the challenge of coping with a foreign culture and perhaps foreign language.

Campus society also heightens pressures to conform. Young people are naturally susceptible to peer influence anyway, but insular "youth ghettos" (Pavela, 2003)—dormitories, Greek houses, student apartments—aggravate the contagiousness. Not that peer influence is necessarily bad. On the contrary, peer influence can help students separate from families and pave the way to take their place in adult society. But peer pressures do push vulnerable students in dangerous directions—drinking games, pill popping, unwanted sex, restricted eating, purging, self-cutting, and suicidal attempts. More insidiously, competition with peers can reinforce vulnerable students' tendencies toward perfectionism and self-dissatisfaction. Sometimes the treatment of choice for self-destructive or perfectionist students is to separate them from their equally self-destructive or perfectionist friends.

A new, far-reaching influence on campus is the explosion of cell phones and text messages, e-mail and instant messaging, web logs ("blogs"), virtual communities, multiplayer computer games, and the like. On the plus side, these developments do helpfully bring together unacquainted students and keep physically separated friends and relatives connected, and for isolated students chat rooms provide at least an attenuated form of socializing. But electronic tools can reinforce social avoidance. Obsessed with computer games, virtual communities, or, most ominously, online pornography, some students hole up in their rooms at the expense of face-to-face socializing or real accomplishment. Also, students often relate on the Internet through aliases or false identities. While trying out different personas may be freeing and identity building, such posing is, again, no substitute for genuine relating and makes it easy for individuals to misrepresent themselves and deceive others. In addition, solitude and reflection are compromised with cell phones incessantly ringing (even in therapy sessions!), privacy is often violated by tell-all web logs, and damaging messages—hate mail, slander, threats of suicide or violence, electronic stalking—are as easy as clicking on a keyboard.

All in all, the contemporary revolution in communications, like the advent of television a half century earlier, would seem to be a mixed blessing for students' relationships and emotional development.

Self-Care   Many students trip up in their courses because there are no parents on the scene to monitor and nag. Now it's up to them to turn off the TV or video game and get to work. Likewise, it's the student's job to plan meals, manage finances, clean the bathroom, make the bed, do laundry, get exercise, take showers, arrange transportation, and get a good night's sleep. For young scholars used to being told what to do, self-care may be more demanding than taking French or calculus.

Unfortunately, the college environment isn't conducive to acquiring self-care skills. Regular sleep habits are hard to establish with slamming doors, late-night parties, and midterm exams. Healthy eating is complicated thanks to all-you-can-eat cafeterias and crazy-quilt class schedules, and financial budgets can fall prey to credit card temptations and cell phone excesses. Loss of control in any of these areas—academics, sleep, eating, finances, exercise, cleanliness—can be the first domino toppling other areas of functioning.

Self-care may also fall apart because of stress. Many students today juggle full-time jobs and full-time course schedules, or pile on course credits, campus activities, and internships. Their overloaded schedules are often necessary; perhaps they can't afford college without working 40 hours per week. Sometimes, however, stressed-out students do it to themselves. These are the undergraduates who can't, or won't, let themselves rest, whose sense of self depends on relentless self-driving. No wonder they can't sleep or eat well or that at some point they stop in their tracks like an exhausted marathoner.

Change   One of the most striking features of college students' lives is that nothing stands still for long. Every year brings new roommates and rooms, classes and teachers, friends and lovers. The span of a single semester ushers in a transition to school and a transition out of school, with academic peaks and valleys in between. So, if students are emotionally labile and impulsive, perhaps partly it's due to their fluid circumstances.

Students' lives change, but are the changes orderly? Past writings by various observers, including this one (Grayson, 1989), tied developmental challenges to certain pressure points over the 4-year college life cycle. Freshman year was said to feature separation struggles; sophomore year emphasized the identity concerns of self-examination and choice; junior year stressed different identity concerns—achievements and disappointments; and senior year again roused separation anxieties because of graduation. Aside from being tidy, this stage theory was appealing due to its explanatory power. Class year provided a key to students' underlying difficulties.

The trouble with this neat schema is that today's students no longer spend four straight years at a single institution. Instead, they often transfer colleges or even "swirl" among several different schools (Bailey, 2003), study abroad, drop down to part-time status, and take time off to move back home before returning to college later. Starting and ending college are still reliable milestones, but in the intervening college years we can no longer be quite so precise about when developmental struggles unfold.

Diversities   Along with their developmental status as late adolescents/young adults and the college pressures they face, a third defining feature of students is their heterogeneity. Many students are, in one way or another, members of a minority.

Recent years have seen dramatic increases in diversity on campus in terms of race, ethnicity, and country of origin, including a growing demographic of bicultural and biracial students (Choy, 2002). For clinicians of any background, this development presents a fascinating challenge. While diversity training, firsthand experience, and empathy go a long way, no clinician can be an expert on every culture, much less know every language. Inevitably, some meaning gets lost in translation. And quite apart from the particular culture, it's often a puzzle figuring out the source of a minority student's problems. Is the student struggling academically due to adjustment problems, lack of support structures or campus role models, the negative role of racial (and gender) stereotypes, "real life" family or financial stresses, poor secondary school preparation, or limited aptitude? Are a student's complaints of discrimination reality based or rooted in cultural or social misperceptions? In general, are the student's problems due to being a member of a minority group on campus, or would this same individual founder even back in his or her home community?

It's a truism that every group (and every individual) is unique, but it's also true that different minority groups face similar struggles. An African American from a working-class background, an Indian international, a "1.5 generation" Korean American, and an Orthodox Jew may have more in common than they realize. One familiar theme for all minority-group members is feeling different from other students. (Of course, middle class whites can feel that way too.) Another is feeling different, and at times estranged, from their parents, punctuated by clashes over dating choices, an academic major, religious practices, and plans after college. These are the usual late-adolescent battlegrounds anyway, but the conflicts tend to be fiercer now for minority-group students because the generations' positions tend to be further apart, with parents sometimes issuing ultimatums: "Stop dating him (or her), or you're barred from the family." In addition to the external conflicts with parents or their peers at school, students often experience fierce internal conflicts, feeling torn between cultures. The greater the gap between a student's past and present, between the original culture and the cultural values and practices prevalent on campus, the more wrenching the student's internal struggle.

College students have also dramatically diversified in regard to sexual orientation and gender identity. Of course, it's impossible to quantify sexual diversity historically, since at one time lesbian, gay, bisexual, and transgender (LGBT) students hid their identities for fear of expulsion. Even the campus mental health office wasn't safe back then, when "sexual deviation" was considered a "basic character disorder" (Blaine & McArthur, 1971). Today, by contrast, the *Princeton Review* lists colleges that are most accepting of the gay community, and almost every school has some office or club for LGBT students. Many students, LGBT or straight, seem nonchalant about whom they sleep with and how they identify themselves.

Yet being a sexual minority is still not a ho-hum issue. Discrimination, harassment, and rejection have not disappeared in society or on campuses (Rhoads, 1994), and neither have students' internalized negative feelings and identity struggles. Coming out to parents still sometimes courts emotional rejection and financial cutoffs. Even on tolerant campuses, sexual and gender minorities can have trouble making friends and finding partners. As for students who are unsure about their desires or identity, this uncertainty can feel intolerable, driving some confused individuals to declare their identity or sexually experiment before they are ready.

Still another rapidly expanding campus population includes older students. In many ways, nontraditionally aged students differ from their younger classmates just as one would expect. They tend to live off-campus and to be emotionally closer to spouses and partners than to classmates or parents. They generally have more perspective than younger classmates, are less impulsive and prickly with authorities, and are simply less like teenagers. In sessions, they may talk about marital problems, mortgage payments, child rearing, baldness—not your usual college counseling material.

But college has a way of bringing out the late adolescent in everyone. Financially pressed older students may have to take money from parents or move back home, reviving old conflicts around separation and individuation. Dealing with professors re-creates parent/child dynamics too. Poor grades and the lowly status of being a student may lower their self-esteem, and choosing courses, digesting readings, and making career plans may prompt self-examination—all classic identity themes. In short, treatment of older students doesn't require a whole new skills set. Sometimes these relatively mature adults are uncomfortably wrestling with the same insecurities as 20-year-olds.

Disturbance   A final salient fact about students is that many exhibit psychological disturbance. Quite a few warrant diagnoses from the *Diagnostic and Statistical Manual of Mental Disorders* (DSM). Many, however, have short-lived crises rather than fixed disorders. Awful as they look for a while, weeks or days later they may be symptom free—until, perhaps, the next eruption. What their troubles lack in chronicity, they make up for in acuity. Everything seems to go haywire at once—sleep disturbances, feelings of hopelessness, missed classes, mood swings, substance abuse, self-cutting, suicidal urges, unprotected sex—and every symptom exacerbates the rest. But the good news is that progress on even one front—say, cessation of marijuana use or completion of a term paper—can bring quick across-the-board benefits.

Students' plasticity has been cited as an argument for the developmental model over the so-called medical model, for a normative perspective over a pathological perspective. But we shouldn't push these distinctions too far. If pathology is defined by impairment in functioning, subjective distress, and/or risky behavior, then with or without a clear diagnostic label a sizable number of undergraduates surely display pathology.

Are students psychologically worse off than they used to be? College counseling-center directors certainly think so. In a 2004 survey, 86% of directors detected an increase in severe psychological problems over recent years (Gallagher, 2004) (as had 84% of respondents 10 years earlier [Gallagher, 1994]), and the consensus was that 41% of patients had "severe problems." As corroborating evidence, a longitudinal study of college therapists' assessments conducted at Kansas State University from 1988–89 to 2000–01 found increasing numbers of students had problems in 14 of 19 areas, including depression, personality disorders, suicidal thoughts, and sexual assault (Benton, Robertson, Tseng, Newton, & Benton, 2003). (Substance abuse, eating disorders, and, curiously, chronic mental illness showed no significant increase.) The picture is no brighter from the students' perspective. According to an American College Health Association (ACHA) survey of 47,000 students, 94% had felt overwhelmed at least once in the past year, 63% had felt hopeless, 45% had been so depressed that they had had difficulty functioning, and 10% had seriously considered suicide (ACHA, 2004).

What is behind all the crises, acting out, and despair? Obviously, developmental strains, college stressors, and the pressures on minority-group members each play a role. So undoubtedly does the increased enrollment in college of chronically disturbed persons, thanks to new pharmacological treatments for psychiatric illnesses and to disabilities laws prohibiting discrimination against the psychiatrically disabled (Thomas, 2000). Though many chronically disturbed students succeed, some, unsurprisingly, fold under college pressures. (Not helping are their home doctors' loose follow-up plans, in effect: "Take these pills and call me over Christmas vacation.") Other theories for students' disturbances include chaotic upbringings and rising parental divorce rates, the psychological impact of terrorism and political upheavals, the unrelenting pressure to excel from kindergarten onward, and the alienating effects of technology (Berger, 2002; Sharpe, 2002; Silverman, 2004; Sontag, 2002). We can also speculate about the impact of soulless and attention-deficient popular entertainments, rampant consumerism, and the splintering of society into relatively isolated subgroups. Plausible explanations for students' distress are not hard to generate.

Whatever the causes, something is deeply upsetting many of our students, and the pressure on college mental health services has grown commensurately.

Aspects of Treatment

Treatment on the Fly

The larger the institution, the more likely it limits the number of counseling sessions (Gallagher, 2004). But even without formal session limits, most schools have a short-term approach anyway, due to financial restraints and bulging caseloads that have grown dramatically in recent years (Arehart-Treichel, 2002). Offering unlimited sessions is a luxury few colleges can afford. Of course, the academic calendar imposes its own time restrictions on treatment, allowing a maximum of 15 or 16 weeks of uninterrupted sessions over a semester.

There are college therapists who endorse brief therapy as the treatment of choice for most students (e.g., Steenbarger, 1992), and therapists who decry session limits (Whitaker, 1994; Wolgast, Lambert, & Puschner, 2003). But in practice, session limit debates are beside the point, because usually the student has the final say about the course of therapy. Yes, some patients do show up dutifully until the semester ends or a session limit is reached. But quite a few students come for only a session or two, dropping out for any number of reasons, not necessarily from dissatisfaction. Many others pursue idiosyncratic treatment courses—no-showing and rescheduling, frequenting walk-in hours or demanding emergency appointments, shopping around for clinicians, perhaps vanishing and reappearing unpredictably over their college career. Their treatment is more akin to random drop-in sessions than a coherent and consistent course of therapy.

Such erratic therapy patterns make sense if you're a student. Going to the campus therapist is usually not a commitment to ongoing therapy, but rather a snap decision to get symptom relief, or, as Webb, Widseth, and Bushnell (1991) point out, a short-lived desire to explore within. Just as they make appointments with academic advisors and campus physicians on an as-needed basis, students check in with clinicians when something's amiss. If you're a therapist, though, haphazard scheduling is a tough way to do business. You can't count on a set number of sessions to develop a relationship, conduct a full evaluation, define and later work toward treatment goals, and build toward an orderly termination. There's no time for an assessment period prior to a treatment period. Every session has to be helpful in its own right, since it may be the last (Grayson, 2002).

Because students are chameleons, you also can't count on a stable clinical picture. An apparent crippling depression may quickly morph into a less serious adjustment problem, or vice versa. A treatment focused on a parent's death may soon veer off into friendship problems and career direction and self-esteem. Students' clinical fluidity calls for great therapeutic flexibility. To meet students where they are and make them feel heard, therapists must be prepared to respond to whatever is currently important to them, which may have little to do with last week's topic or mood. Yet, in order to be more than just a supportive presence or problem-solving consultant, therapists also want to show the connections between apparently remote topics, directing students' attention to core themes or pervasive patterns. Ideally, clinicians attend to the trees while helping students discover the forest.

Crises

If colleges had their way, crises would be prevented before they ever happened. That is the idea behind educational programs teaching healthful habits such as stress management, letters to incoming students and parents describing campus support services, outreach programs targeting underserved and vulnerable populations, screening days for depression and other disorders, training initiatives teaching campus personnel to identify and refer high-risk students (Arenson, 2004), and online educational and assessment tools to reach otherwise hard-to-reach students. Though all these prevention efforts are worthwhile, it's impossible to know just how much they actually prevent, since you can't tally the number of crises that don't happen or confidently measure trends for a rare event like completed suicides on a single campus. No matter; prevention programs, like therapists, do what they can. We know anecdotally that mental health efforts prevent crises and tragedies—just as we know that no program can ever eliminate them.

When crises do happen or are on the verge of happening, enter the counseling service. In the eyes of the campus community, nothing the service undertakes is more important. Nothing is more difficult, either. People want black and white answers in crises—is the student safe or not?—but undergraduates' behavior is notoriously hard to predict (as are suicidal and homicidal behaviors at any age). Often, a suicide attempt, alcohol intoxication, or drug episode comes out of the blue, surprising and confusing even the student: "I never did that before. It just happened." What's more, students in crisis don't necessarily welcome assistance. Some have to be practically strong-armed in by parents, deans, or residence hall administrators. As for what to do with them, the various crisis management measures all have benefits and costs. Every intervention meant to protect a student is a judgment call that runs some risk of making matters worse.

Crisis measures fall along a continuum of aggressiveness, from therapy-as-usual to radical interventions. On the quiet end of the scale are steps taken within the confines of the therapeutic relationship—in-depth assessments of safety, problem solving, support, discussion of coping skills, possible arrangements for between-session contacts, and safety contracts. (Opinions differ as to whether and when safety contracts work.) Such steps may be just what, and all, the crisis-ridden student needs. At the same time, it takes nerve to place full trust in such steps. You have to rely on your judgment about the student, endure uncertainty, and brace yourself for second-guessing if the plan backfires. For the college clinician, restless nights after letting a shaky student walk out of the office are an occupational hazard. Are the student's safety assurances credible? Will he or she make it safely through the weekend? Will the campus wonder later why you didn't do more?

A somewhat more aggressive crisis plan is to bring in others—housing personnel, trusted advisors, families—for additional support and monitoring, and, not incidentally, a sharing of responsibility. Similarly, making a psychiatric referral, aside from the benefits of medication, provides additional monitoring and evaluation and the comfort of collaboration. Sometimes this step of bringing in helping partners is a no-brainer: why not ask an on-call residence hall director to check in once on a lonely and suicidal student during a long holiday weekend? However, including others in the safety plan can also have unintended consequences. Students may interpret the additional troops as a sign that their problems are too much for therapy or for their own resources.

Multiple helpers also can make for confused or diffused or divided treatments—especially with patients who are gifted at splitting. More subtly, the existence of extra helpers changes the dynamic in the therapy office. The exclusiveness, confidentiality, and privacy that are integral to the therapy experience are now compromised, or at least watered down.

Another tack is to mandate sessions, as in the University of Illinois's four-session program following a suicidal threat or gesture. Proponents would argue that there may be no other way to reach and break through the defenses of some at-risk students, and no doubt some mandated students do respond favorably (Pollard, 1995). Experience suggests, however, that enforced treatment can be grudging treatment, a going-through-the-motions until patients have fulfilled their obligations. It seems safe to say that students generally benefit most when treatment is their choice.

Inpatient treatment, a still bolder response, can be literally a lifesaver, providing medical treatment following a suicide attempt, alcohol intoxication, or severe food restriction and keeping students safe while self-destructive urges abate and perspective returns. Hospital stays allow psychotherapy and medication regimens to start and set the stage for ongoing treatment. Beyond this, the very fact of going to the hospital can be like a good slap in the face, jolting students and families awake after years of denying problems. The aversiveness of the experience can be curative, too: one taste of the emergency room or inpatient psychiatric ward, and some students' suicidal or substance-abusing careers are over. Sometimes even the little things make a hospital stay worthwhile. One student said the doctors and nurses seemed preoccupied, but the kindness of the aides and the poignancy of other patients' stories assuaged her isolation and despair.

But you can never know beforehand the lasting impact of sending a student to the hospital. Some hospitalized students aren't really any better afterward—many are in and out within a day or two, or aren't admitted at all—and meanwhile they're saddled with hospital bills and possibly shame, demoralization, and bitterness: "I came to talk about my problems, and you sent me to a psych ward." The ante is raised still higher with involuntary hospitalizations, which, though occasionally necessary, are as far from the usual consensual therapeutic arrangement as you can get. It's not pretty when burly men and women in uniform force handcuffed undergraduates into an ambulance. But again, there's no predicting. The very same students who were last seen wailing or cursing on the way to the emergency room may later return to thank the therapist for caring enough to secure their safety.

Another strong crisis response is to persuade students to take a psychological medical leave (the nomenclature, procedures, and conditions for this step vary across schools). In theory, medical leaves remove students from the stresses of college in favor of a supportive environment and permit reinstatement later when students are academically and emotionally ready. Trouble is, sometimes there is no supportive alternative; going back home, the obvious choice, would only make matters worse. And some chronically disturbed students are poor bets to be any more stable following time off and treatment; a medical leave merely postpones the problem of adjusting to college. Moreover, many students and parents resist medical leaves because of lost time, money, scholarship or visa opportunities, or academic work, or because they can't or won't acknowledge a problem.

In short, despite all the crisis intervention options, college clinicians are unable to pacify, or induce to leave, all the students who are risky and make the campus nervous. I shall have more to say about this stubborn reality shortly.

Medication

According to surveys of college counseling-center directors, 24% of college-counseling clients today (Gallagher, 2004) take psychotropic medications compared with 9% in 1994 (Gallagher, 1994). At one college clinic, more patients are on medications than not (Young, 2003). Why all this drug taking? Partly it's because more psychologically disturbed students are entering college, and medications have grown safer and more effective. However, these aren't the only factors. Family practitioners and psychiatrists have lowered their thresholds for prescribing medications to children and adolescents (though the warnings from the U.S. Food and Drug Administration [FDA] about antidepressants' suicide potential may arrest this trend [Mahler, 2004]). Limited insurance benefits favor medication management over costlier psychotherapy. Most important, the culture has embraced taking pills. Decades ago, college students recoiled at the suggestion of drugs, which surely meant they were crazy. Today medications are as unthreatening as cough medicine. High school and college students demand prescriptions from clinicians for their "chemical imbalance," and if that fails, they may get nonprescribed pills from friends, parents' medicine cabinets, or dealers for self-medicating or recreational purposes (Amsden, 2004); or, in the case of stimulant medications, they may use them as a study boost (Hall, Irwin, Bowman, Frankenberg, & Jewett, 2005).

The widespread use of nonprescribed medications is alarming, of course. But the prevalence of even prescribed medications troubles some observers as well (e.g., Whitaker, 1992). According to Carter and Winseman (2003), students today are overmedicated and overdiagnosed, and a quick biochemical fix for isolated symptoms and behaviors too often takes the place of understanding the "multi-layered messiness of human development."

As drug treatment has become widespread, college psychotherapists have had to adjust. To be a college clinician today requires knowing when to refer students for a medication consultation, and that in turn requires familiarity with the once often neglected or scorned DSM. Clinicians also have to discourage students who want drug treatment but don't need it, while encouraging reluctant students who do—such skeptics do still exist. And while collaborating on treatments is usually a positive experience, clinicians have to learn to work with prescribers. With conjoint treatments there is always the risk of mis-communications, complicated negative transference and countertransference reactions (the usual treatment dyad is now a triad), and frankly divided treatments (Grayson, Schwartz, & Commerford, 1997).

Most of all, college therapists have to educate students about the benefits of psychotherapy and, equally important, believe their own words, since therapists too can be seduced by medications' mystique. For most college patients, there really is no substitute for talk therapy. It takes skill and faith to get this message across to anxious undergraduates who insist on pills to make the bad feelings quickly go away.

Passing the Baton

Since many students need more assistance than counseling services can provide, a chief goal of college mental health interventions is making a referral (Medalie, 1987). Referring may not be the most intriguing or emotionally rewarding activity, but it's no small accomplishment. To refer well, you have to quickly engage and then disengage, and sell the virtues of therapy without overselling yourself as the only qualified therapist. Patience is required in working through resistances to ongoing treatment, identifying the right treatment options, if necessary enlisting parents' financial and emotional support, and describing the workings of clinics, private practitioners, and insurance companies. To make sure a student hooks in, it's advisable to contact the referral source beforehand, and essential to follow up with the student and therapist afterward. But even after following all these steps to the letter, the referral still may not stick. A certain percentage of students can be counted on to reappear after being referred out—once again the mental health service's responsibility.

Referrals have always been a struggle in communities that lack affordable and accessible treatment resources. When students lack insurance or have restricted mental health benefits, the choices are further narrowed. And scarce as community psychotherapy resources may be, psychiatric resources tend to be still scarcer, especially in rural communities. Where do you refer a student who needs medication management but claims to have no money? Too often, college clinics are caught in a bind, unable to serve every student on-campus, unable to find off-campus alternatives, yet somehow expected to manage the mental health needs of the entire student community.

The Campus Context
The Individual Student and the Community

Troubled students trouble others as well. They ruin suitemates' sleep and studying, disrupt class discussions, and make friends monitor their safety and keep secrets about their self-destructive behavior. They monopolize the time and exhaust the patience of residence officials, faculty advisors, administrators, and clinicians. If really on the edge, they jeopardize the entire student body—suicides prompt copycat attempts—and ultimately the college's reputation and ability to attract applicants. For college administrators, the thorny question is, At what point do these individuals no longer belong in school? When should troubled students be dismissed for their own safety and well-being? When should they be dismissed because of their negative impact on the community?

In the easy cases, these considerations are clear-cut and neatly coincide. The student clearly needs to leave school, and the well-being of suitemates and friends just as clearly depends on the student's leaving. Often, though, these considerations aren't so straightforward, and what's best for the community doesn't suit the individual. Though others might breathe easier if a troubled student is dismissed, the student may be better off at college than if sent away, demoralized and at loose ends, particularly in the absence of a supportive family environment. In these hard cases, college administrators must make difficult dismissal decisions, factoring in the community's welfare, the student's safety, the student's alternative living options, and the student's right, according to the Americans with Disabilities Act (ADA), to be in school despite psychological disturbance. These decisions are value laden, contentious, and slippery. It's too easy to rationalize getting rid of a difficult student as being for his or her own good.

As for college clinicians, the question is whether these sticky decisions should be their concern. Specifically, should clinicians dismiss at-risk and disruptive students by recommending mandatory psychological leaves of absence? Pavela (1985) and Amada (2004) have argued persuasively in the negative. With rare exceptions, they say, campus administrators should be the ones to dismiss at-risk or disruptive students, based on overt behavioral violations of the campus disciplinary system, not therapists, based on presumed underlying pathology. That way there's no danger of discrimination, since the mentally disturbed do have a right to attend school so long as they don't threaten themselves or others or violate reasonable community living standards. That way, too, clinicians won't be put in the ethically unsavory position of making administrative judgments about the students' rights to remain in school.

A well-reasoned argument, but in my experience it often falls on deaf ears. "This student has a psychological problem," dissenters say. "Who else should make this decision if not trained mental health professionals?" And in fact, there is a case to be made for clinicians' taking part in dismissal decisions, at least as consultants, if only to counteract others' knee-jerk inclinations to send a student packing. Because clinicians can see the clinical big picture, they are, at least theoretically, less likely than nonprofessionals to overreact to a crisis. Some colleges finesse these tricky dismissal decisions by appointing a team to make them, composed of administrators, a clinician, and a campus attorney.

The ultimate criterion for dismissal is still violation of community standards, and the ultimate decision is still the administrators', but the team approach ensures that clinical and legal opinions are given their due.

The Mental Health Service and the Community

In calmer times, college mental health services had to justify their existence within the academic community. The public relations challenge was explaining why an institution of higher learning should bother funding a fringe activity like psychological treatment. In today's climate of acting-out students and the negative publicity and lawsuits that follow suicides (Franke, 2004), the need for psychological assistance is no longer in question. Now college services have a different selling job: proving that their interventions work. More precisely, their task is to demonstrate effectiveness in curbing disruptions and averting tragedies.

But how, exactly? The normal activity of therapy, conducted invisibly behind closed doors, doesn't exactly project a robust image. To impress the community, the pressure is on clinicians to flex their muscles—to hospitalize, initiate contact with others around safety planning, check up on shaky students between sessions, contact parents, and yes, remove students from school. And so, despite their expertise, clinicians may find themselves bowing to external and self-imposed pressures and responding overaggressively to troubled students. Treatment decisions may be influenced by public relations and political considerations.

The irony, of course, is that aggressive measures initiated in response to community fears are no assurance of protecting the community. Sensing clinical overreactions, current patients may lose trust and be turned off to treatment. Other students, hearing about questionable hospitalizations and enforced leaves, may hesitate about coming forward for treatment. Ill-considered interventions may drive away the very students the community is most concerned about reaching.

Even in the absence of blatant overreactions, therapists who are distracted by community anxieties may be prone to clinical tone-deafness, lapses in empathy, and understanding. It takes one's full clinical powers to sit with suicidal, eating-disordered, substance-abusing, and self-cutting students. You have to be able to assess and tolerate risk and explore the motives behind the risky behaviors. You need faith in students' ability to eventually overcome their self-destructive patterns. But this mindset is incompatible with a mandate to keep the campus safe at all costs. You can't listen with the third ear while community anxieties are ringing in your head.

Decision-Making Power

Deciding on medical leave is hardly the only occasion when clinicians may wield administrative power over students. Clinicians may also join administrators in consultation teams to address behavioral concerns (Marsh, 2004). They may evaluate students' fitness to return to dormitories after a hospitalization or a reported suicide threat. They may communicate with professors about giving extensions, incompletes, or reduced course schedules; with the housing office about granting single rooms or release from housing contracts; or with judicial officers about negotiating disciplinary sentences. Sometimes it's others who ask clinicians to weigh in on these decisions. At other times clinicians pick up the phone first to advocate for their patients.

As for the merit of these administrative forays, it all depends. Clinicians' assessments seem warranted—although hardly infallible—in decisions about a student's readiness to return from a psychological medical leave or a hospitalization. And pulling strings to reduce academic stressors or change a bad living situation may be a clear necessity if a student's safety or well-being is in jeopardy. Far less compelling is the case for a therapist's intervention in mundane matters like course extensions or judicial sentences. One would think that an intelligent professor or administrator could (and should) make these decisions without needing a clinician's testimony. Rulings on whether students are fit to be resident assistants or to study abroad, even if students sign a release form for this, also raise questions for an office that, all things being equal, wants to preserve administrative neutrality.

On this last point, while sometimes therapists have good reasons to use their clout, generally they shouldn't. The accreditation guidelines of the International Association of Counseling Services (2000) require counseling services to be "administratively neutral," lest students refrain "from seeking services for fear that such information may negatively affect their college careers." Equally important, administrative involvements tend to debase therapy even for those students who do seek treatment. Patients may then slant material so decisions are made in their favor. They have less incentive to solve their own problems, since the therapist promises to do it for them. In a larger sense, they lose out on what makes the counseling experience unique—the opportunity to examine motives and patterns of behavior with an impartial adult who won't pass judgments or act on disclosures. For all these reasons, therapists should wield power only if it's clearly necessary. Otherwise, the best response for struggling students is to support their efforts to fend for themselves.

Confidentiality

College clinicians uphold confidentiality because students won't speak openly or even visit the service otherwise. Confidentiality and privacy are central tenets of mental health professionals' codes of ethics, mental health services' accreditation standards, and legislative acts, i.e., the Family Educational Rights and Privacy Act (FERPA) and the Health Insurance Portability and Accountability Act (HIPAA). There are exceptions to confidentiality, of course, which, depending on state laws, generally have to do with imminent or significant danger to self or others, court-ordered subpoenas, and suspected child abuse. But the essence of confidentiality policies, the way they're explained in informed consent agreements, is that these are truly exceptions. What's said at the counseling center, even the fact of going there, isn't shared with outsiders.

That being said, confidentiality, like administrative neutrality, has always been something of an uphill fight for college mental health services. Campuses are small and interconnected communities whose members find it natural to pump clinicians for information. Often the questioner starts with the disclaimer "I don't want to know anything confidential" and then proceeds to ask for just that: "Just tell me if he came in," "Just tell me if she's okay," or "I just got this distressing e-mail from her. What do you make of it?" The request for information may come from the professor or academic advisor who referred the student for counseling. Or a residence hall director, vice president, or dean may call, who can claim information on a need-to-know basis and may be in a position to help the student—and certainly won't appreciate hearing a priggish or withholding answer from a colleague or subordinate. (Again, college mental health services ignore campus opinion at their peril.) Parents call too, of course, and while their input can be famously intrusive and off-the-wall, more often than not they are rightly concerned about their child. Finding a diplomatic and helpful response to these various questioners without inappropriately divulging confidential information has been a perennial struggle for college practitioners. And deciding when to take the initiative in revealing information or when safety or community concerns should override confidentiality is equally confounding.

A trio of legal developments has put further pressure on upholding confidentiality practices. The first, the Tarasoff case of 1976, made clinicians more likely to warn potential victims about patients' violent intentions (VandeCreek & Knaff, 2001). Then in 1987, the drinking age was raised to 21, after which privacy laws were amended so that colleges could notify parents about drinking violations by underage students (Sontag, 2002). Now comes the Elizabeth Shin shocker, finally settled after a period of great uncertainty (Hoover, 2006), in which the parents of an MIT student who immolated herself sued the university for negligence. Particularly as a result of "Elizabeth Shin"—like Tarasoff, her name has entered the student affairs idiom—colleges are likelier now to notify parents and other campus personnel about risky students, even (if deemed necessary) without the students' permission. And while administrators and clinicians have different thresholds and criteria for divulging information, plainly the bar has lowered for everyone, clinicians definitely included. Fifty-five percent of counseling-center directors now report that it is legally permissible to notify parents if a family-dependent student is hospitalized—a whopping 22% increase over the prior year's survey (Gallagher, 2004).

The oft-repeated rationale for disclosing privileged information about a student is convincing: Better a lawsuit for violating confidentiality than a lawsuit for letting the student die. And better to protect a vulnerable student than respect his or her autonomy. But as with forced hospitalizations and forced medical leaves, this reasoning assumes that disclosing information makes students safer. Once again, that's not always true. Some parents play a toxic role when told about a crisis. And while some students may feel protected when clinicians breach confidentiality, other students lose trust in treatment, and so are at greater risk.

The problem goes even deeper than that. Once exceptions to confidentiality become established practice, they stop being exceptional. Pretty soon, more people on- and off-campus insist on their need to know confidential information. More occasions seem to demand it—the definition of imminent or significant danger is widened. Such chipping away at the foundation of confidentiality undermines the mental health service's credibility and ultimately its ability to reach students, as Hanfmann (1978) powerfully argued nearly three decades ago.

In the end, there are no absolute answers. Legal and ethical obligations and clinical reasons line up in support of confidentiality. They may also, along with community concerns and political circumstances, justify breaking it. In confidentiality matters as with other aspects of college mental health, the judgments only grow tougher.

References

ACHA. (2004, June). *National College Assessment Web Survey.*

Amada, G. (2004). The highly self-destructive college student: Some clinical, ethical, and disciplinary considerations. *Journal of College Student Psychotherapy, 18,* 7–24.

Amsden, D. (2004, October 4). Pop. Snort. Parachute. *New York Magazine.*

Arehart-Treichel, J. (2002). Mental illness on rise on college campuses. *Psychiatric News, 37,* 6.

Arenson, K. W. (2004, December 3). Worried colleges step up efforts over suicide. *New York Times.*

Arnstein, R. L. (1984). Developmental issues for college students. *Psychiatric Annuals, 14,* 647–652.

Bailey, D. B. (2003, December). "Swirling" changes to the traditional student path. APA *Monitor on Psychology, 34,* 36–38.

Benton, S. A., Robertson, J. M., Tseng, W-C, Newton, F. B., & Benton, S. L. (2003, February). Changes in counseling center client problems across 13 years. *Professional Psychology: Research and Practice, 34,* 66–72.

Berger, L. (2002, January 13). The therapy generation. *New York Times, Education Life.*

Blaine, G. B., Jr., & McArthur, C. C. (1971). *Emotional problems of the student.* New York: Appleton-Century-Crofts.

Blos, P. (1979). *The adolescent passage.* New York: International Universities Press.

Carter, G. C., & Winseman, J. S. (2003). Increasing numbers of students arrive on college campuses on psychiatric medications: Are they mentally ill? *Journal of College Student Psychotherapy, 18,* 3–10.

Choy, S. (2002). *Access and persistence: Findings from 10 years of longitudinal research on students.* Washington, DC: American Council on Education.

Erikson, E. H. (1968). *Identity: Youth and crisis.* New York: Norton.

Frammolino, R. (2004, September 17). China discovers the couch. *Los Angeles Times.*

Franke, A. H. (2004, June 25). When students kill themselves, colleges may get the blame. *Chronicle of Higher Education.*

Gallagher, R. P. (1994). *National Survey of Counseling Center Directors.* Alexandria, VA: International Association of Counseling Services, Inc.

Gallagher, R. P. (2004). *National Survey of Counseling Center Directors*. Alexandria, VA: International Association of Counseling Services, Inc.

Grayson, P. A. (1989). The college psychotherapy client: An overview. In Grayson & Cauley.

Grayson, P. A. (2002). Psychodynamic psychotherapy with undergraduate and graduate students. In J. J. Magnavita (Ed.), *Comprehensive handbook of psychotherapy* (Vol. 1). New York: John Wiley & Sons.

Grayson, P. A., & Cauley, K. (Eds.). (1989). *College psychotherapy*. New York: Guilford.

Grayson, P. A., Schwartz, V., & Commerford, M. (1997). Brave new world? Drug therapy and college mental health. *Journal of College Student Psychotherapy, 11*, 23–32.

Group for the Advancement of Psychiatry. (1990). *Psychotherapy with college students*. New York: Brunner/Mazel.

Hall, K. M., Irwin, M. M., Bowman, K. A., Frankenberg, W., & Jewett. D. C. (2005, January/February). Illicit use of prescribed stimulant medication among college students. *Journal of American College Health, 53*, 167–174.

Hanfmann, E. (1978). *Effective therapy of college students*. San Francisco: Jossey-Bass.

Hoover, E. (2006, April 14). In a surprise move, MIT settles closely watched student-suicide case. *Chronicle of Higher Education*.

International Association of Counseling Services, Inc. (2000). *Accreditation standards for university and college counseling centers*. Alexandria, VA: Author.

Joffe, P. (n.d.). *An empirically supported program to prevent suicide among a college population*. Unpublished manuscript.

Mahler, J. (2004, November 21). The antidepressant dilemma. *New York Times*.

Marano, H. E. (2004, November/December). A nation of wimps. *Psychology Today*.

Marsh, K. (2004, March). Emerging trends in college mental health. *Student Health Spectrum*, 3–7.

Marsh, H. W., & Hau, K.-T. (2003). Big-fish-little-pond effect on academic self-concept. *American Psychologist, 58*, 364–376.

Medalie, J. D. (1987). Psychotherapy referral as a therapeutic goal of college counseling. *Journal of College Student Psychotherapy, 1*, 83–103.

Pavela, G. (1985). *The dismissal of students with mental disorders*. Asheville, NC: College Administration Publications, Inc.

Pavela, G. (2003, November 19). *Student suicide: Institutional policy, liability and prevention*. Audio conference.

Pollard, J. W. (1995). Involuntary treatment: Counseling or consequence? *Journal of College Student Psychotherapy, 9*, 45–55.

Rhoads, R. A. (1994). *The struggle for a queer identity*. Westport, CT: Bergin & Garvey.

Sharpe, R. (2002, January 24). Suicide at MIT raises parents' ire. *USA Today*.

Silverman, M. M. (2004, March). College student suicide prevention: Background and blueprint for action. *Student Health Spectrum*, 13–20.

Sontag, D. (2002, April 28). A suicide at M.I.T. *New York Times Magazine*.

Steenbarger, B. N. (1992). Intentionalizing brief college student psychotherapy. *Journal of College Student Psychotherapy, 7*, 47–61.

Thomas, S. B. (2000). College students and disability law. *Journal of Special Education, 33*, 248–257.

VandeCreek, L., & Knaff, S. (2001). *Tarasoff and beyond: Legal and clinical considerations in the treatment of life-endangering patients*. Sarasota, FL: Professional Resource Press.

Webb, R. E., Widseth, J. C., & Bushnell, D. (1991). Further comments: Facilitating students' going into and stepping back from their inner worlds. *Journal of College Student Psychotherapy, 5*, 67–80.

Whitaker, L. C. (1992). Prescription psychotropic drugs and psychotherapy: Adjunctive or disjunctive? *Journal of College Student Psychotherapy, 7*, 79–82.

Whitaker, L. C. (1994). Managed care: Who cares about psychotherapy? *Journal of College Student Psychotherapy, 9*, 7–17.

Wolgast, G. M., Lambert, M. J., & Puschner, B. (2003).The dose–response relationship at a college counseling center: Implications for setting session limits. *Journal of College Student Psychotherapy, 18*, 15–30.

Young, J. B. (2003, February 14). Prozac campus. *Chronicle of Higher Education*.

2
Developmental Considerations

RICHARD J. EICHLER

A bright and intellectually ambitious young woman of 18 sought therapy, complaining of migraines, a nervous cough, social withdrawal, bouts of depression, and thoughts of suicide. She traced the onset of her most problematic symptoms to an incident 2 years earlier when her father's friend, whom she had known since childhood and with whom she had long enjoyed a warm relationship, made sexual advances, which she rebuffed. When she told her parents of the incident, her father confronted his friend, who in turn dismissed the young woman's allegations as a flight of imagination. Her father accepted this explanation and insisted his daughter seek professional help. When she recounted the episode to her therapist and went on to report that her father was having an affair with the wife of her would-be seducer, the therapist focused on how gratifying she must have found the older man's interest in her, as well as on her buried erotic feelings. After 11 weeks of this, she abruptly terminated treatment.

The year of this encounter was 1900, the patient was Ida Bauer, better known to history as "Dora," and the therapist was, of course, Sigmund Freud (1953). With this dismal clinical failure, we have one of the earliest recorded instances of the psychodynamic treatment of a college-aged patient. Notable both for its centrality in helping Freud formulate the importance of transference in treatment and for what it reveals of his profound misunderstanding of women—it has been called an "urtext" for feminist psychoanalytic critique (Chodorow, 1989, p. 221)—the case also highlights the hazards of failing to take account of developmental considerations in the conduct of psychotherapy. In treating Dora, Freud made no special efforts to accommodate to her youth, and, as Erikson (1964) was to point out decades later, neglecting the fact of her adolescence was a major source of his therapeutic failure. Freud famously ended his account of the case by wondering what kind of help Dora wanted of him.

What does any adolescent or young adult, as distinct from patients more firmly established in adulthood, require of a therapist? That question is the broad subject of this chapter. More narrowly, I will try to apply what we know about late adolescent and young adult development to the formulation of a distinctive approach to college mental health practice, which I take to mean the generally time-limited treatment[1] of students on the college campus where they study and often reside. The campus context and time constraints of college mental health practice distinguish it from psychotherapy undertaken with college students in all other settings and are integral to understanding the developmental opportunities—and potential pitfalls—of this special work.

The Developmental Tasks of Late Adolescence and Young Adulthood: An Overview of the Literature

Blos (1967) formulated the critical tasks of adolescence in terms of separation-individuation theory. He suggested that by disengaging from intrapsychic parental object ties, adolescents continue the processes that begin in infancy of differentiating and stabilizing self and object representations. This leads to ego maturation, a better-defined character structure, and less susceptibility of mood and self-esteem to external events. The loosening of family dependencies is prerequisite to taking one's place in the adult world but is inevitably conflictual. Even as adolescents strive to establish their independence, they struggle, if only unconsciously, to resist regressive yearnings to recapture the gratifications, security, and sense of omnipotence of early childhood.

Critics of Blos's influential individuation model contend that it emphasizes separation at the expense of the fundamental human need for belonging and connection (e.g., Galatzer-Levy, 1984). Marohn (1998) believed that ties to parents are better understood as transformed than as repudiated in adolescence, although it is a matter of some debate as to whether the separation-individuation model really suggests otherwise (Levy-Warren, 1999). In contrast to the developmental importance assigned to disengagement and differentiation in separation-individuation theory, Kohut (1977) stressed the lifelong need for *selfobject* relations—that is, for inner relationships with others who are not clearly differentiated from oneself. Thus, he described the developmental importance of transformative interpersonal interactions with parents in organizing self-experience. In childhood, parents ordinarily fulfill needs for mirroring and idealization but are inevitably de-idealized as adolescents develop sophisticated critical faculties and a wider breadth of experience by which to measure them. New selfobject relations now must be found for development to proceed (Goldberg, 1984). Therefore, undergraduate, and especially graduate, students may turn to mentors to help them organize and consolidate their own emerging "professional selves" and professional values.

Doctors (2000) recasts adolescent development as a process of attachment-individuation. Secure attachments serve as a platform for developmental expansion, while insecure attachments engender the familiar upheavals of adolescence in efforts to amend and improve emotional connections. Especially cogent to this argument is a burgeoning research literature correlating secure attachments with successful adjustment and maturation during the college years (e.g., Bernier, Larose, Boivin, & Soucy, 2004; Rice, FitzGerald, Whaley, & Gibbs, 1995).

In contrast to the often transient, fungible relationships younger adolescents employ to help diminish the intensity of family ties, during the college years relationships are increasingly substantive, discriminating, and valued for their own sake (Adatto, 1991). Thus, whereas Erikson (1963) characterized the pivotal developmental struggle of adolescence as one between identity and role confusion, he conceived of the struggle to achieve mature intimacy and to avoid isolation as the central task of young adulthood.

Erikson's (1956, 1963, 1968) account of the process of identity formation involved a reformulation of Freud's familiar psychosexual stages into a psychosocial progression in which the interplay between the person and the social surround is accorded far more prominence. The successful passage into adulthood requires that there is some correspondence between the young adult's conception of self and the community's view of the young adult (Erikson, 1956). Adolescents therefore audition various identity choices, seeking validation through the judgments of their parents, teachers, partners, peers, and other representatives of the larger culture. In the ideal, the conflicting identifications of childhood are variously discarded, altered, or subsumed under a superordinate, but "forever-to-be-revised" (Erikson, 1968, p. 211) "ego identity,"[2] which bridges the past and the future and enables a sense of authenticity and personal continuity (Erikson, 1956).

The identity of adulthood, in contrast to that of childhood, is of a mature sexual being. Thus, a successful passage through adolescence requires modifying the body image to accommodate the physical changes accompanying and following puberty (Blos, 1962; Greenacre, 1971a) and requires, as well, integrating new sexual feelings, experiences, and emerging sexual competencies.

According to Erikson (1968), only with the attainment of a cohesive identity is true intimacy possible; until then, intimacy, with its unconscious undercurrents of fusion and loss of boundaries, is too threatening. However, Erikson's description of the progression from adolescence to adulthood better fits the course of male development than female, since, as he acknowledged, intimacy and identity are typically interwoven for women. Gilligan (1982, p. 164) found that women define themselves through "relationships of intimacy and care," and proposed that a more appropriate characterization of the transitional phase to adulthood, which subsumes both male and female developmental issues, is "integrity vs. care." By this, she described the conflict between compromising in order to preserve relationships, on the one hand, and remaining true to oneself and one's desires, on the other.

A further transformation vital to the transition to adulthood involves the relationship to work and career. Pine (1985) suggested that just as in early adolescence sexuality is experienced as foreign to the experience of self, in late adolescence and early adulthood work is often experienced as alien to and an interference with the rest of life. As younger adolescents must integrate the biological and psychological changes attendant upon puberty into an adult body image, older adolescents and young adults must expand their self-image to embrace work as something they do for themselves and in their own way, rather than something imposed from without.

While the major psychodynamic theories attempt to articulate general developmental lines, how development unfolds along these lines will vary, of course, with variations in life experience. For example, adolescents and young adults of color, confronted with inequities, often have to grapple with complex, conflictual attitudes toward their own group and toward the dominant culture in their pursuit of a positive racial identity that still permits them to selectively embrace elements of the majority culture (e.g., Cross, 1995; Sue & Sue, 1990). As another example, children who express same-sex attractions often encounter silence, discomfort, or contempt in parents and, later, in age mates, which may lead these children to link a sense of "otherness" to their same-sex attractions and sexual identities (Drescher, 2002; Isay, 1989). This, in turn, may influence later adolescent identity struggles. Meyer and Schwitzer (1999) found that during the college years, students with minority sexual preferences are preoccupied, in a way that heterosexual students are not, with "confronting, resolving, and integrating *difference* from others in their interpersonal world" (p. 58).

I hope that this necessarily brief and uncritical snapshot of late adolescent and young adult developmental theory serves to illuminate that most psychodynamic formulations, however otherwise divergent, have this much in common: a psychological reorganization of some kind is a developmental imperative of adolescence, and the intrapsychic shifts of late adolescence can occur only within an interpersonal matrix. In addition—and this is an especially crucial point for the college counselor—virtually all developmental theories share the view that while failures in earlier developmental stages may complicate the passage through later stages, the restructuring that accompanies adolescence and young adulthood also affords unparalleled opportunities to rework and improve upon flawed adaptations to adverse developmental influences.

A Developmental Approach to College Counseling

The foregoing perhaps suggests a realistic mission and therapeutic orientation for college counselors. In an era when college counseling centers are challenged both by the volume of students seeking services and by the severity of many students' pathology (Benton, Robertson, Tseng, Newton, & Benton, 2003), few centers can provide the depth and breadth of treatment necessary for students to resolve deep-seated conflicts, reconcile to early trauma, or modify rigid self-defeating character traits. Efforts to assume these traditional therapeutic assignments within the time constraints of college mental health are likely to frustrate therapist and patient alike. What counselors can strive to do, however, is support and promote developmental plasticity at those moments of transition or stress when students are tempted to retreat from the uncertainties and strains of the passage into adulthood.

If the essence of successful development is internal reorganization, then hallmarks of pathognomic development are surely rigidity, unyielding attachments to the choices of earlier developmental stages, and lack of receptivity to new relational patterns. When development preempts new possibilities, adolescents who had previously achieved only tenuous adjustments are likely to deteriorate, and even those who had previously accommodated well are likely to struggle, in keeping pace with the new and changing sociocultural expectations of their age. In specifically concentrating on helping students weather change without resorting to fundamentally pathological "solutions" to life's challenges or prematurely foreclosing on further developmental possibilities, as counselors "we have to rely more heavily on the inherent restorative capacities that [our adolescent patients] bring to their psychological distress," activating abilities that are "often dormant under the weight of an . . . insecure future and an unworked out relationship to the past" (Noam, 1999, pp. 62–63).

This approach to college mental health emphasizes consistency in philosophy and focus, rather than in technique, and, depending on the immediate impediments to developmental progression, may suggest a range of quite dissimilar interventions. For instance, techniques that promote self-regulation and affect tolerance may be appropriate for students who are unable to manage the anxiety of transition and change except by recourse to self-destructive acting out. By contrast, treatment that challenges students' beliefs about themselves and their past may be appropriate for those who are in jeopardy of constricting their choices in life, as illustrated by the following vignette.

An exceptionally sincere and likeable 19-year-old student, Harry, sought counseling at the urging of friends, who were troubled by his increasing "negativity." In recent months, Harry had come to feel progressively more fraudulent and uncomfortable around others, and had withdrawn somewhat from his social circle. More and more, he was given to negative rumination on being essentially defective, unworthy, and fated to fail in life, especially in relationships. He had held these beliefs for as long as he could recall, but they weighed on him now more than usual, despite his record of unblemished academic excellence and his warm friendships in college. He had several girlfriends but usually broke off the relationship after only a few weeks, since he "knew" they would end poorly. Similarly, he had convinced himself that no quality professional school would have him and accordingly contemplated dropping out, since he could no longer "justify" the cost of his education.

Harry's depression began to lift after I invited him to consider the origins and functions of self-denigrating and fatalistic beliefs he had long taken as self-evident "givens." For example, I called his attention to the curious fact that he was most certain he would fail and took steps to ensure that he would, just when he had the most reason to believe in his own capabilities. Harry entertained the possibility that he might be guilty and ambivalent about "moving on," while his parents, both of whom suffered from serious psychiatric illnesses, continued to lead lives of desperation. He was able to consider as well the possibility that his appraisal of himself as unworthy might have been a childhood construction designed to justify his parents' erratic behavior toward him and, in turn, help him manage his anger toward them, stay connected, and maintain some faith in the world. He began to see in his chronic sense of futility echoes of the childhood experience of trying to make sense of, and influence, the more unpredictable and irrational of his parents' behaviors. Finally, he considered for the first time that his view of himself as damaged and helpless might derive, in part, from an identification with his parents and from the real worry that he, like they, might be vulnerable to psychiatric illness.

I suspect that at least part of what contributed to Harry's turnaround was that he was able to turn passive to active. Perhaps for the first time, he began to understand that at this point he himself—not a malevolent universe—was conspiring against him. Harry could now see that he was not merely the product of misfortune; as much as he had genuinely and unavoidably been scarred by what had happened to him, he had also actively managed his experiences in a way that offered him protection in childhood but which had now outlived its usefulness and instead become an independent source of his difficulties. Increasingly, he felt a sense of personal agency, like a person who had done the best he could with the very bad hand that life had dealt him, a resourceful person at that, who, now that he was older, could perhaps do something better.

None of this is to suggest that my brief interventions with Harry were sufficient to work through the trials of his childhood or to substitute for the longer-term treatment I urged him to seek when circumstances permitted. However, in revising his view of himself, Harry could reengage and profit from the rich developmental content of his college experience. My goal with Harry was just that: to interrupt his precipitous retreat from new possibilities into an increasingly closed-down world, in which a grim future was the inevitable product of a failed past. As Schafer (1986) has commented, short-term treatment can often help create a more coherent life narrative, in which personal strengths are recognized and feelings of helplessness, passivity, and unworthiness are dislodged "just enough" so that patients begin to "function in a somewhat more resourceful, adaptive, and happy way . . . [and] are then in a better position to invite and get more positive responses from family members and others in the environment, or at least, to end some of the dreadful interpersonal stalemates that played a part in their becoming psychotherapy patients in the first place" (p. 156).

Of course, many students arrive at the counseling center already significantly "shut down" due to some combination of biological and/or psychological vulnerabilities, and the counselor will have to assess whether it is possible to reawaken developmental strivings and resources within the time parameters and other constraints of the counseling center. If not, successful referral for more intensive and longer-term treatment may emerge as the goal of counseling.

Applications of a Developmental Orientation

In this section, I will comment on several frequently encountered clinical problems that may be understood, from one angle, in terms of the age-expectable transitions of the college years. In doing so, I hope to illustrate the application of developmental thinking to interventions both at the level of the individual and at the level of the organization (i.e., service delivery arrangements). I will draw freely from competing developmental models, with little effort at reconciling their differences, because it is a general developmental perspective, rather than a particular developmental model, that I suggest is most helpful in informing work with our college-aged patients.

Ambivalence about Treatment

Veteran college mental health professionals are almost all familiar with this scenario: A student presents at the counseling center describing a usually ill-defined, but urgent need for treatment, becomes intensely engaged within a session or two, and then abruptly withdraws from treatment. In fact, a recent study found that more than 17% of students seen at a college counseling center did not return after their initial intake and that more than 40% were judged by their therapists to have terminated prematurely (Hatchett & Park, 2003).

Of course, ambivalent attitudes toward treatment may be found in patients at all stages of life, and may arise from several factors, including social stigma associated with mental health services, the negative experiences of friends or family members with mental health professionals, and cultural barriers to care. In late adolescence, however, ambivalence toward treatment is often that much greater, reflecting more general ambivalence toward entering relationships with adults, especially those relationships that have a dependent flavor.

While it is rarely the intent of college counselors to promote a regressive, dependent transference, students often arrive at the counselor's doorstep already under the sway of regressive fantasies aroused by even the anticipation of treatment. Greenacre (1971b) has written of a universal primary transference, originating in the caregiver/infant dyad, in which the experience in infancy of being fed and nurtured is revived in an attitude of "expectant dependent receptiveness" (p. 628) toward the therapist. This mindset provides the unconscious foundation that allows one stranger to approach another with the belief, or at least hope, that needs will be recognized and met. Without the elemental foundation of trust it provides, treatment is nearly impossible.

However, because of its origins in the relationship between infant and caregiver, the primary transference may also be unconsciously experienced in late adolescence as a menace to autonomous strivings and inflame ambivalence about treatment. Ironically, some of the very qualities that make therapy compelling, such as the therapist's empathic attunement and compassion, threaten some students because of their resonance with early mother/infant relations.

From the perspective of theorists who regard continued attachment, rather than separation, as the prime motivation in development, ambivalence toward early object ties to parents, and by extension toward actual parents and other adults, is not an inevitable concomitant to late adolescent development. Rather, ambivalence, when it occurs, is better understood as arising from failures in attachment. For instance, for an overly controlled child or a child who has had to enliven and coax involvement from a depressed parent, attachment may come at the cost of excessive conformity to the needs of others, and a submergence of "true self" feeling states beneath "false self" organizations (see Winnicott, 1965). A yearning for connection may attract students with this sort of developmental history to counseling, while the expectation that it will prove impossible to be authentic and remain connected may lead them to recoil from treatment. From this perspective, ambivalence toward treatment is not a universal problem, but a problem nonetheless likely to be encountered in a significant portion of the college therapy population.

Age-specific preoccupations with consolidating occupational, social, and sexual identity may further intensify ambivalence toward treatment. Some students unconsciously fear that psychotherapy will define them as "a mental patient," now and forever. In the extreme, the irrational underlying syllogism goes something like this: "I see a counselor, so I must be sick. If I stop seeing a counselor, I will stop being a mental patient and will be well, so I'd best stop seeing the counselor."

Ambivalent about treatment, students may seek to titrate down its dosage. For example, some students resist weekly sessions, preferring to schedule appointments every 2nd or 3rd week, or not to schedule future appointments at all, but rather arranging sessions only as needed. While these arrangements often represent an excellent compromise, they frequently meet resistance from therapists whose own training, interests, professional culture, and identity may converge on an investment in longer-term treatments, and on the sanctity of regularly scheduled appointments, at least once weekly.

Many premature terminations occur because college counselors insist students commit to a structured course of treatment at an age when it is normative to defer commitments. Therapists invite a dependent relationship precisely when students are invested in asserting their autonomy, and ask that they become "patients" just when students need to be recognized for their strengths, not their vulnerabilities. While some students unquestionably require the predictability and security of an explicit long-term treatment plan, others do better with a less defined, more fluid counseling approach, which allows them a greater sense of control and does not force them to confront dependency conflicts prematurely. This is not to dispute the importance of setting and maintaining treatment boundaries. It is, rather, to draw a distinction between parameters appropriate to treatment models with adult patients in longer-term therapy, on the one hand, and college counseling, on the other. While most treatments are probably best structured along conventional lines, I am suggesting that it is a mistake to be bound *a priori* to a given set of arrangements in the college counseling setting. Inquiring early on about students' expectations of treatment and otherwise encouraging realistic collaboration in treatment planning may help temper students' fear of being overwhelmed by adult authority and of recapitulating in therapy earlier dependent relationships.

Even when successfully engaged in counseling, and clearly reaping its benefits, many college students pronounce themselves cured once an immediate crisis has been surmounted, despite the persistence of obvious underlying vulnerabilities. In an adult, such behavior might be appropriately characterized as a flight into health, and, of course, it may be in college students as well. In these cases, particularly when students are at elevated risk, it is natural to encourage them to continue in therapy to work toward preventing future crises.

In many cases, however, an abrupt decision to terminate counseling is best understood as an expectable developmental phenomenon, most effectively and appropriately met not with interpretation of resistance, but rather, with an invitation to return when and if a student likes. Afforded this opportunity, a surprising number of students will use counseling intermittently, attending a few sessions, disappearing for months or even years, resurfacing for a few more sessions, only to disappear again until the next major life transition.

Intermittent treatment is often more than just an accommodation to students' ambivalence. At times, it is the optimal complement to their efforts at individuation. Just as toddlers taking their first steps literally and figuratively check back to reassure themselves of their caregiver's continued presence (Mahler, Pine, & Bergman, 1975), college students best venture into the wider world of new experiences when confident of a secure home base to fall back upon in a crisis. Students who drop in and out of counseling sometimes are not so much resistant or ambivalent as they are adaptive in using their attachment to the therapist to support their development. Long gaps in treatment do not necessarily imply gaps in the therapeutic relationship, which may be very much alive for students during their absences from treatment. Students may draw sustenance from their therapists' constancy and ongoing availability, the knowledge that they are there to be found again when needed. For this reason, among others, when counseling centers find it necessary to impose limits on visits, as most do, I favor arrangements that allow students the possibility (though not necessarily the assurance) of at least a few sessions each year they are enrolled. Ideally, centers preserve clinical latitude to offer students an ongoing, if intermittent, connection. This may involve setting annual, rather than "lump sum" session limits (i.e., an annual limit of 8 visits, rather than a limit of 20 visits overall) to ensure that students do not exhaust their allotment of visits in a single year. Case management models that eschew strict session limits altogether in favor of administrative reviews after a specified number of visits may be more preferable still in preserving clinical flexibility and optimizing a center's capacity to provide developmental support.

Many students adjourn counseling by simply failing to appear for an appointment. This mode of termination may be an expression of resistance, or an enactment in which the therapist is prompted to seduce the patient back into treatment or to abandon the patient by failing to take up a heated pursuit, or, as I have said, may be understood in developmental terms. In almost every instance, however, there is aggression implied in the act, not only because it violates social convention, but also because separation is inherently an aggressive behavior. Whatever other forces may be at work, in leaving treatment, students communicate that at that moment they don't really have a need for their therapists, who are therefore diminished in value or importance. Even when a student's newfound readiness to go it alone testifies to his or her therapist's effectiveness, there frequently develops a sense of having outgrown or surpassed the therapist, having exhausted his or her capabilities. Just as teenagers often devalue their parents in an unconscious effort to separate, so too do many students devalue their therapists at the point of separation.

Because of the aggressive elements in separation, some students are unable to assert wishes to leave treatment directly. Unfortunately, when there is no opportunity to work through the aggression implicit in termination, students may subsequently feel too guilty or ashamed to return should life events warrant it. When a student vanishes from treatment, it may therefore be useful to call or write, affirming the therapist's ongoing availability should the patient wish to return later. The point of such a communication is, other than in high-risk situations, not to urge the student to reconsider terminating, but rather to convey the therapist's emotional constancy and capacity to absorb and survive the aggression intrinsic to the patient's leaving.

Centers that offer walk-in hours or provide quick telephone access to counselors[3] tacitly recognize the profoundly mixed feelings with which many students approach treatment. By drastically reducing or eliminating the waiting period between scheduling an appointment and meeting with a clinician, the center minimizes the opportunity for ambivalence to tip the scales against counseling. Informal satellite offices, operating on a drop-in basis and housed, for example, in undergraduate residence halls, similarly address ambivalence and impulsivity and promote access. In addition, locating therapists in non-traditional spaces helps normalize counseling and combat the stigma associated with mental health clinics.

Action Orientation

The tendency to revert to an action orientation is an age-expectable characteristic of adolescence (Blos, 1967, 1979). While acting out in adolescence is sometimes, as in adulthood, symptomatic of psychiatric disorders or of character pathology, often it is a transitory concomitant of developmental events. College is the first time many students live away from home and must manage impulses without direct parental supervision. The adaptive strategies of childhood frequently prove inadequate to managing the stimulation and temptations of college life. The situation is compounded as efforts at individuation lead adolescents to reject, at least temporarily, morals that feel imposed from without, with a consequent loosening of previously internalized social restraints (Blos, 1967). Paradoxically, adolescents' increased capacity for thinking abstractly about mental states can be a source of additional strain. Simplistic, but comforting, childhood beliefs about self and others give way to an appreciation of the complexity of motivation and of the moral ambiguity that may stimulate anxiety, inducing a temporary retreat from thought into action (Fonagy, György, Jurist, & Target, 2002).

Acting out frequently fulfills defensive functions during the teenage and even early adult years. For instance, adolescents may take flight into action as a defense against passive regressive wishes, or to assert an illusory sense of mastery over external reality (Blos, 1979) when their move into the more competitive social and academic arenas of college life press upon them increasing awareness of personal limits. Self-destructive and reckless behaviors may involve, in part, frantic efforts to maintain omnipotent defenses against the narcissistic injuries that are an inevitable part of finding one's place in the adult world. By self-mutilating, starving themselves, driving too fast, provoking fights, or exposing themselves to any number of other unnecessary risks, some adolescents seem to be trying to convince themselves of their invincibility, as well as proclaim their ability to do whatever they want to whomever they want (Novick & Novick, 2001). Recourse to drugs and other thrill-seeking behaviors may, as well, relieve a thirst for stimulation and enliven a self that feels emptied out and deadened when deprived of selfobjects, as these selfobjects undergo the revisions and restructuring necessitated by late adolescence (Goldberg, 1984).

But in its milder forms, acting out also serves progressive development. For example, by engineering symbolic reenactments of early developmental failures, adolescents sometimes call upon the greater internal resources now at their disposal to master the residual effects of the overwhelming situations inevitable in every childhood (Blos, 1967). According to Blos (1979), this is one of the crucial tasks of the late adolescent years: Mitigating the adverse impact of early developmental failures, conflicts, and danger situations is an essential part of transitioning to adulthood.

As discussed earlier, adolescents do not become their adult selves through calm reflection, but rather through trial action through which they seek validation and mirroring. This sort of experimental activity is ordinarily transitory and benign, but when the sense of self is fragile, reliance on action to affirm identity may become extreme. For example, some students rely on the pain and blood from self-cutting to verify that they are alive, or they self-cut in order to control physical pain and in this way assert autonomy when they otherwise feel out of control.

A challenge in working with acting-out students is to resist the unconscious temptation to minimize their potential for self-harm in order to relieve the anxiety of feeling responsible for their survival. Also quite important is taking care not to overreact to milder forms of acting out or to confuse the trial experimentation of late adolescence with pathological behavior. In fact, tolerating adolescent experimentation is a critical therapeutic activity, a point perhaps best made by Winnicott (1984), who wrote that in order to "feel real . . . not to fit into an adult-assigned role," adolescents need to antagonize and defy the representatives of the social order "in a setting in which their dependence is met and can be relied upon to be met" (pp. 152–153). This is not to suggest that all acting out is to be abided, but rather that adults, and therapists in particular, meet the challenges posed by adolescent enactments "rather than set out to cure what is essentially healthy" (Winnicott, 1984, p. 155). External pressures, such as worries about liability or negative publicity should a patient come to harm, may blind therapists to the developmental possibilities inherent in even mildly risky behaviors and cause them to exaggerate the hazards they pose. Countertransference may also cloud therapists' responses to adolescents acting out. For example, middle-aged counselors may envy youthful attractiveness and sexuality or be uncomfortably aroused by it and therefore unconsciously seek to stifle its expression.

The pathological elements in the more sensational forms of acting out sometimes overshadow the functions and meanings of these behaviors and become the exclusive focus of therapeutic attention. Notwithstanding the importance of managing symptoms, it is important that the ends served by acting out also be recognized and addressed. To offer a commonplace example, some college students resort to actions ranging from academic neglect to suicidal gestures as a compromise between aggressive, rebellious feelings toward parents, on the one hand, and wishes to command renewed parental attention and involvement, return home, and regress to a state of dependence, on the other. If these conflicts cannot be translated into language, students are at risk for continued acting out. Discussions of acting out almost invariably include some reference to "setting limits," although the term is rarely explained except by reference to the behavioral demands made of patients. However, setting limits is, in my view, less about creating concrete goals than about clarifying the terms of the therapist–patient relationship, particularly the limits of therapists' capacity to tolerate patients' self-destructive behaviors and the limits of therapists' influence over these behaviors. Adolescents need to understand that therapists are relatively powerless to stop them from hurting themselves if they are intent upon doing so and that they themselves must share in the responsibility for *trying* to get well. Perl (1998) has wisely observed that in assuming the role of quasi-omnipotent protector or selfless caregiver rather than the more realistic role of collaborator, therapists may unintentionally reinforce regressed fantasies and behaviors in their adolescent patients. Under these conditions, Perl notes that adolescent patients may become locked into hostile-dependent struggles in which they elicit attention and nurturance by self-destructive behavior while simultaneously expressing their autonomy and power by defying their therapists' efforts to keep them safe.

Externalization and Mistrust of Authority

Among the characteristic means by which college students seek at least a temporary respite from the ambivalence that accompanies the passage into adulthood, externalization figures prominently. By externalization, Anna Freud (1965) referred to the process whereby patients attribute one aspect of their personality or one side of a conflict to their therapists, whose "opinions" they then hotly contest. This defensive maneuver is prompted by an intuitive appreciation that it is generally easier to struggle with an identifiable external antagonist than with one's own conflicted desires.

The reality that they are capable of taking full responsibility for their actions overwhelms many adolescents and prompts them to externalize accountability, conscience, and judgment (see Novick & Novick, 2001). Consider, for example, the adolescent who demands that her therapist supply "one good reason" why she ought not to continue drinking excessively and engaging in high-risk sexual activity, when these are her only avenues to pleasure in an otherwise empty life. The act of asking the question implies the wish for a convincing response, which, in turn, suggests that these risky behaviors are not as conflict free as the student would like to believe. However, the student's wish is not primarily to be persuaded; rather, it is to provoke the therapist into containing and voicing her more cautious inclinations, so as to free the student to act out, with only the therapist rather than her own common sense to battle.

In the treatment situation, externalization often exacerbates adolescents' age-expectable mistrust of authority. Leaving aside all the legitimate reasons that youth may question authority, young people's wariness is typically founded in a fear of succumbing to an external agent of control at just that development moment when they are struggling to establish their own authority and independence. By exporting the exercise of judiciousness and restraint to authority figures, while maintaining psychological ownership of their more adventurous and independent sides, adolescents may contribute to the experience of authority as repressive, demeaning, and hostile to efforts at pleasure and self-expression.

A sophomore majoring in one of the physical sciences evidenced numerous symptoms of a debilitating major depressive episode, which caused him to stop attending classes and completing assignments. Despite pervasive fatigue and apathy, he was punctual to sessions, quickly became attached to his counselor, and expressed eagerness to salvage his semester. The counselor was therefore taken aback by the sudden hostility and suspicion with which he reacted to her suggestions of a medication consultation. He derided medication as a crutch that would turn him into an automaton, protested that he would not submit to "mind control," and entertained vaguely paranoid notions about the counselor's motives.

This ordinarily curious and open-minded young man could not engage the question of medication rationally. His fear that medication would alter his experience of self was consistent with age-expectable concerns with authenticity, which, in his case, were heightened by a long history of difficulty in staking out his own territory in life. He had repeatedly acquiesced to the wishes of his very traditional family, sensing that failing to do so would compromise family ties, but had done so resentfully and at great cost to feelings of genuineness.

Apart from his concern that medication might blunt his affect, reality-based considerations, such as fear of side effects or worries about long-term health consequences, figured little in the patient's reluctance to consider medication. Rather, his objections appeared to arise principally from unconscious worries that "submitting" to medication, and to the therapist who had suggested it, would recapitulate his submission to his parents' authority and would substitute one form of dependence (medication) for another (family). Beyond this, he experienced the counselor's recommendation of a medication consultation as a betrayal—as the introduction of demands into a relationship in which he had previously enjoyed the novel experience of unconditional acceptance.

Focusing on the student's developmental impasse, the counselor quickly came to understand the futility of trying to persuade the student of the potential benefits of medication. Not only did this replicate his experience of parental domination and fuel his sense of betrayal, but it also played into the dynamics of externalization. The more the counselor attempted to dispel his misconceptions about medication, the more the student bickered with her rather than grapple with his own ambivalence. Accordingly, on my advice, the counselor shifted her focus to some of the reasons he might wish to remain depressed, notably that while his depression might arise largely from biological factors, it had come to serve as a somewhat welcome, if ultimately self-defeating, means of asserting independence from his family, while at the same time eliciting their concern and care. As for the medication itself, she no longer tried to answer his objections, but suggested that as a student of science he was well equipped to research the literature and come to his own opinions. This stance helped the counselor disengage from a doomed "debate" predicated on externalization, and concurrently appealed to the student to activate his ego resources in the face of depression.

As adolescents often externalize conflicts, so too do many externalize responsibility for their troubles. During the long childhood period of dependency, it is natural enough to attribute responsibility for actions and even thoughts and feelings to one's parents (Novick & Novick, 1996). Thus, we have the familiar childhood complaint, "Now look what you made me do!" Adolescents are still on the road to assuming adult levels of responsibility for their actions and therefore are still prone to defensively ascribing difficulties of their own making to external misfortunes. A failure to make friends may be blamed on a cold social milieu at college, poor academic performance may be blamed on unreasonable grading, and so forth.

Until students believe that they contribute to their problems, they are obviously unmotivated to examine, much less change, their behavior. However, interpreting externalization is often a delicate clinical exercise, as externalization usually involves subtle distortions rather than gross misconstructions of events.

A gay Asian-American student had alienated friends and lovers by his entitlement, disregard for their feelings, and combativeness, and had been cited for several infractions of university rules. In counseling, he spoke bitterly of being stereotyped and ostracized on campus, and disclaimed any responsibility for his plight. Successful therapy with this young man had to begin with an explicit acknowledgment of the social realities of which he complained. Racism and homophobia are indeed sad and persistent realities and contributed importantly to his troubles. Before he could feel safe in examining his own participation in his difficulties, it was critical that his therapist affirm the legitimacy of his complaints as both an Asian American and a gay man. Only then could he see, as Sue & Sue (1990) have written, "that although many problems of minorities are rooted in the shortcomings of society, there is no inherent contradiction in viewing society as racist and having personal problems" (p. 208).

Prolonged Adolescence

Even under ideal circumstances, adolescents are ambivalent about moving into adulthood. Adulthood brings new responsibilities and anxieties and the loss of many childhood gratifications. It implies rooting oneself more firmly in reality and increasingly confronting the finiteness of life, as well as the finiteness of personal abilities and choices. As one moves through late adolescence, with every choice made, other possibilities begin to recede: Selecting one major effectively rules out all the others. Applying to medical school makes it less likely that one will go to law school or become a journalist or painter. Committing to a particular partner requires, at least for the time being, bypassing other liaisons and love possibilities. Moreover, with every choice, time passes. As young as they are, college students commonly complain of "falling behind" or having "wasted too many years."

For many, the concern with time is attendant upon a vague awareness that as they approach graduation, the era that Erik Erikson (1956) has felicitously described as a "psychosocial moratorium" is rapidly drawing to a close. In college, there is social sanction to defer adult levels of commitment and responsibility, so that students may try on different future occupational, social, and relational roles. However, the implicit social compact of the college years also requires that experimentation progress toward self-definition. The injunction to gradually delineate a future social and occupational identity is concretized in such events as pledging a fraternity, declaring a major, entering into exclusive relationships, interning, applying (or not applying) to graduate or professional school, and graduating itself.

For most adolescents, the privileges and pleasures that adulthood confers and the wish to fulfill social expectations more than compensate for the loss of the seemingly limitless possibilities of youth. However, some students, often those with narcissistic vulnerabilities, are less equipped to surrender the open-endedness of adolescence. For them, all choices fall short; all realistic options pale beside the grand aspirations and self-idealization of their childhood fantasies (Blos, 1979).

Often these students seek socially sanctioned means of extending the developmental moratorium of the college years. Graduate study, undertaken not out of conviction that one has found one's life calling, but precisely because one has not, represents one of the more common and generally benign means of extending the inconclusiveness of the adolescent years. Some graduate students founder, however, upon discovering demands for focus, specialization, and dedication that outstrip those encountered in college and that are antithetical to the longing to remain uncommitted.

In its most extreme and pathological forms, prolonged adolescence entails an overriding dedication to remaining unsettled. These young people make repeated and ultimately haphazard and futile attempts at new beginnings but refuse to relinquish the gratifications of childhood and lapse into a state of perpetual neediness, restlessness, shame, and dysphoria (Blos, 1979).

Some theorists find nothing inherently pathological about a lack of resolution in late adolescence. In this view, selfobject relations are not supplanted by autonomous ego functions or by a fixed character structure, and the grandiosity of childhood need not give way to more attainable goals at the end of adolescence. Rather, selfobject relations undergo continuous revision throughout the life span, and the magical beliefs of childhood remain in permanent, if evolving, dynamic tension with more realistic ambitions (Lage, 1997; Marohn, 1998).

In a related vein, Noam (1999) wrote that the notion of identity consolidation, and by extension, that of an endpoint to adolescence, is the product of an earlier historical and cultural moment. Lifestyle choices are not as etched in stone as they once were. For instance, Noam pointed out that midlife career changes, geographic relocations, divorce, remarriage, and childbearing and adoption later in life are now all commonplace.

While there is clearly merit to these criticisms, they are best regarded as correctives or qualifiers that do not contradict the essence of Blos's notion of prolonged adolescence, distilled from its metapsychological and cultural framework. Although development surely does not end with the transition to adulthood, at the heart of prolonged adolescence is actually stasis, in which a frenzy of activity masks a determinedly directionless and stagnant way of life unconsciously designed to sustain the fantasy of limitless time and choice. Avoiding even provisional commitments may give the impression of receptivity to life's possibilities, but in fact ensures that all possibilities are rejected. Living one's life as it is and as it might realistically become is rejected in favor of maintaining a state of expectant, if futile, hopefulness for a perfect future.

The treatment of the most severe cases of prolonged adolescence often overlaps with the treatment of narcissistic personality disorders and generally requires referral for open-ended therapy. However, many students who present with the beginnings of what might evolve into prolonged adolescence, or with mild versions of the syndrome, may be excellent candidates for a developmental approach intended to avert a descent into limbo.

Chronic procrastinators and perfectionists, for example, may be on the way to consolidating a strategy for handling narcissistic vulnerability that foreshadows a prolongation of adolescence. Perfectionism and procrastination, although superficially quite different, often share a common underlying motive: to withhold work from the judgment of others and, in this way, avoid taking the true measure of one's capabilities in the world. That grandiosity is at work in perfectionism is evident enough. What is sometimes less obvious is that the perfectionist's endless research, editing, and revisions often serve the unconscious end of forestalling the completion of work and therefore ensuring that it is not evaluated (Philip, 1988). Similarly, completing assignments at the last minute affords procrastinators a prefabricated rationalization that disappointing grades are the product of insufficient effort (ibid.), thus insulating them from feedback that might otherwise disturb narcissistic overvaluation of their intelligence.

The problem with these strategies, apart from their obvious practical limitations, is that they are self-perpetuating. In failing to test their capabilities, perfectionists and procrastinators have little opportunity for realistic self-appraisal, which might otherwise serve as a counterpoint to childhood grandiosity and better align ambitions with reality considerations. When aspirations are not attenuated in late adolescence, real achievements generally wither in comparison, and thus accomplishment and mastery do not provide a source of self-regard (Blos, 1979), promoting an even greater reliance on grandiosity to regulate self-esteem, which leads to an even greater avoidance of discovering limits, and so forth.

In therapeutic work with students who "solve" narcissistic vulnerability by retreating from developmental challenges, it is sometimes productive to redirect attention from the pleasurable aspects of grandiose fantasy life to its oppressiveness—to the relentless and unachievable standards that follow from an unmodulated ego ideal, and to the tendency to sacrifice intimacy in the pursuit of admiration.

Of course, conflicts between autonomous and dependent strivings also frequently play a part in prolonging adolescence. In mild cases, students may become paralyzed by indecision in, say, declaring a major or deciding upon postgraduate plans, because of unconscious preoccupations with whether their choices are motivated by their parents' wishes or their own. Ironically, neither answer would likely resolve their dilemma, since, fundamentally, it originates from conflicting desires to individuate from, and remain connected to, parents, and from a developmental failure to discover a means of doing both.

Concluding Remarks

I would like to conclude by returning to Dora, and to the problem of technique in working with college-aged students. Dora came to Freud, we might imagine, distraught, disillusioned, psychologically orphaned, and in search of adult validation of her experience of betrayal and corruption. However, in single-mindedly pursuing the vicissitudes of her erotic feelings, Freud refused Dora the affirmation of historical actuality she required in order to legitimate her experience and restore her faith in adult society (Erikson, 1964). He denied her as well empathic mirroring of the person she was striving to become and a sustaining relationship with an adult who might provide the source of positive values and identifications she could not find in her parents or the other adults in her life. Instead, Freud may well have conveyed to Dora the same devastating message she had received before from the important men in her life: that all they could see in her was sex.

As Dora needed Freud to acknowledge the historical truth, when students complain in counseling of adult neglect, hostility, or exploitation, they require us, even as we listen for the transferential possibilities in their communications, to be equally attuned to historical actuality and to remain very humble about our ability to discriminate between the two. Fears of uncertainty, of failure, and of disappointing patients' hopes and fantasies place all therapists at risk for dealing in false clarity of the kind Freud imposed upon Dora, but college counselors may be especially at risk. Adolescence, as we have seen, is a time of reorganization and of a transient loss of cohesiveness, which may stimulate therapists' own fears of fragmentation (e.g., Lage, 1997; Laufer, 1996). This, in turn, may lead therapists to retreat from empathic immersion in their patients' experiences and to seek reassurance in theoretical "certainties." Moreover, as Schafer (1986) has observed, short-term treatment limits what can be known and accomplished, adding to the temptation to rush to conclusions. In addition, dedicated counselors sometimes feel guilty for "depriving" students of ongoing care and may attempt to compensate by reaching beyond the limits of their understanding and influence (ibid.).

While college mental health professionals understandably feel challenged by the genuine limitations of their work, this challenge may be met, in part, by managing the countertransferential barriers to recognizing and mining the abundant potential of the setting to complement adolescents' developmental needs. By applying a developmental perspective to college counseling, capitalizing on intrinsic assets such as the connection to the university, and thoughtfully rationing visits and other resources, counseling centers can formulate treatment models that are uniquely suited to supporting students in utilizing the richness of the college experience to foster their entry into adulthood.

Notes

1. The average duration of treatment at 339 college counseling centers polled in a recent nationwide survey was 5.6 sessions (Gallagher, 2004).
2. Schafer (1973) cautioned against the reification of concepts of 'self' and 'identity.' While I will employ these terms freely for simplicity's sake, following Schafer I do not mean them to suggest entities, but rather ways in which people think about and experience themselves. From this perspective, revisions in the sense of self or identity refer to changes in self-representations; in the consistency or inconsistency of the feelings that one has toward these representations; in the relative constancy of the representations, and so forth. True constancy—the state of self-sameness described by Erikson—is, Schafer argues, impossible, in that self-representations are subject to radical shifts with changes in mood or life circumstances (p. 52).
3. A small, but growing, number of universities have adopted systems that offer students telephone appointments with a clinician, usually within 24 hours after first contacting the counseling center (Rockland-Miller & Eells, 2005). Designed to promote early recognition of acute psychiatric problems, such systems have the incidental advantage of fostering an early connection with the center.

References

Adatto, C. P. (1991). Late adolescence to early adulthood. In S. I. Greenspan & G. H. Pollock (Eds.), *The course of life, Vol. 4: Adolescence* (Rev. ed., pp. 357–375). Madison, CT: International Universities Press.

Benton, S. A., Robertson, J. M., Tseng, W., Newton, F. B., & Benton, S. L. (2003). Changes in counseling center client problems across 13 years. *Professional Psychology: Research and Practice, 34*, 66–72.

Bernier, A., Larose, S., Boivin, M., & Soucy, N. (2004). Attachment state of mind: Implications for adjustment to college. *Journal of Adolescent Research, 16*, 783–806.

Blos, P. (1962). *On adolescence.* New York: Free Press.

Blos, P. (1967). The second individuation process of adolescence. *The Psychoanalytic Study of the Child, 22*, 162–186.

Blos, P. (1979). *The adolescent passage.* New York: International Universities Press.

Chodorow, N. J. (1989). *Feminism and psychoanalytic theory.* New Haven, CT: Yale University Press.

Cross, W. E. (1995). The psychology of nigrescence: Revising the Cross model. In J. G. Ponterotto, J. M. Casas, L. A. Suzuki, & C. M. Alexander (Eds.), *Handbook of multicultural counseling* (pp. 93–122). Thousand Oaks, CA: Sage Publishing.

Doctors, S. R. (2000). Attachment-individuation: I. Clinical notes toward a reconsideration of "adolescent turmoil." *Adolescent Psychiatry, 25*, 3–16.

Drescher, J. (2002). Invisible gay adolescents: Developmental narratives of gay men. *Adolescent Psychiatry, 26*, 73–94.

Erikson, E. H. (1956). The problem of ego identity. *Journal of the American Psychoanalytic Association, 4*, 56–121.

Erikson, E. H. (1963). *Childhood and society* (2nd ed.). New York: W. W. Norton.

Erikson, E. H. (1964). *Insight and responsibility.* New York: Norton.

Erikson, E. H. (1968). *Identity: Youth and crisis.* New York: W. W. Norton & Co.

Fonagy, P., György, G., Jurist, E. L., & Target, M. (2002). *Affect regulation, mentalization, and the development of the self.* New York: Other Press.

Freud, A. (1965). *Normality and pathology in childhood.* New York: International Universities Press.

Freud, S. (1953). Fragment of an analysis of a case of hysteria. In J. Strachey (Ed. and Trans.), *The standard edition of the complete psychological works of Sigmund Freud* (Vol. 7, pp. 7–122). (Originally published 1905.)

Galatzer-Levy, R. (1984). Adolescent breakdown and middle-age crises. In D. D. Brockman (Ed.), *Late adolescence: Psychoanalytic studies* (pp. 29–51). New York: International Universities Press.

Gallagher, R. P. (2004). *National Survey of Counseling Center Directors.* Alexandria, VA: International Association of Counseling Services.

Gilligan, C. (1982). *In a different voice.* Cambridge, MA: Harvard University Press.

Goldberg, A. (1984). Depression and the unstimulated self. In D. D. Brockman (Ed.), *Late adolescence: Psychoanalytic studies* (pp. 191–210). New York: International Universities Press.

Greenacre, P. (1971a). Early physical determinants in the development of a sense of identity. In *Emotional Growth* (Vol. 1, pp. 113–127). Originally published in 1958 in the *Journal of the American Psychoanalytic Association, 6*, 612–627.

Greenacre, P. (1971b). The role of transference: Practical considerations in relation to psychoanalytic therapy. In P. Greenacre (Ed.), *Emotional Growth* (Vol. 2, pp. 627–640). New York: International Universities Press. (Originally published 1954.)

Hatchett, G. T., & Park, H. L. (2003). Comparison of four operational definitions of premature termination. *Psychotherapy: Theory, Research, Practice, Training, 40*, 226–231.

Isay, R. A. (1989). *Being homosexual.* Northvale, NJ: Jason Aronson.

Kohut, H. (1977). *The restoration of the self.* New York: International Universities Press.

Lage, G. (1997). Self psychology perspectives on adolescents. *Adolescent Psychiatry, 21*, 305–316.

Laufer, M. (1996). The psychoanalyst of the adolescent. *The Psychoanalytic Study of the Child, 51*, 512–521.

Levy-Warren, M. H. (1999). I am, you are, and so are we: A current perspective on adolescent separation-individuation theory. *Adolescent Psychiatry, 24*, 3–24.

Mahler, M. S., Pine, F., & Bergman, A. (1975). *The psychological birth of the human infant.* New York: Basic Books.

Marohn, R. C. (1998). A re-examination of Peter Blos's concept of prolonged adolescence. *Adolescent Psychiatry, 23,* 3–19.

Meyer, S., & Schwitzer, A. M. (1999). Stages of identity development among college students with minority sexual orientations. *Journal of College Student Psychotherapy, 13,* 41–65.

Noam, G. G. (1999). The psychology of belonging: Reformulating adolescent development. *Adolescent Psychiatry, 24,* 49–68.

Novick, J., & Novick, K. K. (1996). *Fearful symmetry: The development and treatment of sadomasochism.* Northvale, NJ: Jason Aronson.

Novick, J., & Novick, K. K. (2001). Trauma and deferred action in the reality of adolescence. *American Journal of Psychoanalysis, 61,* 43–61.

Perl, E. (1998). Snatching defeat from the jaws of success: Self-destructive behavior as an expression of autonomy in young women. *Adolescent Psychiatry, 23,* 143–167.

Philip, A. F. (1988). Parents, sons and daughters: Growth and transition during the college years. In L. C. Whitaker (Ed.), *Parental concerns in college student mental health* (pp. 17–32). New York: Haworth Press.

Pine, F. (1985). *Developmental theory and clinical process.* New Haven, CT: Yale University Press.

Rice, K. G., FitzGerald, D. P., Whaley, T. J., & Gibbs, C. L. (1995). Cross-sectional and longitudinal examination of attachment, separation-individuation, and college student adjustment. *Journal of Counseling and Development, 73,* 463–475.

Rockland-Miller, H. S., & Eells, G. T. (2005). *The implementation of mental health clinical triage systems in university health services.* Manuscript submitted for publication.

Schafer, R. (1973). Concepts of self and identity and the experience of separation-individuation in adolescence. *Psychoanalytic Quarterly, 42,* 42–59.

Schafer, R. (1986). Discussion of transference and countertransference in brief psychotherapy. In H. C. Meyers (Ed.), *Between analyst and patient: New dimensions in countertransference and transference* (pp. 149–157). Hillsdale, NJ: Analytic Press.

Sue, D. W., & Sue, D. (1990). *Counseling the culturally different* (2nd ed.). New York: John Wiley & Sons.

Winnicott, D.W. (1965). *The maturational processes and the facilitating environment.* New York: International Universities Press.

Winnicott, D. W. (1984). Struggling through the doldrums. In C. Winnicott, R. Shepherd, & M. Davis (Eds.), *Deprivation and delinquency* (pp. 145–155). London: Tavistock Publications. (Originally published 1963.)

3

Legal and Ethical Issues

ROBERT MAY

First a disclaimer: I do not consider myself an expert on mental health law. What authority I have here comes from close to 40 years in the field (30 of those as director of a counseling and mental health service), from a recent review of relevant books and articles, and from consultation with people who know more about these things than I. Also, it is important to remember throughout what follows that most mental health law is state law. It is my impression that there is considerable similarity across states in the issues I'll be discussing, but in the end I can vouch for my summary of the law only as it applies to psychologists in Massachusetts. Anyone outside Massachusetts should verify the situation in his or her state (the American Psychological Association [APA] has been putting out a series of books summarizing mental health law for each state). It is also true that there are variations, usually minor but possibly important, in the laws governing the various mental health professions. And while the code of ethics for psychologists is nationwide, states may differ according to whether the legislature has adopted that code of ethics as law (Massachusetts has).

We would like to think of the legal, the ethical, and what's fair or right as concentric circles: At the core would be the law, specific and clear, around that a more general code called ethics, and surrounding both a much larger and vaguer area of opinion about what's fair or right. This ideal picture would also mean that everything that is legal is also ethical and that both of those terms are included in our definitions of what's right. In life we are not so lucky. While I think it is true that as we move out from the central circle things become less precise, less codified, and more a matter of opinion, the very fact that lawyers (and appellate courts) exist shows us that even decisions in the center circle involve judgment and potential disagreement. The problems that trouble us persistently come in areas where there is conflict between these three guides to what we should do.

We can assume for the most part that when it comes to professional behavior, what is illegal is also unethical (as my tax adviser said when I wanted to deduct a parking ticket I got while at a professional lunch: "Breaking the law is never tax deductible"). But the opposite, that if it's legal it's ethical, is not necessarily true. Certainly we could imagine laws that it would be more ethical to violate—we will consider such an instance later. It is not hard to think of hypothetical situations in which one could behave legally but *not* be doing the right thing (e.g., ignoring a drowning person); it seems these days that we are presented with an endless stream of examples, especially from the worlds of business and politics, of behaviors which may be legal but don't seem right. Or take the question of whether it would be ethical for a psychologist to accept a gift of a million dollars from a grateful patient who has won the lottery. It would be legal, but is it ethical? A psychologist who worked on revising the APA ethics code has recently assessed this as "a difficult question" (Walker, 2005). It seems to me not the least bit difficult, and I am baffled that anyone could even imagine that accepting this kind of gift from a patient would be ethical. So it seems both that acting within the law is no guarantee of being ethical and that when it comes to professional ethics, much is left to opinion and interpretation.

Here's a conflict which may be familiar to directors of college and university mental health services: When the president of the college tells you that your concern with confidentiality is "legalistic" and suggests you drop it in favor of "working together with the administration in the best interests of the student," he or she is asserting a claim which is supposed to take precedence over the law. Another conflict we will consider shortly is whether, as some therapists working in colleges think, parents have a "right" to know about a student's suicidality or psychiatric hospitalization regardless of legal and ethical injunctions concerning confidentiality.

We are going to examine a number of these areas in college mental health practice that are to some degree troublesome, and possibly controversial, because of conflicting ideas about what is right. I will first take up issues of confidentiality, with a focus on two lawsuits, one by now as close to "the law of the land" as we are likely to find (*Tarasoff*) and the other already the subject of much anxious conversation among college therapists (*Shin v. MIT*). The second section focuses on the Americans with Disabilities Act (ADA), a law which I believe has important implications for our practice, notably in terms of limiting the use of diagnostic and therapeutic considerations in administrative decisions such as mandatory medical leave. This discussion will also touch on the tension between clients' rights and the rights of other students or the interests of the institution, and on the risks to the counseling service of developing a reputation for making administrative decisions. And finally I will mention a few larger social and professional issues to which thinking about what is right may lead us.

Confidentiality

Confidentiality is not a luxury or a legal nicety for a psychotherapist. It is the basic condition that allows us to do our work. If any one of us doubts that,

I suggest trying the test of talking with students with the office door open (perhaps it would be better just to *imagine* doing this). My neighbors in the English Department do it all the time and in fact seem most comfortable that way. For therapists it typically has a strongly limiting effect on what we feel we can ask and what we can expect to hear. The reason colleges and universities need psychotherapists in addition to, for instance, sensitive and involved deans, many of whom also have counseling skills and training, is that we are able to offer a situation of confidentiality which allows a different kind of work to happen.

It has been recognized all the way up to the Supreme Court (in *Jaffe v. Redmond*, 518 U.S. 1, 1966) that privacy and confidentiality are vital for the effective provision of psychotherapy. Since effective psychotherapy provides a benefit to society, the courts have by and large respected the patient's rights in this regard (and it is important to remember that the right of confidentiality belongs to the patient, not the therapist). But this support is not without limits. In *Tarasoff*, the judges of the California Supreme Court ruled that "the protective privilege [of confidentiality] ends where the public peril begins" (see Bersoff, 2003, and Behnke Hilliard, 1998, for a fuller summary of the case and the rulings). The two *Tarasoff* rulings (1974 and 1976) established a new duty for psychotherapists, a duty of care to a third party with whom the therapist has no professional relationship, and probably never even has met. This was a major expansion of the legal duties of the mental health professions (and it was opposed by our major professional organizations). The duty established in *Tarasoff* is to use reasonable care to protect an identifiable potential victim when in the therapist's best professional judgment there is a clear and present danger of serious bodily harm. In this situation confidentiality takes second place, though even then the California court said that protective action must be taken "discreetly, and in a fashion that would preserve the privacy of [the] patient to the fullest extent compatible with the prevention of the threatened danger" (Bersoff, 2003, p. 168). *Tarasoff* is not a blank check to disregard confidentiality, but rather a very specific exception. Thus it joins the various other conditions that states specify as justifying a breach of confidentiality (in Massachusetts those other conditions are significant danger to self and abuse or neglect of a child or an elderly or disabled person. See Behnke Hilliard, 1998, for more details).

Tarasoff is often described as prescribing a "duty to warn," but warning the intended victim is only one way of carrying out the duty to protect. Other ways (states may vary on this) are to notify a law enforcement agency near the patient or victim, or to arrange a psychiatric hospitalization. The great irony of the *Tarasoff* case is that had it gone to a full trial, the actions of the therapist involved might well have met the requirements of the court—they certainly would meet the current requirements in most states. The therapist, a psychologist at the clinic at the University of California, Berkeley, came to believe that his client was a serious threat to a fellow student with whom the client was obsessed. The therapist then wrote a letter to the campus police stating his concerns. The police interviewed the young man but let him go. At this point, the therapist wanted to initiate an involuntary hospitalization. The director of the clinic, a psychiatrist, was apparently of the absolutist school regarding confidentiality. He vetoed hospitalization, had the letter returned from the police, and ordered all records in the case destroyed.

The rulings that we refer to as *Tarasoff* were actually only preliminary and procedural, concerning whether the parents had legal standing to sue. Once it was established by the California Supreme Court that they did, the university decided to settle out of court (I assume that it did so in part because of the actions of the clinic director, whose extreme definition of confidentiality had been thoroughly undercut by the court's decision).

A lingering awkwardness of the *Tarasoff* decision is that it requires us to do something we don't do very well: predict dangerousness. The MacArthur Violence Risk Assessment Study, the latest comprehensive study of prediction of violence in people with mental disorders, concludes, "It is no longer reasonable to expect clinicians unaided [by actuarial methods and computer support] to be able to identify the variables that may be influential for a particular person, integrate that information, and arrive at a valid estimate of the person's risk for violence" (Monahan et al., 2001, p. 143). Reasonable or not, that is what the courts expect us to do. In spite of knowing that a clinical interview is not an accurate way to assess risk, we still have to take every explicit threat seriously (including, according to a recent ruling by the California Supreme Court, reports from a patient's parents about threats made), err on the side of caution, and hope for the best. The situation is the same in evaluating suicide risk, and this brings us to the *Shin* case.

The best available published description of the sad events here is that by Sontag (2002) in the *New York Times Magazine*. Her report is based largely on information from the parents and their lawyer. Sontag frames the story within the question of whether universities, in giving up *in loco parentis*, have stepped back too far from taking responsibility for their students. That may be an important philosophical issue and is certainly of concern to university administrators, but it is not, I think, a prime concern for college mental health personnel. Our responsibilities are much more clearly defined, and the most troublesome issue in the *Shin* case for us has to do with a potential conflict between our responsibility to try to prevent suicide and our obligations of confidentiality.

Elizabeth Shin set herself on fire in her dormitory room and died in April 2000, in her sophomore year. Her parents sued Massachusetts Institute of Technology (MIT) for wrongful death, claiming that the school did not provide adequate, coordinated mental health care for their daughter and that MIT should have informed them of the deterioration in their daughter's condition in the month before her suicide. That there may well be valid questions of continuity of care can be seen by the fact that Elizabeth had seen, by the time she killed herself, seven different therapists and psychiatrists, all either at or arranged by the university mental health service. There had already been one psychiatric hospitalization (freshman year), an overdose, repeated cutting, calls from friends to campus police and deans, and reports of continuing suicidal thoughts and threats. Aside from the overdose in her freshman year, which Elizabeth promptly minimized, none of the particular incidents seemed quite to rise, in the judgment of the clinicians involved, to the level of imminent risk. One sympathizes with a large service attempting to cope with a difficult and troubled student, who was thought of by at least one clinician as "borderline." At the same time, it's puzzlingly unclear whether there was any one clinician who had the responsibility of putting together all the pieces of this complicated picture. That kind of coordination would seem to be an important part of providing adequate care, and is especially needed in a large mental health service with many part-time staff members. As the case played out in the courts, a judge initially ruled that the Shin family did have grounds to sue, not the university but those deans and mental health staff who in the judge's view should have known that there was an "imminent probability" of suicide and then "failed to secure Elizabeth's short term safety" (Hoover, 2005). Ultimately, the university settled the case with the parents, failing to arrive at a definitive conclusion (Hoover, 2006).

But the primary question for us here is whether the mental health service should have contacted Elizabeth's parents, overriding what seems to have been her refusal of permission. Would this be a justified violation of confidentiality? As human beings, and especially if we are parents, we may feel that parents *do* have a right to know if, for instance, a child is suicidal or for some other reason requires psychiatric hospitalization. We can readily imagine the shock and hurt of finding out about such things after the fact, perhaps long after. We intuitively believe that parents' caring for a child gives them some right to such information. So, should we just set aside the legal and ethical requirements of confidentiality when they conflict with our sense of what is right? After all, Winston Churchill is often quoted as saying that at times it is important to rise above principle and do the right thing (and in a more modern vein is Bob Dylan's "To live outside the law you must be honest"). I have heard college therapists maintain that they *would* notify parents regardless. I have been told by the director of mental health services at a prestigious university that the director of the health service instructs the staff to the effect that the university insures each of them for $3 million and that they are to do what they think is best and let the university lawyers worry about the rest. But this strikes me as cavalier, even arrogant. If you're not Winston Churchill (or Bob Dylan), it behooves you to be cautious about assuming you know better than the law. This is one of the problems with the presidential comment

I mentioned above: to call the laws about confidentiality "legalistic" and to assert a principle of "the student's best interest" is to do just what the law exists to prevent: arrogate to ourselves what should be the patient's right to decide. Putting ourselves above the law won't do as a general solution. Though we do still need to recognize rare instances in which individual conscience overrules the law, this issue doesn't seem to rise to that level.

There certainly is a rationale at the institutional level for breaching confidentiality. College and university administrators may believe, and may be told by their lawyers and insurance companies, that it is better to risk being sued for breach of confidentiality than to risk a wrongful death claim. Such advice may also include statements about getting the student the treatment he or she needs, or even about saving lives, but the context and emphasis usually seems to suggest that the main concern is to protect the institution from financial loss (see e.g., United Educators, 2005). It is easy to understand why administrators, lawyers, and insurance companies would take this position. It would be more difficult to defend against an accusation of wrongful death concerning a student, since the death of a young person will always to some degree strike a jury as a tragedy that should have been prevented, than to have a complaint of breach of confidentiality, which will seem more of a professional technicality. But we shouldn't forget that in the latter case the clinician bears more risk than does the institution (assuming, as may be the case, that the institution doesn't insure the therapy staff against professional malpractice). In accusations of breach of confidentiality, it is the clinician's license and livelihood which are at stake, not the institution's. But most importantly, these understandable institutional concerns do not put the wishes and welfare of the individual student first, and they cannot take precedence over the legal and ethical obligations of our profession. Thus the college clinician may find himself or herself caught between obligations to the student and the wishes of the administration.

Another attempt to resolve this conflict between the law and our sense of what is right is apparent in remarks attributed to a mental health service director shortly after Elizabeth Shin's death and in the context of a discussion of this issue (Greenwood, 2002). This very experienced clinician is quoted as saying that if he believed a student were in danger, he would contact a parent regardless of the student's wishes. One reason he cites is that students in trouble who can't notify their parents are also letting us know that there is a family in trouble. The language here is interesting because it seems to broaden the definition of who the patient is. We go from a troubled student to a troubled family. If the family *were* the patient, then there would be no breach of confidentiality. But this is rare in college work; almost always it is the student who is our patient. The rhetorical shift aims at lessening the unease about violating the student's legal and ethical rights. In the end it fails.

None of these justifications for violating confidentiality is strong enough. What about safety? Safety would be the usual justification for notifying parents against the student's will. But as we saw in *Tarasoff*, risk does not give us carte blanche in setting aside confidentiality. The courts have held that even in situations of serious risk, confidentiality may be breached only to the extent necessary to meet the immediate danger. As the APA ethics code (Bersoff, 2003) has it, "Psychologists disclose confidential information only as mandated by law, or where permitted by law for a valid purpose" (Standard 4.05). We must have a narrow definition here. *How* exactly does notifying parents increase the student's safety? In some families and situations it would, in others it would not (given the story of the Shin family, particularly the parents' earlier reactions when they *were* informed of their daughter's difficulties, it's not at all clear that notification would have offered much protection). Is there another alternative to ensure safety? The Massachusetts law in this regard allows breach of confidentiality in instances of clear and present danger to self and a refusal to accept further appropriate treatment (Brant, 1991). Certainly one can imagine a situation in which notification makes absolute sense: for instance, a treatment-reluctant student discharged too soon (the norm these days) from a psychiatric hospital and headed home without the parents being at all aware of the possible suicide risk. But this would be a rare example, especially since it assumes that neither the hospital nor the deans had contacted the parents. In the end, the test of notifying parents must be, it seems to me, whether it is the *only* way to ensure safety in the circumstances.

Lest I sound like an advocate for keeping parents in the dark, let me say that the ideal at Amherst has always been that in cases of suicide attempt or psychotic episode, there should be a meeting involving the student, someone from the counseling and mental health service, a parent (or representative of the family), and a dean, for the purpose of considering issues of risk and what to do next. In my experience most students will see the usefulness of this. But if the student is simply not willing, then I think that overriding his or her right to confidentiality is not only a legal and ethical violation but also runs grave risks for the reputation of the service. Thus on balance we rightly choose not to notify parents without permission. It may seem that notifying the family is a purely benign and helpful thing to do. Those of us who are parents are likely to assume that other parents would be as helpful and concerned as we (on a good day) would be. But we may forget that most of our students are in a developmental phase in which separation, even moments of estrangement, from parents is absolutely normative. Few things could have as chilling an effect on students' willingness to use the mental health service as a rumor that the service will notify their parents without their permission. Many of us who worry about the outcome of the *Shin* suit fear that the court might establish a parental "right to know" that would put us in just that untenable position.

And finally in the area of confidentiality, I want to state my concern that the confluence of the Health Insurance Portability and Accountability Act (HIPAA) and the so-called Patriot Act may have seriously altered the degree of confidentiality that we can offer students. For decades at Amherst we have given an information sheet to students coming for first appointments, much of which is taken up with our policy on confidentiality. It says that their coming to our center will not be made public in any way unless they themselves choose to do so, that the very fact of coming to see us is their own business, that students can trust that what they say here will remain here, and that they can be assured that no outside agency will have knowledge of their contact with us unless they give their explicit permission. I fear that we can no longer honestly make these assurances and that to do so is arguably a violation, at least by omission, of the APA ethical injunction to discuss the limits of confidentiality with clients (Standard 4.02).

At Amherst we maintain our own records under lock and key, not on any electronic network, and destroy all records 5 years after the student graduates. The problem, as I see it, is with those students (at least 20% of those we see) who get lab tests or medication, or use insurance to pay for mental health treatment. Any of these actions will create a file in an electronic database over which we have little or no control. Although HIPAA is supposedly aimed at protecting privacy and confidentiality, it also is an act that facilitates, and eventually will require, the electronic transmission and storage of health information in a uniform format. Electronic databases are increasingly hard to protect. Our government has a seemingly insatiable hunger for information, and those few intrusions that are too extreme for the government to undertake can easily be contracted out to private "data mining" companies. Anyone who doubts the enormity of these invasions of what we have thought of as areas of privacy need only read O'Harrow's (2005) *No Place to Hide*. And now we have the USA PATRIOT (Uniting and Strengthening America by Providing Appropriate Tools Required to Intercept and Obstruct Terrorism) Act, which, to quote an editorial in the *New York Times* (April 10, 2005), "allows the government to demand library, medical, and other records, and makes it a crime for the record holders to reveal that the request was made." My colleagues at Amherst see me as a bit alarmist about this, saying that we should wait until there is actual evidence of violations of confidentiality. But of course when it comes to computer searches at a distance, and especially given the gag rule which is part of the "Patriot Act," the fact is that one is unlikely to even know that a search has been done. This is an extreme example of the more general truth that the age of electronically encoded data has made it much more difficult to ensure confidentiality. I believe that students using our services (especially those who may be interested in a career in politics or government or any job requiring a security clearance) have a right to know the limits to which we can guarantee confidentiality. The Patriot Act is, in my view, a good example of the fact that not everything legal is ethical. Certainly a clinician served with an order to divulge information will be placed in a cruel dilemma, caught between this law and its penalties on the one hand and his or her obligation of confidentiality on the other. Only future legal challenges will clarify this conflict.

The Americans with Disabilities Act

One of the effects of the *Shin* case, along with other highly publicized suicides at Harvard and New York University, has been to increase anxiety about suicide among college and university administrators. There seems to be an increase in "risk management" strategies and the use of mandatory psychiatric leave as a way of separating potentially suicidal students from the institution. The ADA has, I believe, important implications for this sort of activity. But before getting into that, I want to put the ADA in a larger context. The law is, I believe, a helpful reminder of the difficulties we can get into when we begin to use diagnostic and therapeutic language to address what are basically administrative issues. I want to outline a number of such difficulties, starting with the most general and returning at the end to the specifics of the ADA.

Compared with diagnostic categories in, say, internal medicine, psychiatric diagnoses are more general, tied less to physical signs and more to people's statements, more changeable in reaction to social circumstances (as in the removal of homosexuality as a diagnostic category), and more stigmatizing. Thus there is a risk that these categories can be used to "diagnose" political dissent or unpopular ideas. Lest we think that this could be true only of Soviet psychiatry or foreign, totalitarian regimes, I want to mention an example closer to home that has only recently been acknowledged in print. Robert Bellah (2005) writes that when he was recommended for tenure in the mid-1950s, the dean of the faculty of arts and sciences at Harvard asked him "to visit the director of the Harvard Health Service, where I had received some counseling as a freshman, to have my mental health examined" (p. 42). Why? Not because of the counseling while an undergraduate but rather because he had, as he freely admitted, been a member of the campus Communist Party for two of those (pre-war) undergraduate years. Now members of the Harvard Corporation (the equivalent of the board of trustees, which had to approve tenure) were concerned that an ex-Communist must be "crazy," and they needed to be reassured in that regard. The shock for me is not so much that Bellah consented—a tenured professorship (which he eventually got) is a powerful prize—but rather that the director of the health service would agree to play his part in such a travesty. Obviously it seemed all right, perhaps even charitable, at the time. The trouble with these mistranslations is that they *always* seem all right at the time. Only the distance of years or a different culture forces us to see them for the muddle they are, with the mental health service wading inappropriately into complex political and administrative questions.

It is often tempting to label troubling behavior as an illness, needing treatment (as in "she needs to get help," when she herself may have no such wish). As Gary Pavela (1985), a lawyer who has spent his career in universities and writes the Association for Student Judicial Affairs newsletter, points out in his cogent book on dismissal for mental health reasons, another danger of this translation is that it can undermine the disciplinary system at the college or university. It may seem kinder to the deans, or to us, to require someone to leave because they (in our view) "need" treatment than to name the disruptive behaviors and require the student to stop them in order to remain at school. But Pavela usefully details the many ways in which keeping the focus on the problematic behavior and respecting the disciplinary system can be better both for the institution and for the student in question.

Another problem with using therapeutic language for dealing with essentially administrative issues is that there's no evidence that we're any good at answering the question once it's been translated into mental health terms. Will this particular student be able to cope well enough with his depression to remain in school? Will that student become suicidal again? Is this student, as I've heard it put by deans and health service staff, "psychologically ready to return to school"? I don't believe these are answerable questions. We have enough trouble assessing imminent risk, or trying to come up with helpful treatment strategies. The more we extend ourselves toward these larger questions, further off in the future, the more we enter the arena of illusion. It's a tempting illusion. There's a bureaucratic satisfaction and ease for the institution in defining certain students as mentally ill (or whatever gentler euphemism one prefers) and then leaving the decisions to us. And, eager to help and eager to be seen as helpful by the administration, we may ourselves come to believe that these terms make sense.

The final difficulty, and here we come to the heart of the ADA, is that engaging mental health language in administrative decisions is quite likely illegal. The ADA aims to protect students from being denied access to a college or university on the basis of the existence, or history, of any mental or psychological disorder. Thus any sort of mental health screening as part of the initial admission process would be illegal, as would a dismissal from school based on diagnosis or supposed need for treatment. Any exclusion must be based on clear evidence of behaviors that violate or fail to meet the reasonable standards of the institution. If safety is the issue, there must be evidence of direct threat to self or others. Direct threat is defined as "a significant risk of substantial harm to the health or safety of the individual or others that cannot be eliminated or reduced by reasonable accommodation" (Pavela, 2003). And there must be an occasion for the student to challenge the factual assumptions and to allay concerns about the apparently threatening behavior. This is a very high standard. I suspect many of our current systems for mandatory psychiatric withdrawal fail to meet it. To the extent that the mandatory withdrawal process centers on a mental health assessment, and to the extent that modifications to the student's situation that could reduce risk are not explicitly considered, the process is arguably in violation of the ADA.

When mandatory withdrawal is a possible outcome, the procedure should not be one that gives the counseling and mental health service the central decision-making power. To do so suggests that this *is* a diagnostic question, to be answered by a mental health evaluation (and isn't it a bit odd that we think it's acceptable to decide *re*admission on the basis of a process that would be clearly illegal for the original admission?). This sort of procedure puts the emphasis in the wrong place, and, it seems to me, all it would take would be a sufficiently assertive lawyer to put the institution in potential difficulty with the U.S. Department of Education Office of Civil Rights (Pavela, 2003). If the issue is, as it should be, one of evaluating the problematic behaviors, then the administrators most likely to be familiar with those behaviors and most widely knowledgeable about the institution—and here I mean the deans or their equivalents—should have the central role. (A particularly bad process would be, as some colleges do, to have an outside psychiatric assessment. An outside evaluator typically knows very little about the institution, and the less one knows the institution, the less one is likely to be able accurately to predict functioning.)

A procedure in line with the ADA would have the counseling/mental health service in a clearly advisory role, would focus in documented detail on the problematic behaviors, would consider whether any reasonable accommodation (e.g., changes in living situation or course load) could be made to allow the student to continue, and would set sensible terms for readmission at the time of leaving. These sensible terms would stem, at least in part, from the best understanding of where the problems were. For example, if the student's capacity to do work had been impaired, then a readmission requirement of completing some courses elsewhere would make sense; if the student had seemed unable to tolerate dormitory life, then some evidence of the ability to live with peers and away from home might be expected; and so forth. And it would be the student's responsibility to persuasively describe, in a readmission interview with a dean, how the situation would be different this time. Certainly experience in therapy while away could be evidence of change, but so could many other things. While I realize that opinions differ on this, my view is that requiring therapy makes little sense.[1] Our position and experience at Amherst have been that mandatory therapy is usually a waste of everybody's time and money and that readmission letters from outside therapists are uniformly useless (if it's going to be negative, it won't get written).

One of the troubling things one sees these days is a very low threshold for suicide risk and a resort to rapid dismissal and reluctant readmission. To take an extreme (but true) example, a system whereby a student who has overdosed for the first time is told, while still in the emergency room of the local hospital, that she has been "put on medical leave," appears to be more aimed at protecting the institution than respecting the needs of the student and is unacceptable. It's also the case that strict risk-management policies like this are probably miscalculated. As Pavela puts it, "Colleges that invoke mandatory withdrawal policies to avoid litigation over liability for suicide face a much greater risk of litigation for an ADA violation. They're jumping from a cold frying pan into a hot fire" (personal communication, e-mail, March 9, 2005).

Beyond these legal issues there are concerns which, if not directly addressed by codes of ethics, have at least what I would call an ethical aspect. The reason I have focused on the implications of the ADA for mandatory leave is that I think here we often feel, for good reason, that we are trying to serve two masters in these situations. The student's wishes and the institutional interest are by definition in conflict—thus the words "mandatory" or "involuntary." We psychotherapists are used to thinking of ourselves as helping students to get more of what they want, and these situations of conflicting rights make us uneasy. We sometimes try to ease this discomfort by telling ourselves that to remove a disturbing or disruptive student from campus is respecting the rights of *other* students (rights to a quiet dorm, rights not to be distracted from their work, etc.), but it seems to me that these rights are properly addressed through codes of conduct rather than through mental health interventions.

There is a real tension here. The administration will expect us to do all we can to protect the college from the legal risk and social pain of a student suicide. But it may be better for the student to have a chance to stay. This is often the case, for instance, with students for whom there is little support at home, or students whose families are struggling economically and culturally and for whom being at college represents an important opportunity in our increasingly economically stratified society. For such a student, a mandatory semester or year away may be a real setback. Returning home is not a positive experience for all our students. An interrupted education is often hard to resume. If the rationale for the interruption is that the student can find more adequate treatment at home than we can provide at college, then we have to ask ourselves whether, given the inadequacy of public mental health resources in most areas of our country and the limitations of insurance, this is a realistic expectation for any but our well-to-do students. Certainly my experience has been that many instances of a first overdose can be safely and successfully treated with the student remaining at college.

In terms of this conflict between the interests of the student and the interests of the institution, the generalities of the APA Ethics Code are of little help. We are left trying to decide what is right. For me the right balance leans toward respecting the interests of the weaker side, which is to say the student rather than the institution. I say this not only out of a concern with fairness and a temperamental tendency to side with the underdog. It seems clear to me that both ethical standards and the spirit of the law would support the idea that the clinician's *first* commitment must be to the welfare of the client. This is exactly why *Tarasoff* represented a break with tradition and is stated as a very specific exception. Of course we will feel other pulls: a wish to please (or as the case may be, to oppose) our immediate supervisor, sympathy for administrators facing difficult decisions, an understandable preference for having this difficult student disturb the sleep of a hometown therapist rather than our own, an anxiety about being unemployed, and the like. But these natural concerns must be secondary, at least for a clinician directly engaged with the student (priorities may be different for someone whose role consists of consultation to administrators).

There is also a risk here to the reputation, and therefore the functioning, of the counseling and mental health service. We sometimes try to distinguish between "administrative" and "clinical" interventions and hope that the students will too. But that's a lot to ask. An example of what we fear appeared in a long piece in the *New York Times* (Arenson, 2004) on colleges' concerns about suicide. The article begins and ends with the story of a first-year student who, according to her account, was required to see a psychologist at the counseling and mental health services and was then "forced to take a medical leave." The student eventually returned to campus but remained bitter, calling the process a "charade" and saying that she had thought the interview with a therapist was to help her figure out what she needed to stay in school but now regrets being honest because "he worked for the school, not the patient." Since returning to the university, she has not sought any psychotherapy. Whether or not this account is entirely accurate, stories like this circulating on a campus can do a lot of damage to students' willingness to use our service. When I first came to Amherst, there was a rumor circulating that if you went to the counseling center, the person you were talking to might, to your surprise, pick up the phone and tell the dean that you were leaving school. Whatever might have happened to create such a story, it seemed to me a cardinal rule to try to avoid doing anything to justify it. Being centrally involved in mandatory mental health withdrawals puts us at high risk for provoking these kinds of rumors.

Anyone who has spent a decade or two working in a college or university has probably come to realize that diagnosis is rarely the determining factor in whether a student can make it. Students with depression, anxiety, eating disorder, even thought disorder, can, under the right circumstances, manage to graduate. Diagnosis tells us important things, but *not* typically how someone will do in school. The ADA can help us retain a useful modesty about how well we can predict.

Final Thoughts

We often have, I think, an unfortunate tendency to think of legal and ethical issues in a negative way, as a list of liabilities, a burden, a thicket of rules that hems us in. Certainly the prospect of a lawsuit or a complaint to the licensing board can trigger a rush of anxiety in all but the pathologically self-assured clinician. But we're better off at least trying to take these admonitions as opportunities to think about what's right. It may be hard to have much faith in an ethics code which says, for instance, that in the case of conflicts between ethical imperatives and institutional demands, "psychologists clarify the nature of the conflict, make known their commitment to the Ethics Code, and to the extent feasible, resolve the conflict in a way that permits adherence to the Ethics Code" (Bersoff, 2003, p. 31). We might wish for a little more specificity. About the only clear injunction in the APA code is that you have to wait at least 2 years to be sexually involved with an ex-client. When confronting a complicated and disturbing issue such as the participation of psychologists in the abusive interrogation of detainees at Guantanamo (see Mayer, 2005, for details), our ethics code yields what is to my ear an embarrassingly equivocal statement (Lewis, 2005). Our colleagues in medicine and psychiatry are able to speak more clearly, perhaps because their ethics code has a fundamental principle: First, do no harm. In the psychologist's code, doing no harm is only one of five rather abstract and idealized principles, which are clearly identified as only "aspirational in nature" and *not*, as the ethical standards are, "obligations" or the bases for imposing sanctions (Bersoff, 2003, p. 30). When faced with a demanding administrator or institutional superior, these pious generalities can sound like an invitation to declare one's principles and then compromise them as soon as is convenient.

Although both *Tarasoff* and the ADA may have initially provoked a good deal of professional complaint, it seems to me that by now we must acknowledge the basic rightness of both. It *does* seem right that when we come to believe that a client of ours is a serious threat to someone else, we do something. It *does* seem right that the presence, or history, of a psychiatric diagnosis should not be held against someone seeking educational opportunity. Professionally we are better off having been required to think about these things.

I hope by now it is clear to the reader that I do not favor a narrow, what-can-get-me-sued view of these matters. Quite the contrary. I think that a consideration of what's right will inevitably take us into broader areas of social issues and moral responsibilities. My first college counseling job was while the Vietnam War was still grinding on its merciless and meaningless way. The counseling and mental health service staff on which I worked was painfully split between those who believed it was our moral *and* professional duty to do anything we could to spare our students (e.g., letters to the draft board for any student who asked) and others who believed it was a perversion of our professional role to do so. While it's probably true that neither side was absolutely in the right, it was important that we were wrestling with that social issue. Nowadays, when the absence of the draft seems to have largely removed war as a focus for protest on campus, social and moral issues may be less obvious. But what about the ways in which the economic stratification of our society affects our campus? Or, more immediate for most of us, do we have a professional obligation to speak up when we believe our institution is not providing adequate resources for the counseling and mental health service? One hears of respectable institutions that limit students to so few sessions that all that can realistically be provided is a triage and referral service. When staffing is inadequate (see May, 2000 and 2003, for some standards here) and students are being deprived of the tremendous benefit which developmentally attuned brief therapy can provide for this age group, do we have a professional obligation to do all we can to change that situation, even at the risk of disturbing the institution's complacency or public image? These are only some of the issues with which we should be concerned.

So, in the end I imagine this discussion may only have raised more conflicts and questions than the reader had in the beginning of this chapter. I hope so. Nobody ever said that trying to do the right thing would be easy.

Note

1. My argument against requiring treatment would go as follows: There is little evidence that mandatory therapy works (as opposed to much evidence that various psychotherapies done in the usual voluntary way do work), and the areas in which mandated treatment has been used most often (substance abuse, sexual offenders, batterers) are those in which the results are generally acknowledged to be poor; requiring therapy limits the choices available to the student, since many good therapists would decline to be involved in a situation of mandatory reporting; it is often the case, especially with the college age group, that the main thing that a requirement of therapy does is to create a client whose only commitment to the work is showing up for appointments and who is likely in the end to come away cynical and disillusioned about the usefulness of psychotherapy; and finally, in terms of confidentiality, although the letter of the law is observed in these procedures by having the student give permission for the therapist to convey information to the institution, the spirit is not observed, in that it is hardly a free choice when the alternative is potentially severe disciplinary action—we cannot ignore the coercion here and the likelihood that the counseling and mental health services will come to be seen as an arm of the administration.

References

Arenson, K. (2004, December 3). Worried colleges step up efforts over suicide. *New York Times*, A1.

Behnke, S. H., & Hilliard, J. H. (1998). *The essentials of Massachusetts mental health law.* New York: Norton.

Bellah, R. (2005, February 10). McCarthyism at Harvard. *New York Review of Books*, 42–43.

Bersoff, D. N. (2003). *Ethical conflicts in psychology.* Washington, DC: American Psychological Association.

Brant, J. (1991). *Law and mental health professionals: Massachusetts.* Washington, DC: American Psychological Association.

Greenwood, K. F. (2002, December 4). When college life overwhelms. *Princeton Alumni Weekly,* 11–13.

Hoover, E. (2005). Judge clears way for trial of MIT administrators in high-profile student suicide case. *Chronicle of Higher Education, 51,* 49, A1.

Hoover, E. (2006, April 14). In a surprise move, MIT settles closely watched student-suicide case. *Chronicle of Higher Education, 52,* 32, A41.

Lewis, N. (2005, July 6). Psychologists warned on role in detentions. *New York Times*, A14.

May, R. (1986). Boundaries and voices in college psychotherapy. *Journal of College Student Psychotherapy, 1,* 3–28.

May, R. (2000). Basic requirements and survival strategies for a college psychotherapy service. *Journal of College Student Psychotherapy, 15,* 1–14.

May, R. (2003). How much is enough? *Journal of College Student Psychotherapy, 17,* 3–10.

Mayer, J. (2005, July 11 and 18). The experiment. *The New Yorker,* 60–71.

Monahan, J., Steadman, H., Silver, E., Appelbaum, P. S., Robbins, P. C., Mulvey, Edward P., et al. (2001). *Rethinking risk assessment.* New York: Oxford University Press.

O'Harrow, R. (2005). *No place to hide.* New York: Free Press.

Pavela, G. (1985). *The dismissal of students with mental disorders.* Asheville, NC: College Administration Publications.

Pavela, G. (2003, June 18). *Association for Student Judicial Affairs Law and Policy report, 6.*

Sontag, D. (2002, April 28). Who was responsible for Elizabeth Shin? *New York Times Magazine.*

United Educators. (2005, April). *Risk research bulletin.*

Walker, L. (2005). Responses to questions. *National Psychologist, 14.*

4
Medications

VICTOR SCHWARTZ

While there have been some papers discussing increased use of medications in college mental health services (Grayson, Schwartz, & Commerford, 1997), actual discussions of prescribing practices have been lacking. In fact, a Medline search performed in the summer of 2004 cross-referencing "university students" and "psychotropic drugs" yielded results related only to substance abuse.

The ideas presented in this chapter grow out of nearly 15 years of overseeing psychiatric prescribing at New York University Counseling Service, where I worked and consulted with staff members and supervised over 200 senior psychiatric residents. Working with staff and helping these young psychiatrists understand the differences between college counseling services and hospital clinics forced me to examine these issues in my own thinking.

This chapter attempts to present a comprehensive approach to the prescribing of psychiatric medicines for college students, paying special attention to those issues that are unique to prescribing in college mental health services. There are issues that therapists should understand and consider when asking for a medication evaluation for college students. There are also considerations important for prescribing clinicians.

Setting the Stage

As recently as 15 years ago, many college counseling services did not have a psychiatrist on staff or a psychiatric consultant available and had to send students to private psychiatrists in their communities or use nonpsychiatric physicians or nurse practitioners affiliated with their college health services to prescribe psychiatric medicines. Since that time, this picture has changed dramatically. Now, 54% of schools offer psychiatric services on campus (Gallagher, 2004). Further, the number of counseling-center clients on psychiatric medication nearly tripled from 1994 to 2004 (Gallagher, 2004), and more students arrive on campus already taking medicines (Carter & Winseman, 2003). How do we account for this change?

In the past 15 years, mental health care in general and particularly for children and adolescents has come to rely much more heavily on medication-based treatments. Developments in psychopharmacology created a great sense of optimism regarding the ability to treat psychological difficulties quickly, safely, and relatively inexpensively. Emerging research technologies led neuroscientists to imagine that we were on the verge of a revolution in our ability to understand the function of the brain in both normal and pathological states. This sense of optimism led the first President Bush to declare the 1990s the "Decade of the Brain" (Lemonick & Nash, 1995; Library of Congress/NIMH, 2000). There was hope that all problems could be solved by research, technology, and the proper adjustment of neurotransmitters through medication.

This shift to a more biological, medical model of psychological illness has had several practical results. On the positive side, it may have helped reduce the stigma associated with psychiatric diagnoses. This in turn has probably led to parents having greater comfort in seeking mental health care for their children. So, it is possible that more cases are coming to light and being treated. Further, a medical intervention must of course be based on making diagnoses. Training in all mental health disciplines has come to depend more heavily on making diagnoses based on the *Diagnostic and Statistical Manual of Mental Disorders,* fourth revision (DSM-IV), and this would unquestionably lead to more people receiving diagnoses, and as a result medicine.

Economic and market factors have also had an impact on prescribing practices. Many managed-care programs have encouraged medication treatments at the expense of talk therapy. The claim seemed to be that if the patient—child, adolescent, or adult—was "sick" enough to require treatment, there must be a need for medicine. The aggressive marketing of psychiatric medications by the pharmaceutical industry to both physicians and the general population increased people's comfort with the idea of prescribing and taking these medicines. Medications' improved tolerability and safety allowed people to consider taking medicine for problems that would not have seemed severe enough to justify a less well tolerated medicine in the past. The result of all of these considerations has been increasing reliance on psychiatric medications.

Specific Considerations in Medicating College Students

Population

College students live in a transitional developmental world. They are no longer quite adolescents, nor are they yet adults. Most have never really lived on their own, and many have never seen a physician or therapist without a parent present or at least involved in the process. While students may be intelligent, their identity and emotional world may still be quite fluid. Even their cognitive world may have strong remnants of adolescent and childhood thinking. These factors can interfere with the ability to present a clear and coherent history. Many college students have not thought carefully or talked deeply about their feelings. Many tend to have a very narrow sense of personal history and time. Often, those who may be feeling sad on a particular day as a result of a breakup or an unpleasant conversation with a parent present as always having had a miserable life. Two or three days later, when things have improved in their love life or family situation, all is well and their whole life has been just fine.

To complicate matters further, the developmental challenges and even stress levels of college students fluctuate dramatically during their college years. A freshman may be struggling with a first separation from home and family, while a sophomore may be experiencing a first relationship or challenges related to finding an academic major and defining life goals. Stress levels vary dramatically over the course of a semester and school year. Relationships can be fickle and tempestuous. So, the way a young person appears today may be quite different from even a few days later.

With regard to treatment, many students who have been in treatment as children or adolescents were sent by others or coerced into these therapies. These childhood and adolescent treatments often go badly, leaving the student with a bad taste and pessimism about the possibility of treatment being a cooperative and helpful process. Thus, even students who now come for help willingly may be hesitant to share with adult therapists and psychiatrists their deepest secrets.

Feelings of shame and embarrassment about sexual feelings or activities or about illicit activities such as substance use also can frequently lead to inaccurate reporting and difficulties assessing students' needs for medicine. Often symptoms that are initially presented as occurring without precipitant become less mysterious after a bit of patient exploration—or prying. As a rule, when a student's story doesn't add up, it is reasonable to wonder whether information is being withheld.

Young people are often quite impatient. As a result, problems are presented with great urgency and there is often pressure placed on the therapist to make things better immediately. This can result in premature consideration of medicine when a bit of time, exploration, and support may be all that are needed. Discussions about the effects of medication may also be colored by patients' desire for immediate relief. If the medicine is not working right away—most, of course, do not—they conclude that it is no good.

Setting

College mental health programs generally follow a short-term treatment model. Session limits are common. Further, college students are often on the move. There are frequent breaks throughout the year during which students often leave school. These time limitations again create a sense of pressure to treat and stabilize students quickly, and also present a challenge for monitoring responses carefully.

Further, while student mental health services are better covered by psychiatrists than in the past, typically they are still not heavily staffed by psychiatrists or psychiatric nurse-practitioners. As a result, many college psychiatrists see large caseloads in brief sessions. And many treatments are split between a therapist and a prescribing psychiatrist. Practices vary among services as to how treatments are shared: whether the service will medicate students who have private therapists, whether students are required to be in therapy in order to receive psychiatric care, and how communication between clinicians are handled. These questions will be discussed in greater detail later in the chapter.

Recommendations for Therapists Considering Medication Consultations

Indications

In which clinical situations should a therapist consider a medication consultation? There are some circumstances when it is imperative to at least consider prescribing psychiatric medications. If a student is suffering from psychosis (independent of the etiology) or is severely depressed to the extent of serious functional impairment or significant suicidal ideation or impulse, a consultation should be sought as soon as is feasible. Acute manic symptoms are also an indication for urgent psychiatric consultation. (Of course, these situations also require consideration as to whether the student requires admission to an inpatient psychiatric service.) While there may be instances in which the student might not benefit from medicine, a consultation should definitely make that determination.

Psychiatric consultation should also be considered when a student presents with moderate depression, especially in the absence of apparent environmental precipitants, or when depression is chronic and has been unresponsive to talk therapy. The same is true with panic or significant anxiety in order to prevent a sense of helplessness and lack of control, which would only exacerbate the anxiety (Schwartz, 1994). Medication, especially short-term use of benzodiazepines, can be quite helpful in restoring a sense of control. With obsessive-compulsive disorder (OCD), impulse control problems (including some eating disorders), performance anxiety, attention-deficit/hyperactivity disorder (ADHD), and significant personality disorders, it is prudent to consider medication and obtain a psychiatric evaluation. At the same time, it is important to remember that there are few absolutes. While these clinical problems may be helped with medicine, there may also be good reasons to delay treating pharmacologically in particular cases.

As noted earlier, it can be very difficult to obtain a clear history and to get a clear clinical snapshot from college students. Especially for clinicians who have been raised on the DSM-IV approach to assessment and diagnosis, it is easy to forget that poor or inconsistent nutrition and poor sleep not only may be symptoms of depression or anxiety, but can also cause these problems or simply present like them. It is always imperative to ask about sleep, nutrition, medical problems, pregnancy, and other issues that might be affecting the student's level of physical or emotional stress. Further, substance use or abuse, whether acknowledged or not, must be assessed in every patient and should be included in any differential diagnosis. Almost any psychiatric problem may be exacerbated by substance use, and most diagnoses can be mimicked by a substance-induced problem (American Psychiatric Association, 1994; Nichols, 2004).

There are also disadvantages or problems with college students taking psychiatric medications, and therefore one should hesitate prescribing for minor symptoms. While many of the newer psychiatric medications—whether antidepressants, mood stabilizers, or newer "atypical" antipsychotic medicines—are better tolerated and probably safer than the previously available medicines, they are still not completely free from side effects or risk. The *selective serotonin reuptake inhibitors* (SSRIs) have been implicated in increased risk for suicide (more on this later) and can induce mania in susceptible individuals. Atypical antipsychotics have been associated with electrocardiograph (EKG) and metabolic abnormalities. The putative mood stabilizers are associated with a variety of endocrine and metabolic problems. People can be either sedated or agitated with any of these medicines. No medication is completely safe or free of side effects. Additionally, medications can add significantly to the cost of treatment.

Timing of Medication Consultations

It is important to consider the psychological impact of being on a medicine. Since many of the problems that students present with at college mental health centers are brief and self-limiting, a patient who is quickly medicated may feel better several weeks afterward. But then patients and clinicians are presented with a tough decision: Has the improvement resulted from the medicine (in which case it should probably be continued for several months) or from some circumstantial change in the student's life? Complicating the decision, the student may *believe* that medication explains the improvement, so stopping it may cause anxiety about symptoms recurring. A more general problem is that most people imagine that response to medication implies an illness, and this in turn implies chronicity. Many college students now present to counseling services stating, "I have clinical depression" or "I have panic." In fact, however, late adolescents' and young adults' diagnoses tend not to be stable. And it is important to bear in mind that any person who experiences an episode of major depression has a significant chance of never having another episode (Kessing, Andersen, & Mortensen, 1998). Further, there are suggestions in the literature that treating people with medicines can lead to a decreased appreciation for psychological factors and a devaluing of psychotherapy as a component of treatment (Bolton, 1996).

In light of these considerations, except in urgent cases such as psychosis or severe depression, or if the student is already on medication and is doing well, it is a good idea to do a careful assessment and try a few sessions of talk therapy before considering medication. When there are environmental precipitants for the problems, they will often shift or resolve in a few weeks. Developmental issues (like homesickness) *and* personal crises will also often begin to improve with a few weeks of support and adjustment. Many people who have never been in psychotherapy need a few sessions to get the hang of it, but will often begin to show improvement after 2 to 6 weeks of therapy. If the symptoms persist or worsen during this time, a psychiatric consultation can be obtained. Also, after several visits, the therapist is in the position to pass along useful information to the psychiatrist. By this time there should also be the beginning of a therapeutic alliance in the treatment, so that the patient has a greater sense of trust that consultation is being suggested for good and therapeutic reasons.

Discussions with Students

How should the consultation be presented to the patient? As part of any assessment, it is helpful for the therapist to discuss impressions and goals with the patient. This is especially important in college mental health services, since students usually present with acute (if not specific) concerns, and time is almost always limited. The discussion may or may not include specific reference to DSM diagnoses, but problems and plans should be elaborated as directly as is clinically feasible. If this discussion has been occurring, then the mention of medication should not be a great surprise. If, for example, a student presents with moderate anxiety or depression, the first session might end with an agreement that there will be two or three more meetings to talk about, attempt to understand, and develop strategies for dealing with this problem—and if things are not better, a trial of medication will be considered at that time. Similarly, in cases of acute symptoms, at the close of the sessions the therapist might review the student's complaints, with particular attention to functional difficulties, and then explain that medication consultation may be helpful to further elucidate the problem and to make sure the student understands the full range of treatment options.

Medication should not be presented as a panacea. Most medications help to some degree. None resolve everything. Further, it is important that the treating therapist *not* create a sense of nihilism about talk therapy. Most medication-responsive problems do best with a combination of talk and medicine. It is helpful to remind people that in most cases a positive response to medicine does not mean that the person will need to be on medicine forever. As life circumstances (and our understanding of mental illness) change, need for medicine might change as well. Further, it is useful to remind patients that psychiatric medicines are by and large nonspecific. A response to medicine does not imply a specific diagnosis or pathological state (Slaby & Tancredi, 2001). I have found it useful to present these ideas using an analogy to type II, or adult-onset, diabetes, a syndrome that has multiple and complex causes including genetic predisposition and lifestyle/environmental factors. Type II diabetes can in fact be managed by medication, but often making lifestyle changes such as losing weight and exercising regularly can decrease or eliminate the need for medicine.

What if the student refuses to consider medicine? Then the therapist needs to consider how urgent the clinical problem appears. If a student is grossly psychotic or depressed and/or suicidal, posing a significant short-term risk, a decision needs to be made whether to pursue an emergency hospitalization. Whenever possible, it is best to review the case with another clinician to evaluate choices and alternatives. If the student is not urgently or seriously troubled, there are several options to consider. It is certainly worthwhile to explore the patient's fantasies and fears about medicine. Any medication, and particularly psychiatric medication, carries powerful psychological meanings. Has the student been on medicine before? Has a friend or family member been on medicine and done badly? Does this mean that the student has the same diagnosis as the other person? What will parents think? Students have many questions of their own: Will I have to take the medicine forever? Does this mean I'm crazy, weak, or sick? Will I lose control of myself and be like a zombie? These thoughts can be quite frightening to a young person who may never have made a personal medical decision before. A bit of psychoeducation may help to dispel these concerns.

It is useful to avoid getting into a power struggle over medication. Refusal to take medicine can be explored as any other resistance might be. While lauding the student's desire to be independent and tough it out, one can also explore what may lead the student to choose to be in pain, or what makes it difficult to accept help. Medication should be held out as one more way to feel better and a potential catalyst for therapy, since when someone is quite anxious or depressed, sessions often revolve around only the symptoms. It is helpful to remind hesitant students that the psychiatric consultation can be used as an opportunity to get another opinion about problems and get information about the pros and cons of medicine. They should be reminded that the psychiatrist cannot force them to take medication.

What about a student who is only interested in medication? College counseling services differ in their approach to this question. Sometimes it is clinically sensible to work with a student in a medicine-only treatment—for example, if a student has ADHD, has had good response to medicine, and has no other complaints or problems. Another example is an older student who despite many years of outside therapy still has persistent anxiety or depressive symptoms and has chosen to stay on medication. In general, though, psychiatric problems (even DSM Axis 1 problems) tend to do better with a combination of medicine and therapy. If a student wants medications but refuses therapy, the service or psychiatrist needs to make a therapeutic and policy decision whether to work in this manner with the ultimate goal of "analyzing the resistance" and getting the student to reconsider therapy. To do so the psychiatrist must have time, skill, and the inclination to work on these psychodynamic or therapeutic issues.

Psychiatric Medications: A Very Brief Overview

A brief review of commonly prescribed medications may be helpful. For those interested in more detail, there are several excellent texts on psychiatric medications, including those by Stahl (2004) and Schatzberg and Nemeroff (2001) and the very accessible if slightly outdated handbook by Salzman (1996). It is important to remember that these medicines are not diagnosis specific. There is no medicine that specifically treats schizophrenia or social phobia. Rather, with the possible exception of ADHD medications, the psychiatric medicines treat the *symptoms* of disorders, i.e., psychosis, anxiety, depression, or agitation (Healy, 1997; Slaby & Tancredi, 2001).

The psychiatric medications may be broadly grouped into several categories: antidepressants, anti-anxiety and sedative medicines, antipsychotics, mood stabilizers, and ADHD medicines.

Antidepressants

While there are several different chemical categories of antidepressants, the *selective serotonin reuptake inhibitors* (SSRIs) and the closely related *serotonin/norepinephrine reuptake inhibitors* (SNRIs) have become the most commonly used antidepressants. These medicines became available in the mid-1980s with the release of Prozac and have been the focus of much attention (and some controversy) ever since. The SSRIs/SNRIs have the advantage of a very broad range of effects and in general are quite well tolerated. These medicines (whose brand names include Prozac, Zoloft, Paxil, Lexapro, Effexor, and Cymbalta) are effective in most depressive syndromes and most of the anxiety disorders, including panic disorder, generalized anxiety, and OCD. While different members of this class carry approvals by the U.S. Food and Drug Administration (FDA) for different diagnoses, they in fact mostly are equally effective across the whole range of anxiety and depressive disorders, and there is reason to suspect that FDA approvals for specific indications have generally been sought by pharmaceutical companies based on sales and marketing strategies rather then true differences in efficacy. In general, these medicines are rather well tolerated. Early side effects such as nausea, restlessness, and insomnia can usually be managed by decreasing or changing the dose. Later side effects such as diminished libido, delayed ejaculation, and decreased energy are usually tolerable.

There are several other categories of antidepressants and several novel medicines. The *monoamine oxidase inhibitors* (MAOIs) (such as Nardil and Parnate) were the first recognized antidepressants. While quite effective, they carry the risk of potentially lethal interactions with several types of foods and with many medications, which has drastically limited their use. The *tricyclic antidepressants* (which include Elavil, Tofranil, and Pamelor) may be somewhat more effective than the SSRIs, particularly in severe depression, but have many troubling side effects, including potentially serious cardiovascular problems and a relatively small difference between the clinically effective and the lethal dose.

The novel medication Remeron, while quite effective in depression and anxiety, has been limited in popularity by its frequent side effect of significant weight gain. Also, Wellbutrin (bupropion hydrochloride), a distant chemical cousin of amphetamine, is an effective antidepressant that is quite well tolerated. Its popularity was initially hampered by a slightly higher rate of seizures than with the other antidepressants. Nevertheless, when dosed properly, it can be quite useful for many people and is reported to be quite helpful for ADHD. It should be avoided with those who have eating disorders, and it seems to be less effective for anxiety than the other antidepressants.

It is important to remember that all antidepressants take several weeks to work. Often, patients feel slightly worse before they feel better. Most require dosage to be monitored and adjusted from time to time. These medicines are generally effective in about 60% to 70% of cases. Finally, it should be noted that any antidepressant can induce mania in susceptible individuals.

Anti-Anxiety and Sedative/Sleep Medicines

Although the antidepressants are quite effective in the management of chronic and long-term anxiety, they do not help immediately. In contrast, the anti-anxiety medications, which consist primarily of the benzodiazepine compounds such as Valium, Librium, Ativan, and Xanax, are effective soon after a single dose is taken. These medications are ideal for short-term, acute anxiety. While they are very safe for short-term use, they can be quite sedating, which limits their utility for exams or musical performances. Further, these medicines are addicting when used regularly for extended periods of time. These medications can be quite effective in the short-term management of insomnia, especially when anxiety is a main contributor to the sleep difficulties. The differences among the drugs in this class mostly derive from different rates of absorption and metabolism/excretion.

There are some other medicines marketed or used for anxiety. Buspar (buspirone hydrochloride) is an anti-anxiety medicine effective with mild to moderate anxiety. Because it takes several weeks to work, it is used infrequently. The beta-blocker Inderal is quite helpful for performance anxiety but should be used with caution because it can cause fatigue and has a potential to decrease blood pressure.

Several medicines are marketed specifically for short-term insomnia and are in the benzodiazepine class. Among the nonbenzodiazepine sleep medicines are Ambien and Sonata. Ambien is quite effective, but because it stays in the body for a fairly long time, it should be taken early in the night; it may cause fatigue early in the morning. Sonata, which has a much shorter effect, is a good medicine for people who have initial insomnia or who must be alert soon after awakening. It is less helpful for those experiencing early morning awakening.

Antipsychotics

The antipsychotic medicines are effective across the whole range of psychotic disorders, i.e., schizophrenia, affective psychosis, paranoia, and psychosis secondary to dementia or other medical problems. The development of the antipsychotics (also called *neuroleptics* or *major tranquilizers*) led to the deinstitutionalization of the severely psychiatrically ill in the 1960s and the subsequent dramatic drop in patients requiring chronic psychiatric hospitalization in the United States.

Though quite effective, the older medicines, such as Thorazine, Haldol, and Stelazine, had many troubling side effects, particularly significant neurological ones, including a persistent movement disorder called tardive dyskinesia, which is manifested by involuntary movements of the tongue, face, or upper body. These medicines could also cause significant sedation, stiffness, and feelings of emotional emptiness.

More recently, newer or second-generation antipsychotics have become available, including Clozaril, Zyprexa, Risperdal, and Seroquel, which appear to cause less stiffness and emotional emptiness. There are suggestions that these medicines may be less likely to cause tardive dyskinesia as well, but this is not clear because the incidence of tardive is related to length of exposure; these medicines have not been available for very long. These medications do have other associated problems. Several can cause decreased white blood cell count, some cause weight gain and increased risk for diabetes, and some cause changes in cardiac conduction.

Mood Stabilizers

While the antipsychotics are effective in the management of manic psychosis and agitation, because of the risk of tardive dyskinesia there was a need to find other, safer medications. Long known to have calming effects, lithium was found to have a salutary effect on manic patients and became commonly used in the 1970s. Lithium, though, also has problems. There is a narrow range between the therapeutic dose and dangerous or lethal doses. Blood levels therefore need to be monitored. Its level in the body may be affected by other medicines, food, or metabolic status. There are numerous troubling side effects, including possible kidney problems.

More recently, several medications originally used to treat seizures, including Depakote, Tegetol, and Neurontin, have become common in treatment of bipolar disorder. These medicines also have general sedative effects, and some have been used in other situations such as severe borderline disorder. While free of some of the problems of lithium and the antipsychotics, they pose different difficulties, such as possible endocrine and reproductive effects, liver toxicity, and lowered blood counts. Another seizure medicine, Lamictal, is the first medication approved by the FDA for bipolar depression. It is associated with dangerous skin complications, so must be dosed and monitored carefully.

ADHD Medicines

Stimulant medications such as Ritalin and amphetamines have been the mainstays of ADHD treatment and can be dramatically effective. When diagnosis is done carefully and the medicines are well monitored, they are safe and effective. Problems associated with them are potential insomnia, increased anxiety, stunted growth in children, and potential abuse. A black market has developed around these drugs, and prescribers must thoroughly assess to determine whether students intend to use these medications as prescribed. Recently, several nonstimulant alternatives, such as Strattera and Wellbutrin, have become available, but they may not be quite as effective as the stimulant medications.

Considerations for Prescribers

Psychiatric practice in a college mental health service integrates elements of an emergency room, a walk-in clinic, a private practice, consultation-liaison duties, and adult and child-adolescent psychiatry. As such, it requires versatility and flexibility and a preparedness to work in ambiguous circumstances. Psychiatrists also may have a consultative role to play because college counseling clients have often already been in psychiatric treatment or on medicine before arriving at the college counseling service (Grayson et al., 1997). College psychiatrists may therefore attempt to work with the health center or other university offices to make entering students and their families aware of the need for ongoing treatment planning for those students. Some schools send letters informing entering students about campus mental health and health resources and their limitations.

On many campuses, prescribing is done primarily by psychiatric nurse-practitioners or nonpsychiatric physicians or nurse-practitioners. It is important for these clinicians to be knowledgeable about psychiatric medications and students' psychological and developmental issues. Ideally, they should have access to psychiatric help for consultation about complicated cases.

Students Already on Medication

Because many people have come to be (over)reliant on medications, students often come to school with a bottle or bottles of medicine and an appointment to see their doctor back home over Thanksgiving or winter break, but little else in the way of support. If a student has a fairly chronic and stable condition or is easily able to go home for psychiatrist visits, this may suffice. For others, it is certainly worthwhile to establish a relationship with a counseling-service psychiatrist or, if this is not practical or available, a psychiatrist in the community. Counseling-service psychiatrists need to find ways to work with students who have other clinicians. It is helpful for individual counseling services to define fairly clear policies around shared treatments and lengths of treatment. At the same time, it is important that the service be flexible enough to be able to help students who have an acute need. If a student will be remaining in contact with the doctor from home, it is best if there is a decision as to who will be the primary caretaker and who will manage emergencies. Ideally, this should occur after discussion among the clinicians, the student, and, if appropriate, the student's family.

Students who have private psychiatrists may benefit when a college mental health service has the capacity to function as an acute care psychiatric or psychopharmacology service and fill brief prescriptions, since many forget to refill medications or to contact their doctor back home to order refills in time. Filling brief prescriptions saves students problems with abrupt discontinuation of medicines or long waits in emergency rooms. However, some campus psychiatrists are uncomfortable with this practice, because it involves assuming responsibility for a patient that they may know little about. Instead, they advise students to schedule reevaluations in the community. At the very least, a service should have clearly stated policies for this and should be able to help a student obtain expeditious care so that there is no unnecessary lapse in treatment.

If a student already on medication presents to the counseling service, the prescription usually should be continued at least in the short term, unless the medicine is ineffective, inappropriate, or dangerous, or the diagnosis seems obviously wrong. If there are questions about the advisability of the medicine, it is best to contact the treating psychiatrist, since the student might not present an accurate picture or explanation as to why the medicine was given, or circumstances might have changed. The psychiatrist always needs to evaluate the student's psychological relationship to the medicine. Is the student feeling forced to be on the medicine? Now that the student is some distance from home, family, and treating psychiatrist, does he or she have a strong desire to go off it and paint it as unhelpful? Is the student so attached to the medicine that it is portrayed as all he or she needs, even though there are obvious psychodynamic issues at play? Much might hinge on how the student had come to be on medicine and relates to the psychiatrist back home. For these reasons, it is a good idea to get permission to consult with the previously treating psychiatrist.

Students New to Medication

For students who are new to psychiatric care and are being sent by the therapist for an initial consultation, a full psychiatric assessment should be undertaken—and indeed some campus psychiatrists would argue that even renewals of medication call for a full assessment. Keeping in mind the developmental challenges of college life, the psychiatrist must attend not only to symptoms and diagnoses but also to the context in which the complaints are arising. For example, homesickness may present as anxiety or depression or a combination of the two but is probably best addressed as a specific adjustment issue. Since the student's ability to present a clear chronology of symptoms may be limited as a function of emotional and intellectual maturity, anxiety, difficulty trusting the psychiatrist, or intense desire for urgent help, time must be taken to review therapist notes and do a thorough evaluation. A service may also use written "consult requests," filled out by the therapist, so that the psychiatrist is presented with a thumbnail sketch of the therapist's concerns.

College psychiatrists should acquaint themselves with the common developmental issues that college students encounter. To work effectively in a college setting, psychiatrists not only must have expertise in diagnosis and medication, but also should be versed in and sensitive to psychological issues relating to common developmental and psychodynamic themes and conflicts in college students.

Keeping in mind that traditionally college-aged students are at the border between adolescence and adulthood, there should almost always be discussion about the parents' relationship to the treatment. Do they know about the student's problems? Has medication consultation been discussed with them? What are their comments or feelings about medication? Parents do not necessarily need to be included in the discussion, but their engagement or lack of engagement or their support or resistance to treatment will be significant factors in the student's relationship to medicine and treatment and may have practical implications in terms of referral options and affordability of ongoing treatment. Both college psychiatrists and therapists are often in the position of negotiating, or helping students negotiate, with families. At times, it may also be appropriate to offer to speak to or meet with the student's parents. With rare exceptions, notably acute life-threatening emergencies, this should be done with the agreement and participation of the student. Many resistances can be effectively addressed in this manner. Students are often pleasantly surprised and relieved to find that their parents are indeed concerned and supportive, and parents are often relieved to find that their obviously suffering children are seeking help. When parents are not helpful or overtly undermine treatment, having this information can at least help clinicians formulate a practical plan of action.

In the assessment, the possibility of substance use, including abuse of prescription drugs, should always be kept in mind, since such use can mimic or exacerbate psychiatric problems. For the same reason, medical problems should also be considered. If the student has not had a recent medical exam, it is best if that can be done at least concomitant with the assessment or at the start of medication. (In this regard the psychiatric nurse-practitioner and nonpsychiatrist medical doctor are at an advantage, as they may be able to perform a physical exam right away.) The psychiatrist should inquire about all other medications taken, including herbal or homeopathic remedies, since these can have psychoactive or metabolic effects—students often will not mention herbal remedies on their own, seeing them as natural substances and not medications. It is essential to review students' sleep and nutrition statuses and take a sexual history to check for any possible contribution to the presentation. Finally, female students should be questioned about the possibility of pregnancy or plans to become pregnant in the near future, since these issues may influence the decisions around prescribing.

If a decision is made to start medicine, timing factors should be considered. Since most services provide time-limited care, it's probably best to avoid starting on medicine just before a referral off-campus will take place, assuming the problem is not urgent. This will allow receiving psychiatrists to make their own choice about which medicine to use. In some hospital-based clinics, not every medicine is on formulary, so if the campus psychiatrist prescribes a nonformulary medicine, it might need to be switched almost right away and delay effective treatment.

The time of the semester should be considered from both diagnostic and treatment perspectives. A student experiencing panic before a first set of midterms or finals should be managed differently from a student having panic with no obvious precipitants. In the former case, a short-term treatment with a p.r.n. (taken as needed) benzodiazepine may be all that is necessary, whereas in the latter case an SSRI might also be indicated. Further, since many medications, notably the antidepressants, do not take effect right away and can actually make students feel worse in the first few weeks, they should generally not be initiated within two weeks of midterms or finals unless the situation is urgent. A new medicine started just before an exam period is more likely to impair than improve student function. In any case, winter or spring breaks in a stress-free environment will often have a very salutary effect on a seeming major depressive episode.

As a general rule, it is prudent to try short-term management in cases of significant anxiety, most often with a p.r.n. benzodiazepine, even when there are also depressive symptoms. In my experience, most students are quite conservative and careful about overuse of these medicines. In this way, ongoing medication can be avoided as symptoms resolve. Also, it is often helpful to address prominent sleep problems first, since if students get enough sleep they often feel much better, and long-term medication can be avoided. Obviously, caution should be exercised when there is a history of substance abuse. As a note of interest, after the events of September 11, 2001, many students at New York University, which is close to Ground Zero in lower Manhattan, suffered some degree of posttraumatic response. Aggressive management of sleep difficulties with acute medication was very helpful to most of them and, in conjunction with supportive psychotherapy, got them back on track.

With all medications, it is a good idea to start with lower doses than those recommended by the prescribing information and increase dosages slowly. Not only does a cautious initiation tend to prevent unpleasant side effects, but if the student is surreptitiously abusing substances which interact with the medicine, there will be less danger. Starting slowly is particularly wise with the SSRIs and related medicines, since raising the dose too quickly can lead to akathisia (a very unpleasant sense of inner, physical agitation), insomnia, increased irritability and impulsivity, or an increase in the likelihood of mania and suicide.

Students started on medicine should be seen often enough for the practitioner to monitor for side effects and make decisions about how rapidly to increase the dosage. Follow-up visits can be brief, especially when the student is regularly seeing a staff therapist. It is important to ask specifically about common side effects and about changes in medical status or new medications started and to briefly ask about drug or alcohol intake.

ADHD

There is much current controversy about the diagnosis and management of ADHD. Some reports indicate that this syndrome is being overdiagnosed and that treatment is being too quickly provided to young people, while others claim that ADHD is rather common and often missed and untreated or undertreated (Belkin, 2004; Elia, Ambrosini, & Rapoport, 1999). The feelings are further polarized by the fact that the main medicines for ADHD treatment are stimulants, which are controlled substances and have some potential for abuse. To further complicate matters, most people feel somewhat more alert and focused after having taken small to moderate doses of mild stimulants, and hence the frequent use of caffeine-containing drinks such as coffee, tea, or colas. Therefore, a patient's improvement on medication does not necessarily support the diagnosis of ADHD. Further, there is no definitive test for ADHD, which is a presumptive diagnosis that overlaps with other problems; both anxiety and depression can cause concentration problems. Additionally, in many cases the diagnosis is made by family practitioners, pediatricians, or child psychiatrists based on very brief contact and very superficial evaluation. The question of what happens to children with

ADHD as they grow up is not resolved either (Steinhausen, Dreschler, Fold-enyi, Imhof, & Brandeis, 2003). Does it ease up with maturation? Do people find ways to adjust to it? Does it continue unchanged?

It helps to remember that by the time people have reached college age, most cases of true ADHD have *probably* been identified. Exceptions might be students from other cultures or those who have grown up in unstable families, been home-schooled, or attended schools in communities that have large classes and little individual attention. It is also possible that a student who has ADHD is so intelligent that the condition went undetected prior to the rigorous academic pressures of college. On the whole, however, it is unusual to find new cases of true ADHD in college students.

As a result, when a student presents to a college mental health service asking for evaluation and treatment for ADHD, some skepticism is warranted. If available, thorough evaluation and testing at a specialized ADHD program should be pursued. If not, a thorough psychiatric history and assessment should be done with careful attention to the differential diagnosis of ADHD at this age, including, but not limited to, anxiety disorders, depressive disorders, adjustment problems, drug seeking, factitious disorder (intentional production or feigning of symptoms), pure academic problems, or learning problems. ADHD should be approached as a diagnosis of exclusion rather than a quickly accepted likelihood.

If a student who has previously been evaluated and diagnosed with ADHD presents for continuing treatment, medicines should certainly be maintained for the short term. But whenever possible it is prudent to assess the reliability of the diagnosis by communicating with previously treating clinicians and reviewing reports. When the previous assessment appears to have been superficial or of questionable reliability, an ADHD reassessment is warranted at a suitable agency or program. (This is often quite costly.) It is useful to refer students who have ADHD for academic support and tutoring and to the school's disability program for extra academic support and/or accommodations.

Substance Use and Medications

Dually diagnosed or mentally ill chemically abusing (MICA) students, who have both substance abuse and psychiatric problems, present a special challenge for colleges and college mental health programs. Many students are less than completely forthcoming when discussing substance use or abuse with clinicians. As a rule, clinicians should have a high index of suspicion for substance use when students present with rapidly fluctuating states, have atypical presentations, or have unexplained symptoms or rapid deterioration. Drug abuse should also be kept in mind in the differential of psychotic symptoms, since drug use, which can precipitate psychosis, is more prevalent in this age group than is functional psychosis (SAMHSA, 2004).

In many cases, it is difficult to discern whether drugs are exacerbating an underlying problem or are a separate and independent problem. In the best of circumstances, when students admit to drug use and accept the possibility that their use is exacerbating their problems, they may agree to stop or curb drug use so that psychiatric status can be assessed without substances muddying the presentation. If the student does succeed in cutting back or stopping drugs, a proper assessment can be made. If the student is unable to decrease use (or feels worse upon trying to stop), discussion should then focus on the severity of the substance problem. A referral for alcohol or drug treatment, and possibly inpatient detoxification or rehabilitation, might then be necessary.

When a patient denies suspected substance use, it may be worth asking if the student will agree to a toxicology screen. Few agree or comply. At this point, it may be necessary to begin medication treatment, proceeding slowly and carefully with frequent follow-up visits. The psychiatrist should continue asking about substance use but avoid antagonizing and turning away the student. It is often useful to invite the student's participation in the treatment with the reminder that the withholding of information about substance use can lead to getting the wrong kind of help.

There are no absolute contraindications against using most psychiatric medications in the context of surreptitious substance use. (One exception is the MAOIs, which should, in any case, be prescribed only for patients who are highly responsible and compliant with care.) Nevertheless, substance use may interfere with proper response to medication and prompt the psychiatrist to augment or change medicines unnecessarily or unhelpfully. It has also been my clinical impression that some students have intensified responses to marijuana when they are on SSRIs, and so warnings are in order about mixing these medications with marijuana or any of the hallucinogens. For further information on substance abuse in college students, visit the National Institute of Drug Abuse website at www.nida.nih.gov.

SSRIs and Suicide

There is strong evidence that suicide rates have dropped in the United States since 1986, which many researchers claim is a direct result of increasing prescriptions of antidepressants, especially the SSRIs (Grunebaum, Ellis, Li, Oquendo, & Mann, 2004). Recently, however, the FDA added a "black box" danger warning to all antidepressants in order to warn doctors and patients about the increased risk of suicidal thoughts and behavior in children and adolescents being treated with antidepressants (*FDA News*, 2004). How are patients and doctors to make sense of this confusing information? In many ways, neither of these findings is very surprising. There is no doubt that the antidepressants have helped many people, both young and old, overcome problems with depression and anxiety. Yet no medication is without potential problems or side effects.

When the tricyclic antidepressants were the mainstay of antidepressant treatment, it was recognized that the early weeks of treatment were especially risky, since patients sometimes began to have more energy before their mood started to lift. As a result, energized but still miserable patients ran a higher risk for self-harm. It seems reasonable to assume that the same thing may happen with SSRIs as well. In addition, some patients experience akathisia when they begin SSRI treatment, especially when they receive higher doses than are tolerable. To compound matters, many clinicians have prescribed SSRIs to children and adolescents at full adult doses, which increases the likelihood of akathisia. This phenomenon may be the central cause of increased irritability, impulsivity, and suicidal thoughts and feelings at the start of treatment.

Additionally, any antidepressant can evoke mania in vulnerable individuals. There is controversy as to whether someone who develops mania while taking an antidepressant is truly bipolar. In any event, this response may also be dose dependent, and since children frequently receive doses that are too high, there are probably more cases of mania in children than in adults. Manic reactions following SSRI treatment also may lead to increases in dangerous and impulsive behavior, especially among children.

Finally, it may be that the apparent increase in danger in children and adolescents sometimes reflects the synergistic combination of SSRIs and unreported illicit substances. As noted above, some patients have brief, intense responses to marijuana and serotonergic hallucinogens (e.g., LSD) while taking an SSRI. These reactions may present as brief mania, psychosis, or an intensified response to the drug; some people respond to marijuana as if they had ingested LSD. For a thorough and accessible discussion of this topic, see Mahler (2004). For a more scholarly discussion and a fascinating history of antidepressants, see Healy (1997).

Psychiatrist and Therapist Collaboration

With the rise in drug treatments and financial pressures from managed-care programs, it has become increasingly common practice in the past 10 to 15 years for mental health treatments to be split—with social workers, counselors, or psychologists doing talk therapy, and psychiatrists (or health service providers) managing medication. While this arrangement may be efficient and cost effective, it also presents challenges to the treating clinicians. Changing the treatment from a dyadic to a triadic relationship has profound psychological impact on the patient. Further, the therapist's role is relatively passive, while the provider's role is to do or give something. Making this collaboration work requires thoughtfulness, tact, and a certain degree of artistry.

The decision to request a consultation is not a simple event. While the patient's serious symptoms are the most obvious precipitant, often the patient is also making the therapist anxious or frustrated. Sometimes there is a desire, perhaps not fully recognized, to have someone else take a look at the student. In any case, the therapist should avoid communicating a sense of therapeutic nihilism to the student. The message needs to be, "Medication might help the therapy to help you better," not, "There's nothing I can do for you, so you'd better take medicine." At the same time, the therapist needs to avoid overselling the medicine as the solution to all of the patient's problems. The therapist needs to carefully listen for patients' reactions and responses to the suggestion of consultation. Are students pleased that their complaints are being taken seriously? Do they fear that this means that they are sick and not just worried or sad? These reactions should be thoroughly discussed.

The psychiatrist must avoid the temptation to be the powerful helper who is actually doing something, while the therapist is portrayed as passive and peripheral. Both the therapist and the medicating psychiatrist need to be aware of the more obvious transference and countertransference problems that tend to emerge in shared treatments. If medication is to be prescribed, there should be a mechanism for regular communication between the clinicians involved in the treatment. There must also be clear lines drawn as to who is responsible for which aspect of treatment and planning. Will the therapist manage the full referral plan, or will the psychiatrist take care of the medication follow-up plans? There are probably strategic advantages to having one clinician manage the total referral plan, since one person can carefully track and clarify the cost of ongoing treatment. In some services, the therapist and psychiatrist may work at different hours or sites, which requires an organized system of communications. Voice mail or written messages allow for frank discussions of planning, goals, and medication strategies between therapist and psychiatrist, limiting the problems inherent in split treatments.

While clinical charts should reflect that all clinicians are aware of treatment plans and are in contact, charts can be requested by patients, insurance companies, and potentially by other parties as well, and so are best treated as not completely private. In light of this, the clinical chart is not the best place for thorough discussion of all clinical and planning issues. It goes without saying that the clinical chart is not the place to record disagreements between clinicians regarding the treatment plans.

Finally, many students now request that college mental health services provide medication management alone or medicate them while they pursue therapy from a private practitioner. The service needs to consider the burden that this may place on its resources. A college counseling service must have adequate psychiatric staffing to promptly see new students needing evaluation for medicine. Since many students do present to college services in fairly acute distress, it seems sensible to have the greatest resources set aside for acute care. Of course, the school's location and availability of affordable psychiatric care in the community must also be considered in setting policy.

References

American Psychiatric Association. (1994). *Diagnostic and Statistical Manual of Mental Disorders* (4th ed.). Washington DC: American Psychiatric Association.

Belkin, L. (2004, July 18). Office messes. *New York Times Magazine.*

Bolton, G. (1996). Distinguishing borderline personality disorder from bipolar disorder. *Journal of the American Psychiatric Association, 153,* 1202–1207.

Carter, G. C., & Winseman, J. S. (2003). Increasing numbers of students arrive on college campuses on psychiatric medications: Are they mentally ill? *Journal of College Student Psychotherapy, 18,* 3–10.

Elia, J., Ambrosini, P., & Rapoport, J. (1999). Drug therapy: treatment of attention-deficit-hyperactivity disorder. *New England Journal of Medicine, 340,* 780–788.

FDA News. (2004, October 15). *FDA Launches a Multi-Pronged Strategy to Strengthen Safeguards for Children Treated With Antidepressant Medications.* #P04-97.

Gallagher, R. P. (2004). *National Survey of Counseling Center Directors.* Alexandria, VA: International Assoication of Counseling Services, Inc.

Grayson, P. A., Schwartz, V., & Commerford, M. (1997). Brave new world? Drug therapy and college mental health. *Journal of College Student Psychotherapy, 11,* 23–32.

Grunebaum, M., Ellis, S., Li, S., Oquendo, M, & Mann, J. (2004). Antidepressants and suicide risk: 1985–1999. *Journal of Clinical Psychiatry, 65,* 1456–1462.

Healy, D. (1997). *The anti-depressant era.* Cambridge, MA: Harvard University Press.

Kessing, L. V., Andersen, P. K., & Mortensen, P. B. (1998). Recurrence in affective disorders. *British Journal of Psychiatry, 172,* 23–28.

Lemonick, M., & Nash, M. (1995, July 17). Glimpses of mind. *Time, 146.*

Library of Congress/NIMH [National Institute of Mental Health]. (2000). Project on the decade of the brain. Retrieved April 9, 2006, from: http://www.loc.gov/loc/brain

Mahler, J. (2004, November 21). The antidepressant dilemma. *New York Times.*

Nichols, K. (2004, December 17). The other performance enhancing drugs. *Chronicle of Higher Education,* A40-1.

Rosack, J. (2003). Prescription data on youth raise important questions. *Psychiatric News, 1.*

Salzman, B. (1996). *Handbook of psychiatric drugs.* New York: Henry Holt and Co.

SAMHSA [Substance Abuse and Mental Health Services Administration]. (2004). *2003 National Survey on Drug Use and Health.* Retrieved April 8, 2006, from http://oas.samhsa.gov/nhsda/2K3nsduh/2K3Results.htm#toc

Schatzberg, A., & Nemeroff, C. (2001). *Essentials of clinical psychopharmacology.* Washington, DC: APA Press.

Schwartz, V. (1994). The panic disorder psychodynamic model. *American Journal of Psychiatry, 151,* 786–787.

Slaby, A., & Tancredi, L. (2001). Micropharmacology: Treating disturbances of mood, thought and behavior as specific neurotransmitter dysregulations rather than clinical syndromes. *Primary Psychiatry,* 28–33.

Stahl, S. (2004). *Essential psychopharmacology.* Cambridge, England: Cambridge University Press.

Steinhausen, H. C., Dreschler, R., Foldenyi, M., Imhof, K., & Brandeis, D. (2003). Clinical course of attention-deficit/hyperactivity disorder from childhood toward early adolescence. *Journal of the American Academy of Child and Adolescent Psychiatry, 42,* 1085–1092.

5
Family Problems

DAVID S. HARGROVE, SUSAN H. MCDANIEL,
ELIZABETH MALONE, AND MARTHA DENNIS CHRISTIANSEN

Most problems presented by college students in a campus counseling center are, in some way, family problems. Thus family systems theory is a useful point of view for clinicians who work in college and university settings. In many cases for the first time, traditionally aged college students are removed from their family residence and the strictures of parental control. From a family systems perspective, the primary developmental challenge for these students is to establish an identity separate from their nuclear families. To achieve successful individuation, the student and the family (especially parents) must adjust their roles and identities. As a result, the relationship between student and family is dynamic and sometimes emotionally volatile.

This chapter focuses on counseling college students who have problems that relate to their families and who seek help from college counseling centers. Although students' families may not be available in the counseling session, a family systems orientation is helpful for both case conceptualization and treatment. It is also important to stress that the presenting issue may not be an explicit expression of the family system problem. However, even if the problems apparently do not concern the family, family systems theory helps the therapist understand the interpersonal aspects of the student's distress and provides a more holistic treatment intervention.

In this chapter, we will first briefly describe the conceptual basis of family systems theory. Then, we will summarize key psychotherapeutic principles from the family systems perspective and present case studies to illustrate clinical and consultative work from within this framework. We will also discuss some particular family problems: divorced and divorcing parents, over-involved parents, emotionally distant families, rigid family environments, and abusive relationships. While there are many approaches to family systems work, we will draw primarily on transgenerational family systems theory (Bowen, 1978; Roberto, 1992) and an ecosystemic, integrative approach (Mikesell, Lusterman, & McDaniel, 1995).

Key Concepts

Most family therapists use some version of *family systems theory,* which is an application of general systems theory to the family or other close relationships. Family systems theory is based on the belief that the most effective unit of analysis for treating behavioral and emotional problems is the family and the relationships among family members. Nichols and Schwartz (1998) identify five central concepts from various psychotherapy approaches based on family systems theory:

1. **Interconnectedness** asserts that change to any part of a system will result in change in the rest of the system. Nichols and Schwartz comment, "The essence of systems thinking is seeing the patterns of connection where others see only isolated events" (p. 128).

2. **Triangulation** refers to two persons in conflict bringing in a third person. Family triangles are also important when two members form an alliance to exclude a third.

3. **Circular thinking** emphasizes the interactional aspect of most problems. No cause is assigned to an individual's behavior. Rather, most interpersonal difficulties have a "chicken or egg" character. For example, it is not uncommon for one parent to be more lenient and the other parent strict in responding to a child's difficulties. An effort to assign cause likely will be futile, since each one may be responding and trying to compensate for the other. Arguments about the parenting approach may result in inconsistent parenting and increased anxiety and behavior problems in the student. So the important question in such a case is how both parents can behave differently to help the student.

4. **Emotional cutoff** refers to the way individuals separate themselves from uncomfortable relationships. For college students, this may be a strategy to create distance from the past generations and start their lives in the present generation. Cutting off is a process of separation, isolation, withdrawal, running away, or denying the importance of the parental family, even after leaving home (Bowen, 1978). Individuals who cut off emotionally may relieve immediate pressure (Kerr & Bowen, 1988). Ironically, this strategy perpetuates emotional dependency rather than true independence from the family.

5. **Family structure** is defined as the rules and boundaries that govern family relationships. These frequently unspoken rules and alliances influence the way life is lived in the family. For example, a mother may be very close to a child but distant from her husband. It is not unusual for such problematic family structures to underlie students' difficulties. The therapeutic task in family therapy would be to change the family structure itself. For the student in individual treatment,

the goal becomes individuating and separating in such a way as not to get drawn into and perpetuate these problematic patterns.

In addition to Nichols and Schwartz's five concepts, we should also mention several others. **Enmeshment** refers to a condition where two or more people lack appropriate boundaries so that it is difficult for them to function independently. In contrast to students who have been damaged by being emotionally cut off from their families, enmeshed students aren't free to develop because they are so emotionally bound up with one or both parents. Related to this is **overfunctioning,** in which one member takes over for another (who is underfunctioning), fostering unhealthy dependency and robbing that person of a sense of agency. For example, parents may try to handle aspects of student's lives that students are developmentally ready to manage on their own.

Another concept is the **family life cycle.** Just as individuals pass through predictable developmental life stages, so does the family. Family life cycle stages include: leaving home, the new couple, families with young children, families with adolescents, launching children and moving on, and families in later life (Carter & McGoldrick, 1999). For obvious reasons, the life cycle stage most relevant to college students is "leaving home." In Western culture, young adults in this stage accept emotional and eventually financial responsibility for themselves (while parents let go of those responsibilities), achieve differentiation of self in relation to families of origin, and develop intimate peer relationships. Of course, there is great variability in the ways in which individuals and families pass through this stage. For some students, "leaving home" may involve trying to emancipate while their single mothers remarry or have a new baby, or while one grandparent retires and another has a terminal illness. These stages are grounded in transgenerational family systems theory, which places the nuclear family in the context of the extended family and emphasizes the interrelationships of individuals and all units. Transgenerational family systems theory seeks to identify patterns of development and behavior that may be repetitive across generations.

Two interacting transformations take place during the adolescent period and the launching of adolescents into college. The first is the impact on the family system itself, and the second is the influence on the person who departs. While families face new challenges (developmental tasks) that affect the way in which college students manage their growth, students face their own developmental tasks (Preto, 1989).

Psychotherapy from a Family Systems Perspective

Several important points should be made about using a family systems perspective. First, family systems theory is a point of view from which a clinician conducts treatment, whether the clinician sees individuals, couples, or families. This perspective does not define the number of people who are in the room, but rather describes a paradigm that understands human problems as rooted in relationships (Bowen, 1978). Second, the importance of the family system to the college student is not diminished when the student lives away from the family. Rather than signaling dissolution of family influence, leaving home reflects a new stage in the family's development. The way in which separation occurs influences students' adjustment to challenges at college and in the future. Third, a deterioration of a student's functioning at college may reflect disturbance in the family system. As the cases we shall shortly discuss demonstrate, students who come to college counselors struggling with managing anxiety or some other symptom often have families of origin that have comparable problems. Finally, the family systems approach can be combined with other theoretical orientations and interventions. The cases in this chapter show successful integration between family treatment and behavioral approaches, academic counseling, relaxation methods, psychodynamic approaches, and psychopharmacological treatment.

College clinicians who work from a family systems perspective will focus on the adjustment of students, their relationships to parents and other significant family members, and the functioning of these family members. Clinicians will also be sensitive to students' other relationship systems, including relationships with roommates, romantic and sexual partners, and others on campus. Family problems inevitably manifest themselves in relationships beyond the family itself.

Therapeutic Principles

Four key family systems therapeutic principles are applied to the cases presented in this chapter. These consist of therapists' efforts to (1) maintain neutrality, (2) help clients manage triangles and, more generally, understand parallels between their family patterns and current difficulties, (3) encourage clients to establish effective contact with the family, and (4) help clients achieve differentiation of self.

Neutrality may not be a position accepted by all clinicians who work in college mental health. Some college clinicians may believe in assuming a position of advocacy, or side taking, on the grounds that students are in a relatively powerless position in relation to multiple authorities both on campus and in their families. While students who are in crisis due to violence, suicide, or psychosis must be protected, generally we hold that advocacy or protection is not advisable for psychotherapists. Rather, therapists should pursue a neutral stance, or what Boszormenyi-Nagy (1972) calls *multi-partial alliances,* which involves not taking sides but instead developing positive connections to all relevant parties. Therapeutic neutrality then enables students to take responsibility in their relationships.

Triangles are a common feature in family problems, since they create the possibility of two persons who are in conflict drawing a third into the battle, or two persons allying themselves to exclude the third. Many students have had the anxiety-provoking experiences of feeling caught in the middle when parents are at war, feeling like outsiders when parents or other family dyads reject them, or finding themselves allied with one parent against the other. Clinicians can assist students by explaining the concepts of triangles and triangulation and helping students understand their own positions and other family members' positions within family triangles. Therapists can further assist by helping students analyze the positions they wish to take within the family structure and practice taking those positions. Explaining the role of family triangles is part of a larger therapeutic goal: helping students see the parallels between their families of origin and their current difficulties. Understanding the parallels helps students make thoughtful choices in their current relationships rather than blindly repeating dysfunctional patterns from the past.

Because many psychological problems have their roots in students' nuclear and extended families, family therapists also generally encourage students to **establish contact with their families.** (Exceptions may be necessary in cases of physically or sexually abusive parents or siblings.) Establishing one-to-one personal relationships with each member of the family system is a part of achieving differentiation of self. The goal is for students to establish healthy contact, as opposed to the extremes of enmeshment or cutoff. Doing so changes not only the real relationships with these important people but also changes students' "introjects," the aspects of these people that they have incorporated into their psyches.

Embedded within the three principles mentioned above is the fourth, **differentiation of self.** For older adolescents and young adults, this principle is the relational parallel to developing an identity. Coming to college is often a prime opportunity to work on this fundamental developmental goal. Differentiation requires that students define themselves and find a proper balance between remaining connected with their families and affirming their individuality. Work on differentiation of self requires students to remain in contact with their parents while learning to evaluate and plan their own courses of actions in response to situations at college. It is a move toward independence from parents while remaining in healthy contact with them. Either extreme cutoff or enmeshment is inimical to successful differentiation.

In employing these principles, an effective clinical technique is to draw a family diagram, or *genogram* (McGoldrick, Gerson, & Shellenberger, 1999), early in psychotherapy. This diagram is a graphic representation of the nuclear family, the family of origin (if different from the nuclear family, as with married students), and the extended family. It allows both clinician and student to observe relationships, repeating patterns, significant losses, symptomatology, ways of managing anxiety, and over- and underfunctioning. This information may then illuminate similar relationship patterns at college. It also allows students to take note of what they do not know about their parents and other family members. Gathering this information often helps students view their parents as humans with strengths and weaknesses, a process that facilitates their emotional development.

Case Examples

Students who come from troubled families do not necessarily enter counseling with that particular topic in mind. Their presenting concerns may be academic or social difficulties, substance abuse or eating disorders, unexplained depression or anxiety. In the following case, the student's presenting concerns were depression, academic anxieties, and conflicts with her English professor, who referred the student, seeking assistance from the counseling center.

Luann, a 19-year-old first-year student majoring in English, came to class regularly, turned in most assignments on time, and demonstrated passable ability in writing. During one in-class written assignment, however, after the instructor commented that Luann's writing was significantly poorer than her usual assignments written outside of class, she verbally blasted the teacher for accusing her of "cheating" and vowed not to return, even though it would result in her failing the class. After a consultation with the counseling center, the instructor arranged for Luann to come to the center for an appointment. The initial assessment indicated that she was highly anxious and was possibly experiencing a major depression. Luann explained that her strong reaction to the instructor's comment stemmed from her fear of failure at college, which had driven her to poor eating habits, lack of sleep, deterioration of interpersonal relationships, and inadequate preparation for her classes despite spending inordinate amounts of time trying to prepare. Thus, Luann presented her problems from an individual perspective.

Incorporating the family systems perspective, the psychologist suggested that understanding Luann's family and family environment might help explain her fear of failure. Since she was initially interested, the psychologist began by taking a three-generational family history, organized into a family diagram (McGoldrick et al., 1999). He discovered that Luann was the older of two daughters and that her parents were divorced, the father having remarried. When the psychologist suggested that she contact the father for information about his own parents, who also had divorced and had been estranged from the father for a number of years, Luann strongly objected. The intensity of her reaction and her refusal to contact her father revealed a cutoff from her father and an unwillingness to consider any effort to resolve it. Continued work on the family diagram revealed other problematic or cutoff relationships as a significant theme in this young woman's life.

The psychologist developed a treatment plan that involved reducing her anxiety regarding her schoolwork, connecting with significant persons in her family, and ultimately reconnecting with her father. Thus, the treatment plan was based on the perspective that the presenting complaints and the cutoffs were related. Success in college and a reduction in anxiety and depressive symptoms would be dependent on some resolution of Luann's family problems.

The course of therapy was characterized by the rise and fall of Luann's anxiety, usually in the context of her relationships with faculty, particularly males. She dismissed critical faculty responses to her schoolwork with a flurry of accusations about their animosity toward her and her need to drop the class. After three such incidents, the therapist helped her see the parallels between her family situation and current difficulties, specifically how her responses to faculty were influenced by her ambivalent relationship with her father. She believed her father's only concern was that she should successfully complete her education so she could marry or join the workforce and "get off the family dole" as quickly as possible. Likewise, she believed that faculty weren't interested in her and were ready to pounce with criticism. Both her fear of academic failure and her reluctance to contact her family were rooted in anxiety about self-sufficiency and expectations of rejection.

The work of the therapist was designed to enable her to achieve differentiation of self, both in the classroom setting and with her family. For the classroom setting, the therapist helped Luann find ways to clarify faculty expectations, since her anxiety had muddied her perceptions of what was expected of her. With behavioral rehearsal procedures (role playing) reducing her anxiety, she was able to ask faculty members what was expected of her. These procedures helped her control her emotional expression. Now she was taking sufficient time to think through her responses to others rather than responding impulsively based on her emotions. This new behavior later proved helpful in helping her clarify her father's expectations as well.

As far as reconnecting with her father, the course of therapy did not result in a happy relationship but did enable her to communicate with him more comfortably. That in turn alleviated her depression, furthered her self-differentiation, and helped her perform adequately in class without flaring up inappropriately with professors.

While the preceding case illustrates the far-reaching consequences of emotional cutoffs, the following case demonstrates how academic problems can be associated with overinvolved parents and enmeshed relationships, and also how experiences that affect one family member have far-reaching and often unacknowledged influences on other members.

Brad, 19 years old, was considered less intelligent than his older sister, based on early test scores. However, after his sister rebelled against her family's high expectations and underperformed at a small, liberal arts college, Brad was left feeling obligated to excel academically and so fulfill the family's dreams. During high school he studied night and day, and as a result he was admitted to one of the country's highest-ranked colleges, his father's alma mater, to study biomedical engineering, his father's major. During his second semester, though, his grades dropped and he became increasingly anxious, prompting a decision to visit the counseling service.

In the initial assessment, in addition to teaching Brad techniques to relax and focus, the therapist took a family history. For reasons unknown to Brad, the father had dropped out of the prestigious college during his junior year and had abandoned his dream of being a scientist. The mother was a homemaker who phoned Brad multiple times a day to check on his schoolwork and try to calm him down. Brad felt that she gave contradictory messages, showing support but at the same time expressing concern that he might fail. In response, he typically either became angry and yelled at her or hung up the phone. The clinician then received Brad's permission to call his parents on a speakerphone during one session. This interview shed light on the father's college experience: He had experienced his own performance anxiety back then, which had caused him to drop out. During the call Brad's mother described her concerns for her son and explained she felt it necessary to call often to provide support. Brad's father mentioned, though, that his wife also spoke many times a day to her own mother; tellingly, Brad's sister refused to take her mother's calls.

This information helped Brad and the clinician put his symptoms in context. In relation to his father, Brad was evidently trying to live out the father's unfulfilled dream, which put a great burden on him, and apparently was also unwittingly repeating the father's pattern of becoming anxious and setting himself up for failure. In relation to his mother, it appeared that her excessive concern was robbing him of confidence and impeding the process of self-differentiation. The therapist asked questions designed to help Brad achieve proper separation from his family: What were his academic goals? Did he want to become a scientist for his own sake or that of his father? And what did he want in relation to his family? How frequently did he wish to be in contact with his mother? How could he be close to her without absorbing her anxiety regarding his school performance? Though final answers were not yet possible, merely asking these questions was an important step toward differentiation of self.

That summer, Brad went with his parents and sister to a local family therapist, who communicated with the college clinician to assure coordination of care. (Because of his ongoing anxiety and sleep problem, Brad also was referred to a physician for antidepressant medication, undertook an exercise program, and focused on healthy eating.) The family therapist began by eliciting the family's participation to draw a family diagram on easel paper, which highlighted the multigenerational patterns of anxiety and performance. It wasn't that Brad alone had a problem at school; he was in a sense carrying out a family tradition of performance anxiety. The therapist provided separate sessions for the parents to work on improving their relationship and help the mother manage her anxiety and communicate with Brad in a more supportive manner. The treatment targeted the structural problem—the dysfunctional triangle—of Brad's mother being closer to her son than she was to her husband. The couple took these issues seriously and made progress in solidifying their own relationship and so putting less pressure on Brad.

The family therapist also met individually with Brad to discuss his reactivity to his mother and his approach to summer school. Brad reflected on how his relationship with his mother was very similar to her relationship with her own mother. He began to recognize that his angry attempts to get his mother to treat him more like an adult were in fact having the opposite effect. With coaching, he began to reassure his mother about his capabilities; while at the same time, she began to communicate more confidence in him. As the mother–son relationship calmed down, Brad was able to focus more on studying. He practiced new strategies for his schoolwork during the summer while attending a less pressured college near home. In combination, family treatment, medication, exercise, and the healthy living plan provided a successful biopsychosocial family systems treatment (McDaniel, Hepworth, & Doherty, 1990).

Upon his return to school, Brad saw the college counselor eight times, with the goal of applying what he learned over the summer to schoolwork and relationships. His parents saw the family therapist five times during the same period to discuss how to parent an emerging adult and continue their more positive relationship with each other. By the spring semester, Brad felt successful at school, had discontinued his medication, and no longer felt the need for counseling.

A third case provides another example of an unhealthy triangle, a structural problem in which a mother was very close to her daughter and distant from her husband. Changes in family structure are not easy—it's not simple to bring distant parents together, for example—but are often necessary for effective therapeutic change to occur. Even if the basic family structure can't change, a student can at least learn to change interactions with the family structure, with the goal of individuating and separating, and so not getting drawn into the parental problems.

Carrie, a 23-year-old undergraduate who was the first member on either side of her family to attend college, came to the campus counseling center to manage her symptoms of obsessive-compulsive disorder (OCD). The counselor began by taking Carrie's previous treatment history. Carrie had been treated in mental health settings on and off since age 10 for her fears of contamination and her compulsive hand washing and other cleaning behaviors, but nothing (including systematic desensitization) had been successful. The counselor next gathered information about Carrie's nuclear and extended family. The older of two sisters, Carrie described her family life as unpleasant, with her label of "OCD" being a stated fact among family members, who joked and demonstrated overfunctioning when Carrie was home, treating her as if she couldn't manage for herself. Carrie also sought relationships with friends who saw her as flawed. She said she expected others to ridicule her for her "disease."

At college, Carrie had begun as a pre-medicine major because her parents said she would excel in it and medicine was a respectable profession. But because of poor performance in biology, she switched majors and floundered until ultimately settling on a psychology major. She expressed disappointment in herself for her inability to excel in the field that her family had "chosen" for her.

Usefully employing psychoeducation, often integral to family systems therapy (Gilbert, 2004), Carrie's clinician discussed systems theory in an effort to help Carrie see herself in the context of relationship systems. The clinician explained dysfunction as a way for the individual to take on the anxiety in a system. Since Carrie's parents' marriage was not happy, Carrie had absorbed some of the anxiety and tension of their relationship by being "sick." Her anxiety and inability to function distracted her parents from their own flawed marriage. She saw too that she was enmeshed with her father, calling him at least once a day on the telephone to ask questions about contamination ("Should I wash?"). Depending on his mood, her father vacillated among soothing Carrie ("You will be all right, honey"), overfunctioning ("No, you shouldn't wash because . . ."), and being annoyed ("You shouldn't need me for this!"). In this way, Carrie's father completed a triangle between Carrie and her anxieties about contamination. When she could not contact him, she became increasingly anxious, searching for another person to "triangle" into her stress in order to bring it to a more manageable level.

Carrie's approach to therapy was passive, expecting the counselor's direction and advice while she talked about her stressors and negative self-worth. She believed that she "had a problem" and would require regular counseling forever to keep her from being too much of a burden to her friends and family. Though she stated goals of separating from her parents and becoming a fully functioning member of society, she believed that her OCD symptoms would prevent her from succeeding. After gathering initial information, the counselor encouraged Carrie to think about her OCD symptoms as symptoms of anxiety. She helped Carrie see that she might learn ways to manage anxiety better instead of labeling herself as "disordered" and beyond hope. The clinician gathered more information about Carrie's family and learned of at least two generations of unhappy and distant marriages with a heavy focus on the eldest child. Accordingly, most of the eldest children in Carrie's extended family were highly driven and very anxious, with none of them having had a successful relationship outside the family. Like Brad, Carrie was unintentionally following an entrenched pattern within her family.

The counselor suggested that Carrie could better understand the nature of her relationship to her parents, as well as those to her younger sister and her paternal grandfather, who lived with her parents, by maintaining regular contact with them. Through observation, trial, error, and reflection, Carrie learned what positions she wanted and didn't want to take in relation to these people. Crucially, she decided that she did not "have" a problem. As a way to express her adult position, she dramatically reduced the amount of time spent talking to others, especially family members, about her contamination concerns and instead became interested and involved in other aspects of the family's life. Carrie determined it was not her father's or anyone else's responsibility to fix her anxiety for her. As she moved toward defining herself, her symptoms dramatically reduced and she was able to live off-campus for her last semester of college, a particularly important victory for this young adult who previously was unable to cook for herself because of extreme fears of contamination.

As Carrie took more responsibility for herself, she also noted a shift in the focus of her parents. Though her father reported being happy that Carrie did not need him as much, he predictably called more often, revealing his part in the reciprocal relationship. Carrie was able to distinguish more clearly anxiety that belonged to others, namely her parents and friends, from her own anxiety as a reaction to stress, and in this way was able to assume more responsibility for her anxieties and symptoms. Similarly, she was able to avoid assuming responsibility for her family and friends and their anxieties.

For the counselor, this case presented challenges. It was easy to feel anxious about Carrie in the way family members felt anxious about her, and it was tempting to overfunction for her. As the clinician became aware of Carrie's tendency to pull her into the father–daughter relationship, the counselor "detriangulated"—moved out of the triangulated position—by refusing to solve Carrie's problem for her. Instead, the counselor helped Carrie effectively manage her anxiety rather than cope by being a flawed person riddled with OCD symptoms. With the counselor providing support rather than solutions, Carrie directly solved her problems with her father, decreased "symptom talk," and increased her interest in others.

Specific Family Problems

We assume that family issues are implicated in the full range of concerns students present to college counseling services. In addition, college clinicians likely will encounter certain specific family problems. One is a history of abuse—physical, sexual, or emotional—from a parent or other family member. An often related but sometimes separate problem is that a child is growing up with a substance-abusing caretaker. Substance abusers not only may be abusive to others in the family, they also of course are unpredictable, irresponsible, and in need of caretaking themselves—placing children in the role of parenting their parents. Sometimes family abuse or substance abuse is an ongoing issue. Some college students still live with physically abusive or alcoholic parents, and others may be physically out of harm's way but have younger siblings who are in the care of these parents. In these cases therapists must help students sort out how to assure the safety of themselves or their siblings.

But even if the physical, emotional or substance abuse is historical, students still must deal with the varied consequences for their own emotional development. Some students adopt the same tactics as their parents in their own relationships. They may become abusive toward others or become victims of abuse or the dominance of others. They may develop substance-abuse problems. They may be unduly anxious, mistrustful, lacking in confidence, erratic in their behaviors, and inexplicably depressed. They may still be consumed by rage at the abusive parent and at other caretakers who failed to intervene.

James, a 21-year-old sophomore, came to school after several years of abuse by his alcoholic father. His mother, fearing the father's anger, denied the abuse was happening. In high school, James had worked as an automobile mechanic to financially support the family, which caused him to postpone completing high school by 2 years. Afterward he went to an affordable college that was as far away from his hometown as he could arrange. After a successful adaptation during his first year, however, the university judicial board referred James to the college counseling center the next year following several fights with other students. In each instance, he'd been drinking and had interpreted other students' behavior as "bullying" toward him.

James reluctantly completed the family diagram in his first session at the counseling center. He stated that he'd been responsible for the fights and wanted to put the problem behind him. He vowed to stop drinking as well, blaming the intoxication for his problems. It was clear that he did not want to discuss his family, his hometown, or his high school experience. But as the counselor waited patiently over several sessions, occasionally referring back to family experiences, James did reveal the past abuse, paternal alcoholism, and excessive demands placed on him during his adolescence. He told his counselor that he had not seen his parents or had telephone contact since coming to college over a year ago. He had worked in another city during the summer to finance his education.

James initially reacted with hostility and ridicule to the counselor's suggestion that he contact his parents to reestablish a relationship with them. As therapy proceeded, however, he became less resistant to discussing his family and began to see roots of his difficulties lodged in these relationships. At this point, his counselor again encouraged him to contact his parents to seek information about their own parents, a suggestion that was intended to avert the intensity of a direct confrontation with them over the past. Focusing on the grandparents would engage his parents as allies in the mission of information gathering. The counselor wanted to help James establish a different relationship with his parents in order to work on defining himself. In agreeing to communicate with his parents, James learned that his father had experienced considerable abuse from his own alcoholic father and had been cut off from him for over 30 years. For that reason, James had not known his grandparents.

Reestablishing his family relationships, "bridging the cutoff" in his family, appeared to have a calming effect on his relationships with others in the university community. He now understood his peer difficulties as related to his family experiences and so was able to respond to others without suspicion and hostility, no longer treating them as stand-ins for his parents. As often happens, the reestablished relationship with his father didn't become close, but ending the cutoff did help James work on his differentiation of self.

Another common family problem is parental divorce and separation. Similar to the problem of parental abuse, divorce can have varied and far-reaching effects on students. They may have blamed themselves for the divorce, believing that their parents' failed marriage meant that they weren't lovable. And, indeed, students may not have received sufficient love and attention if their parents had been more intent on their own conflict than on their children's welfare. Students may have been forced to side with one parent against the other, creating the sort of unhealthy triangle that leaves them possibly cut off from one parent and enmeshed with the other. They may have been burdened with caring for a depressed parent or an emotionally neglected younger sibling. They may have had to adjust to parental remarriages, relocations, new half-siblings, and step-siblings. Not every parental breakup leads to such consequences, but in many instances the children of divorced parents carry lasting wounds and suffer problems adjusting to college.

One of the thrusts of transgenerational family therapy is to encourage students who have cutoff parental relations to establish contact with both parents. Managing the triangle with parents, whose own marital relationship may be hostile or nonexistent, becomes an important therapeutic task.

Bernadine, a 22-year-old third-year student, was the only child of parents who divorced when she was 12. Her mother had been granted custody in a bitter dispute and her father had left town the following year; she had little contact with him since. She sought assistance at the college counseling center for depression, poor grades, and social withdrawal. Bernadine spent an increasing amount of time in her room, frequently in bed.

In completing the family diagram with her, the therapist noted the cutoff from the father and the overly dependent relationship with the mother. The counselor also discovered that Bernadine's mother planned to remarry for the fourth time. It was to be a casual ceremony and Bernadine was encouraged not to attend. Bernadine suddenly felt that she had lost her mother as well as her father, and she felt utterly alone.

The counselor coached Bernadine to reestablish contact with the mother, helping her to express her wish to attend the wedding and be a part of that ceremony. When she did, the mother welcomed her, explaining that because of her embarrassment at having three failed marriages, she simply wanted to remove herself from her daughter's life. This positive experience prompted the counselor to encourage Bernadine to recontact her father and establish a realistic relationship with him. With the help of his friends, she tracked him down and called him, but, though cordial, he didn't seem receptive to further contact. Devastated by this, Bernadine worked with the counselor on her expectations about other people's behavior. In sum, she worked toward defining herself in relationship to her father and becoming more realistic with her mother. These experiences gave her a sense of control over herself and in turn helped her reengage in her social and academic life.

Summary

Many problems presented by college students who seek counseling are, explicitly or indirectly, family problems. Given this perspective, we advocate that campus clinicians incorporate principles of family systems theory into their therapeutic approaches. This approach does not legislate who or how many family members are in the therapy room. The concepts of interconnectedness, triangulation, circular thinking, emotional cutoff, enmeshment, overfunctioning and underfunctioning, and family structure are valuable for analyzing problems and planning treatment interventions. The use of the family diagram, or genogram, is a particularly helpful technique. In this work, counseling that employs family systems principles strives for therapeutic neutrality, management of triangles, establishment of contact with the family, and, above all, differentiation of self.

References

Boszormenyi-Nagy, I. (1972). Loyalty implications of the transference model in psychotherapy. *Archives of General Psychiatry, 27*, 374–380.

Boszormenyi-Nagy, I., & Sparks, G. (1973). *Invisible loyalties*. New York: Hoeber & Harper.

Bowen, M. (1978). *Family therapy in clinical practice*. New York: Aronson.

Carter, B., & McGoldrick, M. (1999). *The expanded family life cycle: Individual, family, and social perspectives* (3rd ed.). Boston: Allyn and Bacon.

Gilbert, R. (1991). *Extraordinary relationships: A new way of thinking about human interactions*. New York: John Wiley.

Gilbert, R. (2004). *The eight concepts of Bowen theory*. Alexandria, VA: Leading Systems.

Kerr, M. E., & Bowen, M. (1988). *Family evaluation: An approach based on Bowen theory*. New York: W. W. Norton.

McDaniel, S. H., Hepworth, J., & Doherty, W. J. (1990). *Medical family therapy: A biopsychosocial approach to families with health problems*. New York: Basic Books.

McGoldrick, M., Gerson, R., & Shellenberger, S. (1999). *Genograms: Assessment and intervention*. New York: Norton.

Mikesell, R. H., Lusterman, D., & McDaniel, S. H. (1995). *Integrating family therapy: Handbook of family psychology and systems theory*. Washington, DC: American Psychological Association.

Nichols, M., & Schwartz, R. (1998). *Family therapy. Concepts and methods* (4th ed.). Boston: Allyn and Bacon.

Preto, N. G. (1989). Transformation of the family system in adolescence. In B. Carter & M. McGoldrick (Eds.), *The changing family life cycle: A framework for family therapy* (2nd ed., pp. 255–283). Boston: Allyn and Bacon.

Roberto, L. G. (1992). *Transgenerational family therapies*. New York: Guilford.

Stierlin, H. (1977). *Psychoanalysis and family therapy*. New York: Aronson.

6

Relationships

LEIGHTON C. WHITAKER

College psychotherapists are in an ideal position to help students with their relationship concerns. This chapter will mostly consider current relationship problems with peers and parents but will necessarily also make reference to historical relationships and the therapeutic relationship.

Whether students using campus counseling and mental health centers present relationship concerns per se, past and present relationships inevitably play powerful, though sometimes subterranean roles, in their college and university careers. What may appear, for example, simply as academic problems or as troubling symptoms of anxiety or depression may often be helpfully considered in the light of interpersonal relations. Thus, regardless of the presenting complaints, therapists should always be mindful of the role of relationship issues. After all, human beings live in a social universe. The quality of students' relationships affects all aspects of their lives.

But not all students are prepared to see their relationships as important. For that matter, they aren't prepared to examine themselves developmentally or to be curious about the underlying meaning of their problems. Instead, sometimes students now view themselves as having one or another "disorder" whose cause is inherently genetic or due to "biochemical imbalances," and whose treatment requires medication in addition to, or instead of, counseling or psychotherapy. Students generally are more likely now to assume that their "disorders," though they do have a negative impact on their relationships, are not at all caused by their relationship problems. Rather, their disorders are independent of the quality of their human connections.

Shy students, for example, may believe that they don't need to learn relationship skills. If told that they suffer from "social anxiety disorder," they may simply want the "anxiety" part treated without having to work on the "social" part. They have seen television ads suggesting that social anxiety disorder is a genetically or biologically determined "illness," perhaps even a disease entity. Consequently, while they can see that their problem impacts relationships negatively, they believe that it must be treated chemically rather than viewed as a relationship problem per se. Similarly, "depression" is often facilely considered an entity with no causal link to relationships. This kind of influence is now so endemic to American culture that the idea that relationships and personal issues matter, and can be dealt with in psychotherapy, may be hard for students to grasp.

Electronic Communication and Media Messages

Whether it is MTV, magazines directed at teens and young adults, or computer websites and chat rooms, the media and the Internet strongly influence how college students view and conduct their relationships. Cell phones are now almost standard equipment. Some students are on their phones with parents, friends, or boyfriends and girlfriends a dozen times a day. Most recently, logging in to chat rooms has created the possibility for what some observers regard as an addiction (Applebome, 2004). Brief interactions through IMs (instant messages) and their related "away" messages have become commonplace. Sometimes these electronic vehicles facilitate connection and sometimes they create misunderstandings and even animosities. For better *and* worse, when students relate to one another these days, much of it is electronic, not face-to-face.

On top of this, the popular media teems with relationship advice, particularly for heterosexual relationsips. Television and radio present a vast assortment of relationship gurus, each pitching an approach designed to have emotional appeal and therefore commercial success. Writers offer readers techniques for getting what they want out of relationships by manipulating the other person—for example, feigning disinterest by "playing it cool." A popular magazine for men provides technically accurate, elaborate, step-by-step procedural instruction on how to bring a woman to orgasm but says nothing about how to cultivate a relationship. In an article on relationship advice columns that reviewed studies of media influence on young people, Lori Kogan and Julie Kellaway (2004) found that popular magazines promote "centerfold syndrome" and "appearance obsession." These are some of the influences that we therapists must confront when students come to our offices. Therapists would do well to pick up some magazines to understand what students are experiencing.

On Theoretical Orientation

Paying therapeutic attention to relationships does not depend on one's theoretical orientation. Years ago, a psychoanalytically trained psychiatrist and I asked colleagues to comment on two manuscripts we had written. Their responses were revealing. A Gestalt therapist claimed adamantly that our work was an excellent example of Gestalt therapy. A prominent behavior therapist claimed that our work exemplified behavior therapy. Some psychoanalysts insisted that our work was consistent with their own orientation. Meanwhile, my colleague and I felt that our work had been strongly influenced by psychodrama and milieu therapy!

In my view, various orientations can work so long as they foster caring and positive human interactions. Whatever the problem areas, and whatever the therapist's theoretical orientation, psychotherapy is most effective when the therapist cultivates a positive connection between client and therapist and emphasizes learning about past, present, and prospective relationships.

Sociocultural Context

It is important to understand relationship problems within the context of various sociocultural trends. For example, the increased sexual freedom beginning in the 1960s obviously has had an impact, as has the increase in sexually transmitted infections and diseases, including HIV and AIDS. Other trends that have had an impact on students' relationships include the women's movement and reactions to it; the increased (but not total) acceptance of sexual minorities; increased ethnic and racial diversification; increases in enrollment of foreign students and older, returning students; the increased cost of higher education; the exponential growth in communications technology; increases in mental disturbances among young people; and colleges' earlier abandonment, and subsequent partial reclaiming, of their *in loco parentis* responsibilities and authority. These trends color the kinds of relationship problems college therapists see and the approaches they take.

One sociocultural phenomenon that deserves particular mention for its impact on relationships is the problematic use of alcohol and other drugs on campus, a phenomenon that is not going away despite innumerable educational programs and a vast literature on the topic of student drinking.

Kimberly Williams (1998) has provided an especially valuable report on the complex and usually underreported ways alcohol and other drug use can determine and complicate relationships. Most of the women in her study tended to find and keep friends who used drugs at similar levels to their own. Further, both users and nonusers were expected to engage in caretaking of debilitated users, including in dangerous situations for both users and caretakers. Often caretakers enabled further hazardous use and dangerous behavior by users, especially since the caretakers usually concealed the problem from authority figures, including resident advisors (RAs) and college therapists. "Men's violent behavior in many instances of sexual assault when using drugs or when drunk was excused or forgiven" (Williams, 1998, p. 71).

The common mix of alcohol and sex, especially uncaring sex, often precedes date rape, especially when both parties have been drinking heavily. A study by Inaba and Cohen (1996) involving college men and women found that 75% of rapists and most of those raped were using psychoactive drugs, including alcohol. All of the gang rapists in their study were under the influence of alcohol. Unwanted sex in the context of substance use is also a problem within the lesbian-gay-bisexual-transgendered (LGBT) community.

A Word on Biology

The extent to which differences between men and women stem from biology as opposed to social and cultural forces has been an ongoing debate. Shlain (2004) provides an ingeniously constructed biological foundation for understanding the challenges of relations between the sexes, highlighting how "the kaleidoscopic, maddening, exciting, enchanting, and baffling man–woman dance, more commonly referred to as 'a relationship,' evolved" (p. ix). Employing insights from evolutionary biology, Shlain points out how the two genders have become different in such complex ways that they inevitably find it difficult to match up to their mutual satisfaction. Biologically, men peak sexually in their late teens, while women peak in their thirties. Women have greater connections than men between their intellect and emotions because of their brain structure, notably a thicker corpus callosum mediating more connection between the cerebral hemispheres. Due to the hazards of pregnancy and childbirth, as well as their typically greater responsibility for infants and young children, women tend to be more concerned than men about the security of a relationship. Meanwhile, for men the expectations to empathize with women and take on a long-term commitment may be at odds with roving instincts.

Of course, biological differences hardly account for all the differences between men and women or all the problems of heterosexual relationships. And gay and lesbian relationships have their own challenges, even in the absence of biologically derived gender differences.

General Treatment Issues

Assessment and Treatment

Guidelines for assessing and treating students who present relationship issues have to be structured in accordance with the limitations of the mental health or counseling services, not only due to preordained limits on the number of sessions but also to undergraduates' tendency to come and go rather than sustain therapy (Widseth & Webb, 1992). The modal number of counseling sessions for students is 1, the next highest frequency is 2, the next highest is 3, and so on, with the average number of sessions less than 10 for nearly all institutions of higher education. In most cases, therefore, the relationship between therapist and student, which itself is a powerful determinant of therapeutic success, has only a very brief time to develop. Considering this brevity, formal assessment is seldom possible. Typically, assessment of students and their relationship concerns is done as soon as counseling or psychotherapy begins—assessment and therapy are conducted together, and indeed reinforce one another. Thus, asking pertinent questions about students' past and current relationships can provide the therapist with ideas as to the nature and origins of the problem and simultaneously help the student realize what ingredients may solve it.

As an example of the therapeutic impact of asking the right questions, a second-semester freshman came to the mental health service with simply an "academic problem," due, he said, to the difficulty of his courses. In asking about his family background—a question the student at first thought was irrelevant—the therapist discovered that the student's father had died suddenly the year before. Permission was then sought to talk with the mother, who documented her son's subsequent social withdrawal. In subsequent sessions, both the student and the therapist focused on his relationship with his father, and he began to mourn the loss. His concentration now improved, and even though there had been little direct discussion of academics, he earned a top grade in his most challenging course.

Similarly, a first-year graduate student, a lesbian, couldn't understand her recent concentration difficulties in light of her stellar undergraduate academic career. When the therapist inquired about her current relationships, the student said that she was putting friendships and romance "on hold" in order to devote herself wholeheartedly to her rigorous program, and for that reason had broken off a relationship with her college lover. The therapist wondered aloud about the consequences of neglecting her personal life. Acknowledging that she often caught herself dwelling on her prior relationship and her current loneliness, she determined to take steps to end her isolation. Not surprisingly, as she began to enrich her personal life, her ability to concentrate improved.

Motivation and Readiness to Change

Part of the assessment process consists of estimating the student's willingness to look at what needs to be changed. Quite often, the student's initial frame of reference may not be conducive to change, but subsequently the student becomes more ready to look at underlying issues.

Good psychotherapy for relationship problems often must change the student's perception of not only *what* but *who* needs changing. Commonly, a student in a problematic relationship is trying mainly to get the other person to change, saying in effect, "If only my boyfriend (or girlfriend, parents, or roommate) would treat me better, everything would be fine." Thus, the therapist is implicitly asked to change someone who is not present and who, moreover, may have no inclination to change, let alone enter into psychotherapy.

Such was the wish of George, who presented with depression and alcohol problems for which he felt his father was responsible. His stated goal was to have a better relationship with his father, which would happen by somehow changing this emotionally distant person. The father, on the other hand, wanted his son to reduce his drinking and be more responsible, but wanted no part of any psychotherapy for himself. As the student gradually began to realize and accept that his father was not going to change, he decided to work on himself, stopped drinking entirely, and did in fact become more mature and responsible. The father appreciated the change in George and responded by giving him somewhat more attention, although still without much of an emotional connection. In this case, the relationship itself did not dramatically improve. What did change was the student's acceptance of the relationship's limitations and recognition that any change would have to come from within himself.

The Importance of Historical Relationships

The quality of students' prior relationships must be explored to understand their current relationships as well as other problems. People do not psychologically live only in the present. They generalize from past relationships, expecting to be treated by new people as they've been perhaps problematically treated in the past—indulgently, neglectfully, critically, exploitively, inconsistently, or abusively. They also may try to compensate for disappointments in previous relationships—for example, by idealizing a new relationship or taking vengeance on a new person for an old hurt. Often, the new person has unwittingly auditioned, as it were, for the part of a figure from the past.

Several kinds of historical relationships should be explored: How did the student relate to primary caregivers, siblings, and other key relatives? How did these people view the student; what was his or her image in their eyes? How did the primary caregivers relate to each another? How did the student fit in socially with friends, classmates, and romantic partners prior to college? Discovering parallels to prior relationships helps both therapists and students to understand the current difficulties.

Confidentiality and Privacy

Confidentiality and privacy concerns can be especially challenging in cases of problematic relationships. For example, when one or both parties are making allegations of harmful or life-threatening behavior, such threats or evidence of physical harm must be taken seriously, which may require the therapist to breach confidentiality, albeit in a stringently limited way.

Another problem can arise if the same therapist happens to do individual psychotherapy with two students in a close relationship, a not uncommon situation at a small college. In many such cases, it is possible to refer one of the students to another therapist. A tougher dilemma to resolve arises when two previously uninvolved students seen individually by the same therapist begin an intense problematic relationship. It may be best to discuss the issue with each student and negotiate a referral for one or both, or for them to consider couples therapy. But if it is impractical to refer one of the students, then the therapist needs to clarify the ground rules: "You are free to discuss whatever you like in our sessions. I will not reveal anything you say to anyone else, nor will I reveal anything to you that another person brings up in a confidential session. Our sessions are just between us and they are just for you, to help you understand and work through issues, including your relationship."

Transference and Countertransference

When dealing with relationship concerns, particularly in couples treatment, but also in individual counseling, transference and countertransference reactions are rife. One key question for students is how the therapist is reacting to them in relation to the other person. Does the therapist appear to be on their side, or is he or she siding with the other person—the romantic partner, friend, roommate, or relative? For the therapist, a complementary question is whether these instances of perceived favoritism are solely in the student's mind or are in fact an accurate reflection of the therapist's true feelings? For example, has the therapist been unsuccessful in relationships, and so is unduly negative toward the student's current relationship? Is the therapist attracted to, or turned off by, either partner? Does the therapist have strong and perhaps biased views regarding what constitutes healthy and unhealthy relationships? Does the therapist's sexual orientation influence his or her views of heterosexual and gay and lesbian relationships? For gay and lesbian students, what are their assumptions about the therapist's sexual orientation and the therapist's views regarding same-sex couples? These and other themes may subtly influence how the student and therapist approach treatment. If the therapist senses that he or she is bringing in a biased perspective or is unduly influenced by personal issues, then of course receiving good supervision or peer consultation is recommended.

Individual Versus Couples or Family Treatment

In cases of troubled relationships, an important question is whether to work with the individual or with both (or all) parties. Motivation, readiness, and responsibility are important considerations. If one person in the relationship has no inclination to be involved in psychotherapy, efforts at multiple-party treatment may be unproductive or even harmful. And in some cases, the presence of both partners or the whole family may distract from the real issue, such as when one person needs to take individual responsibility or deal with serious individual problems. But where everyone is in agreement about sharing responsibility to improve the relationship, and no one has such serious individual emotional problems as to doom the effort, couples or family work can be quite helpful. Though distance sometimes makes these sessions impractical, at times even that obstacle can be overcome.

Mary came to an East Coast university, while her father, who had divorced her mother several years before, continued to live on the West Coast. She felt emotionally abandoned by her father and said that perhaps the therapist could help by seeing them together. The father surprised both Mary and her therapist by immediately agreeing to fly east for one or more sessions. The first session alone was immensely gratifying to both. The father was very forthcoming and said he would be glad to make the long trip again if Mary would ask him. He assumed responsibility for having been distant since the divorce, and Mary likewise admitted that she hadn't made it easy for him to reach out. His obvious caring and their mutual acceptance of responsibility made it easy for them to repair their relationship.

Individual Versus Group Therapy

Another therapeutic question in dealing with relationship issues is whether to refer the student for group treatment. Most students come to the college counseling center wanting and expecting to meet one-to-one with a therapist—a predilection many therapists share. However, group therapy may well be the treatment of choice when the presenting problems involve students' habitual ways of relating. Groups give students a laboratory in which they can interact, obtain feedback from their peers, and try out new ways of relating.

Once students actually get started in groups, generally they grow fiercely attached to them. The trick is getting them to start. Most students are reluctant to join a group, explaining that, among other reasons, they are intimidated by groups and would feel too shy to discuss their problems with other students. The best response to these objections is that working on feelings of intimidation and shyness is exactly the point. *Of course* they have these feelings—that's the purpose of the group! The therapist can add that other group members have similar feelings, the group leader will help them feel safe, and furthermore they are soon likely to feel more comfortable once they give group sessions a try. Much depends on therapists' own belief in groups. When therapists truly have faith in the modality, often they can persuade reluctant students to give groups a try. For students who are too resistant or reticent at first, some individual sessions may prepare them for a group referral later.

Specific Problem Manifestations

Shyness and Social Isolation

Shy students are probably more common on campuses than their counseling-center representation might suggest, partly because their shyness makes them hesitate to ask for help. In residence halls and classrooms, their needs may easily go unattended—they rarely cause problems that would attract professional notice. Yet shyness can be an acutely uncomfortable and even disabling problem. Shy students have trouble making friends and finding relationships, are unable to participate in classroom discussions, and, at the extreme, may be unable even to continue in college.

One such extreme case was Don, a withdrawn freshman who had attended a Midwestern university for less than a month when he was found hallucinating on the roof of a fraternity house. He was then admitted to a psychiatric hospital, where he was sullenly withdrawn and immediately became openly angry when assigned to a therapist, saying he felt like punching his therapist in the nose.

Don's family history was characterized by extreme lack of communication, leaving him unprepared for relating to anyone. He hadn't made friends in high school, and he'd scarcely spoken to anyone during his brief stay in college. The therapist suggested, to his surprise, that his anger showed spirit and could be used constructively. A combination of individual and group therapy with other late-adolescent students succeeded in drawing him out to the point that he accepted a challenge to make a speech to the group. But when he delivered his speech, an especially aggressive male member derided him with a loud volley of curses, blamed him for taking up the group's time, and said his speech was the worst he had ever heard. Without hesitation, Don replied that it had taken him courage and hard work to make the speech, whereupon everyone else applauded.

Looking back, Don realized that his psychotic break had been precipitated by his terror at the challenge of socialization. His psychotherapy helped him gradually to develop confidence and social skills. Learning how to use his anger constructively, he returned to the university and became a successful member of the debating team.

Some students may go all the way through college without making any close friends, provided they can do well academically. A woman who survived high school and her 4 years in college in this solitary way found herself on probation in graduate school because she was unable to develop the rapport with others necessary to succeed in group projects. Her psychotherapy required delving deeply into her earliest years to fathom why she had related fairly well within the family but not at all with outsiders.

Typically, shy students expect immediate rejection and need help finding ways to be friendly despite their fear. When their social anxiety is fairly mild, students can be helped with brief psychotherapy that emphasizes preparation and rehearsal for social encounters, first in the safety of the therapist's office and then, if needed, in group therapy with students having similar issues. The therapist's technique can employ cognitive-behavioral methods to help undo unrealistic assumptions, and psychodrama-like role playing to make it possible to try out heretofore "dangerous" friendly advances. The experience of success and of nascent mastery provided by the initial role playing usually becomes a powerful motivator for students to be yet more daring.

In quite mild cases, students can be helped instantly with friendly support and a simple suggestion or two. A beginning graduate student, newly arrived from another state, where he had attended a very small college, succeeded right away after he was encouraged to smile when he went through the cafeteria line. On his first try, he found himself invited to sit with other students and began feeling at home in what had once seemed to him the "strange, impersonal" setting of a huge university.

Typically, shy students are inordinately self-conscious, anticipating that they will be found unacceptable and therefore will be embarrassed, whether by the other person's actual rejection of them or by their own evident awkwardness. Either way, being fearfully self-preoccupied, they may be afraid to take even a first step socially. The best approach then is to find out and build on what the student can already do with some comfort and to encourage the student to shift attention, if possible, from herself to the other person.

Donna was a very bright first-year student admitted to college on the strength of her exceptionally high test scores. She was so shy that she could barely ask for counseling. In her first few sessions, it was difficult for her to look at the counselor, and she would quickly run out of things to say. Her counselor, learning that she liked to draw, then suggested that she simply spend time drawing during the session. They then began talking back and forth while she drew, her eyes still fixed on the paper in front of her. Gradually, she started to describe her discomfort with talking, and recounted some of her history. Becoming increasingly at ease in sessions, she then dared to speak up in some classes, and later mentioned her attraction to a classmate, who turned out to be quite shy himself. She was encouraged to empathize with him, and so to become less preoccupied with herself. The young man was obviously delighted and encouraged by her approaching him and quickly asked her out, which further increased her confidence.

Students can also have problems relating comfortably for reasons other than shyness. Some are very uncomfortable with close human connections due to past intensely hurtful experiences, such as neglect or abuse. They push other people away rather than get too close—and so end up isolated and lonely.

The therapist's manner with these students must be carefully calibrated, neither too warm so as to make the student feel uncomfortable, nor so distant in reaction to the student's coldness and seeming indifference as to be rejecting. Goals with these students are necessarily modest in brief psychotherapy. Ideally, one helps them to establish a degree of relatedness with others that they can tolerate.

Some students are hungry for warm relationships but simply lack social skills. These are the students who may have histories of being teased or shunned, whose efforts at reaching out have consistently failed. Sometimes they are intensely devoted to therapy because it provides their only experience of acceptance and friendship. Such students can benefit from simple social suggestions, such as tips on how to listen to others, ask questions, and even dress appropriately. These students also may find companionship despite their awkwardness if they look in the right places. Therapists can direct them to activities, clubs, religious groups, and organizations that are likely to be accepting. Students made miserable by being outcasts in their dormitories may find more welcoming environments elsewhere on or off campus.

Self-Esteem and Relationships

When students seek friends or romantic partners, their identities and self-esteem are of course involved. Those students who lack self-esteem may fall into the trap famously described by Groucho Marx, "I wouldn't join any club that would have me as a member." These students may be quick to dismiss or disrespect potential friends or romantic partners who accept them. There is always something wrong with the other person, they explain, and they wonder why they simply can't find an appropriate set of friends or a suitable partner, or why all people fall short of their expectations. While it's true that many potential relationships *are* wrong, a consistent pattern of non-commitment and of rejecting possibilities for connection signals self-esteem difficulties—or, according to the psychodynamic perspective, narcissistic difficulties.

Students who lack self-esteem may also gravitate toward people who do not accept them, who instead are critical, self-absorbed, or overtly dismissive. These students may then engage in a long campaign to change the other persons, to win their love and respect. In these cases, not only don't these students feel worthy of someone who might value them in turn, but, from an object relations perspective, they are drawn to depriving "objects"—people who are attractive precisely because they are rejecting. The unconscious hope is that by changing the unavailable and rejecting person's opinion, they can earn self-worth at last. From a historical point of view, of course, they are unconsciously replicating their family history of feeling unloved and rejected, while at the same time hoping to change the outcome.

During her childhood and early adolescence, Michele had suffered consistent neglect from her parents and felt rejected by them. As she started to date young men, she engaged in a kind of repetition compulsion, going after uncaring people who inevitably rejected her. The first stage of treatment helped her to understand this dynamic, to see first the pattern of her going after unavailable men, and then how this pattern was rooted in her early childhood experience. Fortunately, Michele was motivated to understand herself and was soon able to recognize the parallels; indeed, she already half-suspected that she was setting herself up for disappointment in her relationships. The more difficult stage was translating these insights into behavioral change. Michele admitted that other young men were attracted to her, but she had never felt attracted in return. How, she asked, could she go out with someone whom she didn't really like? As therapy continued, however, Michele's sense of herself as an attractive, worthy person gradually grew, thanks in part to the nurturing, supportive therapeutic relationship. If the therapist could find her worthy of respect, then perhaps she was somebody who merited respect from other people too.

Brief college therapies don't always have a clear-cut resolution, but this one did. After a number of weeks, Michele decided that one young man she'd previously overlooked was not, in fact, such a loser. In fact, she discovered that she liked him a lot. Soon they started going out, and she experienced for the first time a mutually respectful and supportive romantic relationship. Not everything went smoothly, to be sure. Michele fretted that this new boyfriend would eventually discover her unworthiness and would reject her too. Sometimes she was excessively needy with him, or became critical; she was testing to see if he would in fact fulfill her deepest fears. Fortunately, however, this time she had chosen a suitable partner, and with therapeutic support she was able to ride out her moments of insecurity in the relationship. When last seen, Michele had become able to accept and return the caring and respect of her new boyfriend and had happily joined a club that wanted her as a member.

Couples Problems

The range of couples' problems is extensive. There are couples who bicker, couples who have violent arguments or engage in cold war, couples who are dealing with jealousy, sexual problems, betrayals, dependency, boredom, and exploitation. Some couples question whether to move in together or get married; others question whether to break up. Further, the problems of couples have complex causes. Usually problems are partly due to his issues, partly due to her issues, and partly due to their issues—basic incompatibilities between them. Adding to the complexity, couples' problems may be exacerbated by stress, academic problems, finances, substance abuse, and a host of other concerns, including the special problems faced by gay and lesbian couples.

For a college therapist working within a brief therapy context, it's obviously impossible to delve into and resolve everything. Whether one is working with an individual having couples problems or with both partners directly, the therapist must try to find a realistic focus and set of goals. One of the early questions to resolve is whether both parties in the relationship truly want the pairing to succeed. If so, then the overall goal is to improve the relationship in some fashion. If not, then the desired outcome may be dissolution, painful though that may be for one or both partners.

How does one help students who are having relationship problems? One way, as suggested above, is by helping them appreciate the negative impact of historical relationships. Quite often, the inevitable reenactments are unwitting. While psychotherapy cannot change the past (sometimes students seem to hope that revisiting their early deprivations and injuries will magically bring about a different outcome), psychotherapy can help students avoid automatically repeating old self-defeating patterns of behavior.

Jack, an older, married student, became aware in treatment that whenever he entered through the front door of his apartment, he immediately expected to encounter the same atmosphere of tension and lack of caring he had experienced in his childhood home. His therapist explicitly encouraged him to hesitate before opening the door in order to remind himself that it was his wife who lived there with him, not his parents. He began to understand that while his marriage had its own challenges, his apprehensiveness was due to his earlier programming, which had exaggerated and exacerbated the actual marital difficulties. When he anticipated coldness and criticism from his wife, he reacted defensively and, of course, provoked her into doing the same; his negative expectations became a self-fulfilling prophecy. This one insight, and the single technique of pausing before entering the apartment, did not, of course, entirely resolve his marital difficulties. However, sometimes one small change can bring important dividends. Both Jack and his wife were encouraged by the progress and continued to make gains in their marriage.

As Jack's example makes clear, students having couples' problems can also be helped with practical suggestions in addition to key insights. For example, consider students who are afraid to express feelings and needs. These students may have been discouraged from doing so as children, whether because they had been placed in a caretaker role and encouraged to put others' needs first or because they had learned that it was necessary to be perfect in order to be loved; showing weakness or need was to incur rejection. While understanding these issues can of course be helpful, such students can also be given practical help in expressing needs and feelings appropriately. This may take the form of assertiveness training: "What would you like to say to him? How could you express it directly?" Role playing and/or giving homework might be utilized. Cognitive-behavioral techniques, designed to ferret out irrational and catastrophic assumptions, may also be useful. Thus one might say to a student afraid to tell her boyfriend that she wants to spend more time with him: "What exactly are you afraid of? What do you think he would do?"

Sometimes relationship problems are clearly tied to serious psychological problems of one of the partners—or, more often, both partners. (More often than not, students choose partners who, though they may have different personality styles and issues, are roughly on the same level in terms of emotional development.) Most notably, if one or both students have borderline personality traits, relationship problems are a foregone conclusion. These relationships tend to be characterized by great intensity and tendencies to act out. The drama may revolve around breakups, suicide threats, cheating, physical violence, and passionate reconciliations. For these disturbed students, or those involved with them, resolving the relationship problems is impossible without intensive individual therapy to address individual problems. These students may present costly dilemmas in terms of time and worry, with demands and needs not possible to meet.

Roommate Problems

Roommate problems can be as intense in their own way as romantic vicissitudes. Students have high hopes for friendship with their roommates but then may find that the other person comes from a very different background and has very different habits and values. Living in close quarters under the stress of academic pressure, sleeplessness, and noise heightens any potential tension. Roommates may squabble about playing loud music, keeping lights lit, cleaning bathrooms, borrowing clothing, or having boyfriends or girlfriends stay over, or about politics, religion, and morality. They may interact with rejection, criticism, teasing, or cold silence. It can be hard living with another person. Sometimes two students who might well get along or become friends otherwise can become mortal enemies when shut in together in a confined dormitory dwelling.

Helping students who have roommate problems again comes down to motivation, to the student's acceptance of some responsibility for problems and for a solution. If the student is willing to make changes, then the relationship may get better. Therapists can discuss and even role-play with students the basics of negotiation, communication, and assertiveness—expressing needs politely and directly, while listening to and respecting the roommate's needs. The goal is compromise. If this plan doesn't succeed, then the student can be advised to have an RA mediate, to spend more time out of the room and with friends, or, if those steps don't work, to arrange for a room change.

All human relationships are, of course, influenced by the principals' distorted perceptions of each other based on earlier life experience, or *transference phenomena*. Roommate relationships are no exception. Another useful approach, therefore, is to help students discover ways they may be misjudging their roommates, exaggerating their flaws, or overreacting to minor or casual offenses. If students can view their roommates in perspective, the relationship is sure to improve.

Abusive Relationships and Stalking

Abusive or stalking relationships arouse great consternation for everyone involved, particularly because they are at the intersection of disciplinary and mental health service concerns. Students, mental health practitioners, college administrators, and others must weigh the seriousness of threats of physical as well as emotional harm in choosing intervention approaches (Amada, 1994, 1999; Whitaker, 2002).

Abusers, including stalkers in particular, tend to have a sense of entitlement, acting as though they have a right to invade their victims' personal space. They may even rationalize their abuse by blaming the victim, like a perversion of the old song, "You made me hurt you, I didn't want to do it." Victims, in turn, may unwittingly encourage the abuse, very possibly because of their own prior history of abuse as children. At any rate, colleges have to respond to all aspects of these poisonous situations. Steps should be taken to protect the threatened person. Disciplinary and legal actions may have to be taken against the abuser. And counseling or psychotherapy should be offered to both parties. In some cases, even *mandated* short-term counseling for the stalker may be effective if it is tailored specifically to enhance impulse control and take into account the abuser's readiness to change (Pollard, 2001). But it should be emphasized that counseling alone is not sufficient in cases of abusive behavior. Unless there are clear disciplinary sanctions against abusive or harassing behavior, mere counseling may in effect aid and abet further abusive and destructive behavior.

Sometimes abusive students can be treated only through disciplinary sanctions. Liz came to a university counseling center asking to be protected from Jeffrey, who had angrily told her he had fallen in love with her against his own wishes and that his plight was her fault. He explained that she was too attractive for him to resist, and therefore she was sidetracking his dedication to becoming a world-famous scientist. The more he followed her, the more agitated he became and the more frightened she felt. Jeffrey was unwilling or unable to stop his menacing behavior or see a therapist, and so was required to leave the university, while Liz was left having to consult a therapist to deal with her traumatic experience.

Fortunately, counseling can sometimes prove effective. Sung was a lonely international student who instantly fell in love when Gail chatted with him one day when they left class together. He interpreted her friendliness to mean that she felt the same way and soon started sending her gifts and e-mail invitations to go out with him. Afraid of hurting his feelings and unsure what to do, Gail joined him for a coffee on one occasion but otherwise tried to avoid him or made excuses to turn down his invitations. Soon, she was afraid to return to her dormitory for fear she'd run into Sung. She finally reported her concerns to a residential education administrator, who arranged for both students to speak to counselors. Gail learned how to politely but firmly say no, to give clear messages that she didn't want to pursue a relationship. As for Sung, despite his unfamiliarity with American culture, on some level he did understand that his advances toward Gail had been unwelcome, and he accepted the dean's mandate that he cease making any efforts to contact Gail. Therapy enabled him to talk about his feelings of loneliness and supported him as he explored new ways, like campus clubs and a local church, to establish a social network.

Breakups

Students today tend not to be as desperate to find a romantic partner, or certainly a husband or wife, as in earlier eras. Still, many students do search for sexual and romantic partners, and many students do form strong emotional attachments. When their relationships break up, particularly if they have been rejected, they can be left with feelings of shock, hurt, and rage. Not only are most students relatively inexperienced at this—this may be the first time their hearts have been broken—but the person who rejected them may be living in the same dormitory, and perhaps going out with someone new who lives right next door. Often there's no escape after a college romance fails. No wonder romantic breakups are the precipitant of many suicidal crises.

Helping students survive breaking up often requires an exercise in crisis management. Safety plans are, of course, necessary if the student feels suicidal, and it may be necessary to enlist family or friends for support or to encourage the student to go home for a weekend if he is unable to function. Students can be asked about coping means that have worked in the past—writing thoughts down, calling parents, e-mailing friends, playing music—and encouraged to resort to these means again. Therapists should try to restore students' perspective, reminding them that the current pain will not last forever, nor will this failed relationship be their last opportunity to find romance. At the same time, it's important to validate the intensity of students' distress. Breaking up is one of the most psychologically painful experiences of a lifetime, and so students' reactions are understandable.

Being rejected romantically can also take a toll on students' self-esteem. They ask themselves, "What's wrong with me? Why am I unlovable?" Therapists should explore this theme and point out the fallacy in the logic that another's acceptance or rejection should determine one's self-worth. It sometimes helps to give esteem-restoring homework assignments: "Your assignment this weekend is to do anything you can to feel good about yourself."

Often, students whose relationships have ended are loath to talk about anything else. If left to their own devices, they would spend their entire course of treatment revisiting what happened, ruminating about the motives of the other person, and fantasizing about a reconciliation or revenge. While the brokenhearted do need an opportunity to vent their feelings, it is not therapeutically constructive for them to endlessly pick over the failed relationship. The conversation should be widened in order to put the breakup in context. What does this experience remind the student of from her past? How has she dealt with misfortunes before? What does he still value in himself and in his life? What else is he looking forward to in the future? Such questions can take a student out of the immediate torment of the breakup and lead to greater perspective and emotional relief.

References

Amada, G. (1994). *Coping with the disruptive college student: A practical model.* Asheville, NC: College Administration Publications.

Amada, Gerald. (1999). *Coping with misconduct in the college classroom: A practical model.* Asheville, NC: College Administration Publications.

Applebome, P. (2004, December 1). On campus, hanging out by logging on. *New York Times,* p. B1.

Inaba, D. S., & Cohen, W. E. (1996). *Uppers, downers, and all arounders: Physical and mental effects of psychoactive drugs* (6th ed.). Ashland, OR: CNS Productions.

Kogan, L. R., & Kellaway, J. A. (2004). Relationship advice columns from two popular magazines: Implications for therapy with women, men and heterosexual couples. *Journal of College Student Psychotherapy, 19,* 35–55.

Pollard, J. W. (2001). Don't go there: Impulse control in stage-specific short term counseling. In S. E. Cooper, J. Archer, Jr., & L. C. Whitaker (Eds.), *Case book of brief psychotherapy with college students* (pp. 65–84). Copublished simultaneously in *Journal of College Student Psychotherapy, 16* (1, 2 ,3, 4).

Shlain, L. (2004). *Sex, time and power: How women's sexuality shaped human evolution.* New York: Penguin Books.

Whitaker, L. C. (1996). Treating students with personality disorders: A costly dilemma *Journal of College Student Psychotherapy, 10,* 29–44.

Whitaker, L. C. (2002). Mental health issues in college health. In H. S. Turner & J. L. Hurley (Eds.), *The history and practice of college health* (pp. 192–208). Lexington: University Press of Kentucky.

Widseth, J. C., & Webb, R. E. (1992). "Toddler" to the inner world: The college student in psychotherapy. In L. C. Whitaker & R. E. Slimak (Eds.), *College student development* (pp. 59–75). Published simultaneously in *Journal of College Student Psychotherapy, 6* (3, 4).

Williams, K. M. (1998). *Learning limits: College women, drugs, and relationships.* Westport, CT: Bergin & Garvey.

Suggestions for Further Reading

Diamond, L. M., Savin-Williams, R. C., & Dubé, E. M. (2000). Sex, dating, passionate friendships, and romance: Intimate peer relations among lesbian, gay, and bisexual adolescents. In W. Furman, B. B. Brown, & C. Feiring (Eds.), *The development of romantic relationships in adolescence* (pp. 175–210). New York: Cambridge University Press. Written in great depth about LGBT relationships from adolescence into the early twenties. Highly relevant to LGBT college kids, who are usually a couple of years behind their heterosexual peers (K. Cohen, personal communication, February 20, 2006).

Eisler, R. (1996). *Sacred pleasure: Sex, myth, and the politics of the body: New paths to power and love*. San Francisco: HarperCollins. A brilliant social and anthropological evolutionary counterpart to the biological account, places man–woman relationships in a highly constructive framework.

Gray, J. (2004). *Men are from Mars, women are from Venus: The classic guide to understanding the opposite sex*. New York: Quill. Probably the best of the psychological self-help books, takes into account predetermined sex differences and gives practical advice.

Wolfe, T. (2004). *I am Charlotte Simmons*. New York: Farrar, Straus, and Giroux. A lengthy but fast-paced novel vividly depicting, in often harsh realistic detail, a myriad of campus relationship conundrums.

7
Depression and Anxiety

PAUL A. GRAYSON AND STEWART COOPER

Every problem area in this volume is intertwined with every other, and nowhere are the mutual involvements more evident than with depression and anxiety. Students who are depressed or anxious are sure to struggle elsewhere—in their studies, in relationships, and with eating and substance use. In turn, problems in other areas betoken and can trigger depression or anxiety. So, in practice, helping suffering students is rarely a straightforward process of targeting a discrete set of symptoms. Treating depression and anxiety requires understanding complex human beings who may need clinical attention on a number of fronts at once.

Matters get just as complicated when we try to pin down a depressed or anxious student's diagnosis. For one thing, there are so many diagnostic categories to consider. According to the *Diagnostic and Statistical Manual of Mental Disorders,* fourth edition (DSM-IV) (American Psychiatric Association, 2000), there are four kinds of depressive disorders—with *major depressive disorders* distinguished for severity and *dysthmic disorders* for chronicity—and nine bipolar disorders, all involving manic or hypomanic episodes, usually in addition to depressive episodes. There are a full dozen anxiety disorders, including panic disorder, posttraumatic stress disorder (PTSD), generalized anxiety disorder, and several kinds of phobias. There are the adjustment disorders: reactions to stress that normally involve anxiety, depressed mood, or both. Finally, we come to a grab bag of other diagnoses in which depressive or anxious symptoms may figure prominently, among them medical conditions, personality disorders, schizophrenia and schizoaffective disorder, pain disorder, hypochondriasis, and body dysmorphic disorder. The list is daunting.

As if so many diagnostic options weren't challenging enough, many college therapy patients don't fit snugly into any of these categories, or, as with the adult population, may warrant dual or multiple diagnoses. Because they are clinically fluid and because unrest and excesses are normative at their age, many have symptoms suggesting first one diagnostic category and then another, or seem quite diagnosable for a while and later not at all. It's as if we're trying to take their pictures but they refuse to stand still. Add to this the fact that there's considerable overlap between diagnostic categories anyway and so ample room for disagreement: One clinician's dysthymia may be another's generalized anxiety disorder or recurrent major depressive disorder or depression not otherwise specified. Given all this uncertainty, assigning diagnoses strikes us as a useful exercise to aid understanding and guide treatment and as a check on sloppy thinking or vague planning, but we shouldn't mistake it for an exact science. Sometimes the best we can do, given our patients' clinical slipperiness and the DSM-IV's limitations, is affix a question mark or a rule-out notation to a handful of categories, hoping to approximate the clinical picture by creating a diagnostic composite.

As a final caution about clinical complexity, we should also stress that depression and anxiety are usually not separate phenomena. Rather, they tend to occur together and to fuel one another, to the point where sometimes it's hard to tell them apart. Their close association is one reason for covering both of them in a single chapter. Another is that certain treatment principles and strategies tend to prove effective for each. In the following section, we will allude to particular depressive and anxiety disorders in a brief discussion of evidence-based treatment (EBT). But in the remaining sections—on assessment, the therapy relationship, and various treatment approaches—though we sometimes focus on either depression or anxiety and occasionally single out particular disorders, mostly our points apply more widely to all students who wrestle with mood and anxiety problems.

Evidence-Based Treatment

In recent years, more and more studies seem to indicate, and more clinicians have been persuaded, that particular therapies are suited for particular mood and anxiety disorders. In several large-scale clinical trials, the National Institute for Mental Health established that drug treatments, cognitive therapy (CT), and interpersonal therapy (IPT) each led to improvements in approximately 70% of depressed individuals, and further that CT was more successful than drug treatment in preventing relapse (Elkin et al., 1989; Shea et al., 1992). Studies of anxiety disorder have supported the following efficacies (Baez, 2005):

- General anxiety disorder: relaxation techniques and CT
- Obsessive-compulsive disorder (OCD): exposure, cognitive-behavioral therapy (CBT), and response prevention
- Panic disorder: *in vivo* exposure, CBT, and applied relaxation
- PTSD: exposure, stress inoculation, and eye movement desensitization and reprocessing (EMDR)
- Social anxiety: social skills training, relaxation methods, exposure, CBT, and group treatment
- Specific phobias: *in vivo* exposure, CBT, and systematic desensitization.

Such findings cannot be ignored. Even Martin Seligman, who raises caveats about the limitations of controlled trials, nevertheless endorses EBT in flatly asserting that failing to provide a mood-stabilizing medication for bipolar disorder is tantamount to malpractice, and one should "beware of any other form of treatment [besides drugs, electroconvulsive therapy, CT, and IPT] for unipolar depression" (Seligman, 1993).

Still, there are reasons to be cautious about jumping on the EBT bandwagon, especially within the college mental health setting. EBT studies generally last for 20 sessions of uninterrupted treatment, whereas college counseling is usually far shorter and hardly regular. EBT clinical trials exclude individuals who have more than one diagnosis, whereas college counseling patients, as noted above, may have several diagnoses, none at all, or at least no consistent diagnosis over time. EBT studies based on randomized controlled trails don't pay attention to individual differences or necessary modifications in treatment (Silberschatz, 1999). EBT treatments are conducted on adults, not college-age people, and ordinarily don't take into account developmental stressors or cultural factors, glaring omissions to any college clinician. EBT studies appear to be unfair to psychodynamic therapies, which, despite some attempts at manualizing, generally don't lend themselves to clinical trials. Perhaps most important, EBT trials concentrate on methods while giving short shrift to the therapeutic relationship. Several leading psychotherapy researchers (Norcross, 2002; Wampold, Lichtenberg, & Waehler, 2002) and most practicing therapists would argue that the bond between patients and therapists is an essential, if not the chief, active ingredient in psychotherapy.

That said, college clinicians obviously should heed any research findings that point the way to successful interventions. Our own centrist view, similar to our conclusion about assigning diagnoses, is that empirically supported treatments offer useful guidelines but must be flexibly applied, bearing in mind that each case is a fresh therapeutic challenge. Many of the principles and strategies discussed in this chapter are in the spirit of EBT practices within CT, behavior therapies, and IPT.

Assessment and Psychoeducation

Good treatment is predicated on accurate assessment. Some clinicians favor formal depression and anxiety assessment instruments such as the

- Beck Depression Inventory (BDI) (Beck, Rial, & Rickets, 1974)
- Beck Anxiety Inventory (BAI) (Beck, Epstein, Brown, & Steer, 1988)
- Hamilton Depression Rating Scale (U.S. DHHS, 1976)
- Public Health Questionnaire–9 (PHQ-9) (Spitzer, Kroenke, & Williams, 1999), a quick self-report assessing major depression
- Zung Self-Rating Depression Scale (Zung, 1965).

Assessment measures have the advantages of informing a clinician's impressions and objectively measuring a student's progress over time. These measures can also open the eyes of students who aren't sure whether to believe a therapist's feedback, and may draw out honest answers from those who aren't ready to open up to a therapist but will tell all on a paper-and-pencil or computer inventory.

But even without formal tests, clinicians can still readily identify mood or anxiety problems simply by listening closely to students' presenting concerns and following up by asking: "What has your mood been like recently?" and/or "How have you felt emotionally in the last few weeks?" When students don't clearly answer these questions—perhaps they are psychologically uncomfortable or culturally unfamiliar with verbalizing feelings—the information can usually be elicited by prompting: "Would you say you've mostly felt happy? Sad? Worried?" "Have you been feeling more happy or sad?" "Have you been feeling more sad or more worried?"

Once mood or anxiety problems are suspected, clinicians should follow up with questions regarding sleep, appetite, loss of interest in activities, hopelessness, and physical or other symptoms, to home in on a diagnosis. Knowing the DSM is obviously desirable, but there's nothing wrong with trotting out a copy of the DSM-IV to aid memory and lend authority to the conclusions: "Let's go through the symptoms of panic disorder to see if your problems fit that diagnosis." If the student is depressed, clinicians should also assess for possible bipolar disorder; and in all cases of depression and anxiety, they should assess for suicidal potential (Chapter 16 in this volume) and substance abuse (Chapter 11). A thorough assessment also covers precipitants and duration of the problem, prior episodes ("Have you gone through something similar in the past?"), and family history of emotional problems. With serious cases therapists should routinely ask about medical conditions and possibly recommend a medical checkup.

All these questions are part of a thorough initial evaluation for mood or anxiety problems. But we must take care not to grill our new patients, since their motivation for treatment is unknown and presumably they came in to talk rather than be bombarded with questions. It helps to explain: "I want to ask about your symptoms so we can understand together what you're struggling with emotionally." It helps too to weave questions into the interview so the conversation is two-way and students have time to express what they want to say.

Some young therapists are so intent on gathering information that they lose sight of the purpose of doing so. One reason for assessment, of course, is to guide treatment choices. Unless we recognize the signs of bipolar disorder, for example, we may fail to arrange a necessary medication evaluation. But an equally important reason for assessment is to educate students. Patients have a right to know what they're facing, and need this information to be informed collaborators in treatment.

For many students, just being given a label for their distress, even the general term "depression" or "anxiety," proves reassuring, validating, and therapeutic. Panic sufferers learn that they're not going crazy or dying or losing control; OCD sufferers and the depressed learn that they're not insane; and anxiety sufferers learn that they're not worthless or to blame for their condition. Labeling also can serve as a wake-up call to take problems seriously: "No, your symptoms aren't trivial. They're consistent with a major depressive episode. It's good you came here today to get help with this."

Jill, an 18-year-old African-American sophomore, told her therapist that she didn't want to make a mountain out of a molehill and was only coming in because her friends pushed her. When the therapist asked what specifically concerned her friends, Jill gave vague answers peppered with many "I don't knows" and added, "But doesn't everyone get sad sometimes?" With her consent, the therapist then systematically went through the DSM-IV criteria for a major depressive episode: Was she depressed most of the day? Did she still have interest in her usual activities? Had she noticed any changes in weight or appetite? After finishing the list, the therapist summed up, "According to the manual, you have almost every symptom of a major mood disorder. It sounds like your friends had the right idea about you." Jill softly sobbed and silently nodded her head, unable any longer to shrug off her distress.

Most students welcome having their problems identified, but not everyone does. Some students view labels as insulting, damning, simplistic, or plain wrong. And so, when therapists assign a label, they should follow up by asking what that means to the student.

When her primary care physician told Cynthia, a 28-year-old Caucasian graduate student who had chronic neck and back pains, that she seemed depressed and should see a campus mental health professional, she felt immensely frustrated and began crying uncontrollably—which, of course, convinced the doctor that he was right and only compounded Cynthia's frustration. Asked later by a counseling-service therapist what it had felt like to be called *depressed* by her physician, Cynthia said it indicated that health professionals weren't taking her or her medical problems seriously and instead viewed her pains as "all in my head." The therapist quickly realized that Cynthia's psychological diagnosis was a minefield from which he'd better steer clear in the interests of earning her trust and permitting her to feel heard and respected.

Once therapists share their clinical impressions, further psychoeducation is possible. Anxiety sufferers benefit from learning that anxiety is a normal reaction to a perceived threat, so common that some star athletes and entertainers are nervous wrecks before every performance, and that a racing heart, palpitations, and other bodily manifestations, though unpleasant, are not physically dangerous. Therapists can explain further that the goal of treatment is not to eliminate anxiety, since this impossible aim is likely to instill anxiety about anxiety—and so elicit it. Rather, a healthy approach is to carry on in spite of it, to cope with anxiety through letting it be. For depressed students, the encouragement is similar: Carry on and make constructive decisions even while caught in depression's grip. We shall have more to say later about this strategy.

Depending on the individual, other educational messages can be helpful. Students who are curious as to why they're depressed or anxious may profit from learning that various factors—genetic vulnerability, biochemical processes, family history, current stressors, maladaptive coping styles, and patterns of thinking—can play a part, and that emotional disorders are not solely matters of "biochemical imbalances" (as noted in Chapter 6 in this volume). Some students need reassurance that treatment can indeed help, just as others need reminding that there are no immediate or magical cures. Students new to therapy, especially if from communities or countries where it is unusual, need explanations about how therapy works and the importance of their active collaboration in getting better.

Therapy Relationship

Depressed students tend to make agreeable patients. True, those who have borderline or narcissistic traits can be exceptions, like one tormenting female student who taunted her therapist: "Probably I won't kill myself but I won't guarantee it, because I want you to worry about me at night." Generally, though, therapists like working with depressed clients. What's not to like about bright and attractive young people who value themselves less than they deserve and who are apt to treat us deferentially and compliantly, searching for our approval? These sympathetic sufferers make it easy to be empathic, accepting, and encouraging—we root for them to get better. Fortunately, such positive feelings on our part usually make for good treatment. Depressed students convert their therapists' empathy, acceptance, and encouragement into self-awareness, self-acceptance, and reason for hope. Generalizing from the therapy relationship, they become open to favorable experiences with other people. The healing power of therapists' genuine acceptance and empathy is, of course, the basis of Alexander and French's (1946) "corrective emotional experience," Rogers' (1951) client- or person-centered therapy, and Kohut's (1977) self psychology, and no doubt constitutes a significant part of what all clinicians, regardless of theoretical approach, have to offer their depressed patients.

Yet, there is a danger in coming across as too positive and approving: Some self-loathing patients feel misunderstood and falsely reassured (McWilliams,

1994, p. 244). What psychodynamic therapists interpret as a "harsh superego" or what CBT therapists interpret as irrational self-blaming cognitions may be viewed by patients as accurate self-appraisals to which their therapists are blind. Alternatively, they may half want to believe their therapists' more forgiving viewpoint and half want confirmation of their own sense of reality. To respond to both sides of this ambivalence, therapists can gently put forward their own perspective while also expressing empathy for the patient's view: "I don't agree with your harsh view of yourself, but I'm starting to understand why you might see yourself that way."

Ralph, a 23-year-old Caucasian senior, obsessively tormented himself for various sins, especially perceived transgressions against his deceased father. The father, an alcoholic and probably schizophrenic, had imposed undue demands throughout the boy's life, until finally Ralph broke away and left for college, provoking a bitter fight. Three months later the father took his own life. To the therapist, Ralph's leave-taking was developmentally appropriate and particularly justifiable given the father's tyranny. After years of self-sacrifice, naturally the young man had moved on. Ralph, however, held himself responsible for his father's suicide and said he'd end up mentally ill like him, "just as I deserve." Ominously, he was starting to miss classes and show signs of mounting depression. The therapist tried many ways to appease his sense of wrongdoing—explaining the developmental inevitability of his separating from his parents, remarking on his support and devotion to his father, and asserting that the father's downward trajectory had been beyond anyone's ability to control. The therapist also gently explored Ralph's hypertrophied sense of responsibility, ambivalence toward his father, and identification with him. But while Ralph listened closely, none of these avenues seemed to reach him, nor would he consider taking medication. "You don't understand," he would say, his face contorted with anguish. "I should feel guilty."

What finally did reach and soothe Ralph was the therapist's allowing room for Ralph's self-judgment, by saying, "I'm beginning to appreciate how in your own eyes you could have done more for your father. Maybe in some ways you did let him down—we're all human." Empathizing with Ralph's sense of wrongdoing, yet still accepting him in spite of it—not unlike a priest hearing a confession—brought him comfort. If the therapist could permit Ralph his guilt, then Ralph didn't have to defend it so fiercely, and he could turn his attention to getting better.

Like excessive self-blame, depressed students' hopelessness can also provoke a therapeutic overreaction. Some patients stubbornly insist that they have no future, treatment will fail, and nothing therapists do will help. On some level maybe they want to thwart their therapists, but also they may be afraid of the unknown, the consequences of giving up their misery: "Being depressed," one female student said, "is all I know." Such hopelessness can jolt therapists' self-confidence. If not careful, we may find ourselves going into overdrive to prove our value, pushing helpful interventions on students who can't or won't be helped, feeling frustrated and critical toward students who already feel quite frustrated and self-critical. At such times, the answer is to take a deep breath, stop working so hard, and empathize with the student's despair. Talking openly about hopelessness may also put it into perspective and sap its strength: "As you know, I believe that with time and treatment you will feel better, but I also understand that this seems very hard to accept right now. It's hard to believe anything will ever change." In a similar vein, the therapist might ask, "What do you think it might take for you to begin feeling a bit of hope?" With certain reflective students, it also may help to bring therapeutic overzealousness out into the open: "I wonder if you're feeling pushed by me to get better, and what that's like for you."

Unlike many depressed students who never expect to get better, anxious students may demand to get better right away. Also unlike depressed students, anxious students are often not so much interested in therapists' approval as they are intent on getting results—therapists exist as a means to an end. These are the patients who may linger after sessions are over and ask for extra sessions because "I'm not better yet." Their sense of urgency tends to be contagious—anxiety begets anxiety. And so even though their "help me now" posture may be nothing like depressed students' passivity and resignation, their effect can be similar, pressuring therapists to provide relief. We may catch ourselves with anxious clients introducing one intervention after another, prematurely scheduling a medication consultation, doling out advice. Since feeling rushed and pressured is unpleasant, we may also notice ourselves getting irritated. *Let me do my job,* one thinks. *I'm helping as fast as I can.* The challenge for therapists here is twofold. Anxious students' sense of urgency is earned—acute anxiety *does* feel intolerable—and we should validate this: "I can appreciate how awful these anxiety attacks feel and why you'd want to make quick progress." But for students' sake and our own equanimity, we also need to set realistic expectations. "Let's see what we can do together. These problems generally require some patience to work through them. But we can try right away to get moving in the right direction."

Other relationship themes play out in work with depressed and anxious students. Worrywart students may bore therapists, and on some level maybe they want to bore them. Traumatized students' stories may be difficult for therapists to bear. Meanwhile, therapists' own traits, insecurities, and unfulfilled needs also enter into the therapeutic relationship. As pychodynamic therapies teach us, such transference and countertransference phenomena are inevitable and, if introduced sensitively, can be used to therapeutic advantage, shedding light on patients' views of themselves and of other people and on how they impact others.

And so, while heavy-handed transference interpretations are inadvisable with college students, who will likely view excessive "how are you feeling about me?" comments to be condescending or irrelevant, an occasional, tactful here-and-now observation can vividly get across a point: "You say you're afraid to speak up with your family, and I wonder if that's going on between us too. Are you keeping your thoughts from me now, the way you do with your parents?"

An even more important reason to closely monitor transference and countertransference phenomena is to preserve the working alliance. If we feel anxious, irritated, or bored with a student, which can happen, we must recognize and analyze the reaction so that it doesn't compromise our professional stance. If a student develops strong negative feelings toward us, we'd better repair the problem before it's too late. All of which is to say that we should always tend to the health of the therapeutic relationship. The interventions that follow will avail us little in the absence of a basically positive human connection.

Behavioral Interventions

Avoidance

You don't have to be a behavior therapist to recognize the clinical significance of maladaptive behaviors. And of all the maladaptive patterns of anxious and depressed students, perhaps the most widespread is avoidance. Anxious students shy away from confronting specific objects or situations (as seen with simple phobias and PTSD), interacting with classmates (social phobia), or talking in class or giving a speech (performance anxiety). Panic sufferers avoid situations associated with their attacks, and some agoraphobics literally won't leave their room or apartment. Depressed students may languish at home rather than visit friends, try out for the swim team, or ask a tutor for help. More subtly, students who have generalized anxiety disorder and OCD are avoiders as well, expending time and energy on their worries or rituals rather than taking constructive action.

Avoidance is detrimental in any number of ways. Many challenges are more difficult in imagination than in reality, but avoiding them makes them seem scarier, like peering down and hesitating on the proverbial high diving board. What's more, putting off challenges can in fact increase their difficulty, whether it's catching up with classroom assignments, breaking into a friendship circle, or paying off credit card debt. Avoidance causes embarrassment and shame, too, which leads to more avoidance; a hypersensitive student may feel too mortified after failing to finish an assignment to show up again in class. Avoidance also frees up mental energy that can easily be channeled into more worries, anxieties, and pessimism. Rather than doing, avoiders have time on their hands to dwell on the worst. Avoidance turns off other people. Shy or demoralized students are often dismissed as snobs or misfits by their classmates or viewed as unmotivated by their professors. In a larger sense, avoidance is the enemy of psychological development. Successfully negotiating life's developmental challenges requires taking risks and testing oneself, not running for cover.

For all these reasons, treating anxiety and depression won't get very far until students stop running away and begin to face up to their challenges. But students don't always see it this way, instead identifying their symptoms as the problem and avoidance as a by-product. *First cure my fear,* they say, *and then I'll talk in class. Restore my motivation, and then I'll study or go out with friends.* One of our main jobs as therapists, therefore, is to sell avoidant students on the merits of taking constructive steps. "I know you're reluctant, but it's very important to your treatment that you get moving again." A popular saying captures the point: It's a lot easier to act your way into a new way of feeling than to feel your way into a new way of acting. Alcoholics Anonymous puts it more concisely: "Fake it till you make it."

As for where to begin with constructive behavior, solution-focused therapy's sagely commonsense advice is to build on positive exceptions, the times when students are already doing a little of the right thing (Walter & Peller, 1992). Even the most socially withdrawn student likely says hello to somebody, and the most despondent student engages in some productive activity. These are the behaviors to reinforce. To find instances of constructive behavior, students can be given a monitoring homework exercise: "Notice the times during the week when you feel even a little less depressed [or frightened or worried]. What are you doing then to make this possible?" (The very act of assigning homework sends the uplifting message that students can do something concrete about the problem, and right away.) Assuming that students do the homework (they may avoid it!) and find constructive examples, the assignment for the following week should be to do even more of the same.

In a similar spirit, the behavioral strategy of graded assignments has students tackle behavioral challenges sequentially, starting with the least anxiety provoking and working up to bigger challenges. Therapists can ask students, "What small goals seem most feasible for you to do this week? What would be a first step telling us you're moving in the right direction?" If students draw a blank, it may be necessary to offer suggestions: "Can you imagine smiling at one person?" "Would it be possible for you to start studying again for at least a half hour at a time?" Since striving and accomplishments are inherently rewarding, even small positive changes can provide a big boost. This get-them-moving-again approach, like a psychological First Law of Motion, posits that people at rest (avoiders) tend to stay at rest, whereas people in motion (doers) tend to stay in motion. Once started, a student feels inspired to tackle harder challenges.

After her new boyfriend broke up with her, Andrea, a Caucasian junior, feared spiraling downward and having a recurrence of a high school depressive episode. She had already passed several days alone in her room, missing all her classes. In her first therapy session, she breathlessly chronicled her relationship and speculated about the boy-friend's motives—until the therapist politely interrupted to ask what constructive steps she could take in the upcoming week to feel better about herself. He also advised keeping a log of her activities and asso-ciated feelings. Next session, as often happens with students, Andrea was in a very different mood. Proudly she reported attending all her classes and reaching out to friends, and said whenever she felt bad she reminded herself to keep busy. Somehow her ex-boyfriend seemed less of an issue. The boost from her positive activity having warded off a deeper depression, she was now ready to move on in therapy and explore her pattern of dependency in romantic relationships.

A more refractory case was Julia, a Caucasian first-year student who'd had an untreated depression for as long as she could remember. Throughout her treatment at the counseling service, Julia expressed strong urges to stop everything—her class assignments, socializing, medication, therapy, and, at one scary point early on, her life. Fortu-nately, she was also resilient and could form an alliance with her thera-pist. Acknowledging how hard it must be, the therapist preached the importance of taking constructive actions: attending class, slogging her way through assignments, saying yes whenever possible to invitations from classmates—and of course staying in treatment and refraining from suicide! Julia complied, reluctantly. "I went out with my suitemates on Friday to get ice cream," she would declare. "But I didn't have a good time." "I did my paper, but it was lousy." Her therapist would reply, "I understand your disappointment. I still believe you did the healthy thing." This therapeutic pas de deux continued for an entire year, with Julia repeatedly protesting her unhappiness and lack of motivation, the therapist just as persistently coaxing her to continue striving anyway. There were no dramatic breakthroughs, but Julia plugged away until she completed her courses and successfully transferred to another institu-tion—no small accomplishments considering her lifelong despair and powerful urges to give up.

Unassertiveness

A subtle form of avoidance is the problem of unassertiveness. Many depressed and anxious students outwardly engage in college life but retreat when it comes to expressing their opinions and feelings, asking for help, or saying no to unwanted requests. Perhaps praised as children for always being good or perfect or selfless (the exact constraints vary), now they fear that acting assertively will lead to aban-donment or retaliation, or to their own out-of-control neediness or rage. Therapists can help here by validating students' rights and needs and encouraging, coaching, and modeling direct communications. Role-playing and homework assignments are also recommended: "What could you say to your mother next time she cuts you off?" "How could you respond if she gets mad?" "Do you want to practice? I'll play your mother dominating the conversation, and you politely but firmly tell me to please listen while you're talking." Like avoidance, unassertiveness tends to be deeply ingrained. But once students experiment with honest communications, they find that it becomes easier to maintain.

Self-Destructive Behaviors

Depression and anxiety are also associated with self-destructive behaviors—alcohol or other drug abuse; disordered eating; excessive gambling or spending; Internet, television, or video-game abuse; self-cutting; or self-destructive sexual activity. Though momentarily exciting or soothing, such behaviors ultimately dig a deeper hole of suffering. As with avoidance, treating self-destructive behaviors begins by assessing students' readiness to change. Denial, minimization, and rationalization are to be expected when people are confronted about their behavior, especially young people, whose idea of a good time naturally runs to experimentation and recklessness. (For a discussion of helping students face up to their damaging actions, and on harm reduction versus abstinence as treatment goals, see Chapter 11.)

Even when students say they want to control themselves, it's hard to quit cold turkey or even cut down when the activity feels good or numbs bad feelings. (To be sure, resisting the impulse to act and withstanding the attendant anxiety until it ultimately wanes is precisely the point of exposure and response prevention, the treatment for curbing compulsive behaviors [Rachman & Hodgson, 1980].) To abstain from a behavior, students need alternative behaviors to put in its place. Brainstorming with students about constructive substitutes is therefore crucial: "What would be realistic for you to do at those moments of temptation?" Thus when tempted to take a drink or gamble or self-cut or binge, students may plan to call a friend (or a sponsor), do a relaxation exercise, take a walk, write in a journal, or count to 10 and then reconsider. Over time, the new behavior becomes more automatic, and the temptation of the original behavior loses its potency.

A subset of self-destructive behaviors that can both reflect and cause mood and anxiety problems is erratic, unhealthy patterns of sleep, diet, studies, and self-care. Unhealthy living habits are, of course, endemic to college campuses, where it seems that everyone gets away with studying and eating and sleeping at odd hours, but such practices can be poison for depressed, anxious, and potentially manic students. Therefore, to the extent they can, these students should be counseled to go to bed and arise at set times, eat regular and healthy meals, and study and socialize according to a fixed schedule—the name for this approach in the treatment of bipolar disorder is *social rhythm therapy* (Harvard Medical School, 2001). Steady habits steady the emotions. Even humble routines like regularly scheduled showers and laundry runs and telephone calls home can counteract a feeling of spinning out of control.

Social Deficits

A final area of behavioral difficulties is social deficits. Some depressed and anxious students shrink away from taking social risks partly because they know from experience that they'll strike out. There's no point urging them to try again until they can improve their prospects. While it's impossible in short-term (or probably long-term) therapy to fully teach the art of making friends, a small tip or two and some in-session practice can sometimes make a noticeable difference. With this thought in mind, one enthusiastic practicum student coached her awkward and painfully shy patient on maintaining eye contact and asking appropriate questions, and then invited in fellow trainees to role-play sample conversations. Her patient made some progress in the sessions and a few gingerly overtures on the outside.

Another tack with awkward students is to steer them away from situations where they're sure to fail toward more welcoming environments, such as church groups, certain campus clubs—and, of course, therapy groups. There's a lid for every pot, and even the least socially adept students may find acceptance if they know where to look. The importance of establishing social connections should never be underestimated. Sometimes the best remedy for a despondent student is simply making one new friend.

Cognitive Interventions

According to the CT model, depressed and anxious people think their way into suffering. Specifically, they have maladaptive basic views, or *schemas* ("I'm unlovable," "I'm helpless"), associated maladaptive rules or underlying assumptions ("Unless I'm perfect, people won't like me"), and related automatic thoughts that misinterpret everyday reality (Leahy, 1997; Sperry, 1999). Depressed people in particular hold negative views of themselves, the world, and the future—the "cognitive triad" (Beck, 1976). Anxious people's negative thoughts revolve around threats, insecurities, and "what if" scenarios.

CT is nothing if not thorough in providing techniques to heighten awareness of and refute negative and irrational thinking. Patients can learn to categorize their errors, such as mind reading, black-and-white thinking, overgeneralizing, or personalizing. They can learn to examine the costs and benefits of their views, analyze the evidence, argue back at their thoughts, and supply more rational and positive alternative explanations (Leahy, 1997). The general approach is well suited for college students, who are bright, verbal, and drawn to the power of ideas. But in our experience it isn't necessary to follow a manual or use multiple techniques, which can come across as intellectualized and formulaic. The important thing is simply to help students recognize and question their self-defeating habits of thought.

Jay, a gay Caucasian sophomore, recited a litany of worries and doubts: What if his best friend didn't like him any longer? What if he wasn't cut out for a career in music? What if he asked out a cute guy who then said no? What if the guy said yes and Jay wasn't really interested? After several weeks of these ruminations, the therapist recapped the topics one by one and pointed out that Jay always found something new to stew about. "You're a gifted worrier. I can't imagine you running out of fresh material. Trouble is, you're using your creativity to make yourself miserable." These observations resonated with Jay. It hadn't occurred to him that he had a choice about worrying. He agreed during the upcoming week to notice instances of upsetting himself and to divert his attention, if possible, to constructive alternatives—the conversation he was having, the text he was reading, the faces he passed on the street. Reporting next session that this exercise was helpful, he agreed to continue it in the upcoming weeks. Before long he noticed a decrease in his tendency to worry.

In a second case, Olga, a bright and attractive international student, was mired in self-disparagement, dysphoria, and shyness. Her therapist asked her during the second session to write down on paper all the ways she viewed herself as inadequate. Ever obedient, she produced a very long list: "I am not pretty enough," "I am not smart enough," "I'm really selfish inside," "Other people think I'm mousy," "Other people think I'm bossy" (self-unfairness doesn't respect consistency), and literally dozens of variations on these themes. Seeing all this negativity cover several densely packed sheets, Olga was astonished. Up to that point she hadn't realized the sweep and relentlessness of her self-denigrations or understood how so much negativity held her back from living. At the therapist's suggestion, Olga agreed to monitor her thinking and replace self-criticisms with self-encouragements, and at the same time to take small social risks. Within a few weeks, she enthusiastically reported reducing her negative cognitions and enlarging her social circle.

Such successes do happen, but habits of mind are difficult to break. Unless students remain vigilant, their worries, self-criticism, and fears will insidiously return. What's more, the success of cognitive therapy depends on students' buying into the idea that their core assumptions and automatic thoughts are actually wrong. Some students reject this notion, insisting that they attack themselves because they deserve criticism and frighten or worry themselves for good reason. They *are* ugly or selfish or unlovable or at risk— it's not in their mind. Taking this argument an ingenious step further, some even fault themselves for being self-critical or worry about their proclivity to worry, as if their negative thinking somehow justified negative thinking. We therapists can point out the self-defeating circular logic of these rebuttals;

but past a certain point, challenging students' beliefs is futile and ends in a therapeutic stalemate.

As the popularity of CBT makes clear, CT works best when coupled with behavioral exercises such as setting behavioral targets, following graded task assignments, and role-playing assertive behavior (Leahy, 1997). In other words, for constructive thought patterns to take root, they must be accompanied by constructive behaviors. Conversely, behavioral changes depend on acquiring healthy cognitions. Thus, it makes no sense to urge avoidant students to ask a question in class, turn in a homework assignment, or start talking to classmates if they are wedded to the idea "I must do everything perfectly or I'm a failure" or "It's devastating to be rejected." Before they're ready to take behavioral risks, students first need to be cognitively inoculated against life's inevitable frustrations and disappointments: "Of course you won't say something brilliant every time," or, "It's possible she won't go out with you if you ask. The important thing is to give it a try." Ideally, avoidant students will learn to interpret striving as inherently rewarding, and will take pride in their *effort,* regardless of the end result. Thus cognitively prepared, they are ready to take behavioral risks.

Still, human beings can derive only so much satisfaction from noble failures and nice tries. Ultimately, everyone needs success sometimes as a reward for effort. And that, in turn, requires another cognitive accomplishment—learning to set realistic goals, so that success is really a possibility. For college-age patients, discovering where and how high to set their sights—neither shooting for the unattainable nor selling themselves short—can be a vital therapeutic step and good protection against depression and anxiety: "Suppose you don't end up making medical school. Any ideas what else you could strive to achieve? What other professions would allow you to enjoy a satisfying career and feel good about yourself?"

Psychodynamic Interventions

Whatever techniques one uses, the treatment of anxious and depressed students benefits from psychodynamic insights, as we've already seen in connection with analyzing transference and countertransference phenomena. Another key psychodynamic insight is the importance of identifying and resolving patients' resistance to change (Greenson, 1967), and in a larger sense taking into account patients' personality style. (In a similar vein, recent CBT writings focus on "maximizing readiness for change" [Sperry, 1999] and the importance of treating comorbid personality disorders [Beck, 2005].) And so, before we reassign homework tasks that a student hasn't completed, first we should explore what may be getting in the way, or why he or she isn't complying. Does the student equate the therapist's involvement with smothering, hectoring, or impossible-to-please parents? Does the student sit back and wait for the therapist to magically wave a wand? Does the student mistrust the therapist? Is the student afraid of change and of giving up the miserable safety of the status quo? The possibilities are many. Once the reasons for resistance are discovered and brought out into the open, the student may respond to behavioral and cognitive interventions.

The psychodynamic perspective also sensitizes us to the "how" of resistance, which is closely associated with personality style. Does a student

- "Forget" assignments?
- Get too easily discouraged?
- Argue and nitpick?
- Make a joke of problems?
- Get lost in confusing details?
- Shift the focus of attention?
- Prefer to blame others?
- Prefer to wallow in self-blame?
- Come late or miss sessions?

Here too, it often helps to point out the pattern: "Have you noticed that whenever I ask about your actions during the week, you bring up some other topic, like right now when you started to criticize your roommate? For some reason it seems difficult for you to focus on your own behavior."

Of course, students won't necessarily like hearing about their opposition to change. A nonjudgmental, sensitive manner when pointing out resistances protects the therapeutic relationship and makes it clear that we're not blaming or grading our patients: "I'm sure there are reasons why you keep coming late, and it would be good for us to discover them." Sometimes it's wise not to mention resistances at all, since doing so may only elicit more resistance. But even when we say nothing about it, gauging the strength of resistance helps us determine when to press ahead with interventions and when to ease up with them. In the face of strong opposition to change, the best course may be to sit back and empathically listen for a while, leaving it to the student to later take the lead in altering behaviors and ways of thinking.

Beyond exploring the hidden sources of resistance, the various psychodynamic perspectives also mine unacknowledged feelings and motives in general. This emphasis is of particular relevance to depressed and anxious students, who often give the impression of not knowing their inner lives, and not wanting to know. Thus, deferential and exaggeratedly nice students may be out of touch with their forceful and aggressive impulses; hypermasculine students may be out of touch with either tender or homoerotic feelings; and hyperrational students may be out of touch with feelings of any stripe. For all such self-deceivers, stifling taboo feelings is a no-win proposition, leaving them feeling depleted when their defenses work well and anxious when their defenses threaten to break down. It follows that helping students recognize and accept underlying feelings is central to the treatment of depression and anxiety. And while all therapies strive to accomplish this goal, the psychodynamic approach, with its historical stress on unconscious phenomena, especially tunes into missing aspects in patients' presentations, what they can't or won't allow themselves to say or fully experience.

Rhonda, a Caucasian graduate student, came to therapy complaining of recent crippling anxiety attacks that visited her "for no reason." Everything was basically fine, she said, and as for the few annoyances in her life—her roommate's moodiness, a friend's leaving the area, and dissatisfaction with her graduate program—these were "no big deal, I can handle it." As she explained all this, her eyes filled with tears. Her therapist wondered aloud if perhaps these events and others she hadn't yet mentioned were more troubling than she let herself realize. It was good to cope with problems, but not at the cost of knowing her true feelings. Rhonda didn't initially relish this idea of owning up to strong emotions. Stoicism had served her well as a child in dealings with her abusive father and melodramatic mother. But as she grudgingly started to allow herself to have human reactions—as she started to accept her true feelings—her anxiety tellingly subsided.

Finally, the psychodynamic approach, especially traditional psychoanalysis, famously looks to the past and especially early family relationships to understand current mood and anxiety symptoms. Here college clinicians need to exercise their judgment. On the one hand, the short-term model used at most campus clinics precludes taking a painstaking history, and delving deep into early life events is probably developmentally inappropriate for present- and future-oriented young people. On the other hand, many depressed and anxious students have been damaged by earlier experiences—neglect or loss; emotional, physical, or sexual abuse; parental substance abuse or emotional illness; teasing or bullying at school—and with this pain often comes a strong need to tell their story. Disclosing hurtful experiences to an accepting and affirming adult can bring catharsis, perspective, hope, and resolve. Without an opportunity to unburden themselves and make sense of their pasts, some students will feel held back from tackling current problems.

Ingrid, a Caucasian senior, shied away from potential boyfriends due to general fearfulness and pessimism and specifically her exaggerated fears of abandonment. Though sensing that all of this was connected to her family, it wasn't until she began talking about her mother's overprotectiveness and her parents' chilly marriage that the full impact of her upbringing sank in. "I can see now that she never let me try anything because I might get hurt," "I've always expected that guys would treat me like my father treated my mother," and later on, "Maybe my mother didn't want me to go out and try things because then I'd have a better life than she did."

The true test of insights is whether they promote change. Ingrid's discoveries about her family prompted the realization that fearfulness wasn't an intrinsic part of her, but rather a learned and potentially remediable point of view, and therefore it was time to move on in her life. She bravely signed up for Internet dating and opened herself to the therapist's questioning of her deep-seated beliefs that she was "unworthy of love" and that "anybody who comes to know me will inevitably reject me." After a couple of computer dating false starts, she started going out with a recent college graduate, and soon, to her astonishment, found herself involved in a mutually devoted romantic relationship. It is unlikely that she would have allowed herself to meet or stay with her new boyfriend had she not first gained perspective on her family's early negative teachings.

Medications

Because pharmacological treatment is covered in Chapter 4, we will confine ourselves here to briefly commenting about the nonmedical clinician's pivotal role in drug therapy. The main task is to determine when a medication consult is warranted, based on careful diagnostic assessment. Medications are indispensable for bipolar disorder, often necessary for major depressive episodes and OCD, and sometimes necessary in cases of panic disorder, PTSD, and dysthymia. Common sense is another factor when weighing a medication consult. When a student's symptoms haven't remitted after a trial of psychotherapy, and especially if the student is growing discouraged and may drop out of treatment, then psychopharmacological treatment deserves a chance.

Of course, medicines do have side effects, and the consequences of long-term use are not fully known and for some may be negative (Whitaker, 2002), and so, if possible, the clinician should try other appropriate treatment remedies before starting a student on drugs. Another common objection to medications is that they undercut students' motivation to understand themselves and learn coping skills, instilling a passive, "I'm not in control" mindset. However, this argument can be turned on its head. Rather than undermining psychotherapy, medications are sometimes a necessary adjunct to it, relieving students of paralyzing symptoms and so making it possible for psychotherapy to progress.

Nonmedical therapists also can play a helpful role by explaining when drug treatment is and is not appropriate, specifying what drugs do and don't do, stressing the dangers of taking substances while on medications, and listening to students' reactions to being on a drug. Since undergraduates can be unreliable about taking pills and may impulsively decide to stop, clinicians should monitor compliance with drug treatment regimens and regularly ask the question, "How are you doing on your medications?" Psychotherapists should also closely collaborate with prescribers and encourage students to consult with prescribers as often as necessary.

Relaxation, Meditation, and Exercise

While bad feelings and low moods are part of life, there are ways to take the edge off of negative effects, as therapists can usefully demonstrate in three short steps. First ask students to rate their level of anxiety or distress on a 100-point scale. Next, have them close their eyes, take slow and deep breaths, and silently recite the word "relax" with each exhalation. Then ask for a new anxiety or distress rating—which, one trusts, has gone down. If the student says, "But I'm still feeling 50," the recommended reply is, "Yes, but you were 60 before." Assuming that the demonstration proves successful, students can be encouraged to do this simple exercise in class, in stressful social situations, or whenever their distress peaks.

Chapter 8 discusses many relaxation and meditation options and physical exercise, all of which benefit body and mind. Relaxation is physiologically incompatible with anxiety (Benson & Klipper, 1976), and exercise has proven physiological benefits. In addition, relaxation methods give demoralized and frightened students the satisfaction of exercising at least partial control over bad feelings, while exercise workouts and getting in shape build self-esteem and inspire constructive action in other areas.

As with every other intervention, results do vary. Students may be too wrought up or despairing to try these methods, or give up when they don't show immediate improvement. When they object, "I did the breathing but I started to feel bad a half hour later," we need to remind them, "It's not a panacea, but it can still provide some relief if you try it." Other objections are that exercise or relaxation methods take too much time, or the student doesn't like these methods or isn't cut out for them. As always, it pays to explore students' reluctance, and sometimes to keep on nudging. One depressed, soft-looking gay student had an image of himself as "a head, not a body." His therapist's suggestion to go to the gym brought back shameful childhood memories of feeling athletically and physically inferior to other boys. Nevertheless, the student courageously agreed to sign up for an aerobics class and before long was rewarded with an unprecedented pride in his body and a newfound sense of optimism.

Environmental Changes

Depressed and anxious students often attribute their problems to outside circumstances, and sometimes they are right. For them to recover from their problems, something in their lives must change. And since students' lives do change rapidly and unpredictably, time is often treatment's great ally. Once midterms pass, the psychological crisis may be over.

When time alone won't suffice, students, with or without therapists' assistance, may have to change their circumstances: getting extensions or taking incompletes, dropping a course or a part-time job, changing majors, transferring to a new school, switching roommates, moving on or off campus, or taking time off from school. It's remarkable how powerful an effect one environmental change can sometimes have, restoring a student's confidence and propelling forward moment.

Mei, an international 4th-year student from Asia, came to the counseling service in a state of desperation. For 3 years she'd been high functioning, sociable, and a model student, but since moving in with a new roommate who kept late hours, she hadn't had a single night of good sleep for several months, affecting her studies and her health. Now her request to terminate her housing contract had been denied, and her reaction was so extreme—uncontrollable crying while expressing hopelessness and insecurity—that her counselor had no alternative but to take her to the hospital for an inpatient assessment. With the counselor's blessing, the next day, the housing office gladly let her void her contract. Mei, promptly released from the hospital and returned to the counseling service for an evaluation, appeared happy, calm, and hopeful—a changed woman. What had accounted for her extreme reaction? Obviously, she had some vulnerability; another student wouldn't have responded to her situation in such unhealthy fashion. At the same time, it's notable that she'd been a well-adjusted student for 3 years prior to this episode, and now gave every appearance of being fully ready to resume her successful college career. At least on the symptomatic level, all it took to resolve her depression (it's not usually so easy) was one favorable ruling by a housing administrator.

Final Thoughts: Putting It All Together

We have taken the position in this chapter that because depression and anxiety are multidimensional, complex phenomena, single interventions and one-dimensional approaches, though evidence based, may not suffice. Thus, behavioral techniques will fall short if a student's maladaptive habits of mind aren't addressed; cognitive interventions will be hollow without addressing maladaptive behaviors; and even a coordinated CBT approach will likely fail in the context of unresolved past traumas, overwhelming current stressors, biochemical imbalances, and comorbid conditions such as substance abuse. And no treatment strategy can overcome the handicap of a flawed therapeutic alliance.

But "pure" treatment approaches do have the advantage of clarity and cohesiveness. Short-term treatments—and college treatments tend to be very short term—require a plan or structure, a clinical focus, and one or two central goals. When there's little treatment time available, one can't be scattershot or aimless. The challenge in working with depressed and anxious students, then, is to be flexible yet focused; to use different perspectives and interventions as necessary; yet to bring them together into a unified, integrative treatment. In the most successful college treatments, one has the sense of zeroing in on a central theme, such as retreating from challenges, shrinking away from open expression, or pursuing goals to satisfy parents rather than inner promptings. Highlighting the central theme not only eases the immediate depressive or anxious crisis, but supports the student's ongoing emotional development.

References

Alexander, F., & French, T. (1946). *Psychoanalytic psychotherapy*. New York: Ronald Press.

American Psychiatric Association. (2000). *Diagnostic and statistical manual of mental disorders* (4th ed., text revision). Washington, DC: American Psychiatric Association.

Baez, T. (2005). Evidence-based practice for anxiety disorders in college mental health. In S. E. Cooper (Ed.), *Evidence-based practice in college mental health*. Binghamton, NY: Haworth Press. Published simultaneously in the *Journal of College Student Psychotherapy, 20*, 33–48.

Beck, A. T. (1976). *Cognitive therapy and the emotional disorders*. New York: International Universities Press.

Beck, A. T., Rial, W. Y., & Rickets, K. (1974). Short form of depression inventory: Cross-validation. *Psychological Reports, 34*, 1184–1186.

Beck, A. T., Epstein, N., Brown, G., & Steer, R. A. (1988). An inventory for measuring clinical anxiety: Psychometric properties. *Journal of Consulting and Clinical Psychology, 56*, 893–897.

Beck, J. S. (2005). *Cognitive therapy for challenging problems*. New York: Guilford.

Benson, H., & Klipper, M. Z. (1976). *The relaxation response*. New York: Avon.

Elkin, I., Shea, M., Watkins, J., Imber, S., Sotsky, S.M., Collins, J. F., et al. (1989). National Institute of Mental Health Treatment of Depression Collaborative Research Program: General effectiveness of treatments. *Archives of General Psychiatry, 46*, 971–982.

Goisman, R. M. (1997, May). Cognitive behavioral therapy today. *Harvard Mental Health Letter*, 4–7.

Greenson, R. R. (1967). *The technique and practice of psychoanalysis*. New York: International Universities Press.

Harvard Medical School. (1998, November). Obsessive-compulsive disorder—Part II. *Harvard Mental Health Letter, 15*, 5.

Harvard Medical School. (2001, May). Bipolar disorder—Part II. *Harvard Mental Health Letter, 17*, 11.

Kohut, H. (1977). *The restoration of the self*. New York: International Universities Press.

Leahy, R. L. (1997). *Practicing cognitive therapy: A guide to interventions*. Northvale, NJ: Jason Aronson.

McWilliams, N. (1994). *Psychoanalytic diagnosis*. New York: Guilford.

Norcross, J. C. (Ed.). (2002). *Psychotherapy relationships that work: Therapist contributions and their responsiveness to patient needs*. New York: Oxford University Press.

Rachman, S. J., & Hodgson, R. (1980). *Obsessions and compulsions*. New York: Appleton-Century-Crofts.

Rogers, C. R. (1951). *Client-centered therapy*. Boston: Houghton-Mifflin.

Seligman, M. E. P. (1993). *What you can change and what you can't*. New York: Fawcett Columbine.

Shea, M., Elkin, I., Imber, S., Sotsky, S. M., Watkins, J. T., Collins, J. F., et al. (1992). Course of depressive symptoms over follow-up. *Archives of General Psychiatry, 49*, 782–787.

Silberschatz, G. (1999, July). The results of randomized controlled trials are useless to clinicians. *Harvard Mental Health Letter*, 5–6.

Sperry, L. (1999). *Cognitive behavior therapy of DSM-IV personality disorders*. Philadelphia: Brunner/Mazel.

Spitzer, R. L., Kroenke, K., & Williams, J. B. (1999). Validation and utility of a self-report version of PRIME-MD: The PHQ primary care study. *Journal of the American Medical Association, 282*, 1737–1744.

U.S. DHHS [Department of Health and Human Services]. (1976). 049 HAMD Depression Scale. In *ECDEU Assessment Manual* (pp. 180–192). Washington, DC: Public Health Service—Alcohol, Drug Abuse, and Mental Health Administration.

Walter, J. L., & Peller, J. E. (1992). *Becoming solution-focused in therapy.* Levittown, PA: Brunner/Mazel.

Wampold, B. E., Lichtenberg, J. W., & Waehler, C. A. (2002). Principles of empirically supported interventions in counseling psychology. *Counseling Psychologist, 30,* 197–217.

Whitaker, R. (2002). *Mad in America: Bad science, bad medicine, and the enduring mistreatment of the mentally ill.* Cambridge, MA: Perseus Publishing.

Zung, W. W. K. (1965). A self-rating depression scale. *Archives of General Psychiatry, 12,* 63–70.

8
Stress

ROBERT McGRATH

Most college counselors agree that there is an increase of students with intense psychological disorders. More students than ever present with major depression, suicidality, anxiety and panic disorders, intense eating disorders, self-mutilation, bipolar disorders, alcohol and other drug abuse, and other serious disorders. Yet, embedded within these disorders, and also a challenge for less troubled clients and for students in general, is a more everyday phenomenon: stress. In my experience, the common estimate that 33% of students experience stress-related difficulties actually seems quite conservative (American College Health Association [ACHA], 2004).

Stress is a familiar concept. Type "stress management" into any Internet search engine and there is an abundance of hits. Yet, with this fairly universal awareness of stress comes a danger of accepting stress problems as inevitable and prosaic and so minimizing them, instead of recognizing their enormous effect. This chapter examines the deleterious influence of stress and presents approaches toward stress management and stress prevention useful for the college student population.

The Basics of Stress

Stress is psychological and physical arousal to the demands of life. A stressful situation is one appraised as taxing or exceeding one's personal resources and endangering well-being. Richard Lazarus states that "stress is a condition or feeling when a person perceives demands exceeding personal and social resource[s]" (Lazarus & Folkman, 1984).

One of the challenges in discussing stress is the diversity of experiences and reactions related to it. What is extremely stressful for one person may be a source of pleasure for another. Thus, moving away from family may be extremely upsetting for one student, but a thrill for the next. Graduating from college may bring joy and a sense of accomplishment, or evoke anxiety. Part-time employment may be a pleasant diversion, or a pressured drain of time. There also may be gender differences in response to stress. While the general response has always been characterized as "fight or flight," the response for the majority of women may be "tend and befriend"; a research team at UCLA found that a majority of women responded to stress with nurturing activities and the development of social networks. This team's biobehavioral explanation is that women secrete a higher level of the hormone oxytocin, which is responsible for reducing anxiety and promoting social behavior. The research team suggests that this difference may explain women's greater longevity and lesser aggressiveness (Taylor et al., 2000). On the other hand, the possible difference in coping strategies does not reduce the need for effective stress management, since research indicates that more female students report feeling stressed than males (Hudd et al., 2000).

Generally, stress induces an arousal of the sympathetic branch of the autonomic nervous system, resulting in increases in blood pressure, gastrointestinal activity, muscle tension, rate of breathing, kidney activity, and sweating. But within this general response system, individual responses are idiosyncratic, and people develop a variety of physical, behavioral, and cognitive symptoms. The most prominent reactions are irritability, anger, disrupted relationships, exhaustion, agitation, headaches, low back pain, hypertension, change in sleep and/or eating patterns, preoccupation, and depressed feelings. Perhaps the most common reaction is a change in sleep patterns, with estimates of 85% of stress sufferers either losing sleep or falling into excessive sleep patterns (Verlander, Benedict, & Hanson, 1999).

The way a person reacts to stress can create further stress. For example, irritability and anger can lead to disrupted relationships. Sleep disruption reduces the individual's ability to carry out daily functions; exhaustion makes completing academic work more difficult. Overeating or undereating reduces the person's ability to function. Perhaps most clearly misguided is the attempt to reduce stress through alcohol or other drugs. All these reactions propel the person into a vicious cycle of escalating problems.

Stress on Campus

Like everyone else, students have individual responses to similar situations. Giving a 10-minute presentation, having a first date, or moving across country to attend college may be experienced as excitingly positive or disturbingly stressful, depending on the individual.

While reactions to potential stressors vary, the situations that tend to put the most pressure on students revolve around academic demands (doing papers, examinations, presentations; being frequently evaluated; having to fulfill academic requirements in areas where a student lacks interest or skill); the pressure of tackling too many tasks (academics, part-time jobs, social activities, family obligations) in too little time; social expectations and fitting in socially; and roommate conflicts.

How stressed are students? In a recent survey by the ACHA, more than 92% of students report feeling overwhelmed occasionally by all that is required of them, and 33% report stress significant enough to interfere with their academic success, often resulting in dropped courses (ACHA, 2004; Kadison & DiGeronimo, 2004).

As is true of the general population, many students develop pathological stress-management strategies. Not only are these strategies ineffective in relieving stress, they create more problems and thus add to the stress level. Excessive alcohol consumption is a prime example, since it involves an assault on the neurological system, lowers coping skills in academics and relationships, and may lead to disastrous consequences such as sexual assaults, disciplinary or legal violations, or suicidal attempts. Smoking and drug use can also be seen as maladaptive responses to stress, and even the excessive use of caffeine clearly qualifies as an ineffective and self-defeating stress reducer. Unhealthy eating, whether overeating or restricting, also results in psychological and physiological problems. Irritability and expressions of anger are natural responses when a student feels under stress, but, again, these tend to make matters worse.

Another common self-defeating stress response is avoidance of responsibilities—for example, putting off writing a dreaded paper by doing something neutral like talking with friends, or negative like drinking excessively. Students who've fallen behind in reading may stop reading altogether, and those who've missed a class may simply stop attending. Avoidance successfully reduces stress in the moment; the student briefly escapes the distressing situation. But since papers must be written, tests taken, books read, and classes attended, avoidance only puts off the day of reckoning and ends up magnifying the student's problems.

It is not difficult to make a connection between ineffective stress management and various psychological disorders. A student who avoids stressful academic situations and then demeans herself for doing so may end up feeling frightened, hopeless, self-blaming—and depressed. A student who responds to pressure with alcohol or drug abuse may develop a chronic problem. Thus psychological disorders interfere with functioning and so cause stress, but stress in turn can be a major factor in the development of psychological disorders.

Stressors by College Year

There are some stresses that tend to apply to all students. A recent informal survey at the University of Wisconsin seems consistent with many other university surveys in pointing to the following most frequently mentioned stressors (McGrath, 2005):

1. Academic concerns, high academic demands
2. Unrealistic expectations in a course
3. Conflict in a living situation
4. Starting or maintaining relationships
5. Interpersonal conflicts
6. Family issues, e.g., separation issues or conflict
7. Financial issues

There are also some stresses particular to different phases of college. Thus in the first year, moving into a residence hall and meeting many new persons is, for many students, a challenging adjustment. Most incoming students are not accustomed to sharing a room, let alone with a new acquaintance. Nor are they used to living in close proximity with a few hundred peers. For some students, these experiences can feel overwhelming.

Some other common first-year stressors are

1. Separating from family (while separation is developmentally appropriate and some students are eager to get away, others find the separation to be difficult.)
2. Separating from friends
3. Taking college-level courses for the first time
4. Living closely with others who may be undergoing personal difficulties
5. Assuming personal responsibility for time allocation
6. Balancing academic demands with other priorities and distractions
7. Dealing with self-induced or external pressure to perform well academically
8. Fitting in and finding a new friendship network

Though the common stressors are not as clear-cut after the first year, a few common stressors can be tied to later phases of the college career:

Second-Year Students
1. Shifting from residence halls to local housing
2. Beginning to feel pressure related to choice of major
3. Dealing with continued academic pressure
4. Dealing with the pressure to contribute to financial costs by taking a part-time job (some first-year students experience this stress, but more second-year students seem to have part-time work expectations.)

Third-Year Students
1. Dealing with heightened pressure to choose a major, if one hasn't been already declared
2. Dealing with increasing concern about grades, if course of studies requires graduate school
3. Again, often dealing with the pressure to take on part-time work, increasing sense of time pressure
4. Coping with an increase in large projects for advanced courses

Fourth- and Fifth-Year Students
1. Making postgraduate decisions
2. Dealing with relationship issues, many of which are accentuated as a result of the imminent change in the student's life situation

Graduate Students
1. Adjusting to a new environment
2. Adjusting to an increased sense of responsibility for being self-productive
3. Dealing with an increased tension between academic and family responsibilities
4. Handling the expectation to produce publishable papers
5. Dealing with a heightened level of self-evaluation related to being at a new academic level
6. Balancing academic demands and social interests
7. If not in a relationship, struggling with the implications of that circumstance

Campus Stressors for Particular Groups

Some stressors particularly affect students from certain groups. Thus, the workload and financial pressures at certain schools probably make them more stress-inducing than others (Greene & Green, 2000). In addition, students of color often mention experiencing the following stressors:

1. Being a minority-group member within the campus community
2. Adjusting to a roommate from a different cultural background
3. Confronting discriminatory or racist reactions
4. Feeling isolated from family and friends
5. Balancing the conflict between family needs and academic demands
6. Coping with an increased sense of pressure, feeling oneself a representative of others from one's group

International students report the following stressors particular to their situation:

1. Adjusting to a different culture and integrating new experiences, or acculturation stress
2. Having language difficulties
3. Resolving conflicts between cultures
4. Confronting discrimination and prejudice
5. Being distant from family and friends
6. Adjusting to different expectations within relationships

Lesbian, gay, bisexual, and transgendered students may experience the following stressors:

1. Being a minority within a campus community
2. Confronting discriminatory or biased reactions
3. Feeling the pressure to hide sexuality from certain persons and in certain situations
4. Forming a positive sexual identity and self-esteem

Stress-Management Strategies

Maladaptive response to stress is typically multidimensional, often involving cognitive distortion, physiologically disruptive responses, and ineffective behavioral choices. For stress management to be effective, an integrated biopsychosocial approach is necessary. A combination of the following techniques is generally more effective than employing a single approach.

Cognitive Restructuring

Addressing the cognitions that increase stressful reactions is essential. Stressful situations are inevitable, but thinking about them in irrational and ineffective ways intensifies the distress. One example is perfectionistic thinking. Granted that most test situations have the potential to be stressful, taking tests is that much harder with the belief that scoring 100% or quite close is a measure of one's personal value. Preparing for the exam becomes more difficult, and the likelihood of good performance is actually reduced. Perfectionism also assures a chronic level of stress, because one of the facts of university life is frequent evaluation.

A very different cognitive set that also makes testing and papers unduly stressful occurs when students angrily focus on the inadequacy of the teacher, resentment toward parents who have put performance expectations on them, or disdain for other students, who are "not very bright, but so compulsive about preparing for the exam." Harboring such negative cognitions can make it impossible to concentrate.

Another irrational and stress-inducing way of thinking is to believe that one must succeed in all social contacts, since, of course, no student will please every potential friend or charm every potential boyfriend or girlfriend. Similarly, the belief that it's necessary to be appreciated and valued by all other students or professors inevitably leads to frustration and unsuccessful relationships.

Clearly, a crucial ingredient in effective stress management is helping students identify their irrational sets of beliefs. Some common stress-inducing beliefs are

> "I need to do extremely well [on exams, in sports, or in club elections] or I am worthless."
> "If I don't do extremely well, there's no point in further trying."
> "If I don't do extremely well, others are to blame."
> "Everyone should appreciate all aspects of me."
> "I should not have to study if I have other things I want to do."
> "These professors should not expect so much from me."
> "My friends and family should never be angry with me."
> "Others should never disappoint me."

In contrast to such stress-inducing beliefs, stress-resistant individuals maintain positive attitudes toward their experience. Some common positive attitudes are an openness to change, a feeling of involvement, a sense of loose control, and an acceptance of the inevitability of certain unpleasant events or required activity.

Discussing more adaptive approaches to experience—thinking about challenges and demands in constructive ways—is an important component of stress management. This includes replacing perfectionistic, black-and-white, catastrophic thinking with reasonable alternatives: "I didn't get an A, but I'm still proud of how I did," "My roommate doesn't seem that crazy about me, but we can still get along, and I have lots of other friends." Constructive thinking also includes recognizing and accepting the inevitability of undesirable events in life. The goal is not to promote passivity. On the contrary, it's to assess whether it's possible to change the situation for the better. Some stressful life events can be effectively managed. Others require a more accepting attitude.

Helping a stressed student understand the difference between situations that can be actively addressed and situations that call for acceptance is a core of good stress management. A fairly common example is a student obsessed and irritated with a professor perceived as inadequate, too critical, or just too annoying. Reviewing the effects of addressing the situation by confronting the professor or transferring from the class versus more passive, but judicial strategies assists the student in making the decision. Either pathway will be stressful. Helping the student identify the beliefs and attitudes that make these situations more stressful is crucial.

A cognitive therapy approach helps the student understand that the majority of stress is self-induced, based on interpretation of events. The clinician should strive to help the student identify dysfunctional, stress-inducing beliefs without coming across as critical. Asking the client to keep a stress log can be extremely helpful. The log should record moments when the client feels particularly stressed, along with who is involved and what the client has been doing and thinking. This exercise may bring to light self-defeating attitudes, such as a striving for superiority; needing to be loved and respected by all, to be competent in all pursuits, and to be right or to win; intolerance of others; and hyperresponsibility.

Reviewing the stress log helps identify cognitions that may be increasing stress or leading to the avoidance of stressful situations. A common example is the student who does very well on examinations but feels more internal pressure to perform well when writing papers. Gently exploring and addressing that student's cognitions about writing papers is a crucial aspect of the student's learning to manage that stressor.

The cognitive approach helps clients become self-assured, not ego focused. It shifts attention away from the self and toward objectively processing information from the environment, and raises awareness of and replaces stress-inducing personal beliefs (like perfectionism) with constructive alternatives.

Progressive Muscular Relaxation

For many stress-management specialists, the core treatment consists of teaching the client progressive muscular relaxation. This technique was originally developed in the 1920s by Edmund Jacobsen, but became well known in the 1960s when the method was incorporated into the behavioral technique of systematic desensitization. As the years have passed, most counselors who employ progressive muscular relaxation do so in a looser manner than the original directions indicate.

The original method involves identifying 16 muscle groups and teaching how to create and release a moderate tension in each. The student is instructed to close his or her eyes and get into a relaxed position (typically by lying back on a reclining stuffed chair). The counselor directs the student to create tension in the first muscle group, encouraging a focus on feelings of tension, and then to let go of all the tension and focus on the feelings associated with relaxation as the muscle begins to unwind. Traditionally, this process is repeated for each muscle group—hands and forearms, upper arms, forehead, upper face, mouth and jaw, neck and throat, upper legs, lower legs, and feet—through two cycles of tension (5–6 seconds) followed by relaxation (40–50 seconds). Many modern practitioners tend to be creative, either combining different muscle groups to make the process quicker and thus more likely to be practiced, or dropping the tension cycle entirely and merely having the client focus on releasing the existing tension. Stressed students are encouraged to practice daily. An important aspect of the practice is to do it with no external distractions. In releasing the tensed-up muscle, students learn to repeat internally a relaxing phrase—perhaps just "and relax." Indeed, just learning to focus one's attention for 15–20 minutes has a very positive effect in itself.

Many students will report that the only time they relax is when they watch television, socialize with friends, or drink alcohol. Obviously these are not authentic or effective moments of relaxation. The notion of quieting oneself with a relaxation procedure is often met with reluctance. A recent case exemplifies both the reluctance and the potential benefits.

A 3rd-year female student was referred by her physician. She reported somatic concerns and sleep-onset difficulties. She had very high academic expectations for herself and was frustrated that her sleep difficulties and somatic concerns were interfering with her academic success. She initially was interested only in medication, but responded to the suggestion that she learn relaxation methods first. She was taught a modified relaxation procedure and encouraged to practice once per day. She was also encouraged to do some minimal relaxation exercise, perhaps when waiting for a class to start or after an hour of studying. As a majority of stressed students discover, the feelings of relaxation are quite pleasant and she became quite regular in her 15-minute relaxation sessions. Within one week, she reported significant improvement in sleep onset, better appetite, and concentration. After weeks, she was still impressed with how much beneficial effect her brief daily relaxation sessions were having.

Meditation

Meditation is taught in many forms and for many different purposes. In the context of stress management, meditation is a skill that promotes a relaxed and patient attitude. Though it is particularly helpful, it is challenging to master for those students who are accustomed to multitasking. The goal of meditation is to shift from a busy, judgmental, critical frame of mind to a more single-focused, peaceful concentration, and so ultimately to achieve greater concentration and relaxation.

Although meditation can certainly be taught in individual sessions, it is very easily taught in fairly large groups, as has been the case with the extremely popular six-session groups at the University of Wisconsin–Madison. These groups begin with a discussion of the benefits of meditation, based on both research and personal examples. Then there is a description of what meditation is and is not, which challenges the misconceptions that meditation is just turning the mind blank, or that it involves gaining psychic power. Rather, meditation is the process of slowing down and exploring one's mind.

Students are then taken through the basic steps:

1. Assuming an upright sitting posture
2. Focusing on breathing, physically and mindfully
3. Possibly employing some minor muscular relaxation
4. Focusing more closely on the breathing process, first in the lower abdomen, then in the upper chest, and lastly in the nostrils
5. Focusing on relaxing images, such as a still lake or blue sky

Another focus in meditation is on the concept of *loving-kindness*. Loving-kindness is a meditation practice that focuses not on changing oneself, but on accepting and befriending oneself. One basic practice is merely to repeat to oneself, "May I be happy and free from suffering." As meditation practice proceeds, the focus on loving-kindness extends to the self, to friends, to neutral acquaintances, and finally to those toward whom the meditator feels anger (Chodron, 1996). Loving-kindness is a concept that is thousands of years old but fits neatly into a modern model promoting self-acceptance.

After the exercise, there is an opportunity for questions and answers. Students are then encouraged to meditate 5 minutes a day, gradually increasing to 20 minutes. The group sessions focus on repeating the meditation exercise and reviewing members' weekly experiences. A fairly high percentage of stressed students enter the meditation group skeptical of the potential benefits but feeling desperate enough to try. They will report common concerns: "I have too much on my mind," "I don't have time," "I am too tired," "My mind is like a tsunami," "My mind won't stop," "I can't sit still." Because the stressed students enter the group with such hesitation, the positive results that typically occur within the first few weeks are very striking to them. The most common effects reported are improved sleep, increased ability to concentrate and focus, and increased feelings of relaxation.

Meditation practices have many variants, but the basic skills of sitting still and focusing attention seem to be universal. The benefits of employing meditation seem to transfer easily to different crucial areas, as studying, sleeping, and eating (Bien & Bien, 2003; Davidson, 2004; Lutz, Greischar, Rawlings, Ricard, & Davidson, 2004). Until recently, the long-standing metaphysical tradition of meditation generated little research interest. Now researchers (Lutz et al., 2004) are collecting electroencephalograph data that indicate that regular meditation may induce short-term and long-term beneficial neural changes.

Aerobic Activity

Many contend that noncompetitive aerobic exercise is the most effective counter to stress, since physical activity fulfills the "fight or flight" aspect of the stress response. Since most modern stress is psychosocial, people normally aren't able to physically respond, even though they're physically aroused. Aerobic exercise allows for this physical release, dispelling muscle tension and strengthening the body for future stressful situations.

Excessive exercise, however, can in itself become a major bodily stressor and may reduce the capacity to respond well to new challenging situations. For many stressed students, exercise represents another demand on their time and energy and so seems counter to their goals. Therefore it's important when recommending aerobic exercise to point out that students should set realistic goals that will not be too demanding of their time and that they should gradually build up to an effective level of exercise.

Choosing an exercise to engage in is an important decision. Competitive sports have some capacity for stress reduction, and they perhaps help most with the "fight" aspect of the stress response. But these sports also have the capacity for being stressful, especially if the participant cares too much about the outcome of the competition. Observing colleagues who recently trained for and participated in a full-distance triathlon—a 2.4-mile swim, a 112-mile bike run, and a 26.2-mile foot run—I was struck by the stress not only of the excessive exercise but also of the cognitive demands related to performance.

Aerobic activities (requiring longer, less intense effort, as in walking, jogging, or swimming) tend to be better for stress reduction than anaerobic activities (requiring short bursts of energy, as in weight lifting or sprinting). The best exercise is also something that the student enjoys. If exercise is perceived as yet another unwelcome demand, it merely becomes another stressor. If the activity becomes a measure of self-esteem—by the person adopting a win-or-else attitude—that too is counterproductive. And if the exercise requires too much time or exertion, that also defeats the purpose. A relatively recent concern expressed by recreational sports professionals is the number of students who are compulsively spending over 3 hours per day on exercise machines. For stress-management purposes, exercise that lasts no more than 30–60 minutes on 5 or 6 days per week is ideal (American College of Sports Medicine, 2005).

Exercising alone and exercising with a group each have different benefits. Solitary exercise has the potential for a meditative focus of attention that enhances the relaxation effect. Yet, those who exercise together, such as runners, find that socializing and humorous conversation add to the sense of relaxation.

Yoga Therapy

Though predating the concept of stress management by centuries, yoga can be a particularly effective stress-management approach. There is certainly a wide range of yoga practices, but the most common ones rely on a combination of gentle physical exertion and focused attention. Many yoga sessions end with a position called *Viparita Karani* ("legs up the wall"), which most practitioners find to be as relaxing and calming as progressive muscular relaxation. *Savasana,* or lying on a folded blanket with calves on a chair, is also a very relaxing pose. As with other approaches, yoga combines mild muscular exertion followed by lessening of the muscular tension, a narrowing focus of attention, and the regulation of breathing, a combination that leads to an extremely relaxed state. Though university counseling services may not traditionally offer yoga treatment, its value for stress management creates a great opportunity for collaboration with the campus recreational sports department. Counseling and Consultation Services at the University of Wisconsin offers two yoga groups that are in high demand.

Another Asian process that has been used effectively for managing stress in college students is Qi-Gong (pronounced: *chee*-gong), which is a combination of easy postures, gentle movements, and simple meditation techniques. Weimo Zhu, a kinesiologist at the University of Illinois teaches a Qi-Gong class for stress management and has conducted research to remove the mystery behind its effectiveness as stress management (Zhu & Chodzko-Zajko, 2006). Common to progressive muscular relaxation training, yoga, and Qi-Gong is the combination of temporary muscle tension, release of that tension, focus on breathing, and focus of attention. The choice of which technique to use is essentially a matter of personal appeal.

Humor and Stress Management

Don't laugh—or, rather, *do* laugh! Cynical readers might snicker at the notion of humor as a significant approach to stress management, but I encourage them to have a good laugh instead, which is better for stress than a snicker. According to a growing body of research, humor results in a general decrease in stress hormones (Berk, 1996; Holden, 1998). Vigorous laughter temporarily increases the heart rate, benefits the immune system, increases alertness, and even exercises skeletal muscles. Levels of both epinephrine and dopamine decrease as a response to humor and laughing. Moreover, laughing has muscle-relaxing qualities very similar to the tensing and release associated with progressive muscular relaxation. Following extended laughter, there is a brief period during which blood pressure lowers and heart rate decreases. Respiratory rate and muscular tension decrease, resulting in feelings associated with relaxation—all positive elements of stress management. Again, humor seems to involve a similar set of reactions to the other stress-management strategies: an increase in muscular activity, followed by a muscular/biochemical release, and a focus of attention on issues other than stressors.

Besides the physiological benefits of laughing, humor promotes a change in cognitive perspective. Much humor is based on the premise that something that seems terribly important is not actually so earthshaking. A good laugh is not self-focused and so, at least momentarily, lessens self-preoccupation. Therefore, incorporating humor in counseling sessions can have a healing effect. Of course, it's important that counselors not convey the idea that they're laughing at clients or at their situations, or that they underestimate clients' suffering. Yet, while remaining empathic and taking clients seriously, counselors can still find appropriate opportunities to incorporate humor. Doing so encourages at least some clients to view their own circumstances differently, to take a more lighthearted and less catastrophic view of their problems.

For many students, the encouragement to focus on humor for 15 minutes per day is more appealing than a comparable period of meditation, relaxation, or exercise. To assure that this approach isn't dismissed as nonprofessional, this suggestion can be incorporated with the other stress-reduction approaches. Once again, however, it is important to convey the value of humor in a manner that does not leave clients feeling that their concerns are being dismissed.

How does one go about recommending humor? Some suggest encouraging the student to start each day with a few minutes of smiling, followed by a brief focus on ridiculousness. Others find late afternoon to be a more ideal time for this exercise. If students are skeptical about it, one can invite them to try it on a brief experimental basis, to see if such a minor shift can have a positive effect. Assuming that this strategy goes well, a next step would be to encourage a minimum of 15–20 minutes of laughing most days of the week. For many individuals, that amount seems minimal. For others, it seems unreachable. The latter should be told that they may have to be creative in their pursuit of a few laughs: computer sites, TV programs, politicians' promises—whatever it takes.

Although offering a counseling-center group based on humor might create skepticism among university professionals, incorporating a time for humorous exchange in stress-management workshops can be very effective and, well, funny. Preceding a period of deep muscular relaxation with a few minutes of humor can be an excellent integrative approach. In the stress-management groups that I have led, the amount of time spent practicing progressive muscular relaxation decreases with each session as the number of muscle groups tensed and relaxed reduces. I have used the extra time to promote discussion of the funniest events of the week. Besides the muscular release, there is a subtle cognitive shift, as many of the stories relate to situations that were previously perceived as stressful.

Stress Management in Groups

There is obvious value to doing stress management in group settings. Since students can learn progressive muscular relaxation training as readily in a group of 10 as in an individual session, the investment in staff time is significantly reduced. Moreover, the opportunity for students to helpfully share the experiences that they find stressful lets them discover the idiosyncracies of certain stresses and the commonality of others. The number of group sessions varies across campuses, but a range of four to six seems most common.

Quieting Reflex

The time commitment in the various stress-management strategies is actually fairly minimal. Yet, if these techniques seem too time consuming, the briefest stress-management strategy may be encouraged, Charles Stroebel's (1982) *quieting reflex*. This procedure takes literally 6 seconds—less time than it does to explain it. You simply inhale an easy, natural breath; think "alert mind, calm body"; smile inwardly; exhale, allowing the muscles through your face and shoulders to go loose; and, finally, attend to the resultant feelings of warmth and looseness throughout your body. Often clients are so impressed with this quick exercise that they become receptive to more extensive methods.

Prevention Strategies

Stress cannot be avoided, nor is a stress-free life healthy. Yet certain personal styles can be promoted to help students avoid unfortunate reactions to stress. Helping students develop these effective styles will result in their experiencing less distress in the future.

Psychological Hardiness

Perhaps the most essential prevention is developing a sense of psychological hardiness, a concept promoted by Salvadore Maddi and Suzanne Kobasa (Maddi, 1999; Maddi & Kobasa, 1984). *Hardiness* is characterized by a sense of challenge, control, and commitment. *Challenge* refers to perceiving stressful situations and problems as opportunities for problem solving, rather than as threats or unwanted demands. The natural response with this perspective is to generate solutions to difficult situations, rather than avoid them. Challenge also involves openness to new experiences.

Control involves the belief that an individual can, in some ways, influence future outcomes. Consequently, instead of avoiding stressful situations, individuals with psychological hardiness strive to confront them. A sense of control does not deny the reality that some outcomes cannot be controlled, but asserts that a positive outlook can still be maintained. It's possible, even in unavoidable circumstances, to control one's reaction. The connection between this concept and cognitive therapy is obvious, since developing a sense of control involves learning to view stressors and difficult situations more positively. The goal becomes to think about situations optimistically and act decisively. *Commitment* is the ability to persevere through difficult situations and retain a sense of purpose in regard to work and relationships.

Generally, the process of promoting hardiness involves setting goals, knowing that they can be reset if necessary, becoming immersed in goal-related activity, and learning to enjoy the experience. I have found self-assessments of hardiness to be engaging for clients. Great discussion and insight have been generated by clients merely being asked to rate themselves on and discuss characteristics like self-discipline, need for achievement, internal motivation, approach to change, openness to new activities, level of optimism, commitment to success in school, and overall self-confidence. Setting valuable personal goals in these areas becomes a natural next step.

Authentic Happiness

Many also consider Martin Seligman's (2002) concept of *authentic happiness* to be a stress preventative. Seligman identifies a set of six personal values that are associated with authentic happiness: wisdom and knowledge, courage, love and humanity, justice, temperance, and spirituality and transcendence. He also asserts that happiness is cultivated by focusing on "signature strengths," which are kindness, originality, humor, optimism, and generosity. Though this approach is not directly about stress reduction, its benefits seem apparent for improving a student's response to stress. As with hardiness, promoting the characteristics of authentic happiness shifts the focus of therapy from pathology to the health state, to strengths. Once again, having the client do an informal assessment of these characteristics is engaging and leads to positive outcomes.

Mindfulness

Mindfulness is the practice of simply paying attention with an open and nonjudgmental attitude. It involves attending to each moment in a very real and immediate fashion—directing attention to only one thing in the moment. Those who promote mindfulness consider the process of *concentrating* on experience, rather than *interpreting* experience, to be an antidote for stress.

Anyone who observes college and university students will notice that in reality the practice of mindfulness is rare. Talking on a cellular phone while walking to class, eating lunch while working at the computer, listening to the radio while taking a shower, thinking about academic responsibilities while talking with friends, thinking about preferred activities while studying—these are just a few examples of students' typical nonmindful activity. It's fairly easy for students to understand the concept of mindfulness, but implementation can be challenging. Thus clinicians who promote mindfulness as part of a stress-management or stress-prevention package do best by starting with small steps.

An example of a common mindfulness exercise would be for the student to become more mindful while eating, walking, or showering. Eating can be an extremely enjoyable activity, but most often the experience is compromised by attending to media, computers, recent conversations, and upcoming responsibilities. Similarly, the sensations of showering can be enjoyable and relaxing, but this experience is typically compromised by focusing on upcoming activities, academic concerns, and so on. Walking provides a great opportunity for attending to the environment, but again is often compromised by cellular phones or preoccupation with past or future responsibilities. Counselors who encourage mindfulness therefore suggest that the student select one of these activities and practice being mindful about it. They are to sense the experience, simply take it in, and not judge it. During the first week, simply doing this for 5-minute periods is sufficient.

Recently, the concept of mindfulness has been creatively applied to the area of alcohol abuse, which could easily be considered a nonmindful ingestion of alcohol and is often an inappropriate and ineffective attempt at reducing stress. Students who drink 8 to 10 beers in a 2-hour period are presumably not doing so mindfully. As a method of harm reduction, then, teaching a student to drink only 1 or 2 beers mindfully can be an enlightening experience and help address problem drinking (Bien, 2002). Typically, students who have been referred to counseling to address alcohol issues deny having a problem. Most commonly, the problem is the manner in which they drink. Proposing the notion of mindful drinking often takes students by surprise, since they are anticipating being told that they should stop drinking. Proposing the concept as an experiment seems to increase the chances of participation. A recent client, very skeptical at first, reported significant changes after only a few weeks. He found that his taste had changed to better, more expensive beers, which he could now afford because he was having 3 instead of a dozen. As he became more mindfully aware, he also lost interest in going to smoky bars with friends who could not maintain a personal conversation.

Biofeedback

Biofeedback, which was so prominent in the late 1970s and 80s, seems to have lost some popularity, yet it remains a valuable method for stress management (Pelletier, 1991). The fact that biofeedback technology is now so portable and affordable makes it very useful; recommended equipment is no larger than a computer mouse. Biofeedback methods demonstrate the effectiveness of the various stress-management techniques in an objective, empirical manner. Particularly for the technologically inclined, biofeedback is an attractive manner in which to attend to the physiological changes resulting from the above approaches.

Conclusion

Stress is a fact of life and has become an extremely well known concept. Perhaps indirectly this awareness has led to a sense of resignation about it, rather than a determination to cope with it in creative ways. Counseling staff have an important responsibility to assist their clients in addressing stress management, utilizing the many techniques that have been developed. Moreover, given the intensity of counseling-center work, I encourage all counseling-center staff to engage in one of the many creative approaches themselves.

References

American College Health Association. (2004). *National College Health Assessment, 2004.*

American College of Sports Medicine. (2005). *Guidelines for exercise testing and prescription.* Philadelphia: Lippincott, Williams, & Wilkins.

Berk, L. (1996). The laughter-immune connection: New discoveries. *Humor and Health Journal, 5,* 1–5.

Bien, T. (2002). *Mindful recovery.* New York: John Wiley & Sons.

Bien, T., & Bien, B. (2003). *Finding the center within: The healing way of mindfulness meditation.* Hoboken, NJ: Wiley.

Chodron, P. (1996). *Awakening loving-kindness.* Boston: Shambala.

Davidson, R. J. (2004). Well-being and affective style: Neural substrates and biobehavioral correlates. *Philosophical Transactions of the Royal Society (London), 359,* 1395–1411.

Greene, H., & Green, M. (2000). *Inside the top colleges: Realities of life and learning in America's elite colleges.* New York: HarperCollins.

Holden, R. (1998). A dose of laughter medicine. *Stress News, 10.*

Hudd, S., Dumlao, J., Erdmann-Sager, D., Murray, D., Phan, E., Soukas, N., et al. (2000, June). *College Student Journal.*

Kadison, R., & DiGeronimo, T. (2004). *College of the overwhelmed: The campus mental health crisis and what to do about it.* San Francisco: Jossey-Bass.

Lazarus, R., & Folkman, S. (1984). *Stress, appraisal, and coping.* New York: Springer.

Lutz A., Greischar, L. L., Rawlings, N. B., Ricard, M., & Davidson, R. J. (2004). Long-term meditators self-induce high-amplitude gamma synchrony during mental practice. *Proceedings of the National Academy of Sciences, 101,* 16369–16373.

Maddi, S. (1999). The personality construct of hardiness: Effects on experience, coping, and strain. *Consulting Psychology Journal, 51,* 83–95.

Maddi, S., & Kobasa, S. (1984). *The hardy executive: Health under stress.* Homewood, IL: Dow Jones–Irwin.

McGrath, R. (2005). *Stress survey of undergraduate and graduate students.* Unpublished manuscript.

Pelletier, K. (1991). *Holistic health: From stress to optimal health.* New York: Delacorte and Delta.

Seligman, M. (2002). *Authentic happiness: Using the new positive psychology to realize your potential for lasting fulfillment.* New York: Simon and Schuster.

Stroebel, C. (1982). *The quieting reflex*. New York: Berkley Books.

Taylor, S., Klein, L., Lewis, B., Gruenewald, T., Gurung, R., & Updegraff, J. (2000). Biobehavioral responses to stress in females: Tend-and-befriend, not fight-or-flight. *Psychological Review, 107,* 411–429.

Verlander, L., Benedict, J., & Hanson, D. (1999). Stress and sleep patterns of college students. *Perceptual Motor Skills, 88,* 893–898.

Zhu, W., & Chodzko-Zajko, W. J. (2006). Qi, aging, and measurement: History, mystery, and controversy. In *Measurement issues in aging and physical activity* (chap. 10). Champaign, IL: Human Kinetics.

9
Diversity Issues

LINDA BERG-CROSS AND VICTORIA PAK

College students who belong to ethnic or racial minority groups or who are international students face a double burden adjusting to college life. While they have to deal with the stressors common to all students, they also experience a variety of challenges peculiar to their minority status both on campus and within the larger society. Culturally skilled college counseling-center clinicians can help these students develop coping mechanisms to adjust to college life and can boost their sense of empowerment and self-confidence. Effective therapeutic interventions can decrease the incidence of serious mental health problems in this population and increase their chances of successfully completing college.

Who Are the Minority Students?

In 2002, 29.4% of all college students in the United States belonged to ethnic or racial minority groups. This population breaks down as follows: 11.9% are African American, 10.0% are Hispanic, 6.5% are Asian or Pacific Islander, and 1.0% is Native American. These numbers have been rising in the past few decades (U.S. Department of Education, 2004).

Racial and ethnic breakdowns vary dramatically at different campuses. At Temple University, in Philadelphia, 27% of the undergraduates are African American, a percentage that soars to 98% at Howard University, in Washington, D.C. At Florida International University, in Miami, 55% of students are Hispanic or Latino; at the University of California at Los Angeles and Berkeley, 45% are of Asian descent; and at the University of Alaska, in Fairbanks, 18% are Native American. The definition of who is a minority student depends very much on the campus context.

"Minority" students who attend a university where they are part of the majority confront fewer social stressors and a large number of social supports and academic incentives (Pennock-Roman, 1993). This results in much higher graduation rates and much lower dropout rates. So, while only 15% of African Americans go to historically black colleges and universities (HBCUs) such as Howard, they account for 30% of all the undergraduate degrees given to black Americans. Indeed, 65% of all African-American doctors and 50% of all African-American engineers have graduated from HBCUs (Wenglinsky, 1996).

Conversely, some students who normally are not considered minorities may have a minority status within a given campus. These students then may find themselves having to deal with the culture shock and marginalization that we normally associate with the traditional minorities. Examples would be women who attend male-dominated technical schools, or white students who attend an HBCU. It should also be noted that lots of students are or consider themselves to be minorities for reasons aside from race and ethnicity, notably students who are lesbian, gay, bisexual, and transgendered or whose age, socioeconomic status, religious background, or political beliefs differ from the majority on their campuses.

Nationwide, the percentage of international students is 4.3%. They too are unevenly distributed across campuses, and they are also unevenly distributed within the strata of higher education. In the United States, international students make up only 2.7% of the undergraduate student body but are 11.4% of all graduate students and 33% of all doctoral students (College Board, 2004). Thus, the average university counseling center is far more likely to encounter significant numbers of international students in graduate school than in undergraduate student bodies.

While international students come from all over the world, the largest numbers come from the Asian countries of India, China, Korea, and Japan; together, they represent nearly 50% of all foreign students studying in the United States. Other well-represented countries are Canada, Mexico, Germany, the United Kingdom, and France. Most African students come from Kenya and Nigeria. Clearly, college clinicians have to learn quickly about many cultures and understand the role that obtaining a higher education in the United States serves in various countries (International Educational Exchange, 2004).

General Issues

Being a minority does not, in and of itself, necessarily place a student at risk. Minority college students are likelier to have social, academic, and psychological problems to the extent that they are subjected to certain pressures and issues. The following are particular themes to explore with this population.

Ethnic Identity

Students lacking in a secure sense of ethnic identity tend to be more at risk. The development of a positive and solid ethnic identity requires nurturance, education, and the opportunity to learn from one's own culture as well as others. Cross (1971) postulated that African-American racial identity develops in a four-stage process:

1. *Pre-encounter stage.* Here, the racism of the current world has been internalized, whites are viewed as superior to blacks, and so assimilating into the white world is seen as the solution to African-American problems.

2. *Encounter stage.* African Americans become aware of their own racial history and their place in it, but they often feel confused and in transition. They no longer just want to assimilate into the white world but haven't decided when or how to make a personally meaningful connection with their own ethnicity.
3. *Immersion stage.* Individuals reject all nonblack values and instead embrace everything labeled "African American" in an effort to prove that they are black.
4. *Internalization stage.* They are sufficiently anchored in their own history to be comfortable exploring other cultures and what they have to offer.

African-American students who enter the college scene are usually in stages 1, 2, or 3, although some do enter with a strong ethnic identity already in place. Those students who come to college in stage 1 may feel the sting of racism and difference at a more profound level than when they were in high school. Students in stages 2 and 3 may be uncomfortable around majority students and not know how to trust or interact with their new classmates. Sometimes, students are still developing an ethnic identity when they graduate college. They may leave feeling like an outsider or a part of a small subset of the university. Other students, who are lucky enough to have developed a strong identity, graduate with an appreciation of how diversity has enriched their lives. They identify with the school and enjoy knowing many classmates, irrespective of ethnic background.

Degree of Alienation

Related to the question of ethnic identity is the extent to which the campus culture seems alien. For some minority students, campus linguistic styles, dress codes, social events, and even food cravings may seem alien—and other students in turn may view the minority student's practices as alien. Other minority students feel more comfortable and accepted on campus. In general, students are more at risk to the extent that they perceive barriers to incorporating their home culture into their campus life.

Social Interactions

Similarly, students differ to the extent that they feel socially included rather than marginalized. Partly this depends on the climate of acceptance on campus. While overt discrimination is rarer than it once was, minority students certainly do confront instances of misunderstandings and negative stereotypes by peers and professors. On occasion, they encounter discrimination and rejection. Partly too, marginalization derives from students' own perceptions and background. Some minority students are relatively comfortable dealing with students from the majority. For others, doing so is not only unfamiliar but stressful. One useful role for the clinician is to help students become comfortable interacting with peers and faculty and so decrease their sense of marginalization. A variety of techniques can be useful here, including role-playing potentially embarrassing or painful social interactions, brainstorming about how interactions can be more satisfying, and assigning homework to try out situations that have a high probability of social success, such as going to an activity or class where everyone is paired off or grouped by the leader.

A related issue concerns friendships and dating with students from different races and cultures. While often such interactions are uncontroversial and indeed commonplace, in some college environments minority students who make friends or date outside their own group face disapproval and rejection—from the majority group, from members of their own ethnic or racial group, or from both.

Campus Supports

Students are likelier to succeed to the extent that there are support systems available on campus. Particularly helpful are faculty, administrators, and friends from the same ethnic group. However, persons from other cultures—notably counselors—can play a helpful supportive role too.

Family Factors

Generally speaking, minority students whose parents have low income are more at risk, if for no other reason than that parents are unable to contribute to college expenses. Minority students also commonly have to assume family obligations requiring time and energy that inevitably interfere with their studies. Minority students also face different degrees of family understanding and support regarding their college experience. If a student is a pioneer—the first member of the family to attend college—he or she may feel alienated from the family, unable to explain the college experience. Similarly, students whose hometowns differ markedly from the college environment may feel not only out of place on campus but also increasingly alienated from the home community.

Employment

Many minority students have to work to pay for their education. For some students, employment is actually a stress reducer, but for others it adds significantly to the burdens of coping at college.

Psychological Factors and Coping Resources

Minority students' emotional resources are obviously a huge factor in determining their college adjustment. Those who are likelier to encounter adjustment problems tend to have a negative worldview, to lack self-confidence, and to be poor at resolving interpersonal conflicts. Other negative indicators are a lack of leadership opportunities prior to college, a lack of definitive career plans, or no religious affiliation (Kerr, 1997; Lucas, 1993; Sanders, 1998; Shadrick, 1995; Ting, 2000). Needless to say, students who have psychological issues such as depression or a personality disorder are at a greater risk of encountering adjustment problems as well.

Academic Background

Ethnic and racial minority students and international students also differ greatly in the degree to which their academic backgrounds have prepared them for college. For minority students who've attended competitive American high schools or prep schools, college academics may not prove much of a shock—or no more of a shock than for majority students. But students from disadvantaged communities or foreign countries may be quite unprepared for the competitiveness and ways of teaching at American colleges.

Multicultural Counseling

Clinicians fall into different camps regarding the importance they place on cultural issues. Some, who tend to minimize cultural issues, have what we would call *beta bias* (Berg-Cross, 2003). This is the tendency to see the universal commonalities among cultures—for example, how all cultures value family. These clinicians assume that all human beings are fundamentally alike and that the core human issues overshadow the strong and distinctive differences among groups. In our view, counselors with a beta bias have a naïve worldview, because they assume that others will surely share their thought processes and values. Minority clients who see such a counselor may find it difficult to form a therapeutic alliance, because the counselor does not understand their roots, their community, and their way of thinking. They may conclude that the counselor is well-meaning but just "doesn't get it."

The opposite bias—*alpha bias*—is the tendency to stereotype others, to tint and magnify one's perceptions based on cultural affiliations. Counselors with an alpha bias risk exaggerating cultural differences and thus overlooking the similarities among different minority groups and between minority groups and the majority culture. Clients who have a counselor with a strong alpha bias may feel that the counselor does not see who they are as individuals—only their race, religion, ethnicity, or sexual orientation. They may see the counselor as racist, naïve, or demeaning.

It takes great skill and sensitivity to find the right balance between universal and cultural themes, to understand the particular role culture plays in the adjustment and problems of a given student. Further, sensitive counseling requires focusing on an individual's multiple group affiliations, including, but not limited to, culture and ethnicity, race, gender, religion, social class, and geography. What's more, individuals differ enormously in their relationship to their various group affiliations. In regard to students' culture, the values, interpersonal styles, and cognitive interpretations associated with their particular group may be bred-in-the-bone, long ago rejected, or irrelevant—not even part of their socialization experiences. One has to examine closely to understand how much a given student's culture plays in his or her problems and is a potential positive force for change.

Culturally competent clinicians strive to use clients' culture to promote change or to challenge distressing aspects of their lives. Some cultural behaviors and attitudes can be mobilized to help clients reach goals. Other cultural behaviors and attitudes may need to be modified. A clinician who knows how to work with cultural concepts in therapy can help clients explore which aspects of their culture should be retained, modified, or rejected in striving toward a particular goal.

Counselors also need to be alert to students' reactions to them, and to their own reactions to students, based on cultural and racial similarities or differences. In psychodynamic language, one must be aware of culturally induced transference and countertransference reactions. Whether explicitly discussed or not, these reactions are always in the room (as are reactions to the other person's gender, age, perceived sexual orientation, level of attractiveness, clothing, and voice). But we shouldn't presume to know beforehand a given client's (or counselor's) reaction to cultural and racial differences. One Latino student may prefer to work with a Latino counselor. Another, for his or her own reasons, may feel more comfortable speaking to a counselor from a different background.

Should white clinicians ask students of color their reactions to working with someone from a different race? Should therapists of color raise this issue with white students? College clinicians have differing opinions. Our own view is that the question should certainly be raised if the student appears to have a negative reaction to the therapist—fear, mistrust, or guardedness: "You seem hesitant talking. I was wondering if you have any feelings about working with a white counselor." It's also advisable to explore this theme if the therapeutic relationship itself is central to the treatment. On the other hand, if the working relationship appears to be solid and the treatment is narrowly focused on specific problems—roommate difficulties, a recent romantic breakup, or career uncertainty—then explicitly addressing reactions to the counselor's culture or race may be viewed as off the topic and distracting. Sensitive counselors should be able to judge when the topic of race and culture ought to be raised.

Listening, Asking, Respecting, and Challenging

The more detailed, concrete, and nuanced knowledge counselors have about a culture, the greater their capacity to promote client empowerment. Clinicians must strive to "hear" cultural expression through the client's verbalizations, reactions, symptomatology, and interaction style. In particular, we advocate the following principles, which may appear easy but in fact require much practice and skill:

- Listen with a "third ear" for possible cultural issues.
- Ask pertinent questions, as appropriate, to reassure clients that a cultural bridge exists between you and them and that they are free to explore cultural issues.
- Respect clients' cultural lifestyle options and limitations.
- If appropriate, introduce worldviews that challenge cultural assumptions and help clients reach their goals (Berg-Cross, 2000).

Shahram, a 33-year-old graduate student, has come to therapy because he is depressed and in particular worries about his failure to find a wife. He is currently a U.S. citizen, who came to the United States in 1990. Although his family is Iranian, they lived in England and various U.S. communities. The close-knit family has always had local friends from diverse backgrounds, but their closest friends are Iranian. Of the dozens of women Shahram has dated at each locale, none has fit his childhood image of the ideal wife. While he has had one or two dates with Western women over the years, the majority were Persians. A number of his closest high school male friends, mostly also Iranian, have serious partners or are engaged, either to very attractive or wealthy Iranian women. Shahram tells his counselor, "My closest friends are all happily married. I go to their weddings and ache for the same type of comfortable happiness. I want my wife to be like the women my father and his friends married—the mothers and wives I remember from my childhood. To find such a match would be bliss. It is so hard to date and so hard to find the right person."

How might a culturally competent counselor proceed in this case?

Listening   A traditional therapeutic approach might explore Shahram's possible fear of commitment or such universal issues as feelings of inferiority, jealousy, or depression. While these themes may be relevant, the culturally competent counselor would also listen for what it means to him to date someone who is or is not Persian, and would be alert to his confusion and stress over possibly using Western values—beauty or wealth—to choose a life partner.

Asking   A culturally competent counselor would ask questions to stimulate Shahram's thinking about family and cultural influences: "What type of women would your parents like you to marry? Is that important to you also? How do you think the type of woman you are looking for is different from a traditional Persian wife? In what ways are you looking for a traditional woman?"

Respecting   A culturally competent counselor would suspect that the client is probably caught between wanting to marry based on love and wanting to find someone from a compatible family. The counselor would be respectful of the client's background, yet challenging of aspects that are not constructive. This counselor might also offer culturally relevant solutions, such as using Persian friends and contacts to arrange introductions, if that seems warranted.

Challenging The culturally competent counselor would present the client with alternative worldviews. For example, since Shahram has been dating primarily Persian women, the answer may be to try dating women from other cultural backgrounds to see if there is a better match. If he would consider marrying only someone who is a virgin, he may need to challenge that rigid criterion. Thus, cultural values and routines that appear to help him reach his goals are encouraged, but cultural baggage that causes distress is challenged. In many respects, the culturally competent clinician uses motivational interviewing techniques, accepting clients where they are now, getting them to weigh the pros and cons of their current choices, and inviting them to change when they are ready to venture outside their comfort zone.

Attitudes about Therapy By and large, racial and ethnic minorities and international students are less likely than majority students to be familiar with and receptive to psychotherapy and to understand how it operates. Therefore, when these students encounter problems, they may not seek help in a timely fashion. One implication is that college counseling centers must do outreach to these populations. Another is that unconventional methods may be useful in attracting students to counseling.

For example, most minority students have at least one other student on campus whom they view as a confidant or social support and is in a sense psychological kin and sanctuary to students. Frequently, this significant person recommends going to the counseling center and may even accompany the client to the first interview. Allowing this to happen—which we call *college kin therapy*—may serve as the intermediate step paving the way for reluctant students to eventually come in for exclusive and confidential therapy sessions.

Particular Minority Groups

Any generalization about a particular racial or cultural group runs the risk of alpha bias, mentioned above—stereotyping the individual based on group membership. Each student who comes to the counseling service brings a unique set of concerns and resources and has a particular relationship to his or her culture. Nevertheless, we can hazard a few general remarks and suggestions for clinicians in relation to particular minority groups.

African-American Students

Racism It is impossible to write about the experience of African-American students without introducing the topic of racism, which, of course, even in the 21st century has not disappeared from American society—or from college campuses. Racism includes everything from discrimination in the classroom to lack of respect shown to students on the basis of their speech, dress, diet, and other cultural ways. Often the racism may be subtle; the person or persons responsible may be unaware of the damage they cause. For example, a resident advisor (RA) who felt he wasn't prejudiced against any ethnic group surveyed which students in the dorm wanted to buy tickets to hear Bruce Springsteen and didn't bother to ask the African Americans, since he assumed they wouldn't be interested. Only later did he realize that his behavior had been hurtful and stereotyping. He apologized and luckily there was still time to get a ticket for a student who very much did want to go.

There are also instances when African-American students may misperceive others' actions and motives as racist. If a student tends to do this, the counselor needs to set up social experiments that can be analyzed in the session. A dramatic example was when a student who earned a C-minus on a paper about the causes of World War I filed a grievance against the white teacher. In the paper, the student had hypothesized that hatred of American blacks had been the prime cause of the war. Refusing to see the teacher's grade as anything but racist, the student only grudgingly admitted that he might have deserved the low mark when a professor from African-American Studies reviewed the paper and explained why it hadn't deserved a higher score.

Stereotype Threat   African-American students at predominantly white institutions (PWIs) are also faced with "stereotype threat" (Steele, 2000)—the feeling that their academic performance is considered to reflect on their entire race and so confirms or refutes their race's supposed lack of ability. Stereotype threat is "the threat of being viewed through the lens of a negative stereotype or the fear of doing something that would inadvertently confirm that stereotype" (Hyde & Kling, 2001, p. 374). The individual experiencing stereotype threat feels pressure to exceed expectations and "prove them wrong," raising anxiety levels and so interfering with performance and lowering academic scores.

Stereotype threat has been demonstrated to disrupt achievement levels (Steele & Aronson, 1995). When students worry about appearing stupid, they are more hesitant to ask questions of faculty or interact with them socially. They are less likely to seek out study circles—an effective studying tool—for fear they'll be judged as unprepared or lost. Avoiding classroom contact with teachers, refraining from asking questions, and avoiding study groups limit their opportunities to learn and achieve.

Counselors need to discuss stereotype threat with clients and assess the degree to which they worry about being flawless and avoiding any show of ignorance. Insight, assertiveness training, and desensitization to anxiety-arousing situations can help empower students who have these concerns. Counselors can begin this process by discussing the following issues: If others use you to judge your entire ethnic group, is this a burden you choose to accept? And if you wanted to accept it, is it realistic to think that you can ever satisfy the judgment of outsiders? In what ways are you a "good example" of your ethnic group? In what ways are you a "poor example"? Is your balance of good and bad traits typical of most people, or do you have special burdens that others would judge more harshly? Are you able to discuss your limitations or weaknesses with classmates, professors, or close friends? When is it useful to do so? Exploring these topics will hopefully desensitize students to stereotype threat. It will also empower them to feel confident in their areas of expertise while promoting help-seeking behaviors when needed.

Racial Identity   Counselors often need to educate students about the stages of racial identity development and how a mature racial identity promotes effective interactions with all races. It may be helpful to direct students to take a course in African-American history or in race and ethnicity. Perhaps the most powerful technique to nurture a positive racial identity is to have students experience an intense, short-term, interracial small-group learning experience (called a "T-group") (Cooke, Michael, Saunders, & Barbara, 1999). These groups promote more openness to feedback and criticism and help individuals learn how to recognize unconscious attitudes and biases and to interact more successfully with people from other cultures. Every counseling center should try to have one staff member highly skilled in this essential technique.

Isolation on Campus   African-American students may feel isolated on campus in a variety of ways. They may feel socially alienated from peers who are not black and feel that there are too few black students available for friendship or dating. Their religious practices and beliefs, tastes in music and clothing, even their ways of relaxation may serve to set them apart. To some extent, isolation may be imposed by the realities of being a minority on campus; to some extent, the individual student may perpetuate his or her isolation. Since isolation is implicated in academic failure as well as psychological distress, clinicians need to address this issue. For example, counselors can urge African-American clients to join a campus organization or activity, experiment with initiating contact with interesting people in their dorm, or encourage them to join a support group offered at the counseling center. At a deeper level, they can help students deal with the fear of rejection, their own prejudices and projections of anger, and the existential need for acceptance found in all of us.

Increasing Utilization of the Counseling Center   As mentioned above, many minority students are reluctant to come to the counseling services. Innovative techniques can encourage at-risk African-American students to take that step. For example, a once-a-month "sister rap" provides the opportunity for female African-American students to come to the counseling center with a friend, since it's easier to talk to a counselor if the friend does so also. If the identified patient decides to continue, she then receives individual therapy. This technique requires that the counselor describe the rules of confidentiality to both parties at the beginning of treatment. A similar idea is to place a counselor for several hours per week within the minority students' office.

Asian-American Students

Culturally competent counselors who work with Asian-American students often need to address several common concerns.

Panethnic Identity "Asian Americans" are an American-made social construct. In fact, there is enormous cultural and linguistic heterogeneity among this population's subgroups. According to the U.S. Census Bureau (2001), there are 43 ethnic subgroups, with the largest being Chinese (25.4% of all Asians) and the smallest Pacific Islanders (4.2%). Some subgroups (e.g., Koreans) are relatively new to this country, whereas Pacific Islanders are endogenous to the United States. Some groups, notably the Chinese, have been subjected to racism and discrimination dating back to the construction of the western railroads in the 19th century. Groups newer to this country have faced only indirect, less severe forms of discrimination.

Some Asian-American students embrace a "panethnic identity"—the coming together of ethnic subgroups into a larger Asian entity—in order to battle racism and xenophobia. Coming together provides support and increases their opportunities to be heard. In addition to the political benefits, panethnic identity can provide important psychological benefits, since some students feel marginalized by their own ethnic culture as well as the majority culture (Rhoads, Lee, & Yamada, 2002).

But Asian-American students identify themselves in various ways, along a continuum from melting-pot American to bicultural to panethnic Asian American to membership exclusively in their original ethnic group (e.g., Thai, Vietnamese, or Chinese). With this in mind, Lee and Davis (2000) stress the importance of assessing cultural orientation. Individuals can be at risk for rejection from their own and other ethnic groups if they adopt an ethnic identity that is not common on their campus, and, like African Americans who lack a mature ethnic identity, they can suffer internally if they feel uncomfortable with their ethnicity. Counselors should help students who lack a positive ethnic identity explore this critical theme. Sometimes, as with African Americans, it helps to encourage joining a club or organization for Asian Americans.

The Myth and Pressures of Being a Model Minority A major issue for Asian-American students is the stereotype of the "model minority"—the belief that all Asian Americans are successful and that they exemplify the American success story. This stereotype assumes that Asian Americans are unlikely to be targets of prejudice and discrimination and are less likely to require assistance. As a result, problems they may face are de-emphasized or ignored. Further, the attempts of elite universities to limit Asian-American enrollment (Chan & Wang, 1991) may make elite Asian-American students reluctant to display any weaknesses that would shatter the image (sometimes self-adopted) of a highly achieving and successful individual. These students may therefore deny problems and refuse to seek help when troubled (Yang, Byers, Ahuna, & Castro, 2002).

Contrary to the myth, Asian Americans report discrimination in varying degrees, ranging from discourteous actions by strangers to lethal violence (Yang et al., 2002). They are often criticized as "not well rounded," a strategy for countering their strong performance on standardized measures of academic achievement (Takagi, 1992). Many Asian-American students over-schedule their athletic commitments, social activities, and campus commitments to prove that they are more than "book smart." In our experience, more than a few Asian-American students end up getting involved with drugs, alcohol, and unprotected sex as a way of proving that they are cool. In fact, So and Wong (in press) found a 94.5% lifetime prevalence and a 78.6% current prevalence of alcohol use among Asian-American college students. Furthermore, 9.5% reported illicit drug use, and 22.8% reported cigarette use.

On the other hand, some Asian-American students, often egged on by parents, do try to live up to the pressure of being straight-A students, sometimes to the detriment of having a full college experience and at the cost of their emotional health. Myths are sometimes misleading but sometimes imprisoning. In order to help these students, counselors can explore what values and activities they most cherish, and how they want to live 10 to 15 years down the road. They can also help students understand the negative consequences of pressures to excel, which can actually hinder performance.

John, a Korean American, came in for psychological testing to find out if he was intelligent enough to pursue a career in medicine. A top student in high school, he was struggling in college. He reported that all the males in his family were medical doctors and that it was imperative that he go to medical school. The testing revealed superior cognitive abilities but very high levels of anxiety. Initially, however, John focused solely on his fear of academic insufficiencies and neglected his emotional issues, which no doubt accounted for his academic underachievement. Furthermore, he attributed all his "psychological" problems to his inability to live up to his parents' standards. Only gradually did he see that this pressure was causing great anxiety, which in turn led to poor performance, and also that he didn't necessarily want to follow in his parents' footsteps. In the end, he expressed interest in studying the epidemiology of viruses and opted to apply to public health graduate programs rather than medical school, a decision his parents fortunately, and somewhat surprisingly to him, supported.

Family Stressors Lee and Liu (2001) found a higher likelihood of reported intergenerational conflict in Asian-American college-age children compared with their white American and Hispanic counterparts. The increased conflict with parents is partly traceable to the fast rate of acculturation among Asian-American youth. Unlike many other minority groups, Asian-American students often stress their American identity, to the chagrin of their parents. Frequently these conflicts center on career goals. Immigrant parents often want their children to pursue economic security, and pressure them not only to excel academically but also to take practical majors such as engineering, business, science, or math. Students, however, may wish to follow their passions and take impractical-seeming majors such as literature, art, or theater. Conflict and misunderstandings ensue.

Intergenerational conflict is a risk factor for psychological distress. Aldwin and Greenberger (1987) found that parental traditionalism was a positive predictor of depression in Korean-American college students, presumably because they despaired about disappointing their parents by failing to follow the traditional path. Counselors first need to convey empathy for the difficult conflict between loyalty to families and their own inclinations. Next, they can help students find ways to express filial devotion and commitment independent of subservience to parents' preferred career choice. In fact, in many cases, if students go after their dreams, their parents will come to admire their perseverance and commitment to ideals. The short-term impasse over choice of careers may be eventually replaced by parental approval and pride in the students' ultimate career choice.

Sexual Behavior   Compared with other ethnic groups, Asian-American women are more reluctant to obtain sexual and reproductive care and have less communication with their mothers concerning sexual and gynecological issues (Okazaki, 2002). In general, Asian-Americans may be more uncomfortable than other groups discussing sexual topics with their counselors. Counselors should ask their Asian-American clients how they feel about discussing these topics. Though it may feel like a game of Twenty Questions, sometimes it helps to refer to specific acts or to sexually transmitted diseases as a means of getting the client to open up about the topic. Also, a gender match between the counselor and the client can often make discussion easier about sexual topics.

Due to the cultural emphasis on interpersonal harmony and protecting the family name from shame, Asian-American women are extremely reluctant to disclose or report sexual abuse. Instead of feeling anger and hostility toward their abuser, they are likely to express suicidal ideation or attempt suicide (Rao, DiClemente, & Ponton, 1992). Further, others within the Asian-American community who are less acculturated may judge the victims of sexual aggression harshly, believing that they share the responsibility for the crime. Consequently, Asian-American female victims of abuse often struggle with feelings of self-blame, self-loathing, and self-castigation. Counselors can help by educating clients about the use of power in intimate relationships and the psychological burdens associated with being a sexual assault victim. Of course, counselors need to be extra-sensitive about avoiding any statements that imply responsibility on the part of the victim.

Roadblocks to the Counseling Center   When faced with psychological problems, Asian-American students are more likely to seek help from social support networks than from professionals. Korean Americans are especially likely to turn to religious leaders or religious groups (Yeh & Wang, 2000). Many Asian-American students cope with mental health issues without turning to anyone else at all, because cultural beliefs suggest that emotional expression is both disruptive to interpersonal harmony and a sign of weakness (Zander, 1983). Given the high rate of suicide in Chinese populations, for example (Phillips, Li, & Zhang, 2002), the stakes are especially high when students are reluctant to seek professional help. Accordingly, these students sometimes need encouragement that talking to a counselor is helpful, is common in America, and is not a sign of weakness.

With Asian-American students, clinical interventions and interviewing styles that demand an emotionally expressive response may be less successful than interventions that require a problem-solving, analytic, or "best fit" solution. Indeed, Li and Kim (2004) found that Asian-American students preferred a directive counseling style, highly structured and focused on providing concrete guidance. Though concrete advice is often seen as too controlling by white students, many Asian Americans see advice as "gift giving" (Sue & Zane, 1987). Of course, not all Asian Americans are averse to insight-oriented or exploratory therapies.

Counseling centers wishing to make the center user-friendly to Asian Americans (and others who are wary of professional mental health services) can create a series of culturally sensitive brochures that explain what happens in a counseling session and can engage in outreach activities—for example, holding office hours in the Asian Studies Department or at other places where Asian and Asian-American students congregate.

Hispanic Students

Although they all share a common language and many share common religious rituals, Hispanic or Latino (Latina) students, like Asian Americans, comprise a wide range of cultural groups who share unique stressors. Many come from families geographically separated because of economic and political circumstances. Some find the traditional male and female sex roles and religious teachings of their community challenged by college experiences (Martinez, Huang, Johnson, & Edwards, 1989). In addition, many struggle with intense family demands and a lack of role models.

Family Demands   Hispanics have the lowest educational attainment of the four major racial or ethnic groups in the United States (Chapa & Valencia, 1993; Gándara, 1995). A possible explanation for this grim fact is *familismo,* defined as providing and receiving support from family members. More than most groups, Hispanics may be willing to sacrifice long-term success for the immediate needs of the family (Keefe & Padilla, 1987). These students feel pressure to prove their commitment to family through daily social interaction, help, and availability. But attending college may interfere with these contributions and almost always limits their financial contributions. The stress and shame of not being able to meet family obligations weighs heavily on these students; they may feel that they are betraying their families by pursuing an education. While counselors must respect students' family ties and sense of obligation, often they can help clients see that ruining their college careers and futures is not in the long-term interests either of themselves or of their families. Family pressures particularly affect Hispanic women. Pidcock, Fischer, and Munsch (2001) found that of all Hispanic students who did not return to school, 92% were female. Most of these women dropped out to tend to family obligations.

Clearly, counselors working with Latino students need to thoroughly explore the pressures at home. In particular, females need support and guidance to avoid being pressured into a traditional martyrdom role. Males and females alike may find that college challenges their traditional sex roles and religious teachings (Martinez et al., 1989), and these issues may need to be addressed as well.

Lack of Role Models   While lack of role models is a problem for most minority students, this issue is particularly prominent among Hispanic students. By and large, Hispanic students accurately assume that they will not find any Hispanic professors to mentor them. When such mentors do exist, the positive impact is profound. Ceballo (2004) found that Hispanic students attending Ivy League universities reported that having Hispanic role models was one of the most important factors in their academic success. When a campus lacks Hispanic mentors, it can be invaluable to link the student to a mentor in the community. Furthermore, encouraging students to find non-Hispanic mentors who share other important characteristics (e.g., love of a particular academic subject, career path, or avocation) can help them grow academically and personally.

International Students

SEVIS (Student Exchange Visitor Information Service)   Developed after September 11, 2001, as a foreign-student database, SEVIS requires international students to register and be cleared before arriving on campus and taking trips abroad. Students attending college can face delays of months before being able to reenter the country if they leave to attend conferences, visit family, or travel. As a result, the number of international students applying to study in the United States has dramatically dropped (Gilman & Schulz, 2004). Those already studying here have heightened anxiety about their ability to start each semester on time, visit home, and attend critical conferences in their field. Like the main character in the movie *Terminal*, they are afraid of getting caught, feel powerless to expedite the governmental visa process, and sometimes watch their dreams of academic training go up in smoke.

Despite their diversity in country of origin and family background, international students share many common stressors and must use common coping strategies to succeed. In particular, counselors should assess how students cope with the following six burdens.

Homesickness and Loneliness   Unlike U.S. students, who are linked to home and old friends by cell phones, low-cost airfares, car ownership, and campus visits, international students more frequently are prone to homesickness and loneliness. For some, e-mail has become a critical way of keeping in touch with families and friends. For those whose loved ones don't have Internet access, the isolation stings even more sharply. Counselors can encourage these students to join local organizations belonging to their particular group (e.g., a Chinese church), mentor youth from their homeland in the United States, or build relationships with local immigrant families from their country.

Culture Shock   Living in the United States is very different from consuming U.S. media products in one's own country. Once here, international students sometimes feel overwhelmed by the differences in values, lifestyles, food habits, and academic work styles. They may be uninterested in assimilating and may even regard American culture on campus with scorn, horror, or amusement. Also, foreign students are sometimes hesitant to share their political beliefs, afraid of biting the hand that feeds them and of further alienating themselves from their U.S. peers. They may be reluctant to talk about the politics in their home country, assuming that U.S. students are uninterested in and oblivious to world politics and nuanced regional and local concerns.

Counselors can help by inviting international students to test their assumptions. They can encourage students to carefully evaluate which elements of U.S. culture are worth experimentation. They can urge students to test the receptiveness of their fellow students to discussions about their culture and politics. Some skeptical international students discover that U.S. students are in fact interested in other cultures and political systems and are eager to make friends from other countries.

Language Barriers   Many international students are not linguistically proficient in English. They feel pressure to read, write, and speak English with a fluency and accuracy that allow them to achieve as well as they did at home. Yet, such fluency is often difficult to master—particularly in a short amount of time. Also, consciousness of having an accent or being difficult to understand leads many foreign students to shy away from interacting with U.S. students. Sometimes, international students find that expressing strong feelings to their counselors in English is frustrating or even impossible.

To bridge the linguistic barrier during sessions, an innovative way that has proved successful in the first author's experience is to encourage students to explain conflicts or feelings in their native tongue, even if the counselor can't understand. After they have expressed themselves, they can translate the essence to the counselor. Another approach, of course, is to refer students, if possible, to therapists who are competent in their native language.

It should be stressed, however, that language barriers don't always doom therapy. For example, one Japanese student who could barely speak English actually expressed a preference to work with an English-speaking therapist. She didn't feel comfortable opening up to a Japanese counselor, because, she said, her native language discouraged emotional expression.

Financial Burdens   Foreign students bear unusual financial burdens. Fluctuating exchange rates may be a benefit to them, but often they're an additional hardship. And because they are prohibited by U.S. law from working off-campus, foreign students cannot easily increase their income by taking a part-time job. Whether the need is for computer repair or dental treatment, each unexpected expense can cause a cascading set of problems and stressors. Here, if possible, counselors must become social workers to help students find needed help and support.

Educational System Adjustments   International students often need to make major adjustments in their study skills, since the U.S. educational system operates differently from many others. For example, it is not unusual for an international student to be unfamiliar with multiple-choice tests, study groups, or the practices of sharing old exams or asking questions in class. Inquiring how college differs from their previous educational settings often will lead to productive discussions. Another common problem for many is that their original educational systems stressed rote memory and repetition. Not only is adjusting to American term papers and essay exams a challenge, but some find themselves inadvertently committing plagiarism when they dutifully copy material they have acquired from another source.

On a very practical level, clinicians can help by educating international students about how the U.S. educational system operates. Often, collecting problematic vignettes that have occurred on campus and walking students through the possible solutions is especially helpful. Counselors can also encourage international students to join study groups with American students so as to learn from example how the American educational system functions.

Biracial and Bicultural Students

The growing number of biracial college students face special problems of acceptance and understanding from other students, since they don't automatically fit in with one group or another. For example, Williams (1999) notes that as a biracial woman, she was never "black enough" for the other black students, yet to the whites she was "not white." The struggle for external acceptance and a place to belong is often paralleled by internal confusion and conflict. At one time, many biracial students may have gravitated toward the identity that had preferred status in society. Thus a light-skinned black might prefer to be seen as white. Today, many biracial (or multiracial) students seem more receptive to claiming all parts of their heritage, a process in which counseling obviously can be of help. Analogous to the Rogerian notion of enabling clients to become aware of previously denied aspects of experience, counseling of these students can help them accept previously disowned aspects of their racial and cultural selves.

Coming to college brings identity issues to a head for these students. As children, their racial identities were often established by their families. Now, however, it's up to them to decide which clubs to join, which groups of peers to befriend, and which identity—or identities—to claim. College presents challenges, but it also provides an opportunity for students to negotiate their own racial identity (Root, 1998).

Also facing particular identity struggles are transculturally adopted college students. Thus a student whose biological parents are black, Asian, or Latino but who was raised by white parents faces both external challenges, in the form of misunderstandings and rejection by classmates, and internal challenges to reconcile disparate identity elements. One such female black student, for example, encountered rejection from other black students because of her supposedly "white" values, tastes in music, and preferences for white friends. On the one hand, she faced the challenge of all African-American students to arrive at stage 4 (internalization) of racial identity development (Cross, 1971). But forming an authentic identity also required not renouncing the obviously sweeping influence of her adoptive parents. There is no shortcut to this process. Only by reflecting on their various "roots" and influences can these students, or any college student for that matter, arrive at a secure and authentic sense of self.

Beyond Counseling

While this chapter has focused on in-house methods of reaching minority and international students, the outreach required by a culturally competent counseling center is significant and continues to grow. Hence, it would be remiss not to mention the importance of such activities as housing a counselor at the Student Academic Center; teaming with the campus ministry;

running groups during orientation on such topics as homesickness, keeping in touch, and changing and staying true to one's roots; sending out e-mails to targeted populations; encouraging minority leadership within departments; promoting multiethnic dance/music weekends; and developing links to the community.

References

Aldwin, C., & Greenberger, E. (1987). Cultural differences in the predictors of depression. *American Journal of Personality and Social Psychology, 37*, 789–813.

Berg-Cross, L. (2000). *The LARI method.* Unpublished manuscript.

Berg-Cross, L. (2003). *Alpha and beta biases in psychotherapy.* Unpublished manuscript.

Berg-Cross, L., & Takushi, R. (1995). Multicultural training models and the person-in culture interview. In J. Ponterotto, M. Casas, L. Suzuki, & C. Alexander (Eds.), *Handbook of multicultural counseling* (pp. 333–357). Thousand Oaks, CA: Sage Press.

Ceballo, R. (2004). From barriosa to Yale: The role of parenting strategies in Latin families. *Hispanic Journal of Behavioral Sciences, 26*, 171–186.

Chan, S., & Wang, L. (1991). Racism and the model minority: Asian-Americans in higher education. In P. G. Altback & K. Lomotey (Eds.), *The racial crisis in American higher education* (pp. 43–67). Albany: State University of New York Press.

Chapa, J., & Valencia, R. R. (1993). Latino population growth, demographic characteristics and educational stagnation: An examination of recent trends. *Hispanic Journal of Behavioral Sciences, 15*, 165–187.

College Board. (2004). *Annual survey of colleges: Data on United States higher education enrollment, 2004.* New York: Author.

Cooke, A., Michael, B., Saunders, C., & Barbara, G. (1999). *Reading book for human relations training* (8th ed.). Alexandria, VA: NTL Institute for Applied Behavioral Sciences.

Cross, W. E. (1971). The negro to black conversion experience. *Black World, 20*, 13–27.

Gándara, P. (1995). *Over the ivy walls: The educational mobility of low-income Chicanos.* Albany: State University of New York Press.

Gilman, V., & Schulz, W. (2004, April 5). U.S. schools losing foreign talent. *Education, 82*, 67–70.

Hyde, J. S., & Kling, K. (2001). Women, motivation, and achievement. *Psychology of Women Quarterly, 25*, 364–378.

International Educational Exchange. (2004). *Leading places of origin: Open Doors 2004: Report on International Educational Exchange.* New York: Author. Retrieved April 16, 2006, from http://opendoors.iienetwork.org/?p=49933

Keefe, S. E., & Padilla, A. M. (1987). *Chicano ethnicity.* Albuquerque, NM: University of New Mexico Press.

Kerr, A. E. (1997). College adjustment: The role of stress, self-cohesion, racial identity development and world view. *Dissertation Abstracts International, 57*(9), 5922B. (UMI No. 9705238)

Lee, R. M., & Davis, C. (2000). Cultural orientation, past multicultural experience, and a sense of belonging on campus for Asian-American college students. *Journal of College Student Development, 41*, 110–115.

Lee, R., & Liu, H. T. (2001). Coping with intergenerational family conflict: Comparison of Asian-American, Hispanic, and European-American college students. *Journal of Counseling Psychology, 48*, 410–419.

Li, L. C., & Kim, B. S. K. (2004). Effects of counseling style and client adherence to Asian cultural values on counseling process with Asian-American college students. *Journal of Counseling Psychology, 51*, 158–167.

Lucas, M. S. (1993). Personal, social, academic and career problems expressed by minority college students. *Journal of Multicultural Counseling and Development, 21*, 2–14.

Martinez, A., Huang, K. H. C., Johnson, S. D., Jr., & Edwards, S., Jr. (1989). Ethnic and international students. In P. A. Grayson & K. Cauley (Eds.), *College psychotherapy.* New York: Guilford.

Okazaki, S. (2002). Influence of culture on Asian-Americans' sexuality. *Journal of Sex Research, 39*, 34–41.

Pennock-Roman, M. (1993). *Differences among racial and ethnic groups in mean scores on the GRE and SAT: Cross-sectional comparisons.* GRE Board Report No. 86-09aP. Princeton, NJ: Educational Testing Service (ETS). Retrieved April 16, 2006, from ETS portal at http://www.ets.org

172 • Linda Berg-Cross and Victoria Pak

Phillips, M. R., Li, X., & Zhang, Y. (2002). Suicide rates in China, 1995–99. *Lancet, 359,* 835–840.

Pidcock, B. W., Fischer, J. L., & Munsch, J. (2001). Family, personality, and social risk factors impacting the retention rates of first-year Hispanic and Anglo college students. *Adolescence, 36,* 803–818.

Rao, K., DiClemente, R. J., & Ponton, L. E. (1992). Child sexual abuse of Asians compared with other populations. *Journal of the American Academy of Child and Adolescent Psychiatry, 31,* 880–886.

Rhoads, R. A., Lee, J. J., & Yamada, M. (2002). Panethnicity and collective action among Asian-American students: A qualitative case study. *Journal of College Student Development, 43,* 876–891.

Root, M. P. P. (1998). Experience and processes affecting racial identity development: Preliminary results from the biracial sibling project. *Cultural Diversity and Mental Health, 4,* 237–247.

Sanders, R. T., Jr. (1998). Intellectual and psychosocial predictors of success in the college transition: A multiethnic study of freshmen students on a predominantly white campus. *Dissertation Abstract International, 58*(10), 5655B. (UMI No. 9812760)

Shadrick, B. P. (1995). Academically successful African-American students on a predominantly white campus: A question of identity. *Dissertation Abstract International, 56*(5), 1615A. (UMI No. 9532116)

So, D. W., & Wong, F. Y. (in press). Alcohol, drugs, and substance use among Asian-American college students. *Journal of Psychoactive Drugs.*

Steele, C. (2000). Stereotype threat and black college students. *AAHE Bulletin, 52,* 3–6.

Steele, C. M., & Aronson, J. (1995). Stereotype threat and the intellectual test performance of African Americans. *Journal of Personality and Social Psychology, 69,* 797–811.

Sue, S., & Zane, N. (1987). The role of culture and cultural techniques in psychotherapy: A critique and reformation. *American Psychologist, 42,* 37–45.

Takagi, D. Y. (1992). The retreat from race. *Socialist Review, 22,* 167–189.

Ting, S. R. (2000). Predicting Asian Americans' academic performance in the first year of college: An approach combining SAT scores and noncognitive variables. *Journal of College Student Development, 41,* 442–449.

Upchurch, D. M., Levy-Storms, L., Sucoff, C. A., & Aneshensel, C. S. (1998). Gender and ethnic differences in the timing of first sexual intercourse. *Family Planning Perspectives, 30,* 121–127.

U.S. Census Bureau. (2001). *Profiles of general demographic characteristics: 2000 census of population and housing, United States.* Washington, DC: Author. Retrieved April 16, 2006, from http://www2.census.gov/census_2000/datasets/demographic_profile/0_National_Summary/2khus.pdf

U.S. Department of Education (2004). Digest of Education Statistics, 2004, National Center for Education Statistics, Institute of Education Sciences. Table 206. Total fall enrollment in degree-granting institutions, by race/ethnicity, sex, attendance status, and level of student: Selected years, 1976 to 2002. Retrieved June 11, 2006, from U.S. Department of Education portal at http://nces.ed.gov/programs/digest/d04/tables/dt04_206.asp

Wenglinsky, H. (1996). The educational justification of historically black colleges and universities: A policy response to the U.S. Supreme Court. *Educational Evaluation and Policy Analysis, 18,* 91–103.

Williams, C. B. (1999). Claiming a biracial identity: Resisting social constructions of race and culture. *Journal of Counseling and Development, 77,* 32–35.

Yang, R. K., Byers, S. T., Ahuna, L. M., & Castro, K. S. (2002). Asian-American students' use of a university students-affairs office. *College Student Journal, 36,* 448–470.

Yeh, C., & Wang, Y. W. (2000). Asian-American coping attitudes, sources, and practices: Implications for indigenous counseling strategies. *Journal of College Student Development, 4,* 94–103.

Zander, A. (1983). The value of belonging to a group in Japan. *Small Group Behavior, 14,* 3–14.

10
Academic Difficulties

CHARLES P. DUCEY*

Subject though it is to numerous other influences, academic performance is at once a consistent outcome, sensitive indicator, and solid predictor of emotional well-being at all stages of development. Hence, the effective college mental health practitioner conceives the task of promoting students' academic performance as just one aspect of enriching their educational and personal experience and hence improving the quality of their lives. This broad aim may seem at loggerheads with students' sometimes explicit, often narrower, and more pragmatic goals: to improve their grades, gain recognition from faculty, or get into prestigious postgraduate programs. Yet, psychotherapy reveals that most students know that their performance is an intrinsic aspect of who they are as individuals and how they approach making sense of life experience.

Achievement motivation is a universal human striving, in that the effort at competent and effective behavior is fundamental to the human spirit (Basch, 1988; Heath, 1965; McClelland, 1961; White, 1963). Many progressive societies capitalize on this striving and instantiate it through a meritocracy, rewarding effective achievement as defined by external standards. Such societies promote early socialization of children's achievement through competitive rating systems that compare children and hold them to the same standards. This approach can have well-known and well-documented consequences for children whose skills vary from or are delayed relative to other children: negative self-evaluation; painful feelings; self-fulfilling prophecies of future failure; and a consequent "downward-mobility" drift toward underperformance and inadequate educational, and perhaps later career, achievement (Vaillant, 1977).

Loving parents and supportive teachers can to some extent offset the impact of these negative early educational experiences. Once children develop and are reinforced for their own unique skills and talents in other areas, some negative psychological consequences of early underperformance—particularly poor self-image, evaluation anxiety, and self-blaming depressive reactions—can be further obviated. Yet it does not take searching questioning of many

---

* I am very grateful to Dr. Barbara A. Ducey, whose penetrating insights, clinical wisdom, and literary expertise contributed substantively to this chapter.

college students to uncover their continuing pain and self-recrimination for academic underperformance.

Insofar as academic achievement is both a cause and a consequence of emotional well-being, college counselors or psychotherapists need to address underperformance through both direct strategies and interventions for the many emotional and psychosocial difficulties that influence achievement. They treat "whole persons" of interlocking and interacting components—cognitive, emotional, psychosocial, psychosexual, and spiritual aspects of self; as well as academic, athletic, social, and extracurricular aspects of college life. These elements bear either parallel or complementary/compensatory relationships with each other. In the case of parallel effects, students' difficulties in one area emerge as difficulties in others; depression, for instance, has a uniformly negative impact on functioning in all areas. In the case of complementary and compensatory effects, altered functioning in one area may effect seismic shifts in others: students' overdevotion to athletic involvement may impair academic performance and restrict social life to sports buddies. Student problems therefore call for a range of interventions that affect diverse realms of college experience.

Aims of Intervention

Depending upon how broadly college mental health practitioners define their responsibility, the following goals may guide their interventions:

- Enhance students' academic accomplishments to implement the college's educational aims.
- Facilitate development of students' full achievement potential by helping them overcome cognitive limitations and resolve psychological conflicts, inhibitions, or affective disturbances.
- Promote students' capacity for autonomous thinking, independent judgment, understanding the world, problem solving, and decision making.
- Promote students' self-awareness and individuation, and hence their more consciously focused and directed life plans and goals.
- Enhance quality of life in other areas, insofar as happiness or unhappiness affects intellectual accomplishment.
- Help students productively utilize the "psychosocial moratorium" of college, the transition from adolescence to adulthood (Erikson, 1968).
- Develop students' skills for future careers and values for informed citizenship.

Making these goals explicit can help practitioners be aware of their assumptions about achievement, guide them in selecting appropriate interventions, and allow them to assess their success. But since these goals are complex, abstract, and not simply measured, it is not easy to arrive at straightforward criteria for success. Sophisticated counselors or psychotherapists tend to hold themselves to more complex standards than improved grades or, for that matter, symptom relief or better study habits. Because of adventitious and uncontrollable factors, such as socioeconomic disadvantage and under-preparation for college work, grades may not faithfully reflect knowledge, learning, or growth. Moreover, college success is only mildly or coincidentally correlated with postcollege success (whether measured by income, quality of life, or positive impact on society). According to the former dean of Harvard College:

> Things that Harvard used to talk about—courage, ambition, mental toughness, integrity, imagination, compassion, capacity to rebound from reversals, a desire to leave the world a better place than you found it—these are the things that matter in real life. Not insignificant varia-tions in grade point average. (Lewis, 2003)

Hence, in assessing educational counseling or personal psychotherapy, counselors must remind themselves regularly of the larger issues of human development at stake.

Fortunately, education and psychotherapy share some fundamental goals: to expand students' awareness; increase their tolerance of frustration, ambi guity, and competing points of view; deepen their care for themselves, others, and the world at large; and improve their capacities for critical thinking, skill development, problem solving, decision making, and conflict resolution. In short, psychotherapy is ideally suited to complement and support the educa-tional mission of universities.

Academic Difficulties: A Taxonomy of Causes

Academic *underachievement* implies the comparative shortfall of students' achievement below a predefined standard. Academic *underperformance* is the tendency for students' academic performance to fall short of their intellectual potential. The mental health practitioner needs to explore not only the con-text, but also the meaning of underachievement to students themselves. At times college students genuinely do not care to do their academic work, pre-ferring to socialize, party, and sample a rich variety of distractions. "Fiddling while Rome burns" is not *de facto* underachievement, but rather scraping by academically while using college for self-expansion and self-expression. There is no known treatment for this ego-syntonic syndrome.

As for ego-dystonic difficulties, a provisional taxonomy of causes is pro-vided here.

Cognitive Limitations

Underpreparation Numerous, often co-occurring factors may cause students' lack of preparation for college work: socioeconomic deprivation, family poverty, life conditions that impair concentration and achievement motivation, inadequate schooling, family underemphasis on education, cultural standards inimical to liberal education, different primary language, teenage pregnancy, or financial pressures to work.

In particular, students from minority ethnic or language backgrounds may face inadequate early schooling, peer derision at joining the mainstream culture (still white dominated), or insecure intellectual self-confidence. Compounding factors at college include overt, covert, and perceived racial discrimination, negative stereotyping and lowered expectations of minority students, paucity of other minority students and mentors, and financial pressures taking time away from academics.

Mismatch Colleges may also diverge from students' accustomed educational systems or modes of learning. For example, students from backgrounds that require rote learning and following inflexible models of right and wrong thinking may find it difficult to write papers, which calls for establishing their own points of view, formulating and supporting a thesis, analyzing arguments and counterarguments, and reaching integrative conclusions. There are many ways in which a divergent educational background may underprepare students for college.

A 20-year-old took a year off after his sophomore year as a result of mostly poor grades. Cognitive assessment helped explain his poor performance on timed examinations but did not account for his overall academic collapse. He had attended a highly selective private secondary school where his teachers had gotten to know him in small classes. At the large research university he attended, though, freshman and sophomore years entailed huge classes, reportedly unapproachable professors, and "assembly-line" grading that did not encourage the nuanced essays and expository writing skills he was used to. Although deeper psychological issues were also involved, his poor performance was partly due to the mismatch between skills he developed in secondary school and those demanded of him in college.

Study Skills Shortcomings Some students arrive at college without knowing how to study, analyze and solve complex problems, write and organize papers, or approach examinations effectively. Aptitude for reproductive high school tasks, dutiful modes of learning (such as word-for-word reading), or derivative writing do not carry over into college, which requires more mindful, flexible, analytical, integrative, and creative skills. Undue devotion to what has worked in the past can block development of sophisticated cognitive skills.

Shortcomings in Specific Knowledge Domains Students differ widely in their intellectual interests, skills, and talents. Often the intellectual challenges of college have a winnowing effect, bringing into sharp relief their talents and shortcomings. Many arrive at college underprepared for or "maladept" at particular areas of study (such as languages or sciences), or resolutely self-convinced of their incapacity, a classic self-fulfilling prophecy. Ordinarily students learn to play to their strengths once in college, and to major in fields in which they are both interested and talented, a significant reason for the average increase of grades throughout students' college careers.

That students specialize in their strengths is not, however, invariably a desideratum. On the contrary, lower-than-ideal grades may indicate students' willingness to take more challenging and broadening courses or to sample courses outside their comfort zone. For example, grades in the natural sciences and social sciences are regularly found to be somewhat lower than grades in the humanities (Lewis, 2005), and so grade-conscious students may avoid science courses. Students who stay in fields that yield lower grades may be manifesting an unyielding love of the subject, long-range career perspective, and intrinsic motivation. The college mental health practitioner wisely supports students' personal passions over evaluation-based performance.

Learning Disabilities   This popular concept accounts for significant deficits in particular areas of learning in students with otherwise average or above-average intelligence. Learning disabilities (LDs) may manifest themselves in verbal performance (leading to reading or writing problems, and difficulties in grammar, spelling, and learning foreign languages), in visual-motor functioning (leading to difficulties in mechanical reasoning, visual-spatial functioning, or various forms of puzzle solving or problem solving), or as slowed processing speed. LDs may be associated with attention deficit disorder (ADD), characterized by inattention, distractibility, and impulsivity.

In my admittedly minority view, this heuristic categorization has eluded consistent empirical validation, despite valiant efforts at systematic definition, typology, etiology, and specification of neuropsychological substrates of LDs and ADD (e.g., D'Angiulli & Siegel, 2003; Obrzut & Hynd, 1991; Rothstein, Benjamin, Crosby, & Eisenstadt, 1988; Rourke, 1985; Siegel & Heaven, 1986). My reading of the literature suggests that there is no evidence of consistently agreed upon categories or even of reliability in differentiating LD from non-LD children. The increased complexity of adolescent and adult cognitive functioning makes reliable identification of adolescent or adult LD or ADD even more problematic. Criteria of the *Diagnostic and Statistical Manual of Mental Disorders,* fourth edition (DSM-IV) for LD or ADD (American Psychiatric Association, 1994), and popular efforts to define them (Hallowell & Ratey, 1994), are nonspecific and overgeneralized and so capture either a narrow or a broad segment of the population, depending on the diagnostician's whim.

This questionable diagnostic status makes the LD/ADD label susceptible to misuse. Following the Americans with Disabilities Act of 1992, diagnosed students may receive academic accommodations conferring preliminary educational advantages, such as extra time on precollege entrance examinations or on examinations once in college. While no doubt these accommodations are sometimes warranted, the higher-than-expected incidence of LDs in affluent suburbs seems attributable more to economic than psychological or neuropsychological reasons (Borow, 1996). The overuse and dealing of stimulants prescribed for LD/ADD on campuses are other unfortunate consequences.

Organizational Difficulties   Students may also have difficulty in organizing their time, physical space, academic work, and lives. These difficulties are sometimes traceable to family patterns of disorganization, childhood neglect, or lack of explicit instruction and mentoring regarding organization. Psychological assessment can be useful in identifying the cognitive substrate of organizational difficulties: impairments in executive functions (attention, concentration, planning, and synthetic organization) through the Wechlser Adult Intelligence Scale (Wechsler, 1997), or subtle problems in information processing (disorganized cognitive coping style, overly broad or narrowed attention focus, or a rigid and inflexible approach) through the Rorschach inkblot technique (Exner, 1993; Weiner, 1998).

Developmental, Emotional, and Psychopathological Interferences

College mental health practitioners must also assess motivational, developmental, emotional, psychosocial, and psychopathological influences on academic performance. These influences show up everywhere but stand out in bold relief at "elite" colleges and universities, where academic failure "almost always" is due to "some interfering personal psychological factor: lack of motivation, unclear academic direction, loss of a sense of purpose, or serious personal problems" (Lewis, 1997, p. 4).

Developmental Challenges   Three interrelated life-transitional psychosocial tasks make college students vulnerable to disturbance: separation from family and community, differentiation of self from parents, and individuation (determination and consolidation of unique personal desires, goals, values, and guiding principles). Students can lose their bearings in giving up a familiar identity—for example, moving from being a big fish in a small pond to being an undistinguished fish in an unfamiliar one, or feeling unprepared to make independent choices and decisions.

Situational Interpersonal Problems   Roommate conflict, romantic relationship problems, parental divorce, or loved ones' illness or death often negatively affect performance. Practitioners should strive to disentangle developmental or situational issues from lasting psychopathological or characterological issues to avoid pathologizing or medicating the former and so reinforcing students' fears or self-fulfilling prophecies of damage or disease.

Lack of Motivation This broad and complex category is perhaps the major psychological influence on academic performance. *Intrinsic* motivation means learning for learning's own sake, from curiosity and for the joy of discovery. *Extrinsic* motivation, by contrast, suggests the pressure of outside forces that demand accomplishment—not an effective foundation for genuine or joyful learning.

Intrinsic motivation arises from the predominance of healthy or mature defenses (Vaillant, 1993) and the availability of a broad "conflict-free sphere of ego functioning" (Hartmann, 1939). The emotional background of these strengths is the internalization of loving, nurturant people in students' early environment who provide the foundation of the sense of self. The connection of early love and learning is brilliantly captured in the title of Ekstein's (1969) *From Learning for Love to Love of Learning.* Learning for love occurs as a result of children's having been loved and having their needs fulfilled. The importance of love—and its prosaic correlate, motivation—for learning is illustrated in this vignette.

Until the early 1990s, Harvard provided students the option of waiving the freshman foreign-language requirement, so long as they could demonstrate a "specific language disability" on the Modern Language Aptitude Test (MLAT). One student was so ill prepared by his rural high school for learning a foreign language that he did not bother to take the freshman placement exam in Spanish, and proceeded to fail basic Spanish, then Latin. As a result of his abysmal score on the MLAT, which showed his "disability," he was granted a waiver of the freshman language requirement. Yet, after falling in love with a French woman while studying abroad in France, he returned as a senior to visit the dean of freshmen and said—in impeccable French, of course: "You see how 'disabled' I am!"

Inadequate intrinsic motivation often manifests itself in broad academic malaise: lack of interest in working, attending class, or completing assignments. This is not necessarily a sign of depression. Rather, students may not want to attend college or a particular college, but hesitate in discussing this issue with parents and so resort to passive modes of showing their dissatisfaction. Open discussion with family, facilitated by a dean of students or a college counselor, may resolve such issues straightforwardly, allowing students either to leave school for a time by mutual consent or to regain motivation by simply airing concerns.

Academically underperforming students (and their families) are often distraught at being required to withdraw. But, a large majority of students in one-year postwithdrawal reentry statements to Harvard College laud time away as very needed and productive. Similarly, a study at Dartmouth showed a significant increase in grade point averages (GPAs) from the semester prior to their leave to the semester of return, an increase three times greater than the comparable GPA increase for students who stayed in school (Meilman, Manley, Gaylor, & Turco, 1992). Time away from college can have a re-motivating effect by supporting students' individuation, developing their identity independent of college demands (Fitzsimmons, McGrath Lewis, & Ducey, 2005).

Characterologic Disruptions These account for a not insignificant proportion of difficulties in learning. Rigidity effectively defeats growth and learning, which are based on openness to change (Shapiro, 1981). Again the analogy of education and psychotherapy is evident: Characterologically inflexible students are difficult to influence in both cognitive and emotional arenas. Rigidity may be a transitory cognitive-developmental phenomenon: Many freshmen construe knowledge as "dualistic" or "absolute" (black-or-white, right-or-wrong, authority-derived) before later recognizing the plurality of knowledge and "relativistic" or "independent knowing" (Baxter Magolda, 2001; Perry, 1970). But rigid stances also may be attributable to psychological factors, such as introjection or accommodation to authoritarian family attitudes, protection from anxiety, entrenchment in immature defenses (Kernberg, 1976; Vaillant, 1993), or restricted motivational experience and consideration of the external world (Shapiro, 2000).

For other characterologic interferences with academic performance, we can apply Stone's (1993) provisional temperamental categorization of DSM-IV Axis II diagnoses:

- Cluster A (the "eccentric" paranoid, schizoid, schizotypal pathologies): significant disruption of rational, decentered, and "conflict-free" ability to think and reason
- Cluster B (the "dramatic" antisocial, borderline, narcissistic, and histrionic pathologies): dissociative interference with executive function, underperformance based on unconscious "unresolved struggle against introjected coercive or abusive figures from early life" (Ducey, 1989, p. 174), or manipulative behaviors
- Cluster C (the "anxious" obsessive-compulsive, dependent, and avoidant pathologies): traits (conformity, neatness, focus on details, obedience to authority, anxiety to please, proneness to isolation) that may promote achievement but only within the context of dualistic standards of evaluation, impaired performance in subjects that call for nuanced and complex thinking, or conflict-driven defensive stances that undermine performance

In contrast to ego-syntonic characterologic difficulties that may be invisible to students, *psychopathological symptoms* are obtrusive and distressing, as they clearly interfere with performance. While major mental illness (e.g., schizophrenia) commonly makes its initial appearance during college years and disrupts all realms of functioning, the most widespread interferences with academic functioning are anxiety and depression.

Anxiety may disrupt academic performance in general through the pressure of evaluation or the stress of extensive academic demands, or in specific subjects. Thus, psychology courses in sexuality or trauma may trigger reactions in students who have been abused or raped. Religion or philosophy courses may set off a crisis of faith in students from a fundamentalist upbringing. Anthropology or sociology courses may engender intense reactions to racial, ethnic, or class-conflict themes. Depending on students' preexisting vulnerabilities, these situational anxiety reactions may develop into full-blown anxiety. Sensitive and prepared faculty members can play a significant role in spotting avoidance or deterioration in performance and ensuring that these students receive psychotherapy.

Depression is the most common symptom that disrupts academic functioning. Transitory depressive reactions to situational causes are common, even expected, affecting fully one third to two thirds of students (American College Health Association, 2002; Kadison & DiGeronimo, 2004), while roughly 12% of students warrant the diagnosis of depression. Among other symptoms, clinical depression robs students of energy, motivation, curiosity, intellectual focus, sleep, and the ability to pay attention to and interact with the world outside themselves and their depressive preoccupations, all of which can seriously impair academic performance. Meilman et al. (1992) found that depression accounted for roughly half of the academic withdrawals and was the major disruptor of students' future performance upon return to college.

Yet, in accordance with the proverbial melancholic nature of scholars (Burton, 1621), many characterologically depressed students do quite well academically. Reasons include their defensive social withdrawal and the consequent beneficial effect of isolation on concentration, their dutiful or perfectionistic devotion to academic success, their effort to improve low self-esteem through academic success, or their bravery in just soldiering on in spite of misery. Determining whether depression is a transient affect, character trait, or clinical syndrome in order to select the appropriate intervention is a common challenge for the college mental health practitioner.

Academic symptoms such as block, procrastination, perfectionism, and academic dishonesty are complex counterintentional behaviors analogous to inhibitions and symptoms in the psychological sphere (Freud, 1926), which have the classic dynamic structure of symptoms based on unconscious intrapsychic conflict (Malan, 2001). Some of their characteristic patterns of action (or passivity) and cognition are briefly identified here.

Students who experience block, whether in writing (Flaherty, 2004), artistic performance, or taking exams, sin by omission rather than commission and then torment themselves for their inability to produce. Counterforces to writing and performing include those that are developmental (immaturity or inexperience in exposing oneself through one's work), behavioral (habits of hiding oneself or refraining from self-expression), cognitive (unbearable self-criticism or negative self-judgment), and psychodynamic (inhibition of sexual, aggressive, competitive, rebellious, or narcissistic motives by defensive anxiety, guilt, shame, or pain). In the calculus of the unconscious psyche, the consequences of being blocked are less dangerous than producing, a major reason for the ineffectiveness of intentional willpower in overcoming block (Lipson & Perkins, 1990).

The time-honored, time-denying technique of procrastination—avoiding anxiety in the short term only to curry painful or disastrous long-term consequences—also has multiple causes and manifestations. Procrastination often involves unacknowledged assumptions about one's competence: "If I were actually to plan ahead and work hard on this paper, a lower-than-desired grade would confirm that I am stupid and incompetent. Putting it off until the last minute will give me a face-saving excuse. Of course I received a B-minus, I didn't have time to do my best work." There is method in this madness for students who have experienced the narcissistic injury of receiving lower grades than they feel they deserved. When self-esteem is unconsciously based on externally judged performance and students fear experiencing shame over another failure, procrastination performs a prophylactic function.

For some risk-taking and thrill-seeking students, procrastination makes possible an anticipated triumph over self-created adversity. But even if they succeed in doing well, as they not uncommonly do as a result of adrenalin rush and perhaps pharmacologic help, the cost may be intense anxiety, lost sleep, and the hamster wheel of relentlessly raising the stakes to achieve ever more intense thrills, which leads ineluctably to a spectacular crash.

Procrastination also occurs when tasks are not truly important to students, who therefore cannot concentrate, put off work, and then experience guilt, which of course exacerbates their lack of motivation. These escapes may be disguised efforts at adaptation and self-expression against demanding authorities but result in overtly self-defeating outcomes (Ducey, 1998).

Another complex manifestation of personality trends is perfectionism, the effort to do work in accord with idealized and unreachable standards. Narcissistic self-aggrandizement often lurks in the background: These students "confess" to perfectionism, much as other students "admit" to being people-pleasers, overtly distressed but presumably self-satisfied with their superior virtue, or as masochists achieve moral victory through suffering (Shapiro, 1981). Yet, the painful consequences of perfectionism are all too real: time mismanagement (e.g., the "80/20 trap" of spending 80% of time on 20% of the assignment, leaving 20% time for the remaining 80% [Stone & Tippett, 2004]), relentless and ruthless internal pressure, and shame over products never good enough to reveal to others or to the demanding, insatiable introject.

Perfectionism has the structure of a rigid characterologic symptom. Students follow rigid rules and standards that alienate them from genuine wishes, feelings, and motives. The "stubborn will is now the spokesman of adult authority" (Shapiro, 2000, p. 73). Students behave as though failure to meet these rigid, alien standards would result in a sense of inferiority, shame, or humiliation. The result of this effort to avoid such painful self-revelation is fluctuating self-esteem (Reich, 1960), unrelenting self-evaluation, and consequent crowding out of any relaxation or enjoyment of work or life.

Students who practice plagiarism, academia's most heinous crime, consciously ascribe their behavior to time pressure (often a result of procrastination), discomfort with asserting their own point of view, and overvaluing of authoritative sources. Less consciously, plagiarists manifest a range of underlying motives. The naïve and dutiful convince themselves that they are being responsible to their sources, while feeling undeserving of an equal voice in academic scholarship (Lipson & Reindl, 2003). The sociopathic have no compunction about passing off others' work as their own, their self-contempt keeping equal pace with their contempt for teachers, motivated students, and the educational enterprise. The self-abasing and ashamed, paradoxically strict moralists disguised as malefactors, present the products of superior others in place of their own derogated offerings. For them, academic dishonesty is the evil twin of perfectionism. Exposure brings the public shame and humiliation they feel they deserve, like Freud's (1916) "criminals from a sense of guilt" (p. 332), compelled to be caught in order to satisfy the introjective demand for punishment. (Psychologists need sit only briefly on a student disciplinary board to observe the aptness of this characterization.) Finally, perhaps most unconsciously, emotionally neglected and oppositional plagiarists enact a mute, passive-aggressive protest against their family's rigid overvaluation of their achievements at the expense of loving them for who they are, warts and all.

Interventions and Their Application

Many simple problems of academic underachievement yield rather quickly to active short-term counseling, tutoring, or workshop interventions, so long as the student is motivated for change and does not have significant cognitive limitations or emotional interferences. Longer-term psychotherapeutic interventions can effectively remove psychological blocks to academic performance but require greater investment of time, energy, and resolvable emotional upset. The central principle is to conjoin *efficiency* and *effectiveness*, conducting whatever intervention is most effective with the least amount of time and effort, with the following refinements added:

1. Interventions must be guided by thorough theoretical knowledge and mastery of empirical research.
2. Counselors' aim should be to help individual students become themselves more truly and deeply. As students do not fit snugly into theoretical boxes, they require individualized responsiveness.
3. No single tradition in psychology, psychiatry, or education has a privileged path to the truth or to effective practice. The main traditions that still speak to practitioners—psychoanalytic, interpersonal, behavioral, cognitive, experiential, and biological—all have important contributions to make. The sophisticated practitioner is neither hidebound nor unselectively "eclectic": The ideal is pluralistic knowledge (Havens, 1973) and understanding of the differential applicability of each of these theoretical models and modes of intervention.

The following overview of educational and psychological approaches may aid in the selection of appropriate interventions.

Educational Interventions

Pedagogic/Institutional   Programs geared to students underprepared for college work have been widely implemented at colleges and universities. Early and careful placement testing, specialized prefreshman or freshman-year workshops and tutoring programs, and early general education courses (e.g., reading, civilizations, and expository writing) go some way toward leveling the playing field for these students. For students from diverse ethnic backgrounds (Justiz & Rendon, 1989; Pounds, 1989), such programs go beyond improving academic skills to providing mentors (faculty, administrators, or senior students) from students' class or ethnic backgrounds, group support in adjusting to college, individual counseling, inclusiveness workshops, and remedial programs that counteract pervasive stereotype threat (Hrabowski, 2005; Steele, 1997; Steele & Aronson, 1995).

Students diagnosed LD or ADD may receive such academic accommodations as extended time and special arrangements for examinations (a specifically quiet room, individual proctors, or verbal rather than written presentation), or note takers in classroom lectures. Despite my reservations—the unreliability of LD or ADD diagnoses, the lack of evidence for the value of extended time specifically for LD/ADD students (Gordon & Murphy, 2001), and the undermining of students' active thinking and learning processes by using others to take notes for them—such accommodations are well established and are clearly appropriate for some students.

For students in general, pedagogical and institutional improvements can promote achievement. While students need to be held accountable for their apathy, personal difficulties, and lack of academic focus, "the principal reason students don't work hard is that the work they are asked to do is not very interesting and has not been made to seem very important" (Lewis, in press). It is universities' responsibility to provide intellectual conditions under which learning and development may ideally unfold.

In this vein, Light (2001) has made a number of recommendations for improving college education, such as promoting integration of in-class and outside-of-class learning, encouraging student interaction with each other and with faculty, proactively initiating support for those too ashamed or defensively self-reliant to seek it, practicing a policy of inclusion and acknowledgment of diverse perspectives, and relating students' academic ideas and work to their personal lives, values, and experiences.

Didactic   Extracurricular didactic interventions include tutoring in specific academic subjects by other undergraduate students or graduate students, and either individual counseling or workshops for improvement of general study skills. Commonly provided academic workshops include time management, exam taking, writing, and problem solving in math and science. These are mainly a matter of common sense, good advice, utilization of students' own work, and applied practice, and can effectively ameliorate students' academic shortcomings.

Individualized tutoring or effective study-strategies courses are valuable for addressing LDs as well. (Indeed, the strategies for resolving LDs were devised before the label itself.) Despite the current focus on accommodations, intelligent LD students have often developed skills for working around and ameliorating their deficits better than their tutors themselves.

Psychological Interventions

If educational interventions by themselves take care of the academic problem, then psychological interventions will not be needed. But since academic problems are usually symptoms of underlying difficulties, then psychological interventions at increasing levels of "depth" (as roughly arrayed here, following Prochaska [1995]) are needed.

Experiential   Since this approach, which includes person-centered, humanistic, existential, and psychoanalytic object-relational and self-psychology traditions, is foundational for all therapeutic interventions, I will mention only two of its main tenets. First, the therapist must at every moment listen empathically and resonate responsively to students' own subjective experience of their difficulty. All students have a reasonable hypothesis about what ails them and why, from which counselors may learn useful directions to guide the conversation. Second, the positive experience of the therapy relationship has been found empirically to be healing in itself, insofar as the therapist is empathically responsive, warm, supportive, collaborative, and involved (Luborsky, Crits-Christoph, Mintz, & Auerbach, 1988; McCullough Vaillant, 1997; Orlinsky, Ronnestad, & Willutzki, 2004).

Behavioral For many "situational/symptomatic" issues, behavioral interventions are valuable for altering problematic habits that interfere with academic functioning, such as sleep disturbances, physical manifestations of depression (e.g., inactivity and psychomotor retardation), and ego-dystonic substance abuse. *In vivo* exposure techniques are often appropriate for treatment of isolated symptoms (phobias, anxiety and panic disorders, or obsessions) that have become "bad habits" and are not entrenched in the character structure. Of course, most symptoms are outcrops of underlying characterologic cognitive attitudes and affective proclivities (Shapiro, 1965).

Behavioral interventions are now ordinarily combined with cognitive ones in cognitive-behavioral therapy (CBT). CBT training is useful in promoting students' assertiveness and communication skills to engage faculty and enhance class participation; relaxation and mindfulness skills to alleviate stress and improve concentration and self-awareness; and anxiety-management skills to cope effectively with tests (Rothman, 2004).

The organizational problem most accessible to cognitive-behavioral amelioration is time management, which in many senses comes down to anxiety management and life organization. Useful advice includes scheduling longer stretches of time for long-range assignments while mindfully using brief time slots; anticipating future demands and working within multiple time frames; and using the "SOS" strategy—breaking down large, amorphous tasks into "specific observable steps" whose achievement can be monitored and measured. The most important strategies promote students' self-awareness so that they can use time thoughtfully and intentionally. For example, students can translate an inventory of tasks and deadlines into an anticipated schedule, and then collaborate with an advisor or counselor to compare their planned schedule with a log of what they actually did. This advice is entirely consistent with the behavioral principle of enactment: Changes in behavior must follow interventions. Yet, even this follow-up is not enough, for self-awareness also requires cognizance of the inevitability of limitations and conflicts, and the necessity of personal choices. Hence, counselors must help students notice what tasks or activities have been consistently omitted or systematically underestimated. They must also promote students' internal negotiation skills—learning to mediate among conflicting internal demands—and so enhance their capacity for making hard life choices.

In other words, time management puts the emphasis on students' awareness of their actual preferences, passions, responsibilities, and commitments. Otherwise, they will be at the mercy of unrecognized forces. Time management is based on personal self-reflection, choices, desires, and anxieties—not a mechanical task but a deeply personal and emotional challenge.

Cognitive Cognitive interventions increase students' self-awareness of "bad thinking habits": catastrophic, irrationally self-critical, defeatist, or judgmental.

As students become aware of their negative self-statements, automatic thoughts, and cognitive distortions, they learn alternative responses through a variety of techniques: rational responding, questioning evidence for unexamined assumptions, reattribution of responsibility, guided association, and self-instructional training (Beck, 1976; Reinecke & Freeman, 2003). Cognitive techniques also promote students' awareness of their intellectual strengths and weaknesses, the connection between healthy habits (eating, drinking, and sleep) and academic performance, and the motivation behind such dilemmas as procrastination. One partly escapes the grip of intractable problems by gaining perspective. Once students can articulate the basis of the problem, they have "made the subject an object" of contemplation and awareness (Kegan, 1982), and so have partly resolved the problem. Becoming able to make conscious choices rather than being forced to enact unconscious patterns makes change feasible.

In my view, the main limitation of cognitive interventions is their tendency to ignore emotionally based inhibitions, which can lead to an intellectualized therapy and temporary, superficial, transference-based compliance with therapists' expectations rather than lasting change. For example, mere focus on counteracting negative self-statements to raise a student's self-esteem is doomed to failure, since "true self-esteem comes from actually mastering something" (Light, 2001, p. 19). Hence, therapists need to promote mastery of conflict-based challenges, which are almost always emotional and relational, not simply cognitive in origin (Luborsky & Crits-Cristoph, 1998). Moreover, since by late adolescence negative patterns of thinking have frequently become deeply defining of the student's character (Beck & Freeman, 1990), more complex psychodynamic interventions that address unconscious defensive attitudes and emotional conflicts (e.g., Shapiro, 1981, 1989) are usually necessary for resolving them.

Interpersonal/Systemic   Interpersonal therapies focus on the degree to which students' current relationships support or interfere with their life adaptation (e.g., Klerman, Weissman, Rounsaville, & Chevron, 1984). Interpersonal or systems interventions may in some cases indirectly make dramatic improvements in students' academic functioning, as these two vignettes illustrate.

In the fall of her freshman year at Harvard, an international Latina student, the first from her traditionally patriarchal family to attend college, was taken to the emergency room after she overdosed on an over-the-counter medication, cut herself on her arms, and became mute. She had been privately cutting and burning herself on her buttocks and legs during her high school years, to "remind" herself that she had to do better. After superb performance in high school, her grades and motivation for schoolwork at Harvard plummeted, and a masked long-standing depression became manifest. She refused the medication offered by the university health service but was able to establish a good, if intermittent, relationship with a male therapist in the counseling center. Her depression waxed and waned but did not abate consistently until, in her sophomore year, her father—reportedly a harsh disciplinarian—called me, as the director of the service, very concerned about her mental health and academic performance. Once I reassured him that we would continue to provide consistent therapy for her, that her condition was curable, and that I recognized his care for his daughter, he relaxed his prideful guard and then opened up about his own difficult adolescence with his demanding father, his anxiety over subjecting his daughter to that same behavior, and his wish to be a better and more supportive parent. This 45-minute conversation had a galvanizing effect on the father–daughter relationship. He subsequently reached out to her in a loving way, opening lines of communication that had long been blocked. Soon thereafter, she became able to cry openly and regularly in therapy (in place of the defensive emotional blockage and mood instability of her depression), express emotions naturally and appropriately, and become more involved in classes, with consequent improvement of her academic functioning and life in general. She graduated a mature and apparently quite transformed young woman.

A male graduate student, successful and accomplished in scientific research, was nevertheless disorganized in time management, unable to plan ahead and multitask, and thus protracted projects and worked numerous late evenings, negatively affecting his marriage. He documented all the indications of his supposed attention deficit difficulties and expressed interest in some organizational strategies that I suggested as helpful, particularly breaking large tasks down into "small observable steps." But couples sessions with his wife—herself a highly organized and efficient law student—threw a different light upon his supposed cognitive limitations. His distractibility turned out to be partly a consequence of ingrained personality patterns. An agreeable, accommodating, conflict-avoidant "nice guy," he was not "selfish" or assertive and hence did not set limits on the demands placed on him by others in the lab. On a deeper level, his wife reported that his mother had always taken the responsibility for planning and organizing his life—and had once wondered, tongue barely in cheek, whether her son's organizational problems were partly due to her not making him pick up his toys or do any home chores, in deference to his academic achievement. His wife believed that he had now inserted her into the maternal role and took for granted her organizing their lives. The therapeutic conversation now having shifted, the three of us worked to help him set limits on others' demands on him and to develop time-organizational strategies that took into account his wife's and his own needs.

Psychodynamic Psychoanalytic interventions remain the only effective strategy for resolution of intrapsychic conflict, not only of symptomatic and characterologic contributions to academic underachievement, but also of academic symptoms. The unconscious dynamic system of academic symptoms includes the following inhibitory affects and the "hidden" desires, feelings, or impulses they defend against:

- Guilt/self-hatred over taking actions unconsciously construed as unacceptably competitive or primitively sexual or aggressive
- Shame/humiliation over self-exposure, unconsciously construed as exposing one's self-assessed narcissistic defects
- Anxiety/paralyzing panic over incurring failure (leading to narcissistic injury) or success (construed as a dangerous Oedipal victory)
- Pain/unbearable anguish over inevitably falling short of introjected demands disguised as idealized, impossible-to-reach standards

Discussion of the psychodynamic approach is beyond the scope of this chapter. Here I merely would like to stress that this approach can be well adapted to the college mental health service. Contrary to the "silent analyst" image, this approach calls for the therapist to be human, warm, involved, and therapeutically active, as well as receptively responsive. Despite the complexity of psychodynamic theory, this approach focuses on feelings. Despite its reputation as long-term treatment that focuses unduly on the past, psychodynamically oriented therapy can be conducted within the context of intensive brief treatment. It can also be successfully combined with cognitive (Weiss, 1993) and behavioral (McCullough Vaillant, 1997) principles.

The provision of intermittent brief or punctuated episodic psychotherapy in college settings is realistic not only in terms of balancing service demands but also in light of the significant developmental strides students make each college year (Margolis, 1989). The following vignette illustrates the increasingly dynamic and expressive nature of punctuated episodes of therapy over four college years.

A cosmopolitan freshman woman who affected a "cool" persona was referred by her academic advisor because of disorganized time management and an off-kilter sleep schedule that entailed doing homework interspersed with unsatisfying catnaps throughout the night. Skittish as she was about therapy, I made hay while the sun shone in our first and only session that year by focusing on what she wanted and enjoyed doing, instead of on what others demanded of her. This approach surprised her: "I thought you were going to tell me how to do a schedule. Adults always tell you what you should be doing."

Returning in her sophomore year for six sessions, she reported feeling depressed, with flagging motivation and inability to deal with competing time demands and keep up even in classes she enjoyed. She was again struck by my determined focus on and support of what she passionately, if subtly, cared about, including even support of her "perfectionist" standards, since these standards were manifestations of genuine care about her work. Her real problems were passive decision making in work and relationships (she once corrected my claim "You take the plunge" to "The plunge is somehow taken") and alienation from natural desires and feelings. (She had had "no feelings at all" and was an "automaton" for several months after a high school breakup.) "Something opening up inside" her in this brief therapy had the effect of turning imprisoning and immobilizing anxiety and shame into a dynamic engagement with her feelings, and led to a burst of energy in doing intellectually alive work and falling in love for the first time that summer.

She returned for therapy in the winter of her junior year, pregnant and clear about terminating the pregnancy. For this episode of therapy, which utilized dream analysis, defense relinquishment, affect experiencing, and expression, she engaged in a now fully feeling way with her pain, loss, guilt, and mixed love and anger for her boyfriend. She handled the intense emotional challenge to her academic work more skillfully and conscientiously than ever before; for the first time, she did not fall behind, except for briefly procrastinating on the final paper in a seminar she loved, because she cared too much, not too little—a desirable shift. She maintained weekly therapy without a break or missing even one appointment, another clear indication of the shift in her motivation and self-awareness.

In her senior year she sustained a 25-session psychotherapy, maintaining her now long-term romantic relationship, fully experiencing her feelings (including the painful anniversary reaction of the abortion), and showing virtually no academic backsliding. Her maturation over 3½ years was astonishing to behold, and showed how psychoanalytic psychotherapy can resolve academic problems that are deeply embedded in dynamic conflict.

Conclusion

Academic underachievement and underperformance have many causes, ranging from cognitive limitations through maturational processes to psychological interferences. College mental health practitioners who recognize the intrinsic intertwining of academic, emotional, and social-interpersonal development, who understand the complex psychodynamics of academic underachievement, and who are capable of treating the "whole person" with a broad variety of appropriately selected and empathically applied interventions are in a unique and privileged position to improve significantly not only students' academic functioning but also the quality of their current lives and future success in work and love.

References

Alexander, F., & French, T. M. (1946). *Psychoanalytic therapy*. New York: Ronald Press.

American College Health Association. (2002). *National College Health Assessment: Reference group report*. Baltimore: Author.

American Psychiatric Association. (1994). *Diagnostic and statistical manual of mental disorders* (4th ed.). Washington, DC: Author.

Basch, M. F. (1988). *Understanding psychotherapy: The science behind the art*. New York: Basic Books.

Baxter Magolda, M. B. (2001). *Making their own way: Narratives for transforming higher education to promote self-development*. Sterling, VA: Stylus.

Beck, A. T. (1976). *Cognitive therapy and the emotional disorders*. New York: International Universities Press.

Beck, A. T., & Freeman, A. (1990). *Cognitive therapy of personality disorders*. New York: Guilford.

Borow, Z. (1996, March 18). The learning-disability scam. *New York*, 34, 38.

Burton, R. (1621). *The anatomy of melancholy*. New York: Vintage, 1977.

D'Angiulli, A., & Siegel, L. S. (2003). Cognitive functioning as measured by the WISC-R: Do children with learning disabilities have distinctive patterns of performance? *Journal of Learning Disabilities, 36*, 48–58.

Ducey, C. P. (1989). Academic underachievement. In P. Grayson & K. Cauley (Eds.), *College psychotherapy* (pp. 166–192). New York: Gardner.

Ducey, C. P. (1998). Student difficulties as disguised efforts at adaptation. *Harvard Parents' Newsletter*, Winter, 6–7.

Ekstein, R. (1969). *From learning for love to love of learning*. New York: Brunner-Mazel.

Erikson, E. (1968). *Identity: Youth and crisis*. New York: Norton.

Exner, J. E. (1993). *The Rorschach: A comprehensive system: Vol. 1: Basic foundations*. (3rd ed.). New York: Wiley.

Fitzsimmons, W., McGrath Lewis, M., & Ducey, C. P. (2005). Time out or burn out for the next generation. In L. Thacker (Ed.), *College unranked: Ending the college admissions frenzy* (pp. 22–34). Cambridge, MA: Harvard University Press.

Flaherty, A. (2004). *The midnight disease: The drive to write, writer's block, and the creative brain*. Boston: Houghton Mifflin.

Freud, S. (1916). Some character types met with in psycho-analytic work. In J. Strachey (Ed.), *The standard edition of the complete psychological works of Sigmund Freud* (Vol. 14, pp. 311–333). London: Hogarth, 1957.

Freud, S. (1926). *The standard edition of the complete psychological works of Sigmund Freud: Vol. 20. Inhibitions, symptoms, and anxiety* (pp. 87–174). Ed. J. Strachey. London: Hogarth, 1959.

Gordon, M., & Murphy, K. (2001). Judging the impact of time limits and distractions on past test performance: A survey of ADHD, clinic-referred, and normal adults. *The ADHD Report, 9*, 1–5.

Hallowell, E. M., & Ratey, J. J. (1994). *Driven to distraction*. New York: Pantheon.

Hanfmann, E. (1978). *Effective psychotherapy for college students*. San Francisco: Jossey-Bass.

Hartmann, H. (1939). *Ego psychology and the problem of adaptation*. New York: International Universities Press, 1958.

Hartmann, H. (1964). *Essays on ego psychology*. New York: International Universities Press.

Havens, L. L. (1973). *Approaches to the mind: Movement of the psychiatric schools from sects toward science*. Boston: Little-Brown.

Heath, D. H. (1965). *Explorations of maturity: Studies of mature and immature college men*. New York: Appleton-Century-Crofts.

Hrabowski, F. A. (2005). Fostering first-year success of underrepresented minorities. In M. L. Upcraft, J. N. Gardner, & B. O. Barefoot (Eds.), *Challenging and supporting the first-year student: A handbook for improving the first year of college* (pp. 125–140). San Francisco: Jossey-Bass.

Johnson, V. E. (2003). *Grade inflation: A crisis in college education*. New York: Springer.

Justiz, M. J., & Rendon, L. I. (1989). Hispanic students. In M. L. Upcraft & J. N. Gardner (Eds.), *The freshman year experience: Helping students survive and succeed in college* (pp. 261–276). San Francisco: Jossey-Bass.

Kadison, R., & DiGeronimo, T. (2004). *College of the overwhelmed*. San Francisco: Jossey-Bass.

Kegan, R. (1982). *The evolving self*. Cambridge, MA: Harvard University Press.

Kernberg, O. (1976). *Object relations theory and clinical psychoanalysis*. New York: Jason Aronson.

Klerman, G., Weissman, M. M., Rounsaville, B., & Chevron, E. (1984). *Interpersonal psychotherapy of depression*. New York: Basic Books.

Lear, J. (1990). *Love and its place in nature: A philosophical interpretation of Freudian psychoanalysis.* New York: Farrar, Straus, & Giroux.

Lewis, H. R. (1997). Bad grades: Their causes and effects. *Harvard College News, 9,* 4–5.

Lewis, H. R. (2003, October 30). Grades. [Harvard University] *Morning Prayers.* Retrieved April 17, 2006, from http://www.eecs.harvard.edu/~lewis/Grades.html

Lewis, H. R. (in press). *Excellence without a soul: How a great university forgot education.* New York: Perseus PublicAffairs.

Light, R. J. (2001). *Making the most of college: Students speak their minds.* Cambridge, MA: Harvard University Press.

Lipson, A., & Perkins, D. (1990). *Block: Getting out of your own way.* New York: Lyle Stuart.

Lipson, A., & Reindl, S. (2003). The responsible plagiarist: Understanding students who misuse sources. *About Campus, 8,* 7–14.

Luborsky, L., & Crits-Christoph, P. (1998). *Understanding transference: The Core Conflictual Relationship Theme Method* (2nd ed.). Washington, DC: American Psychological Association.

Luborsky, L., Crits-Christoph, P., Mintz, J., & Auerbach, A. (1988). *Who will benefit from psychotherapy: Predicting therapeutic outcomes.* New York: Basic Books.

Malan, D. (2001). *Individual psychotherapy and the science of psychodynamics* (2nd ed.). London: Arnold/Oxford.

Margolis, G. (1989). Developmental opportunities. In P. Grayson & K. Cauley (Eds.), *College psychotherapy* (pp. 71–91). New York: Gardner.

McClelland, D. (1961). *The achieving society.* New York: Free Press.

McCullough Vaillant, L. (1997). *Changing character: Short-term anxiety-regulating psychotherapy for restructuring defenses, affects, and attachment.* New York: Basic Books.

Meilman, P. W., Manley, C., Gaylor, M. S., & Turco, J. H. (1992). Medical withdrawals from college for mental health reasons and their relation to academic performance. *Journal of American College Health, 40,* 217–223.

Obrzut, J. E., & Hynd, G. W. (1991). *Neuropsychological foundations of learning disabilities: A handbook of issues, methods, and practice.* San Diego: Academic Press.

Orlinsky, D. E., Ronnestad, M. H., & Willutzki, U. (2004). Fifty years of psychotherapy process-outcome research. In M. J. Lambert (Ed.), *Handbook of psychotherapy and behavior change* (5th ed., pp. 307–389). New York: Wiley.

Perry, W. G. (1970). *Forms of ethical and intellectual development in the college years.* San Francisco: Jossey-Bass.

Pounds, A. W. (1989). Black students. In M. L. Upcraft & J. N. Gardner (Eds.), *The freshman year experience: Helping students survive and succeed in college* (pp. 277–286). San Francisco: Jossey-Bass.

Prochaska, J. O. (1995). An eclectic and integrative approach: Transtheoretical therapy. In A. S. Gurman & S. B. Messer (Eds.), *Essential psychotherapies: Theory and practice* (pp. 403–440). New York: Guilford.

Reich, A. (1960). Pathologic forms of self-esteem regulation. In *The psychoanalytic study of the child, 15* (pp. 215–232). New York: International Universities Press.

Reinecke, M. A., & Freeman, A. (2003). Cognitive therapy. In A. S. Gurman & S. B. Messer (Eds.), *Essential psychotherapies: Theory and practice* (2nd ed., pp. 224–271). New York: Guilford.

Rothman, D. (2004). New approach to test anxiety. *Journal of College Student Psychotherapy, 18,* 45–60.

Rothstein, A., Benjamin, L., Crosby, M., & Eisenstadt, K. (Eds.). (1988). *Learning disabilities: An integration of neuropsychological and psychoanalytic considerations.* New York: International Universities Press.

Rourke, B. P. (Ed.). (1985). *Neuropsychology of learning disabilities: Essentials of subtype analysis.* New York: Guilford.

Shapiro, D. (1965). *Neurotic styles.* New York: Basic Books.

Shapiro, D. (1981). *Autonomy and rigid character.* New York: Basic Books.

Shapiro, D. (1989). *Psychotherapy of neurotic character.* New York: Basic Books.

Shapiro, D. (2000). *Dynamics of character: Self-regulation in psychopathology.* New York: Basic Books.

Siegel, L. S., & Heaven, R. K. (1986). Categorization of learning disabilities. In S. J. Ceci (Ed.), *Handbook of cognitive, social, and neuropsychological aspects of learning disabilities, 2* (pp. 95–121). Hillsdale, NJ: Lawrence Erlbaum.

Steele, C. M. (1997). A threat in the air: How stereotypes shape intellectual identity and performance. *American Psychologist, 52,* 613–629.

Steele, C. M., & Aronson, J. (1995). Stereotype threat and the intellectual test performance of African Americans. *Journal of Personality and Social Psychology, 69,* 797–811.

Stone, D., & Tippett, E. (2004). *Real college: The essential guide to student life.* New York: Penguin.

Stone, M. H. (1993). *Abnormalities of personality: Within and beyond the realm of treatment.* New York: Norton.

Vaillant, G. E. (1977). *Adaptation to life.* Cambridge, MA: Harvard University Press.

Vaillant, G. E. (1993). *The wisdom of the ego.* Cambridge, MA: Harvard University Press.

Wechsler, D. (1997). *Wechsler Adult Intelligence Scale* (3rd ed.). San Antonio: The Psychological Corporation.

Weiner, I. B. (1998). *Principles of Rorschach interpretation.* Mahwah, NJ: Lawrence Erlbaum.

Weiss, J. (1990, March). Unconscious mental functioning. *Scientific American,* 103–109.

Weiss, J. (1993). *How psychotherapy works.* New York: Guilford.

Weiss, J., & Sampson, H. (1986). *The psychoanalytic process.* New York: Guilford.

White, R. W. (1963). Ego and reality in psychoanalytic theory. *Psychological Issues,* Whole Monograph 11. New York: International Universities Press.

11

Alcohol, Drugs, and Other Addictions

PHILIP W. MEILMAN, DEBORAH K. LEWIS, AND LYNN GERSTEIN

Alcohol is a psychoactive drug that has been around for thousands of years and has been the drug of choice on America's college campuses according to virtually every national study on college students' alcohol and drug use (Johnston, O'Malley, & Bachman, 1998; Meilman, Cashin, McKillip, & Presley, 1998; Presley, Meilman, Cashin, & Lyerla, 1996; Wechsler, Davenport, Dowdall, Moeykens, & Costillo, 1994). Used appropriately, it is not a problem except insofar as it may present legal problems for underage drinkers. But used in risky ways, alcohol is hazardous to physical and mental health. Serious injuries and accidental deaths due to alcohol misuse occur every year on the nation's campuses. In addition, alcohol has the potential to create, mimic, or exacerbate psychological and psychiatric difficulties and to wreak havoc on students' lives, academic careers, and future plans (Meilman & Gaylor, 1989). Other illegal drugs and the abuse of prescription medications can do the same. This chapter addresses the use of these substances and briefly comments on addictions to sex, gambling, the Internet, and food. Alcohol will generally be used as the model, but many of the same principles apply to these other addictions.

A Continuum of Use

Alcohol consumption for any given individual can be placed on a continuum ranging from abstinence to late-stage alcoholism. At one end, there is complete avoidance; about one in five college students report being nondrinkers (Presley, Meilman, & Leichliter, 2002). Students may abstain for any number of reasons, including dislike of the taste or the burning sensation in the throat, dislike of the mental or physiological effects, interference with prescription medications, the desire to be in control, or bad associations with alcohol use in the family. When conducting a substance use assessment, it is a good idea to learn a student's specific reasons for abstinence: "You say that you don't drink at all. I wonder what your reasons have been for abstaining?"

Next on the continuum is alcohol use that is social, in moderation, and without any ill effects. In such nonproblematic cases, alcohol may serve as a pleasant adjunct to social situations but is not the primary activity or focus; it is incidental or secondary to the interpersonal interaction and does not take center stage. Slightly further along on the continuum are isolated problematic incidents such as a single episode of driving while intoxicated (DWI), a single blackout (the inability to remember something that happened under the influence of excessive alcohol consumption), or a single embarrassing social incident. While not necessarily a cause for great concern at the time of evaluation, it should be noted that even a single incident of alcohol misuse can result in serious injury or death.

Problem drinking, or alcohol abuse, next on the continuum, is defined by an accumulation of alcohol-related incidents. It is helpful to think about abuse as "abnormal use," or "ab-use"; normal drinkers do not experience repeated negative incidents. If, for example, a student's drinking has led to several blackouts, an emergency room visit, and trouble with campus authorities, it would fall into the category of substance abuse. While such problem drinking may be uncommon in the general population, it is readily apparent in the college environment, where upward of 30% of the population might meet the criteria of the *Diagnostic and Statistical Manual of Mental Disorders,* fourth edition (DSM-IV), for alcohol abuse (Knight et al., 2002).

Further along on the continuum, alcohol abuse shades over into alcohol dependence. An observer senses that the drinker has developed something akin to a working relationship, a bond, with alcohol. Typically, the student has lost control over the amount of alcohol consumed, or loses control over behavior when drinking. Drinkers also display protectiveness with respect to their drinking, responding with anger when drinking problems are discussed, minimizing the effects, or rationalizing the usage, all verbal strategies to fend off others' concerns and to keep drinking. For example, a dependent drinker might say, "I don't drink half as much as my friends do." Students in this category are sometimes hard to detect, since out-of-control behavior is normative in some college circles (for example, fraternity parties), and so their pattern of use may resemble run-of-the-mill misbehavior. And yet it is something more: early stage dependence, or what laypersons label alcohol*ism*. Since there is a common misperception among students that one needs to drink every day or experience withdrawal symptoms to be defined as alcoholic, it's often best to avoid this term. More valuable are psychoeducational strategies that focus on identifying what is and isn't abuse and dependency.

As drinking progresses over time, the drinker develops greater tolerance; he or she must drink more to obtain the same effects once obtained at lower levels. Drinking may begin to affect work and relationships. Middle-stage alcoholism is characterized by frequent drunkenness, and relationships typically become seriously troubled or lost. Interestingly, academic performance is often the last thing to go. Some middle-stage alcoholics are able to perform satisfactorily in their course work while the rest of their lives fall apart.

In late-stage alcoholism, the drinker's life is typically troubled in most every domain. The body's organ systems break down from having been awash in an alcohol bath for years, and overall health is often severely impaired. Friendships, marriages, and other relationships dissolve. Sometimes these individuals demonstrate reverse tolerance, needing less alcohol to become intoxicated than in the past because the liver's ability to metabolize alcohol is compromised. If they stop drinking, late-stage alcoholics risk delirium tremens (DTs), complete with hallucinations and seizures, and so detoxification needs to take place in a controlled setting and be carefully managed. Though infrequent, we have actually seen college students in their early to mid-20s who, after a 5-, 10-, or even 15-year history of heavy drinking, match the description of late-stage alcoholism.

Technically speaking, a diagnosis of dependence on alcohol or other drugs can be made when there is a maladaptive pattern of use within a 12-month period with at least three of the following symptoms: increased tolerance, withdrawal symptoms, consumption of more of the substance or over longer time periods than intended, a persistent desire to or unsuccessful attempts to cut down, substantial time spent using a substance or experiencing its aftereffects, reduction of important activities due to use, and continued use despite knowledge that it causes physical or psychological harm (American Psychiatric Association, 2002).

While this continuum is useful in understanding alcohol problems, an individual's drinking may not always show a "progression" from one stage to the next. In our experience, some who drink very occasionally may still pose significant challenges. On the infrequent occasions when they do drink, they experience loss of control or predictability, and perhaps a blackout or another negative consequence. In many cases, they have innate tolerance, and so can consume large quantities very early in their drinking history, which can sometimes lead to dangerous behavior and consequences. Thus some female students report unwanted sexual experiences under the influence, some males can be verbally or physically aggressive, and both males and females may engage in suicidal behaviors that are absent when they are sober. The fact that these drinkers may drink less frequently than their peers complicates their recognizing and resolving their alcohol problems. College drinking games, which promote excessive and rapid consumption of alcohol, are risky for all students, but especially for these students who have innate tolerance.

As an example of an atypical case, a young woman would "cross the line" and drink to the point of blacking out. This did not happen every time she drank, or every time she drank excessively, and further she had reduced her drinking to only once or twice a month over the course of her treatment. But though her use was infrequent, twice in a blackout she became suicidal and put herself at risk of falling off a bridge or being hit by a car. She had no recollection of this behavior the next day, challenging efforts to address her problem drinking clinically.

We have seen female students who, following a blackout, discovered missing clothing articles and being in another student's bed, with no knowledge of whether or not they had engaged in sexual activity. We have also seen male students who unpredictably exhibit aggressive or even violent behavior, sometimes directed at professional staff who attempt to intervene. While such difficult behavior is rarely life threatening, such students run the risk of being removed from the university for misbehavior they don't even remember. Their memory loss insulates them from truly experiencing the seriousness of their behavior.

Challenges to Diagnosing in a Developmental and Contextual Framework

A complicating factor for diagnosis and treatment of alcohol difficulties is the developmental stage of most undergraduate college students. At this age students typically feel invulnerable, and thus the consequences of substance abuse may have little or no impact on them. Also, since high-risk drinking is normative within some college circles, one might ask, "How do you tell the difference between abuse and dependence?" The simple answer is, "Sometimes you can't." However, as a clinical rule of thumb, true alcohol dependence will declare itself over time. Thus it makes sense to give an assessment time to unfold and to allow a student to "collect data." Clinicians do not have to convince clients that they are alcohol dependent if they're not ready to hear it—the reality may become self-evident later. In the meantime, one time-honored technique to help students' self-assessment is to invite them to set a limit. If they can stick with it for, say, 6 months or more without suffering any adverse consequences, then there is evidence that the problem may be alcohol *abuse* rather than dependence. However, if students cannot maintain drinking within their own specified limit, or they stay within the limit but experience negative consequences anyway, there is evidence for dependence. This conclusion is relevant because there are different treatment implications depending on diagnosis.

Other Drugs

Students are often very interested in information about drugs other than alcohol. In our experience, providing this information is a tricky business. First, it is difficult to find accurate information about the risks of drugs, since conducting empirical research on illegal drugs is challenging. There are no controls for doses or drug purity, and thus the effects and risks are extremely difficult to pin down. Further, we caution colleagues that students will often find some reason to discount "drug information"—for example, saying to themselves, "That's never happened to me, and I smoke up all the time." It is best to give less information and ask students about their own experiences rather than provide information that may not be relevant and so damage one's credibility. With this disclaimer in mind, we address some of the risks and approaches of nonalcohol drugs that we have seen in our students.

Although usage varies across campuses, the most prevalent drug on U.S. campuses other than tobacco and alcohol is marijuana. Some students report extreme reactions to pot, including panic, while others who use it regularly seemingly suffer no ill consequences. Some insist that marijuana is nonaddictive, while others acknowledge physical cravings and withdrawal. When marijuana use becomes frequent or daily, the effects are often insidious, with increasing lack of motivation and nonchalance about responsibilities becoming evident over time. One difficulty in addressing marijuana use is the fact that many students observe no dramatic consequences, and therefore committed users feel less incentive to stop on their own. Sometimes it may be helpful to explain this phenomenon to a client, "It's a good thing you're here now, because if you waited another year, it's possible you wouldn't care enough to look at this situation."

Much has been written in the popular press about abuse of amphetamine, particularly drugs such as Ritalin and Adderal, commonly prescribed for attention deficit disorder but also sometimes taken (without a legitimate prescription) to give students a competitive edge academically (Kadison, 2005). While some students use these drugs to stay up late partying or studying, the problem may be overstated; a national study of college students found that less than 10% of students had ever tried one of these drugs without a prescription (McCabe, Knight, Teter, & Wechsler, 2005). We find that students who report using these drugs are also frequently abusing alcohol or marijuana, and it is partly their chaotic lifestyle that makes them "need" a prescription stimulant to stay awake to complete their academic responsibilities. However, we should not minimize the problem. There is significant risk with stimulant use, which can potentially cause cardiac problems and addiction, weight loss, and severe depressive episodes from the crash.

Another stimulant is the street drug methamphetamine ("crystal meth"), which is reportedly often abused in the gay male community and causes devastating effects in the lives of its users (Graham, 2005), though we have not seen it often in our college practice.

Likewise well known for its stimulant properties as for its high, or initial "rush," cocaine can cause addictiveness and cardiac effects that land students in the emergency room. The most notable thing about cocaine is the rapidity with which use can turn from recreational to addictive, much faster than with many other substances. Concomitant antisocial behavior—for example, thefts to pay for more drugs—is also occasionally seen with cocaine users.

College students abuse opiates or synthetic narcotics relatively rarely, but heroin addicts and students addicted to prescription painkillers do occasionally appear on our caseloads. In serious cases, they need more help than can be provided on campus. Heroin addiction tends to create a downward social drift that becomes quickly evident when one takes a full history.

Occasionally students abuse prescription sleep aids and benzodiazepines. Often this occurs in the context of other prescription drug abuse, outright polypharmacy, or alcohol abuse. Although students sometimes have full-blown addictions, they may also use these drugs for their unique effects or as an inappropriate way to manage stress. We have seen cases where these drugs are obtained legally from physicians, illegally from other students for whom the drugs were prescribed, and on the black market. Careful assessment is needed to understand the context for a given student's use so that treatment can be tailored accordingly.

Ecstasy, a so-called designer drug, and the newer "rave" drugs such as GHB (gamma hydroxybutyrate), rohypnol, ketamine, and various stimulants tend to be used sporadically and are largely associated with after-hours partying. From our observations, Ecstasy use seems to have peaked around 1999–2000. Known as MDMA (3,4-methylenedioxymethamphetamine), it has both stimulant and hallucinogenic properties. When it was new on the scene, students considered it to be the "perfect drug," with a high that facilitated social interactions without having addictive properties. As use became more common, though, depressive symptoms due to irreversible damage to serotonin-producing neurons became apparent (R. Mendola, personal communication, November 16, 2005). A significant immediate risk is that Ecstasy and rave drugs are often used in large crowds or groups that might not be familiar to the user, who then becomes vulnerable to engaging in unprotected sex, becoming injured, being knocked unconscious and coming to in unfamiliar places, being sexually abused or raped, or having a medical or psychiatric emergency.

This brief summary does not cover all the drugs seen on campus—periodically new ones crop up and old ones resurface—but it does include the drugs of abuse most commonly encountered in our day-to-day work.

Leverage

Substance abuse limits an individual's ability to fully grasp its consequences; intoxication and denial both cause an emotional distancing from adverse experiences. In addition, adolescents' sense of invulnerability and widespread acceptance of alcohol and drug use further minimize their awareness of substance abuse. Consequently, some individuals need to experience serious consequences in order to recognize a problem. In the parlance of Alcoholics Anonymous (AA), this is called "hitting bottom." Because of the challenges of diagnosing alcohol problems and students' widespread denial and minimization of problems, institutional leverage is an important tool in getting students' attention. Leverage "raises the bottom," helping individuals experience the consequences of their substance use (Johnson, 1980, 1986). Deans and campus judicial offices can employ this approach by mandating students into treatment lest they face suspension or academic failure (Meilman, 1992). Similarly, coaches can refuse to play a student unless he or she goes for help.

In our work, we have coordinated closely with the judicial office, which can leverage students into alcohol and other drug (AOD) education and counseling services. While students often initially consider this process punitive, by the end of the program, most report finding the experience helpful.

Is leveraging alcohol and drug counseling ethical? Actually, it may be unethical to do otherwise. Without enforced participation, many students would never set foot in a college mental health center, with the likelihood that they would develop more serious substance abuse problems later.

Co-occurring Disorders and Medications

Alcohol and other drug problems have the uncanny ability to mimic psychiatric disorders, coexist with them, and create them. On the one hand, substance abuse can cause one's life to become unglued, which naturally can lead to depression or anxiety. And drugs may even induce hallucinations, paranoia, ideas of reference, and delusions that appear very much like functional psychosis. On the other hand, sometimes an underlying depression or anxiety disorder precedes and precipitates alcohol, marijuana, or other drug use. Once substances are used as self-prescribed medications, they can lead to substance abuse or dependence.

Minkoff (2005) argues that dual diagnoses occur so often that they should be considered the norm rather than the exception, and when mental illness and a substance abuse disorder coexist, both should be considered primary and treated simultaneously. Psychotherapy with dual-diagnosis patients should be started right away, ideally by a mental health clinician who fully understands substance abuse issues.

There are no clear, empirically based prescribing guidelines for treating dually diagnosed patients (Denning, 2000), and so the decision to provide psychiatric medications to a substance-using patient is somewhat controversial. Denning (p. 157) suggests that a treatment team rule out three possibilities when deciding whether to prescribe medication to an alcohol or other drug user: Does the medication cause physiological dependence? Does the medication have street value, so that the patient might be tempted to sell it? Does the medication interact negatively with the person's drug of choice? The second question is particularly important when considering stimulant medications for attention deficit disorder, given that students may abuse such medicines. (For more on medicating clients who abuse substances, see Chapter 4.)

Abstinence-Based and Harm Reduction Models

There are two basic models for treatment, harm reduction and abstinence. Both have their place. Sometimes a student may first try to reduce harm by *curbing* drinking, only to discover later that complete abstinence is necessary.

Harm Reduction Approaches

Most college students are not initially interested in abstaining and so may hesitate to discuss their substance abuse problems with a counselor for fear that the automatic response will be "Stop using." In contrast to abstinence-based treatment, harm reduction may appeal because it lets students choose treatment goals (Larimer et al., 1998, p. 83). The harm reduction approach holds that alcohol and other drugs are neither inherently good nor bad. The role of clinicians is to help students identify how much harm they experience from using and what steps they will take to reduce the harm.

Consider the example of a student who is brought before a dean for disciplinary action because after consuming 22 beers he caused residence hall damage and got into a fight. Careful review of his situation reveals that he typically consumes 15+ beers per drinking event. Rather than focusing on abstinence or diagnosis, a clinician using a harm reduction approach might ask the student, "What changes would you need to make to avoid getting in trouble with the dean again?" The student answers, "I need to keep my consumption to no more than 12 beers." Though perhaps privately groaning with skepticism, the clinician would reinforce the student's response because it represents movement in the right direction and thus reduces harm. Plans are then made to keep track of consumption and to meet regularly to assess the outcome. In all likelihood, the student will still run into trouble, but further trouble presents a good opportunity for consideration of new goals. In this way, the student defines and buys into the changes that are needed.

Abstinence-Based Approaches

Most inpatient and intensive outpatient programs (IOPs) hold that alcoholism and chemical dependency are best conceptualized as a disease. Based on the work of Jellinek (1960), the "disease model" argues that the goal of treatment should be abstinence from all mood-altering substances. While there are cogent arguments against the disease model (Peele, 1989; Peele, Brodsky, & Arnold, 1991), it is also true that some students truly are dependent on alcohol and cannot safely drink. In our experience, students at times need to try and fail at moderation strategies before choosing abstinence as the goal that is right for them. Indeed, Larimer et al. (1998) found that people trained in controlled drinking eventually had increased rates of abstinence. Thus for some students, the end result of the harm reduction approach is to discover the need for abstinence. When students come to this realization, they are more open to the traditional treatment supports of 12-step recovery (AA and Narcotics Anonymous [NA]). College clinicians can help students make this discovery and find resources to support them in maintaining sobriety.

In our view, college mental health programs should provide or collaborate with a range of treatment providers, from those who support moderation to those who offer traditional abstinence-based approaches. Clinicians should be open-minded in assessing a student's substance abuse problems and motivation for treatment, tailoring an approach appropriate for the individual.

Treatment Modalities

The college mental health facility is well suited to offer brief counseling interventions for substance abusers. Brief counseling should not be seen as a poor cousin to more intensive inpatient treatment. Research suggests that brief outpatient counseling can be as effective as inpatient treatment with certain populations of problem drinkers (Miller, 2000).

Motivational Interviewing

Motivational interviewing is a brief counseling technique that provides a research-supported foundation for effective substance abuse treatment. In their book *Motivational Interviewing*, Miller and Rollnick (1991) use the acronym FRAMES to summarize the key elements of effective brief counseling:

- *Feedback* Communicating the findings of assessment is necessary so that the individual has clear awareness of the present situation and the need for change. Feedback sets the stage for goal setting and deciding what steps to take.
- *Responsibility* In effective interventions, responsibility for change is left with the individual.
- *Advice* The clinician acts as a kind of coach who invites change, a more active role than in traditional psychotherapy. The clinician may clearly identify the problem or risk area, explain why change is important, and advocate specific goals.
- *Menu* The counselor discusses with the client a range of strategies or goals for behavioral change.
- *Empathy* An empathic counseling style is associated with lower levels of client resistance and greater long-term behavior change.
- *Self-efficacy* The clinician encourages the client to make successful changes in the problem area, expressing hope and optimism that the client will be able to arrive at the appropriate outcome.

Building on Miller's and Rollnick's work, researchers at the University of Washington designed a program called BASICS (Brief Alcohol Screening and Intervention for College Students), a usually two-session intervention specifically for use with college students who drink heavily (Dimeff, Baer, Kivlahan, & Marlatt, 1999). In the first session, clinicians establish rapport, explain what to expect from BASICS and harm reduction, and guide students to an assessment. Between the first and second sessions, clinicians develop a personalized feedback profile, an individualized report given to students at the second session. Among other items, this profile provides graphic data allowing students to compare their drinking with that of other college students, a calculation of their typical and peak blood alcohol concentrations (BACs), a review of alcohol-related consequences, and an assessment of students' risk for dependency.

During the second session, clinicians guide students through a review of the feedback profile and the various data points. Having previously assumed that everyone consumes the way they do (the "birds of a feather" phenomenon), students are often surprised to discover that their BACs are in a very risky range and that their use of alcohol differs from the norm at their own institution. The written report and the discussion often motivate students to think about what they might do differently in the future. Thus, BASICS can serve as an effective jumping off point for setting usage goals and/or accepting a referral for further treatment. Research has found favorable responses to this approach (Marlatt et al., 1998; Baer, Kivlahan, Blume, McKnight, & Marlatt, 2001). Our experience, mostly with students mandated to the program following a violation of the campus code of conduct, is that most participants report liking the program, and many follow through with more treatment at the counseling center.

Individual Psychotherapy

Psychotherapy with substance-abusing individuals is something of an art. Since denial is commonplace, it is best to find ways to avoid head-on collisions with the client. If, for example, the student starts out by saying, "I don't drink half as much as my friends do," it may be useful to say, "I believe you, although it actually doesn't matter how much your friends drink. What matters is what happens when *you* drink." If when asked if he experiences negative consequences the student responds, "Not really," it may be useful to reply, "'Not really' suggests that something happens on occasion, so tell me what *has* been happening."

Often, a clinician is able to diagnose alcohol or drug dependence from the start, but sharing this feedback may scare off the client and interfere with treatment. It is important to remember that in the early phases of treatment, the relationship with alcohol and drugs tends to be more important than the relationship with the clinician, especially in cases of dependence. If use is threatened, the student may choose the substance over the clinician.

In cases of substance abuse without dependence, moderation of use is a reasonable goal. Standard psychotherapy practices are, of course, necessary: inquiry, reflection, reframing, offering of a perspective, pointing out options, and interpretations. Additionally, one needs to spotlight the connection between substance use and other areas of the student's life: mood, relationships, sex, family life, academics, health, finances, and social life. Normally the student has experienced adverse consequences, which have brought him or her, whether voluntarily or involuntarily, into treatment. Reviewing these consequences highlights the costs involved in misusing substances. Sometimes adverse consequences that are obvious to the therapist are not seen by the student. Pointing these out is essential, gently and nonjudgmentally if possible—but when the consequences are severe, the therapist may wish to be a bit more emphatic, particularly if the student's denial is so blatant as to distort reality. We remember saying to one student who had multiple adverse consequences, including theft, while under the influence, "You claim it's not about the drinking, yet in every situation you've described, alcohol played a prominent role." We came back to this statement, session after session, each time there was another adverse event.

When a student disagrees with the therapist's view, then timing, dosage of interpretation, and discretion are important. Sometimes harping on drinking or drugging and their adverse effects only turns off the student. Instead it may be useful to back off and focus on other topics, only briefly discussing substance abuse each visit. In time, the student may feel less defensive and gingerly approach substance use and its consequences.

In one case, a severely alcoholic student made it clear that she did not want to discuss going into detoxification and rehabilitation. The therapist said that he would state his view once, so that the client would clearly know his professional opinion, but would not repeat it session after session. They focused productively on harm reduction approaches instead, which was all the student could really tolerate. In another case illustrating how substance abuse is often interconnected with other issues, the therapist occasionally mentioned but did not place emphasis on a male student's daily use of marijuana, knowing that doing so would jeopardize the working alliance. With the power struggle avoided, eventually the student revealed that he had a hidden relationship with a male lover and was terribly conflicted about being gay. Working on the student's shame about same-sex feelings and behaviors paved the way for later addressing the marijuana problem—an outcome that would have been impossible had the therapist hammered away at substance abuse from the beginning.

The harm reduction approach proposes that helping students reduce consumption or problematic aspects of use is a positive step, and any such movement should be reinforced. Setting limits on drinking is a good starting point, no matter what number of drinks the student picks. What does matter is to set a limit as a long-term experiment—6 months to a year, or more. If the student can stick to a drinking limit while suffering no further adverse consequences, then there is evidence that moderation can work. If the student cannot maintain the limit or experiences adverse consequences even when drinking within the limit, then moderation is unlikely to be a viable approach. A single lapse would not be definitive—lapses can be used for their educational value and as an opportunity for resetting goals—but multiple slips would be.

Some students try to set nonnumerical limits, saying that they want to "get buzzed" but not be out of control. Our experience is that this approach invariably fails, since "a buzz" impairs judgment, and impaired judgment prevents an objective evaluation of harmful consequences or ability to control further drinking. If students propose such a vague goal, our response is that this isn't really a limit at all and it probably won't work. Generally, a harm reduction approach is reasonable and effective. It speaks to students where they are. However, the promotion of abstinence may be the only reasonable and ethical stance when there are severe or life-threatening consequences, even in the absence of dependence. Consider a student who complains of anxiety, has recently been consuming heavily, had an accident under the influence, gets into fights when drunk, has been subject to disciplinary action, and suffers from an illness which is exacerbated by drinking. In this admittedly extreme case, a harm reduction approach may not work fast enough to spare the student more trauma. Abstinence may be the only viable alternative.

But even though necessary, abstinence can be difficult, especially in the earliest stages of treatment. And even if abstinence is easy at first, students' later urges to drink and difficulties resisting temptation make it difficult to sustain. It is not uncommon then for feelings to surface that substance abuse previously anesthetized or swept away. These feelings, notably depression and anxiety, may be the source of students' usage in the first place, or may represent shame or embarrassment over bad experiences while they were under the influence. Such feelings can be so difficult to manage that people in recovery often wind up using again to make them go away. Some have said, "If this is what it is like to get sober, then I'd rather be drunk." At this point, the therapist needs to voice confidence in the process and indicate that such distress is a sign that the student is getting better, not worse. This reassurance often enables the student to continue moving forward.

Another therapeutic issue is the "screw it" factor (to use the polite term). Often a student has been working for weeks or months, trying so hard to be "good," until finally he or she runs out of patience, says "screw it," and uses again. Typically, immediately afterward the student feels miserable about the slip. The relapse shouldn't be condemned, or else the student may fail to report slips in the future. Rather, a slip should be used therapeutically and explored for educational value. The slip, that precise moment when the usage actually takes place, is typically the last step in a process that may have begun weeks earlier, when frustration and other negative emotions started to build up, leading to a preoccupation with using that now comes to the forefront. Such craving, not unlike hunger for food or thirst for water (rather than the clawing at walls sometimes portrayed in the media), grows over this time and ultimately culminates in the slip.

Psychotherapy can help students make this journey toward abstinence. In addition, AA, NA, inpatient treatment, an IOP, and group treatment may be useful sequentially or in combination with individual psychotherapy to arrive at this goal. Sometimes work done in the college counseling center is preparatory to more intensive off-campus treatment, and sometimes it can serve as follow-up care to such treatment. Inpatient and intensive outpatient programs offering a level of care beyond what is available in the college setting are discussed later in this chapter.

It usually takes 6 months of sobriety—total abstinence from alcohol and other drugs—for substance-dependent students to get back on their feet, and a year to feel solidly in recovery. That is, assuming that they can make it. Some students (and many older adults) need to recycle many times through treatment before they finally succeed.

Group Treatment

Group therapy, alone or in combination with individual psychotherapy, is a traditional mainstay of substance abuse services. In our experience, group therapy provides a mechanism for addressing the unfortunately easy campus acceptance of alcohol abuse as well as the widespread denial and minimization of substance abuse. When individual psychotherapy reaches an impasse, participation in a group can "inspire hope and engender the courage and motivation to try new solutions" (Little, 2002).

Group therapy is particularly appropriate for students given their developmental status. At an age where forming relationships is central, students are naturally receptive to their peers' input and amenable to learning from their experiences and challenges. Listening in a drug-free and serious context to how peers cope with substance abuse and other problems, they can more objectively assess their own situations. Hearing similar stories from others, they become aware of how drinking affects their own lives, and so they slowly relinquish denial. Our students often report that the conversations that take place in a group simply don't happen outside that setting.

Of course, college students, like adolescents, can also be negatively influenced by their peers. Drinkers and users tend to gravitate toward others with similar usage patterns, which can create challenges as well as opportunities for treatment groups. Without proper planning by the therapist, the members in mandated group work (discussed further below) may start telling war stories about their alcohol and drug use, and so reinforce abuse. Therapists can handle this danger by working with cotherapists and using their individual or combined clout to call the process to the attention of the group. Where appropriate, facilitators can also invite group members to challenge each other. Often, students are concerned about their peers' behaviors but need "permission" to say it. Where there are enough referrals, it can be very useful to integrate voluntarily motivated students with judicially mandated students. The former will be able to address denial by sharing their own experiences in facing their problems. Also, women are generally more internally motivated than men, so a coed group often works best. Finally, as a last resort, it may be helpful to remind students in judicially mandated groups that participation is a privilege and if they cannot use the group constructively, a referral may be made back to the judicial office or to an off-campus agency.

Though formal inpatient and outpatient settings utilize many group modalities to support abstinence (see Brook & Spitz, 2002), these modalities aren't appropriate for most students. Outlined below are the types of groups that we have adapted to suit college students' needs.

Psychoeducational Groups   Building on the BASICS experience, these may provide specific information about the nature of dependency and how students can evaluate their own use, including whether or not they are able to manage moderation.

For the mandated population, a time-limited group with clear expectations has proven the most effective. Since students experience the group as a judicial sanction, they need to know what will be asked of them to fulfill the requirement. In our experience, three themes are effective in a four-session, time-limited, structured group experience: (1) environmental influences on drinking and drugging, (2) self-evaluation, including the use of drinking logs, and (3) individual risk factors such as negative consequences of use and signs of tolerance. Each topic takes one full session, with a final session devoted to self-reflection and goal setting for those who are interested in behavior change.

Another time-limited intervention (three to four sessions) utilizes stages of change theory (Prochaska, DiClemente, & Norcross, 1992) and motivational interviewing techniques to raise awareness of consequences and the impact of substance abuse on students' lives. Through a specific cost-benefit analysis of drinking, exploration of students' own values, and discussion of the potential impact of drinking on their lives, this approach can be effective in facilitating movement from pre-contemplation of change to contemplation to action (Walters and Baer, 2006).

Skills Development Groups   These offer moderation strategies—how to change drinking behaviors so as to reduce harm. (Sometimes inability to employ these strategies helps students see the need for abstinence.) Examples of moderation strategies include eliminating "pre-gaming" (drinking before parties) and the use of "hard" alcohol, avoiding drinking games, alternating non-alcoholic and alcoholic beverages, and setting a limit on the number of drinks. It is often helpful to encourage students to evaluate the amount of "energy" it takes to moderate, as students demonstrating loss of control will continue to struggle to meet their own goals. Another important harm reduction strategy is to have a safety plan if moderation fails, such as specifying designated drivers as well as sober friends to help protect intoxicated students from injury and risky situations that might lead to assault or unwanted sexual behaviors.

Beginners' Therapy Groups   Tailored for a more personalized, less structured, and more open-ended dialogue, these groups are useful for students interested in evaluating their relationship with alcohol and other drugs. They can be mandated for students who've had third offenses or significant negative consequences and who've already completed BASICS and the time-limited group. These groups seem to work best when composed of both mandated and voluntary students; everyone is better able to learn from each other about risks they may be taking.

Recovery Groups   These are for clients who want to maintain sobriety, often following formalized substance abuse treatment. These groups are actually easy to run, because members have some sobriety under their belts and a fair amount of wisdom accumulated from treatment and life experiences. By sharing experiences and identifying and processing new challenges, they often do quite well, embracing the work enthusiastically. There is little need for a cotherapist, since the therapist needs to chime in only occasionally.

Groups in college counseling centers can be open or closed, time-limited or ongoing. We recommend that students have a mental health screening, individual motivational work, or individual psychotherapy prior to starting a group.

Intensive Outpatient Treatment and Inpatient Rehabilitation

If the various on-campus treatment alternatives don't address a student's difficulties, the next options are IOPs and inpatient rehabilitation programs. Inpatient rehabilitation usually entails a 4- to 6-week stay at an alcoholism or drug addiction facility and includes concentrated individual and group treatment, family therapy, AA attendance, and psychoeducation. The usual follow-up is a step-down treatment, which may range from placement in a halfway house to individual weekly therapy. Inpatient work is efficient treatment, a full immersion into recovery without outside distractions.

Because insurance coverage for inpatient programs may be lacking, a good alternative is IOPs, which typically take place for 3 or 4 hours, three or four nights per week, and once again feature group and individual work, exposure to AA, and education. Whereas inpatient rehabilitation usually requires taking time off from school, IOP participation may be possible with a reduced courseload.

IOPs exist even in small cities and are generally not hard to find. Inpatient rehabilitation centers, however, are generally found in larger cities. Some of the nationally well-known facilities, such as the Hazelden Foundation, the Betty Ford Center, Sierra Tucson, and the Caron Foundation, can serve as excellent resources. The Association of Recovery Schools and the Center for College Alcohol Recovery are two additional resources that can help identify treatment programs appropriate for college students (see the website of Substance Abuse Recovery on College Campuses, at http://www.sarcc.com).

Generally it is a good idea to investigate and have advance knowledge of these programs. The most helpful method is to call the agency and ask directly about intake, fees, and strategies for integrating college students into its program. Contacting the agency can give a good feel for what a student's experience will be like. Another strategy is to interview students in recovery and ask about their experiences in various treatment facilities.

Medical Leaves of Absence

When a student's substance abuse seriously hampers academics or is a threat to safety and well-being, a medical leave of absence is in order. In our own settings, the counseling service articulates recommendations for treatment and requirements for return. In cases of substance dependence, we usually recommend successful completion of an accredited inpatient treatment program or IOP, followed by a program of less intensive care, including weekly psychotherapy and regular AA or NA attendance. We further require evidence of successful daily functioning (letters of reference from a work supervisor or a transcript of at least three courses from another institution), 6 months of continuous sobriety, an articulated plan for sober support upon return to the university environment, and an in-person assessment.

In one case, a student petitioning for readmission was denied reenrollment because he did not present a viable plan for sober support upon his return. Six months later, still without having taken any steps to address his substance abuse problem, he once again was denied clearance. Finally, he entered treatment, for the simple reason that this was the only way to get back in school. Eventually he became an avid AA member who seriously worked on his sobriety, and he was cleared for reenrollment. Looking back several years later, he thanked us for not letting him return prematurely. Otherwise, he said, he never would have gotten sober and probably would have died prematurely.

Adult Children of Substance Abusers

For many students who've grown up with parents who had alcohol or drug problems, separation from home provides the first opportunity to truly evaluate the impact of their parents' substance abuse. Students' own problems forming intimate relationships or developing a secure and confident identity may also spur self-reflection about what it has meant to grow up in such a home.

Woititz (1983) outlines 13 characteristics of adult children of alcoholics (sometimes referred to as ACOAs). These include lacking a clear sense of what "normal" is, finding it difficult to make decisions or see projects through to completion, judging themselves harshly, taking themselves and life too seriously, experiencing difficulties with intimacy, continually seeking approval, and acting either hyperresponsibly or irresponsibly. While there is no single personality type for adult children of alcoholics, students who've had a substance-abusing parent often resonate with these descriptions and feel motivated to understand and transcend the harm they've endured. Students who are children of substance abusers are also at high risk for substance abuse and dependence and for partnering with alcoholics or drug addicts, thereby recapitulating with which the difficulties they grew up.

Group therapy is often the treatment of choice, allowing these students to evaluate their own behavior, notice dysfunctional strategies, and experiment with new ways of relating. Groups also build trust and provide consistency—both typically in short supply in homes with a substance-abusing parent. Al-Anon, a community-based companion group to AA designed for family members of alcoholics, can be an additional support provided that the particular group welcomes adult *children* of alcoholics, not just spouses and partners. Individual psychotherapy may also be warranted to help these students when they become severely depressed or highly anxious.

Other Addictive Behaviors

There are some commonalities between substance abuse and other addictive behaviors, such as gambling, the Internet, sex, and food (specifically compulsive eating). These behaviors can be thought of as "disorders of relationship," in which the behavior has become a central focus or organizing principle of the individual's life, and almost without fail other relationships have suffered. Recovery typically involves calling a halt to problematic behaviors and restoring connections with other human beings—family members, partners, friends, or supportive individuals in recovery from similar addictions.

Another common aspect with all addictive behaviors, including alcohol and drugs, is the short-term pleasure, or "endorphin rush," they afford. Even if the student doesn't have a high or euphoria, the result may still be a numbing effect that creates a psychic respite from stress, anxiety, rage, or depression. Addictive behavior is reinforcing in the short run. However, it is often followed by significant amounts of guilt or shame—or major adverse consequences such as public exposure or even arrests in cases of illegal activity.

Food addiction can be defined as "the compulsive pursuit of a mood change by engaging repeatedly in episodes of binge eating despite adverse consequences" (Sheppard, 1993, p. 3). It is, of course, closely connected with self-esteem, body image, relationships, and the wish to manage unpleasant feelings, as are other eating disorders (see Chapter 14). Although food addiction involves bingeing, patients may not necessarily demonstrate current purging, restricting behavior, or compulsive exercising, as seen in other types of eating disorders. Primarily we see frequent episodes of huge caloric intake, not in relation to hunger, which lead to significant weight gain. Sheppard (1993) points out that food addicts show typical characteristics of addictions—compulsion, denial, tolerance, withdrawal, craving, and obsession, and she describes food addictions in the way that alcohol and drug addictions are often described, as chronic, progressive, and fatal, if unchecked.

In gambling addictions, one may observe a substantial amount of time spent in gaming activities and the accumulation of mounting debts. Students may gamble at casinos or off-track betting parlors, online or in person. They may gamble on poker games, horse races, sporting events, or any other number of competitive events. In full-blown cases, there is a progression from a winning phase filled with excitement; to a losing phase accompanied by lying, irritability, and restlessness; and finally to a desperation phase accompanied by hopelessness, suicidality, and alienation of family and friends (IIAR, 2005). Gambling problems may be accompanied by strong urges to gamble again, even after winning, and by lying to cover up activities that are seen as embarrassing or shameful. The less severe cases can be addressed in a college counseling-center setting. Gamblers Anonymous, a 12-step program like AA, and residential treatment programs may be of benefit to individuals suffering from severe gambling addictions. In such cases, the college counseling service can help by recommending a medical leave of absence and by preparing students to accept a referral for more intensive treatment.

Internet addiction may begin harmlessly, but eventually the lure of electronic games, easily available pornography, or online relationships begins to substitute for real-world experiences. More and more time is spent online, sometimes to the point where students lose sleep, miss classes, and fail to attend to their assignments. We have seen a number of students who have had to leave school and take medical leaves of absence due to excessive Internet activity. Withdrawn students and students short on social skills are often at risk. While online activity helps them structure their time and provides some comfort in the immediate present, they can become so absorbed in it that compulsive computer activity takes over, consuming vast amounts of their time. These students often come to the counseling center when their academics have hit a crisis point.

Sexual addiction can take many forms, including pornography, cheating with other women or men, excessive masturbation, voyeurism, exhibitionism, anonymous sex, cybersex, and phone sex. While it may be possible to treat mild forms in the college clinic, more serious problems will likely require the services of a specialist outside of the counseling center. Still, a college counseling service can help students identify a sexual addiction and prepare them for more extensive work on the outside, where that is necessary. Sex Addicts Anonymous (SAA) is a 12-step program with similarities to AA and can be a useful adjunct to treatment.

To recover from each of these problematic patterns, a student has to face the reality of his or her addiction. As is true with alcohol and other drugs, this waking-up process can be painful enough to prompt a return to the problematic behavior—a slip or relapse. But as with alcohol, slips can be learning opportunities. Another common therapeutic issue is shame, embarrassment, and guilt. Therapists must work to destigmatize the addictive behavior within the context of the counseling sessions, so that students will be forthcoming about their behavior and their feeling reactions. Without such honest reporting, therapy will be of little value and will come to a standstill in very short order.

Of course, the principles that apply to substance abuse treatment must be modified with other addictions. Thus, while abstinence may be an appropriate goal for severe gambling addictions, it is not appropriate for eating disorders— human beings have to eat! Similarly, abstinence is probably not a realistic goal for most sexual addictions, although abstinence from Internet pornography or voyeuristically peeking into windows at night is an appropriate goal.

Harm reduction could be a useful approach in many cases of behavioral addictions. Thus a problem gambler might set time and financial limits to gambling (for example, 2 hours at the casino or $20 in losses, whichever comes first), and an Internet "addict" might set time restrictions on computer use (for example, an hour a day) or limit or eliminate particular types of websites (for example, sexually explicit ones). And of course, compulsive eaters can work toward a reasonable caloric intake and healthy nutrition.

Since addictive behaviors often involve poor social relationships, interpersonal insecurities, and social skills deficits, group therapy may be especially helpful as an adjunct to individual treatment in order to establish and enhance real-world relationships. By enhancing their social skills, these clients may find less need to resort to their problematic behaviors.

The translation of these behavioral patterns into an addiction paradigm is not perfect, since there are other dynamics and contingencies at work in each case. And yet the study of substance abuse has much to offer the student mental health provider in terms of understanding patterns and conceptualizing treatment approaches for these challenging conditions.

References

American Psychiatric Association. (2002). *Diagnostic and statistical manual of mental disorders* (4th ed., text revision). Washington, DC: Author.

Baer, J., Kivlahan, D., Blume, A., McKnight, P., & Marlatt, A. (2001). Brief intervention for heavy-drinking college students: Four-year follow-up and natural history. *American Journal of Public Health, 91,* 1310–1315.

Brook, D., & Spitz, H. (Eds.). (2002). *The group therapy of substance abuse.* New York: Haworth Medical Press.

Denning, P. (2000). *Practicing harm reduction psychotherapy: An alternative approach to addictions.* New York: Guilford Press.

Dimeff, L., Baer, J., Kivlahan, D., & Marlatt, G. A. (1999). *Brief alcohol screening intervention for college students: A harm reduction approach.* New York: Guilford Press.

Graham, C. (2005, September 27). Special report: Back from the brink. *The Advocate,* 48–50, 52, 55–57.

IIAR [Illinois Institute for Addiction Recovery]. (2005). Pathological gambling: An addiction embracing the nation. Retrieved April 19, 2006, from http://addictionrecov.org/about-gam.htm

Jellinek, E. M. (1960). *The disease concept of alcoholism.* New Haven, CT: Hillhouse Press.

Johnson, V. (1980). *I'll quit tomorrow: A practical guide to alcoholism.* San Francisco: Harper & Row.

Johnson, V. (1986). *Intervention: How to help someone who doesn't want help.* Minneapolis: Johnson Institute Books.

Johnston, L. D., O'Malley, P. M., & Bachman, J. G. (1998). *National survey results on drug use from the Monitoring the Future Study, 1975–1997: Volume I. Secondary school students*. Washington, DC: National Institute on Drug Abuse, NIH Publication No. 98–4345.

Kadison, R. (2005, September 15). Getting an edge—Use of stimulants and antidepressants in college. *New England Journal of Medicine, 353,* 1089–1091. Retrieved April 19, 2006, from http://content.nejm.org/cgi/content/full/353/11/1089

Knight, J., Wechsler, H., Kuo, M., Seibring, M., Weitzman, E., & Schuckit, M. (2002). Alcohol abuse and dependence among US college students. *Journal of Studies on Alcohol, 63,* 263–270.

Larimer, M., Marlatt, A., Baer, J., Quigley, L., Blume, A., & Hawkins, E. (1998). Harm reduction for alcohol problems: Expanding access to and acceptability of prevention and treatment services. In *Harm reduction: Pragmatic strategies for managing high risk behaviors*. New York: Guilford Press.

Little, J. (2002). Harm reduction group therapy. In *Harm reduction psychotherapy: A new treatment for drug and alcohol problems*. Northvale, NJ: Jason Aronson Inc.

Marlatt, A., Baer, J., Kivlahan, D., Dimeff, L., Larimer, M., Quigley, L., et al. (1998) Screening and brief intervention for high risk college student drinkers: Results from a two-year follow-up assessment. *Journal of Consulting and Clinical Psychology, 66,* 604–615.

McCabe, S., Knight, J., Teter, C., & Wechsler, H. (2005). Non-medical use of prescription stimulants among US college students: Prevalence and correlates from a national survey. *Addiction, 99,* 96–106.

Meilman, P. W. (1992). Alcohol education and treatment: On the use of leverage in the college setting. *Journal of American College Health, 41,* 79–81.

Meilman, P. W., Cashin, J. R., McKillip, J., & Presley, C. A. (1998). Understanding the three national databases on collegiate alcohol and drug use. *Journal of American College Health, 46,* 159–162.

Meilman, P. W., & Gaylor, M. S. (1989). Substance abuse. In P. A. Grayson & K. Cauley (Eds.), *College psychotherapy* (pp. 193–215). New York: Guilford Press.

Miller, W. (2000). Rediscovering the fire: Small interventions, large effects. *Psychology of Addictive Behaviors, 14,* 6–18.

Miller, W., & Rollnick, S. (1991). *Motivational interviewing: Preparing people to change addictive behavior.* New York: Guilford Press.

Minkoff, K. (2005). *Comprehensive continuous integrated systems of care: Psychopharmacology practice guidelines for individuals with co-occurring psychiatric and substance use disorders.* Retrieved April 19, 2006, from the Behavioral Health Recovery Management website at http://www.bhrm.org/guidelines/psychopharmacology.pdf

Peele, S. (1989). *The diseasing of America: Addiction treatment out of control.* Lexington, MA: Lexington Books.

Peele, S., Brodsky, A., & Arnold, M. (1991). *The truth about addiction and recovery: The life process program for outgrowing destructive habits.* New York: Simon & Schuster.

Presley, C. A., Meilman, P. W., Cashin, J. R., & Lyerla, R. (1996). *Alcohol and drugs on American college campuses: Use, consequences, and perceptions of the campus environment: Volume IV. 1992–94.* Carbondale: Southern Illinois University Press.

Presley, C., Meilman, P., & Leichliter, J. (2002). College factors that influence drinking. *Journal of Studies on Alcohol, 14*(Suppl.), 82–90.

Prochaska, J. O., DiClemente, C. C., & Norcross, J. C. (1992). In search of how people change: Applications to addictive behaviors. *American Psychologist, 47,* 1102–1114.

Sheppard, K. (1993). *Food addiction: The body knows* (rev., expanded ed.). Deerfield Beach, FL: Health Communications, Inc.

Walters, S. T., & Baer, J. S. (2006). *Talking with college students about alcohol: Motivational strategies for reducing abuse.* New York: Guilford Press.

Wechsler, H., Davenport, A., Dowdall, G., Moeykens, B., & Costillo, S. (1994). Health and behavioral consequences of binge drinking in college: A national survey of students at 140 campuses. *JAMA, 272,* 1672–1677.

Woititz, J. (1983). *Adult children of alcoholics* (expanded ed.). Deerfield Beach, FL: Health Communications, Inc.

12
Sexual Concerns

KENNETH M. COHEN

This chapter highlights contemporary sexual behaviors, challenges, and problems drawn from the author's clinical practice, research, and teaching. I initially discuss the importance of creating a therapeutic alliance, differentiating sexual nomenclature, and collecting a detailed sexual history using unambiguous language to clarify meaning and convey openness. Thereafter, I explore various sexual behaviors and motives, including sexual dysfunction, and issues unique to lesbian, gay, bisexual, and transgender students.

Establishing a Safe Therapeutic Environment

A safe therapeutic environment is essential for establishing client trust and a working alliance. Yet, minimizing resistance and creating a collaborative partnership are particularly challenging when exploring issues in which guilt and shame are often normative. Unlike countless behaviors which young people feel they can control, sexual desire and function are often experienced as arising from beyond self—or even as being "not of self." As a lesbian character in the film *Kinsey* asserts about her first same-sex love, "You have no idea what it's like to have your own thoughts turn against you." Society instructs young people to deny and conceal their once quiescent sexual selves, abandoning them to worry whether their newly evolved and unrelenting sexual lusts are abnormal. Inadequately informed and frightened of pathology, students may live with unspoken feelings of sexual inadequacy that corrode self-esteem, taint self-concept, and diminish their readiness to seek help for sexual concerns.

Sexual conflicts are usually amenable to therapeutic interventions, yet young people are often too uncomfortable to articulate these issues to themselves, let alone others. Therapists must therefore normalize and destigmatize sexual desires and behaviors. This process begins with messages presented in the waiting room and questions posed on intake forms. Thereafter, a therapist models sexual comfort and acceptance by assuring confidentiality and using explicit, at times vernacular, nomenclature to clarify meaning. Precise language is generally preferable to euphemisms and scientific terms. "Have you ever engaged in vaginal or anal intercourse with men or women?" is preferable to "Have you ever had sex?" "Have you ever given or received a blowjob from a guy?" is preferable to "Have you ever engaged in fellatio?" Questions must be specific; penile–vaginal intercourse should be distinguished from vaginal-object and anal intercourse.

It is equally important to clarify the sex of the partner: "Have you ever been sexually active with a male or a female, or both?" or "Are you currently dating someone, perhaps a woman or a man, or both?" These nondiscriminatory questions convey the normality of such behavior better than asking about "significant others" or "partners," which anxious students may ignore for fear of misinterpreting the question and unintentionally outing themselves (Cohen & Savin-Williams, 2004).

Perhaps the largest stumbling block to treatment is a therapist's reluctance to probe sexual matters. Avoidance of sexuality for fear that it is superfluous or inappropriate or because it generates sexual arousal communicates that sex is an unsafe topic and thwarts processing of potentially useful sexual transference. Therapists should remain cognizant of emotional reactions during therapy around sexual issues and seek supervision or make a referral when these responses hinder treatment.

Definitions

Whether clients present with sexual concerns or these concerns arise later in treatment, it is important for therapists to appreciate contemporary sexual lexicons. Students often bifurcate their experiences as "sex" and "not sex"—even though they may disagree about what constitutes "sex" (Reinisch & Sanders, 1999). Whereas traditionally sex has been broadly defined as genital contact of any kind, young people today are more likely to consider only penile–vaginal intercourse to be sex.

Indeed, one fifth of college students do not consider penile–anal intercourse to be sex and four fifths don't consider oral and manual stimulation sex (Sanders & Reinisch, 1999). For some young people, sex's definition depends on whether there has been a date, an emotional investment, and an orgasm, and who did what to whom. Among college students, heterosexual penile–anal intercourse is sometimes considered sex only if the man orgasms—and oral sex is sometimes defined as sex only if the recipient achieves orgasm (Bogart, Cecil, Wagstaff, Pinkerton, & Abramson, 2000). Because active partners in oral sex seldom achieve orgasm, many students don't regard that act as sex. Also of note, same-sex-attracted youth are more likely than heterosexuals to consider use of sex toys, oral–anal contact, penile–anal intercourse, and oral stimulation to be sex.

Sometimes students' sexual identity does not correspond with their sexual behavior or primary sexual attractions (Savin-Williams, 2005). A therapist must cautiously distinguish among these sexual domains. For example, assessing sexual behavior rather than identity is particularly important with homoerotic male international students and North American minority races and ethnicities, who commonly engage in clandestine ("on the down-low") unprotected same-sex behavior while eschewing the labels "gay" or "bisexual." Because they ignore health messages aimed at gay and bisexual men, they are at increased risk for contracting human immunodeficiency virus (HIV) and transmitting it to their female partners (Cohen & Savin-Williams, 2004).

Definitions of sex also have direct implications for physical safety. Whereas broad-based sex education campaigns help students recognize the risks of penile–vaginal intercourse, youth may ignore or underestimate the sexually transmitted infection (STI) risks of seemingly benign "not sex" activities such as oral–anal and penile–anal contact.

Virginity status is similarly dependent on sexual taxonomy. Three quarters of respondents in one study did not consider heterosexual oral sex to constitute loss of virginity, and less than half did not consider anal sex as virginity loss (Carpenter, 2001). Youths who want to maintain their virginity status are increasingly resorting to anal and oral sex to fulfill personal and relational needs. Indeed, women who wish to retain their virginity but fear losing their boyfriends may offer—or be coerced into—anal sex as placation, despite sometimes feeling marginalized or shamed afterward. Of course, some women enjoy anal sex, and its practice should not necessarily generate concern.

In sum, young people with identical sexual histories may arrive at vastly different conclusions about the meaning and implications of their sexual behavior. For therapists, imprecise taxonomy generates flawed conceptualizations and inappropriate interventions. When working with sexual issues, it is imperative to ask specific questions about specific behavior.

Who Is Doing What to Whom?

Despite a seemingly pervasive sexualized youth subculture (witness MTV), there actually has been a gradual decrease in adolescent heterosexual intercourse and pregnancies over the past decade that partly reflects an increase in noncoital sexual activities. These days both females (85%) and males (73%) are more likely to embrace relativistic beliefs that sexual behavior should depend on the particular partner and the nature of the relationship, including degree of caring (Knox, Cooper, & Zusman, 2001). Not surprisingly, although neither sex strongly endorses hedonism (doing whatever feels good as long as it does not cause harm), males are six times more likely than females to do so.

Masturbation

Prevalence of masturbation is difficult to ascertain because of the stigma associated with self-stimulation and its implication of immorality, hypersexuality, or inability to attract a sexual partner. Nonetheless, masturbation is the most frequent sexual activity among young males, with 85% of college men reporting having done it compared with 37% of women (Schwartz, 1999). Partnered women report as much nonintercourse sexual activity as men, however.

Frequency and duration of masturbation sessions vary greatly and are influenced by libido, opportunity, fatigue, stress, and religiosity. Whereas many females self-stimulate occasionally, it is not uncommon for young adult males to masturbate 4–7 days a week, one or two times a day, often shamefully concealing this from others, including therapists.

To enhance masturbation, more males than females utilize sexually explicit images. For many, Internet pornography affords irresistible temptation, especially during periods of stress; chronically anxious students may masturbate more frequently during exam periods. Whereas most are comfortable with this, some experience guilt, and fear that it indicates pathology. Young adults may present for counseling when masturbation evokes disturbing imagery, seems too frequent, or is in opposition to moral or religious dictates.

It is important to recognize the benefits of masturbation for both males and females, including physical gratification, distraction, and tension release. Masturbation poses virtually no risk of pregnancy or STI and may help maintain students' virginity. Masturbating using the start-stop and squeeze techniques trains males to postpone ejaculation, and masturbating to orgasm prior to a date reduces hypersexuality and may promote positive nonsexual interactions or help forestall premature ejaculation. Self-pleasuring acquaints females with their bodies, and so may help them directly communicate to partners their requirements for sexual gratification. For some women, it also demonstrates their capability of achieving orgasm, a sometimes difficult or protracted task with males.

Ego-dystonic or compulsive masturbation is problematic, however. If ego-dystonic, therapists should explore cultural and religious myths or prohibitions (and perhaps identify more acceptable sexual outlets), process objectionable sexual fantasies, and impart information regarding normative sexual functioning. Masturbation is considered compulsive when a student is sexually preoccupied, feels out of control, and possibly has diminishing sexual enjoyment. Injury to the genitals or other body parts and interference with academic or social functioning are also problematic. If determined to be compulsive or otherwise anxiety related, masturbation's meaning should be thoroughly examined and other coping methods taught, such as emotional regulation, distraction, and social skills training.

One female student habitually resorted to masturbation when socially and academically anxious. She eventually learned to distinguish sexual arousal from emotional apprehension and resisted masturbation—a form of distraction and self-soothing—in favor of journal writing, a focusing activity that allowed her to explore underlying fears and strategize coping means such as obtaining academic assistance for difficult assignments and confronting her boyfriend during periods of friction.

Psychotropic medication may be indicated when the compulsive behavior does not respond to psychotherapy.

Disturbing Fantasies

Sexual fantasizing, especially during masturbation, is widespread and is an important tool for gaining insight into sexual preferences, rehearsing anticipated sexual behavior, and developing a sexual identity. For some, though, fantasies reveal disturbing aspects of themselves. When students conceal fantasies they consider shameful, they fail to properly contextualize their needs and erroneously conclude that they are disturbingly unique. Some anxiety-provoking and confusing sexual longings may be deemed inappropriate— close friends, disliked peers, family members, and individuals of particular races and ethnicities. Still more worrisome to some are homoerotic and fantasies of bondage/discipline/sadomasochism (BDSM). Anticipating such conflicts and preemptively alluding to or directly inquiring about them may yield an outpouring of admissions and attenuated dysphoria. Similar to other aspects of sexuality, gender differentiates; male college students are more likely to be aroused by BDSM fantasies and behaviors (Donnelly & Fraser, 1998). Males are also the vast majority of those who meet criteria in the *Diagnostic and Statistical Manual of Mental Disorders,* fourth edition (DSM-IV), for sexual masochism and sexual sadism (American Psychiatric Association, 1994).

It is clinically useful to consider the desire to be sexually dominant or submissive (D/S) an ingrained orientation akin to sexual orientation. Although researchers remain uncertain about its etiology, a D/S orientation often surfaces during childhood or early adolescence and is highly resistant to change. For some, during times of stress the desire to relinquish power (submissives) or assume it (dominants) increasingly dominates sexual fantasies and/or behaviors.

Many young people enjoy their occasional D/S fantasies (bondage, master-slave, biting, scratching), but for others these fantasies troublingly conflict with sex-role expectations or gender politics. Several males I treated found their desires for physical restraint, servitude, or humiliation particularly shameful, interpreting them as unmanly or, "worse," womanly. Similarly, some women who identified with feminism interpreted their fantasies of servitude as betrayals of their political sensibilities and reflections of male fantasies of female domination. As with other manifestations of sexuality, however, attempts at denial or suppression frequently lead to amplified preoccupation, longing, and discontent.

For subclinical levels of BDSM, a therapist can reduce dysphoria with combined psychosexual education and exploration of underlying dynamics that currently fuel the fantasies. (Discovering the genesis of the fantasies is a more nebulous task.) Insight and normalization may produce acceptance even though the fantasies themselves are usually unremitting. Given that D/S needs are usually harmless, therapy can help a client explore ways to request specific behaviors from sexual partners.

Lisa, a 31-year-old undergraduate, requested counseling regarding a relationship that left her feeling sad, angry, and misunderstood. Initially denying sexual difficulties, she eventually vaguely acknowledged a problem, stating that I would lose respect for her if I discovered what she desired. After exploring fears of judgment and abandonment, I responded to her request to "guess" her sexual preference. I shared my views regarding normal sexual diversity, including breadth of same-sex attractions and desire for dominance and submission. At the latter, her eyes lit up, and she admitted having frequent fantasies of bondage and restraint that generated both arousal and guilt. She told her male partner, who initially relented to her requests but quickly grew uncomfortable, leaving her feeling increasingly stigmatized and fearful that they would never share a satisfying sexual relationship. Together we explored her fantasies, which did not involve risky or dangerous behaviors, and the limited meaning she was able to unearth. As she became accepting of her sexuality, she and her partner researched the topic and developed a shared vocabulary that permitted them to understand her needs and negotiate acceptable behavior—hallmarks of BDSM play.

Therapists commonly experience initial discomfort with these issues and wish to prevent students from enacting them. They, like their clients, should challenge stereotypes and uneasiness by reading popular BDSM literature (Brame, Brame, & Jacobs, 1996) and learning community guidelines that emphasize the canon "safe, sane, and consensual."

More problematic is when BDSM fantasies are obsessional or distressing, interfering with daily functioning, or when fantasies if expressed are potentially dangerous, such as anonymous sexual encounters, extreme verbal and psychological humiliation, or severe bodily injury (beating, cutting, mutilating, branding, strangulating) and physical restraint (physical bondage, especially over long periods). Hypoxyphilia, obtaining sexual arousal by oxygen deprivation (by a noose, plastic bag, mask, or chemical), is particularly dangerous and can be fatal, especially when practiced alone during masturbation. Clients who approach DSM-IV criteria for sexual masochism or sexual sadism are best referred to a specialist.

Paraphilias such as exhibitionism, voyeurism, and fetishism are common, especially among males, and not necessarily cause for concern, especially when they do not generate personal discomfort or infringe on the rights of others. Examples are deriving pleasure from collecting someone's worn garments, washing someone's feet, or viewing or being viewed showering. Provided that these behaviors are consensual, don't interfere with functioning, and aren't dangerous to self or others, they can be expressed, explored, and embraced.

Sexual Impetus, Abstinence, and Virginity

Sexual activity may be used to individuate from parents or distinguish one-self from community or religious norms. Some young people engage in sexual behavior because they erroneously believe that their peers are behaving similarly; others do so simply out of curiosity. Many use sex for emotional regulation and may increase their risk for STI if they have multiple encounters outside of a committed relationship or engage in risky sexual behaviors. Thus, it is insufficient for a clinician to determine *whether* sex is occurring; the meaning of sex must also be explored because of its implications for clinical conceptualization and treatment.

Whereas some students elect abstinence simply because they feel developmentally unprepared, others wish to suppress or contain sexual desires which seem like a corrupting force. Influenced by religion and culture, they may see virginity or total sexual abstinence as reflecting moral and personal fortitude, whereas relenting to sexual desires shames self, family, community, and even ancestors. But social pressures—from peer expectations to media representations—may leave abstainers feeling marginalized and isolated, and thus willing to compromise their values by redefining or reinterpreting "sexual behavior." For example, to fit in with peers or please a romantic partner, a person may engage in various sexual behaviors while selectively ruling out penile–vaginal intercourse, or choose sexual relations only if involved in a loving and committed relationship.

It is therapeutic to clarify students' definitions and assess their motives and level of comfort with their sexual decisions. Even students who are secure with their decisions profit from discussing their costs and benefits. For those who feel isolated, a therapist can help establish connections with similarly minded students, such as those in campus religious or cultural groups, to provide support and reduce anxiety.

It is always useful to assess knowledge about safer-sex practices, because students may underestimate their risk of infection and pregnancy. Some self-identified virgins believe that awareness of safer-sex practices is necessary only for those who actively engage in penile–vaginal sex or are sexually "promiscuous." Yet, some of them engage in oral and anal sex without protection and others impulsively have penile–vaginal intercourse without condoms, placing themselves at risk. Indeed, a recent study found that teenagers who take a virginity pledge are as likely to contract an STI as those who do not (Bruckner & Bearman, 2005).

Hooking Up and Anonymous Sex

Once considered a moral transgression, especially for women, single sexual encounters with a stranger or brief acquaintance are increasingly common among college students. Though definitions vary considerably, "hooking up" typically involves two people attending a party and sharing a mutual attraction, flirting, and advancing to unplanned kissing, petting, sometimes oral sex, and often intercourse. Alcohol and other drugs are usually involved, and precautions (e.g., condoms) are seldom or inconsistently used. During the event there is little verbal communication.

Hooking up can be seen as an expression of sexual freedom and self-determination, but numerous outcomes can mar the experience. Females are more likely than males to feel regret, shame, and self-blame for not having known the partner and for having no further contact with him (Paul & Hayes, 2002). Though they *know* hookups do not lead to relationships, they often *hope* they will and so later feel vulnerable and compromised. Males are more likely to later celebrate and brag to friends, though they may regret the experience if the woman is subsequently deemed unattractive or promiscuous. Counselors can help students address the loss of potential relationships, damage to self-concept, male aggression or coercion (sometimes with date rape drugs), and the negative effects of alcohol and other drugs. Counseling also affords an opportunity for students to explore the motivations and consequences of their behaviors.

Oral, Anal, and Penile–Vaginal Intercourse

Among 18- to 21-year-olds, approximately 75% report having received or given oral sex (Mosher, Chandra, & Jones, 2005). Often treated casually, oral sex is increasingly embraced as a substitute for penile–vaginal intercourse that satisfies (mostly) male sexual demands while maintaining virginity. Unfortunately, the potential for contracting an STI is also frequently underestimated. Heterosexual anal sex is less common, averaging 22% (Mosher et al., 2005), but may be underreported because of stigma. Although anal stimulation often produces sexual arousal in males, heterosexual men who desire or enjoy *receptive* anal intercourse may experience emotional upheaval and identity crisis if they believe that these desires imply they are gay. As with other sexual matters, a therapist's ability to convey acceptance allows clients to share these embarrassing desires. Following exploration of possible homoerotic fantasies, a therapist can offer relief by explaining about the proximity of the prostate to the anus and its contribution to arousal.

Chad, a tall, burly college athlete who was vice president of his fraternity, sought counseling for panic attacks, growing depression, and passive suicidal ideation that had begun 3 weeks earlier and for which he could not identity a precursor. During the second session he discussed a new relationship with a sexually adventurous woman whom he both lusted after and feared. He shamefully admitted that during an initial sexual encounter she had inserted her finger into his anus, giving him a powerful orgasm and longing to repeat the experience. After he explained that this meant he must be "homosexual," we explored same-sex attractions (negligible), discussed his fears of peer rejection and need to maintain a hypermasculine persona, and clarified male physiology while normalizing his sexual response. By the following week, his symptoms had abated and his heterosexual identity was reaffirmed. He was able to discuss sexual needs with his girlfriend, who confirmed his heterosexuality and agreed to further integrate anal stimulation into their future lovemaking.

Heterosexual penile–vaginal intercourse is acknowledged by approximately 90% of 18- to 24-year-olds and occurs at increasingly younger ages, especially among females (Laumann, Gagnon, Michael, & Michaels, 1994). Various sex and race differences have been found. For example, young women most frequently report first engaging in intercourse to evoke their partner's love; black youth report first intercourse at an earlier age than white and Hispanic youth (Blum et al., 2000). Compared with young women, young men are more likely to achieve orgasm and highly rate activities other than intercourse, such as viewing their partner undress and giving/receiving oral sex (Laumann et al., 1994). These sex differences may be the consequence of females being socialized to focus on romance, love, and marriage rather than sexuality, which they're taught may be dangerous and lead to pregnancy or rape. It is thus not surprising that following sexual activity young women report greater feelings of regret, shame, and guilt, though less so when sex occurs within an intimate, committed relationship. Age of first intercourse also is important. Early onset of sexual behavior correlates with problematic behaviors—such as substance abuse, delinquent activities, academic misconduct, increased STI, and female depression—and may constitute the primary focus of therapy (Crockett, Bingham, Chopak, & Vicary, 1996).

Inexperienced college students engaging in sexual intimacy for the first time may be unprepared for disappointment and negative emotions, especially if the media is their primary instructor. Conflicting motives and expectations are particularly likely to hurt females, who may benefit from counseling to reclaim sexual agency, demystify and normalize sexual libido, and learn to articulate future needs and establish limits with prospective partners. Among emotionally or socially unfulfilled males, a therapist can downplay the physical pleasures of sex while emphasizing ways in which sexual and romantic intimacy fulfills emotional needs and bolsters psychological resilience.

Pregnancy and Abortion

Failure to utilize contraception, especially condoms, is multidetermined and should be explored whenever discussing sexuality. Many students eschew condoms for fear they preclude spontaneity or imply promiscuity, or because their partner insists or they feel less pleasure with a latex barrier.

Still others succumb to myths ("I can't get pregnant the first time") or believe they are invulnerable. Sex-positive therapists use motivational interviewing techniques to explore the benefits and liabilities of using condoms while suggesting methods for increasing emotional comfort and physical pleasure. For example, students can become familiar with latex by tasting flavored condoms, and men can practice masturbating with internally lubricated condoms, which enhance sensation.

Among undergraduates, pregnancy is often considered devastating and sometimes can precipitate an emotional crisis. Because pregnancy assumes multiple meanings, therapists should suspend moral judgment and social expectations and carefully assess motives. For example, while the impregnation of a promising young academic may seem tragic, some families and cultures expect and support it, especially if college is considered a place to obtain a relationship rather than a degree. Some women may consciously or unconsciously intend the pregnancy to fulfill emotional needs or withdraw from school. Others use pregnancy, real or feigned, to entrap or vent anger toward a boyfriend. Both men and women sometimes disregard or misrepresent their use of contraception to ensure impregnation and/or continuation of the relationship.

The distressed client who reveals that she is pregnant should be assessed for lethality and offered crisis management and medical referral. If a potential pregnancy is due to rape, police should be notified and the student immediately referred to the university health center or a hospital—whichever provides expert postassault examination and specimen collection, aids to criminal prosecution (see Chapter 13). Prophylactics may then be offered to prevent impregnation and HIV infection if too much time has not elapsed. In cases of consensual sex, couples or individuals can be referred for reproductive health counseling at the university's health center or a community clinic such as Planned Parenthood, and to therapy to explore options and anticipated reactions. For those considering abortion, therapy can normalize possible postabortion relationship changes, such as diminished sexual interest in postoperative women and between partners who experience shame or fear a subsequent pregnancy. It is important to clarify the rights and responsibilities of each partner, especially when they disagree about how to resolve the pregnancy, or there may result substantial anger and hurt that may destroy the relationship. Despite the stereotype that males covet freedom, it is sometimes men who discourage abortion or adoption and suffer following the woman's unilateral decision. They can profit from supportive counseling because, as with most issues, men grieve privately and with minimal social support.

Abortion—which correlates positively with higher parent income and education and student academic success and educational aspirations—is usually chosen to conceal sexual activity and permit continuation of education. Some students would embrace parenthood, however, if they had the financial resources or a stable relationship. Contrary to conventional wisdom, abortion does not inevitably lead to current or perimenopausal depression, though stress, violent impregnation (rape, incest), and coerced abortion, especially when combined with religiosity and past mental illness, may generate psychological repercussions. Students who elect abortion are sometimes surprised to find that they ruminate about or grieve the "lost child." Romantic relationships that are terminated further complicate the grieving process. In the absence of parental and peer support, counseling permits a normalization of reactions and exploration of feelings of loss, shame, and regret by both partners. However, therapists must recognize and keep unexpressed their moral and religious values, including bias in favor of or opposition to abortion, which may conflict with clients' values. If this proves too difficult, therapists should seek clinical supervision or make appropriate referrals.

Sexually Transmitted Infections

Few experiences are as disquieting as contracting an STI. Even when curable, students may react with shock and feel dirty and betrayed. Romantic relationships are strained or dissolve when partners lose trust in each other or seek physical distance to avoid spreading infections. Not uncommonly, guilt and the related belief that the disease is deserved punishment for engaging in sex shatter the young person's illusion of invulnerability, and may stimulate ruminations about other threatening or impending disasters. For many, contracting an STI is a traumatic experience that is inflamed by societal prejudice and stigma and prevents some from sharing their experience with family, friends, and even physicians.

When diagnosed with an incurable (herpes) or potentially deadly (HIV/AIDS) STI, a student may be overwhelmed with panic and depression. In such cases, a temporary leave of absence may be necessary. I will limit myself to several cursory comments about helping these students. Those who suspect that they have been recently exposed to HIV must immediately seek medical attention—preferably within several hours but no later than 36 hours—and begin prophylactic treatment that may prevent infection. When diagnosis is recent, an HIV-infected youth may be coping with the illness that prompted HIV screening and a sense of a foreshortened future. Not uncommon is fear of impending death and rumination about informing others and putting affairs in order. Sometimes students temporarily abandon academics and social relationships. When social isolation is protracted, depression and suicidality may worsen and should prompt therapists to encourage social contact and consider psychotropic medication. Frequently, the temporary withdrawal from life decreases clients' motivation for treatment, especially with a therapist who is not identified as HIV positive. Clients then may benefit from a referral to organizations that offer education and peer support from similar others. With time, education, and the realization that death is not imminent, many clients gradually reinvest in life with renewed purpose and appreciation.

Sexual Dysfunction

Sexual dysfunction, which often first occurs in young adulthood and during initial sexual encounters, includes diminished sexual arousal (e.g., male impotence); delayed, absent, or premature orgasm; and genital pain and vaginal muscular spasms. Students seeking treatment may feel embarrassed when sexual performance problems seem to imply diminished virility, desirability, and adult status.

Careful assessment begins with a detailed analysis of the dysfunction's frequency, duration, setting, impairment, and degree of subjective suffering. Occasionally, assessment finds that there is no dysfunction, only unrealistic expectations. This was the case with a patient who self-diagnosed premature ejaculation, despite his ability to forestall orgasm during 30 minutes of continuous intercourse, because he believed he should last for hours.

Determining the cause of sexual dysfunction involves teasing apart medical/physical, intrapsychic, interpersonal, psychiatric, and cultural contributors (Maxmen & Ward, 1995). *Medical* or *physical* conditions must always be ruled out; physicians advise a complete medical workup prior to psychological treatment. Therapists who practice in interdisciplinary medical centers should regularly collaborate with medical professionals for consultations and referrals. Among college students, fatigue due to sleep deprivation or illness commonly undermines sexual arousal and performance, and thus they may benefit from sleep hygiene coaching. Many psychotropic and some nonpsychotropic medications have sexual side effects, as do alcohol and drugs. Regarding the latter, sexual misunderstandings while intoxicated are commonplace among college students and further underscore the need for substance abuse assessment and treatment. In fact, it is often necessary to treat substance abuse before a sexual issue.

Intrapsychic variables may involve anxiety regarding sexual performance, genital appearance, and pregnancy or contracting an STI. Young adults who approach sex with unrealistic expectations may also set themselves up for sexual failure, especially if they excessively self-monitor and are sensitive to rejection. *Interpersonal* factors reflect relationship issues, such as displaced anger and power plays, that are expressed in the bedroom. Frequently, distrust of a partner or fear of abandonment hampers adequate performance or satisfaction. Naive or shy participants may not communicate clearly about sexual needs and preferences, resulting in unsatisfactory sexual performance and pleasuring of the partner. Several *psychiatric* disorders can affect sexuality, such as major depression, obsessive-compulsive disorder, and severe anorexia nervosa and body dysmorphic disorder. Inhibited sexual desire is associated with histrionic personality style in women and obsessive-compulsive personality features in men, and a history of trauma, such as childhood sexual abuse or adult rape, may also diminish sexual interest or performance. Finally, *cultural* values and standards may shape sexual attitudes and prohibitions, which in turn influence sexual expectations and emotional reactions to sexual behavior.

Patterns of substance use among gay and straight students help differentiate diagnosis and treatment. For heterosexual males, excessive alcohol hinders sexual performance, but low to moderate quantities may enhance it by diminishing social anxiety. Among gay males, even low alcohol consumption can dampen sexual responsiveness during undesirable heterosexual encounters. Some lesbians and gays are able to perform adequately with the opposite sex when sober and their libidos are high but may lose the ability when inebriated. When students use drunkenness as a pretext for homoeroticism, they may develop drinking or social problems.

John was referred to counseling by the university judicial administrator after a third incident of fighting with varsity teammates while severely intoxicated. Though he was out as bisexual—hooking up with females while sober and males while intoxicated—he recalled coming out as gay in senior high school. In counseling, he realized that although he usually maintained a tight rein on his behavior to avoid appearing "gay" or effeminate, being intoxicated freed him to indulge in gender-atypical behavior and homoerotic sex play. John eventually accepted that he preferred sex with males but greatly feared rejection from his teammates and that he had far more internalized homophobia than he'd recognized. As he began coming out again, this time as "probably gay," he gradually reduced the binge drinking and fulfilled his homoerotic needs more directly.

Performance anxiety and poor body image can also impact sexual desire and functioning. Unrealistic body expectations are common among heterosexual women and homoerotic males; the latter may compare themselves with media representations showing gay males as exceedingly attractive, perfectly buff gym rats with large penises. A therapist should assess bodily concerns, including comfort with genitals and breasts (size and shape), and explore underlying self-esteem issues. Therapists can also help students manage anxieties with distraction, relaxation, and systematic desensitization and encourage them to become familiar with summary statistics (average breast or penis sizes) and share concerns with their partner.

Therapists are often uncomfortable discussing and treating sexual conditions. Fearing that their inquiries are gratuitous or voyeuristic, they may truncate assessment and steer students in the wrong direction. Closeted lesbians and gays who complain of heterosexual sexual dysfunction may be inappropriately taught Masters and Johnson sex therapy techniques, and those who acknowledge homoeroticism but request conversion or improved heterosexual functioning may receive unsubstantiated, archaic behavioral treatments, such as painfully snapping an elastic band on their wrist when thinking about gay sex. Failed treatments or client requests may prompt referrals to physicians who prescribe Viagra or refer to urologists. Neither Viagra nor urologists can elevate heterosexual interest if a student's orientation is homoerotic.

In addition to conducting detailed assessment and psychodynamic exploration, sex therapies effectively remediate many (especially male) sexual problems by merging couples counseling, homework assignments, Masters and Johnson sex therapies, and sex education (including bibliotherapy). The last is particularly important for challenging myths, such as that foreplay is childish and unnecessary, arousal (lubrication, erection) must precede sexual initiation, and intercourse and orgasm are the only acceptable outcomes. Many therapists are poorly trained and feel ill-prepared to treat these specialized conditions; if so, they should seek supervision or make appropriate referrals.

Sexual Minorities: Lesbian, Gay, Bisexual, and Questioning Youth

The previous decade has witnessed an unprecedented upsurge in the willingness of students to bring lesbian/gay/bisexual/transgender (LGBT) concerns to college counseling centers. This is partly attributable to the high visibility of alternative sexualities in the media (*Will and Grace, Queer Eye for the Straight Guy*) and the coming out of popular figures, such as Ellen Degeneres, Audre Lorde, and Melissa Ethridge (Savin-Williams, 2005). Whereas previously students could dismiss homoerotic longings as mere chumship or benign curiosity, denial is more difficult as cultural discourse increasingly focuses on homoeroticism and gender bending. A case in point is the celebration of the "metrosexual"—a heterosexual man so secure in his sexuality that he can embrace manicures and eyebrow plucking.

To help students resolve sexual orientation issues, clinicians should be knowledgeable about typical homoerotic development (e.g., see Savin-Williams & Cohen, 1996). A thorough assessment begins with a detailed sexual history, including first same-sex attractions, sexual behaviors, coming out to self, coming out to others, relationships, parental reactions and family problems, harassment, stressors, social support network, and coping strategies (substance abuse, eating disorders). A therapist must also recognize that clients' homoeroticism may be incidental to their identifying complaint and that the aforementioned variables may contribute more to dysfunction than does the sexual orientation per se (Cohen & Savin-Williams, 2004). For example, cultural homonegativity can generate self-hatred, distorted self-concept, and relationship instability among sexual minorities. The HIV/AIDS epidemic has created an atmosphere of dread and loss that further contributes to social marginalization and fear of abandonment. Yet, counter to prevailing stereotypes, there is immense diversity among sexual minorities—some are far more similar to heterosexuals of their own gender than to other sexual minorities. Sexual minorities may be sexually inexperienced or promiscuous, suicidal or resilient, gender typical or gender atypical.

Homoerotic clients may be reluctant to disclose their attractions and behaviors for fear of negative responses from providers, as happened in this case.

When he was a sophomore dating women, Neil was treated for genital warts by an especially warm and empathic infectious disease specialist. Suspecting another STI 2 years later, he revisited the physician and was diagnosed with herpes. Following the examination, the physician invited Neil to bring his girlfriend into the office for debriefing and education. When Neil instead introduced his male partner, the physician grew noticeably cold and curt. Neil was quickly dismissed, feeling numbed by the diagnosis and humiliated by the physician.

Anticipated discrimination stimulates hypervigilance for signs of homonegativity and may lead to delayed treatment (Cohen & Savin-Williams, 2004). Therapists therefore must convey support and nonjudgment, or else refer the client to another clinician. Appreciation for diversity can be communicated by gay-affirming posters and symbols (pink triangle), gay magazines (*The Advocate, Out*) and information pamphlets (e.g., "Homophobia" [Thompson & Zoloth, 1990]) in the waiting room, and prominently displayed affirmative gay books in the therapist's office. Intake forms should avoid the assumption of heterosexuality by assessing sexual orientation, identity, and behavior and providing the options "with males, females, or both." Sexual identity terms should include *heterosexual, lesbian, gay, bisexual, questioning, uncertain,* and *other* (space provided for elaboration) (Cohen & Savin-Williams, 2004). A therapist further conveys reassurance by adopting the client's vocabulary (e.g., avoiding the medicalized and pathologizing term "homosexual" in favor of "gay") and rejecting erroneous characterizations, such as that homosexuality is a psychological defense, there exists a single "gay lifestyle" or community, gay and lesbian relationships are predominantly about sex rather than deep emotional intimacy, everyone is really bisexual, or all bisexuals are actually gay or lesbian. Finally, clinicians ought to be aware of community resources and refer to knowledgeable and compassionate mental health and medical specialists.

Confusion

Although homoerotic young adults may present to counseling for reasons unrelated to sexual orientation, one of the most frequent reasons they come in is sexual confusion and related anxieties. For some, confusion begins when same-sex attractions emerge or assume new meaning following a class lecture on homoeroticism. Suddenly having a language to organize previously inchoate homoerotic thoughts and feelings can precipitate a crisis. Students also may feel confused if they acknowledge homoerotic *sexual* longings but deny same-sex *emotional* attractions. Other students may attribute their sexual confusion to not looking or acting like a stereotypical gay person. One female client who'd been attracted to females since age 9 asserted, "I can't be a dyke, I like makeup and wearing my hair long!" Others manage homoeroticism by repressing their sexuality so fully that they claim to be asexual. Because true asexuality is rare, careful assessment of sexual longings is necessary. Some people also mask their same-sex longings amidst BDSM fantasies, as was the case with this client.

Javier recounted repeatedly fantasizing about being sexually shamed and humiliated by women as men watched. He had long thought of these fantasies as heterosexual because females assumed center stage, while the male observer role—which occasionally involved demanding forced sexual servitude—seemed necessary solely to augment the humiliation. After we analyzed the fantasies, however, he recognized that the males were the *primary* objects of lust while the females served to reassure his heterosexual identity. As he grew progressively comfortable with his same-sex longings, he felt less need to incorporate females as well as forced servitude into his sexual fantasies.

Occasionally, clients are confused or distressed about same-sex "thoughts" that do not necessarily represent a homoerotic sexuality. For example, clients with borderline personality disorder may experience sexual identity confusion or instability, and individuals suffering from obsessive-compulsive disorder may ruminate about newly emerged homoerotic thoughts. Dynamic exploration is usually unproductive with the latter, whose thoughts are more a product of biochemistry than intrinsic sexuality.

Jennifer, a successful freshman with a history of relatively mild untreated childhood obsessions and compulsions, presented for counseling reporting apprehension that she was lesbian—despite previously identifying as heterosexual, exclusively dating males, and observing no appreciable attraction toward females. Shortly before our consultation, she began noticing females around campus and ruminating about whether she was aroused and, therefore, lesbian. So upsetting was this unlikely possibility (her frequent checks for vaginal lubrication suggested no genital arousal) that she developed a depressive disorder. Though she insisted she and her liberal parents were "fine" with homosexuality, she declared she would kill herself if she were lesbian. Initial psychodynamic exploration proved fruitless in clarifying her sexuality or diminishing her sadness. Only psychotropic medication was successful in remitting her symptoms.

Educating clients about different sexual domains and challenging stereo-types often helps clarify sexual orientation. An important myth to refute is the polarization of sexuality as gay *or* straight, especially among females for whom sexuality falls along a continuum. A therapist who supports sexual experimentation while remaining impartial regarding the student's eventual discovery facilitates sexual clarity.

Assessing Sexual Orientation

Homoerotic students who present for counseling in the early stages of sex-ual identity development may request a therapist's aid in determining their sexual orientation. But often behind this appeal is understandable ambiva-lence about self-discovery, since acknowledging homoeroticism risks loss of self-esteem and may trigger social rejection. In fact, clients' requests some-times contain the hidden message, "Please assure me that I'm *not* gay." It is a good idea therefore for therapists to empathically inquire whether a student *truly* wants to know "the answer" and to explain associated risks—one cannot unlearn insight or guarantee the desired outcome. Doing so secures clients' collaboration and respects their need for psychological safety.

A therapist begins by discussing three related, but distinct, domains of sex-uality: sexual orientation, sexual behavior, and sexual identity (Cohen & Savin-Williams, 2004, pp. 361–362). *Sexual orientation* refers to the predominance of a person's erotic feelings, thoughts, and fantasies for members of a particular sex, both sexes, or no sex. Sexual orientation is likely to be established by birth or early childhood and is usually immutable, stable, resistant to conscious con-trol, and internally consonant. A person may choose or change behavior and identity, but he or she cannot easily, if at all, choose or change sexual orienta-tion. *Sexual behavior* refers to an individual's sexual activities. Depending on cultural and individual factors, sexual partners may be consistent or inconsis-tent with a youth's underlying sexual orientation. *Sexual identity* is a socially recognized label that names sexual feelings, attractions, and behaviors and is symbolized by such statements as "I am gay" and "I am straight."

These three domains are often confused and may be incongruent. Thus, it is possible for a female to be attracted to both males and females (bisexual sexual orientation), engage in sex only with a boyfriend (heterosexual behavior), and identify as lesbian in order to partake in a women's community. Depending on whether orientation, behavior, or identity is considered, very different con-clusions will by drawn about her.

Further clarification is possible by inviting clients to answer four sexu-ally explicit questions, any of which they can elect to skip. For each one, they are to determine the extent (percentage) to which their experience is toward *both* males and females, where the combined total is 100%. The questions are:

1. To whom are you emotionally attracted? By this, I do *not* mean erotically or sexually attracted, but rather to whom you feel emotionally closest.
2. To whom are you erotically or sexually attracted? When you walk around campus, who turns your head? You need not become physically aroused.
3. When you are home alone, in the privacy of your bedroom, which sex are you thinking about when you masturbate? If you are viewing pornography, where (and at which sex) are you looking?
4. When you are home alone, masturbating in the privacy of your own bedroom, and you are on the verge of coming and then when you come, about which sex are you thinking or looking?

Males and females usually report high emotional connectedness (question 1) toward females, thus confusing some heterosexual females who fear this implies that they are lesbian, and some gay and bisexual males, who embrace this as evidence that they are heterosexual. However, responses to this question are usually quite discrepant from the others. As clients become increasingly aroused—during masturbation or other highly erotic experiences, and especially as orgasm approaches—culturally imposed prohibitions temporarily recede and lust predominates. Questions 2 to 4 incrementally measure authentic erotic and sexual attractions. Thus, a consistent, clear pattern can be observed among gay males. Although they may be 80% *emotionally* attracted to females (20% to males), they are increasingly homoerotic as orgasm approaches—60% attracted to males when walking around campus, 85% during masturbation, and 98% just prior to and during orgasm. This suggests that for males, at least, emotional connectedness is related to, but different from, sexual orientation and should be interpreted with caution.

It is noteworthy that these questions better determine male than female sexuality, because the latter is far more contextual and emotion based (Diamond & Savin-Williams, 2003). Whereas males usually describe homoeroticism in sexual terms and as arising in childhood, females more often recall their homoerotic experiences beginning years after puberty and in the context of preexisting, highly intimate relationships with friends in which sex was often secondary. As females recount their sometimes surprising sexual attractions toward female friends, they often conclude that they fall in love with the individual rather than the gender (personality matters more than body) and that emotional attraction precedes sexual attraction. Further, whereas male sexual experiences correspond to pubertal hormone levels, female behavior is far more variable and often regulated by environmental and interpersonal factors, such as opportunities for experimentation. Although there is diversity among the sexes, when working with females it is prudent to inquire about strong emotional and loving feelings more than erotic lusts. Emotional connectedness is certainly important to males but is less useful for determining sexual orientation than are measures of erotic arousal.

Grief Work

Subsequent prompting is often unnecessary with homoerotic students as they solemnly reflect on their responses to the four questions. Frequently, they sadly acknowledge the pervasiveness of their homoeroticism with the simple statement, "I thought so." Encouraged by the therapist's question, "What if you are gay?" students may then begin a protracted period of mourning. They should be encouraged to articulate feared losses—such as their heterosexual identity, imagined future (husband or wife, children), and heterosexual privilege. Students frequently express the fear that they are mentally ill and insufficiently feminine/masculine. Lest the grieving process be truncated, a therapist should avoid hopeful replies ("Gay people can have children, too") until after students have sufficiently expressed anxieties and mourned expectations. Given several sessions to grieve, many clients eventually begin responding to their fears with realistic options ("I don't need to be miserable and alone; I might just adopt a child!") and reinstated hope.

Clients' own homonegativity, exacerbated by erroneous and stereotypical representations of homoerotic people, contributes to their shame. Though they may be reluctant to articulate their dislike of gay people, realizing that their beliefs are irrational or fearing the displeasure of the therapist, they should be encouraged to express these homonegative thoughts. The question, "What are gay people like?" can elicit their stereotypes—for example, that gay people are promiscuous, unhappy, or pedophilic. Only after these stereotypes are fully mined should the therapist raise questions about their validity. Another invaluable task is for students to recount their sexual history from first memories onward; this helps them reclaim forgotten childhood and early adolescent lusts or crushes that are earlier evidence of homoeroticism than they initially recalled. This exercise is particularly important for students who misattribute the origin of their sexuality to social events.

Dean, an openly gay junior who had great difficulty accepting his homosexuality, reported with deep regret that he himself was responsible for his current predicament. Six years earlier he had "broken" himself by engaging in oral sex with his best male friend, and ever since, he'd been aroused by homoerotic thoughts and images. On reviewing his sexual history, however, Dean recalled with surprise many earlier instances of same-sex attractions. This exploration demonstrated that his homosexuality had begun much earlier than he thought and that the oral sex with his friend was an *expression* of his sexuality, not its *cause*.

The connection between homoeroticism and gender atypicality is exceptionally strong (Cohen, 2002). Many same-sex-attracted individuals have been humiliated by peers because they didn't fit gender stereotypes—for example, males who were poor athletes. Thus, successful treatment of sexual minorities frequently entails reclaiming, integrating, and grieving these shameful memories.

Reparative and Conversion Therapy

If the above interventions fail to improve self-acceptance, caring therapists may be tempted to consider students' requests for changing their sexual orientation. Before undertaking this effort or referring clients to a so-called reparative therapist, it is crucial to recognize that there is no empirical evidence published in peer-reviewed journals in support of reparative therapy (Haldeman, 1994). Whereas sexual *behavior* and sexual *identity* may be amenable to change (Cohen & Savin-Williams, 2003), sexual *orientation* is not. This conclusion is further supported by the innumerable anecdotal reports of young people who desperately but futilely attempted to alter their homoerotic orientation through prayer, abstinence, suppression, and opposite-sex dating.

It should not be surprising that these attempts are futile, because a growing body of empirical research suggests that sexual orientation is biologically encoded, especially for males (Cohen, 2004). Homosexuality is related to genetic endowment, level of prenatal sex hormones, brain anatomy and functioning, cognitive and verbal abilities, gender expression, handedness, finger length ratio, bone morphology, and auditory and visual processing (for a comprehensive review, see Rahman & Wilson, 2003).

Accordingly, the American Psychological Association, the National Association of Social Workers, the American Counseling Association, the American Academy of Pediatrics, the American Medical Association, and the American Psychiatric Association have adopted policies acknowledging that homosexuality is not a mental illness. They advise against discriminatory practices such as reparative therapies, which not only lack empirical support but may even cause harm.

Gender Minorities

Historically, sex-atypical individuals were derided as tomboys and sissies and usually tried hard to conform to culturally mandated notions of female/male, femininity/masculinity. Those who believed they were assigned the wrong sex seldom openly articulated those assertions and simply sought refuge within lesbian, gay, and bisexual communities. As society moves toward greater acceptance of sexual minorities, though, there is growing tolerance for gender minorities and diverse gender expressions. Young people now have role models (RuPaul, k.d. lang) and vocabulary to create meaning from their experiences and to inspire self-acceptance and emboldened self-expression.

Whereas many therapists are comfortable treating sexual minorities, knowledge about gender minorities lags, spawning inappropriate assessment and treatment. A therapist's willingness to nonjudgmentally inquire about gender experiences from the outset of treatment greatly helps these students.

Transgender

Transgender is an umbrella term for individuals who transcend traditional gender norms—behavior and values that society deems appropriate for one sex or another—and includes transvestites, transsexuals, and gender benders. Many students are content with their biological sex, yet because they do not behave in gender-stereotypical ways consider themselves transgender. They often grow up being teased for inappropriate gender role behavior and as adults may continue to harbor feelings of inadequacy that benefit from therapeutic intervention.

Transvestism   Transvestites are sexually aroused by images of themselves wearing "sexy" opposite-sex clothing. Usually heterosexual men with a male gender identity (they like their genitals), they may feel empowered and rebellious by the act. Cross-dressing begins in childhood or adolescence and often increases in frequency (and wardrobe) but has decreasing erotic appeal. Eventually, it may serve primarily to relieve anxiety.

Female impersonators and gay men who dress in drag for fun or entertainment do not necessarily derive sexual pleasure from the act. As such, they are not transvestites. Many transvestites are content and well functioning. If they request counseling, it is often because they want to strategize how best to share their secret with a partner to increase closeness and, perhaps, to permit cross-dressing at home. Others seek counseling when they encounter social difficulty or suffer increasing anxiety. The goals of treatment may include identifying relational and sexual needs, finding alternate sexual outlets, and developing novel ways of managing anxiety. Cognitive-behavioral treatments may help identify avoidable thoughts, feelings, and situations that generate cross-dressing and that can be managed with cognitive restructuring strategies.

Transsexualism   Transsexuals experience severe gender dysphoria and ongoing desire for the social roles and physical traits of the opposite sex. Unlike transvestites, they usually do not derive sexual gratification from cross-dressing. Rather, many feel trapped in an incorrect body and cross-dress to reclaim their rightful persona. Some transsexuals meet DSM-IV criteria for gender identity disorder since childhood and grow up suffering castigation and even violence from family and peers, as illustrated in the movie *Boys Don't Cry*. When they are mandated to conceal their gender atypicality, anxiety and depression may ensue.

Gender identity disorder and transsexualism are almost certainly of biological etiology and impervious to drug and talk therapies. However, counseling is beneficial for mitigating resulting emotional problems. There has been a slight increase in students, usually males, wanting treatment to obtain sex hormones or to fulfill counseling requirements prior to obtaining sex hormones or sex reassignment surgery. Most therapists lack appropriate training for this work and are advised to refer patients to sex reassignment clinics or other appropriate specialists. It is vital to follow through with referrals because frustrated or impoverished students may forgo medical oversight in favor of dangerously impure underground sex steroids. Counselors whose moral beliefs preclude their supporting the transsexual's transformation should refer the case.

Conclusion

Sexual inquiry is challenging because it necessitates acknowledging and exploring themes that clients, and often therapists, have been socially conditioned to experience as embarrassing. Polite people do not speak, or ask, about anal sex and masturbation. Nonheterosexual therapists may feel additionally burdened by the belief that they must conceal their own sexual orientation and behaviors—and this withholding may generalize to inadequate displays of empathy and insufficient inquiries about sexual matters. Such behavior is often pronounced among young and inexperienced therapists who lack practice dialoguing about sex.

It is our responsibility to recognize these limitations and appropriately manage them, if necessary with a supervisor or consultant. College counseling is typically brief. It is therefore incumbent on us to maximize treatment by direct and immediate exploration of sexual issues. We should embrace the opportunity to impart sexual information and clarify myths while normalizing development. Because our treatment can engender greater comfort with sexuality and make it possible for students to act upon their sexual desires, it is also essential to educate clients about contraception and STIs. When appropriate, students should be referred to sex educators, medical professionals, and peer counselors. Perhaps the biggest gift therapists can impart is modeling comfort with sexual issues and honesty.

References

American Psychiatric Association. (1994). *Diagnostic and statistical manual of mental disorders* (4th ed.). Washington, DC: Author.
Blum, R. W., Beuhring, T., Shew, M. L., Bearinger, L. H., Sieving, R. E., & Resnick, M. D. (2000). The effects of race/ethnicity, income, and family structure on adolescent risk behaviors. *American Journal of Public Health, 90,* 1879–1884.
Bogart, L. M., Cecil, H., Wagstaff, D. A., Pinkerton, S. D., & Abramson, P. R. (2000). Is it "sex"?: College students' interpretations of sexual behavior terminology. *Journal of Sex Research, 37,* 108–116.

Brame, G. G., Brame, W. D., & Jacobs, J. (1996). *Different loving: The world of sexual dominance and submission.* New York: Villard.

Bruckner, H., & Bearman, P. (2005). After the promise: The STD consequences of adolescent virginity pledges. *Journal of Adolescent Health, 36,* 271–278.

Carpenter, L. M. (2001). The ambiguity of "having sex": The subjective experience of virginity loss in the United States. *Journal of Sex Research, 38,* 127–139.

Cohen, K. M. (2002). Relationships among childhood sex-atypical behavior, spatial ability, handedness, and sexual orientation in men. *Archives of Sexual Behavior, 31,* 129–143.

Cohen, K. M. (2004). Etiology of homoeroticism. In E. C. Perrin, K. M. Cohen, M. Gold, C. Ryan, R. C. Savin-Williams, & C. M. Schorzman (Eds.), *Gay and lesbian issues in pediatric health care* [Special issue, pp. 355–359]. *Current Problems in Adolescent Health Care, 34,* 355–398.

Cohen, K. M., & Savin-Williams, R. C. (2003). Are converts to be believed? Assessing sexual orientation "conversions." *Archives of Sexual Behavior, 32,* 427–429.

Cohen, K. M., & Savin-Williams, R. C. (2004). Growing up with same-sex attractions. In E. C. Perrin, K. M. Cohen, M. Gold, C. Ryan, R. C. Savin-Williams, & C. M. Schorzman (Eds.), *Gay and lesbian issues in pediatric health care* [Special issue, pp. 361–369]. *Current Problems in Adolescent Health Care, 34,* 355–398.

Crockett, L. J., Bingham, C. R., Chopak, J. S., & Vicary, J. R. (1996). Timing of first sexual intercourse: The role of social control, social learning, and problem behavior. *Journal of Youth and Adolescence, 25,* 89–111.

Diamond, L. M., & Savin-Williams, R. C. (2003). The intimate relationships of sexual-minority youths. In G. R. Adams & M. D. Berzonsky (Eds.), *Blackwell handbook of adolescence* (pp. 393–412). Malden, MA: Blackwell Publishing.

Donnelly, D., & Fraser, J. (1998). Gender differences in sado-masochistic arousal among college students. *Sex Roles, 39,* 391–407.

Haldeman, D. C. (1994). The practice and ethics of sexual orientation conversion therapy. *Journal of Consulting and Clinical Psychology, 62,* 221–227.

Knox, D., Cooper, C., & Zusman, M. E. (2001). Sexual values of college students. *College Student Journal, 35,* 24–27.

Laumann, E. O., Gagnon, J. H., Michael, R. T., & Michaels, S. (1994). *The social organization of sexuality: Sexual practices in the United States.* Chicago: University of Chicago Press.

Maxmen, J. S., & Ward, N. G. (1995). *Essential psychopathology and its treatment* (2nd ed.). New York: W. W. Norton & Company.

Mosher, W. D., Chandra, A., & Jones, J. (2005). Sexual behavior and selected health measures: Men and women 15–44 years of age, United States, 2002. *Advanced Data from Vital and Health Statistics, 362.* Hyattsville, MD: National Center for Health Statistics.

Paul, E. L., & Hayes, K. A. (2002). The casualties of "casual" sex: A qualitative exploration of the phenomenology of college students' hookups. *Journal of Social and Personal Relationships, 19,* 639–661.

Rahman, Q., & Wilson, G. D. (2003). Born gay? The psychobiology of human sexual orientation. *Personality and Individual Differences, 34,* 1337–1382.

Reinisch, J. M., & Sanders, S. A. (1999). Attitudes toward and definitions of having sex: In reply. *Journal of the American Medical Association, 282,* 1918–1919.

Sanders, S. A., & Reinisch, J. M. (1999). Would you say you "had sex" if . . .? *Journal of the American Medical Association, 281,* 275–277.

Savin-Williams, R. C. (2005). *The new gay teenager.* Cambridge, MA: Harvard University Press.

Savin-Williams, R. C., & Cohen, K. M. (Eds.). (1996). *The lives of lesbians, gays, and bisexuals: Children to adults.* Fort Worth, TX: Harcourt Brace College Publishing.

Schwartz, I. M. (1999). Sexual activity prior to coital initiation: A comparison between males and females. *Archives of Sexual Behavior, 28,* 63–69.

Thompson, C., & Zoloth, B. *Homophobia.* Retrieved April 23, 2006, from http://www.endhomophobia.org/homophobia.htm

13

Sexual Victimization

JACQUELYN LISS RESNICK AND NATALIE ARCE INDELICATO

College students experience many types of sexual victimization, including rape and sexual assault, child sexual abuse, sexual harassment, stalking, and intimate partner violence. This chapter will provide a broad overview of conceptualizing and treating these problems and will also briefly address work with perpetrators. To simplify the writing and as a reflection of the prevalence statistics, we usually refer to the victims as women and the perpetrators as men; however, the intent is not to minimize the fact that male victimization and same-gender perpetration also occur.

Prevalence

Determining the scope of the problem is complicated by several factors: Very few incidents are reported to officials or law enforcement, definitions of sexual victimization vary, and research methodology is inconsistent. Fisher, Cullen, and Turner (2000) conducted a comprehensive national study of the sexual victimization of 4,446 college women. Behaviors were categorized to encompass completed, attempted, or threatened rape; completed or attempted sexual coercion; completed or attempted sexual contact; stalking; and visual and verbal harassment. This study found that nearly 5% of college women experience completed or attempted rape in a calendar year, or between 20% and 25% over the course of a 5-year college career. There were even more incidents than the rates for victimization imply, since 22.8% were multiple-rape victims. When the other victimization categories in addition to rape are included, an astounding 15.5% of college women are victimized in a year. Fisher et al. noted that while most women fear assault by a stranger, most sexual victimizations occur when women are alone with a man they know, at night, and in a residence. Fewer than 5% of victims reported the incidents to law enforcement; two thirds told a friend (not a family member or college official).

Specific questioning about sexual victimization is important, since nearly one half of women who have had incidents that meet the definition of rape answer "No" when asked if they considered the incident rape (Fisher et al., 2000); the same applies for sexual harassment. Students commonly will relate disturbing behaviors but resist naming them sexual assault or harassment, particularly if they know the perpetrator.

Factors associated with an increased risk of sexual victimization include frequent and heavy drinking, being unmarried, and prior victimization (Fisher et al., 2000). Several studies examining prevalence rates of sexual assault among women of color found that rates experienced by black, Hispanic, Asian, and white college women were relatively comparable (Abbey, 2002; Koss, Gidycz, & Wisniewski, 1987).

Conceptualization

Conceptualization and diagnosis are complicated, since individuals' reactions, the length of the distress, and events vary widely. The ecological model developed by Koss and Harvey (1991) accounts for the multiple factors that impact victims' responses. Initially applied to rape trauma, the model fits other forms of sexual victimization as well. The model considers interrelationships among personal characteristics of the victim (e.g., age, developmental stage), aspects of the traumatic event (e.g., duration, severity), and the social environment in which recovery occurs (e.g., social supports, attitudes, and values). It also accommodates multicultural considerations (e.g., race, ethnicity, class, and sexual orientation) identified by Sue and Sue (2003) as important variables affecting clients' response.

Since rape, sexual assault, and other forms of interpersonal violence represent traumatic events that overwhelm ordinary functioning (Herman, 1992), the diagnosis of posttraumatic stress disorder (PTSD) is a useful way to conceptualize many victims of abuse (American Psychiatric Association, 2000). People who have PTSD respond to the traumatic event with intense fear, helplessness, horror, reexperiencing of the event, and often other symptoms such as numbing or increased arousal, persistent avoidance of stimuli associated with the trauma, and significant disturbance in functioning. PTSD may be acute (less than 3 months), chronic (3 months or longer), or of delayed onset (a minimum of 6 months). Symptoms presenting and resolving within 4 weeks of the traumatic event have the differential diagnosis of acute stress disorder (ASD).

Complex PTSD may be presented by those who have been repeatedly subjected to traumatic experiences (Herman, 1992). These people experience problems with trust, overwhelming emotions, destructive behaviors, identity confusion, and dissociation. Brown (2003) notes that traumatic experiences may fit broader definitions than the standard diagnoses in the *Diagnostic and Statistical Manual* (DSM) (American Psychiatric Association, 2000), including events or experiences that violate a person's expectations of a just or safe world, betray trust in dependency relationships, or occur as a buildup of small, persistent threats. Now considered a subcategory of PTSD, another useful diagnosis is *rape trauma syndrome,* first introduced by Burgess and Holmstrom (1974). Rape trauma syndrome is characterized by consistent psychological reactions that come first in an acute phase (lasting from several hours to several weeks), and then in a reorganization phase (the long-term process of recovery, including chronic disturbances).

The patterns of response to sexual victimization seen in rape trauma syndrome have been described by several other authors (Koss & Harvey, 1991; Sutherland & Scherl, 1970; Walker, 1994). Koss and Harvey describe four phases of response: (1) *anticipation*, or the earliest recognition of danger, (2) *impact* of the event and its immediate aftermath, (3) *reconstitution*, or attending to basic living considerations and outwardly adjusting despite ongoing symptoms, and (4) *resolution*. These phases do not necessarily play out in a smooth or predictable steplike progression. During the reconstitution phase, which varies from a few weeks to several months, the victim may experience anxiety, fearfulness, nightmares, depression, guilt, shame, sexual dysfunction, somatic complaints, and helplessness. Ideally, the victim is eventually able to seek help; identify anger; have altered cognitive schemas; experience safety, trust, power, and esteem; enjoy intimacy; and develop resilience. Unfortunately, for some, resolution is long delayed or may not occur.

While some students present directly with sexual victimization, commonly other problems are identified as the primary concern: alcohol or substance abuse, eating disorders, depression, anxiety, difficulty in relationships, dissociation, or self-mutilation. Sexual victimization may have happened a long time ago and not have been considered victimization by the client and/or not have been recognized as being connected to current problems (Koss & Harvey, 1991); therefore, to recognize and treat sexual victimization, routine screening and questioning about experiences, using specific, nonjudgmental language, is essential. The case of Laurel illustrates how other presenting issues can disguise sexual victimization.

Laurel, a 29-year-old single white female who enlisted in the army following high school and subsequently put herself through college, was referred by a professor concerned about her erratic behavior in the research laboratory. She admitted drinking too much, consuming 8 to 12 beers in an evening. She was severely self-critical, lacked self-esteem, and had little insight into her behavior, regarding emotions as evidence of weakness. Laurel felt that fears regarding her commitment to a long-distance relationship had precipitated the drinking. However, the counselor did not regard this as a sufficient explanation for either her alcohol abuse or self-hatred. After several sessions of gentle but focused exploration of her self-punishment, Laurel reluctantly revealed that at age 11 she had been sexually involved with a teenaged neighbor. Ashamed and guilty, she had never told anyone, especially because she'd had some pleasurable physical response and wanted the attention. She was confused and horrified by her reaction and felt she had to be punitive to keep herself in check.

Her counselor emphasized the coercion and the fact that her neighbor had been several years older. Laurel became able to reframe her neighbor's actions and her response into a more acceptable schema, finding compassion for the confused child she had been and still carried inside. With some effort, she stopped being so self-punitive and learned more constructive ways to self-regulate than alcohol abuse. Instead of having to keep her painful secret, Laurel was now able to integrate the experience and understand its impact on current relationships. By termination in the 10th session, when she left for a postdoctoral position, Laurel had reduced her excessive drinking, was more self-accepting, and was functioning at work. She remained ambivalent about intimate relationships and indicated that she would consider future counseling to address her relational needs. The counselor's understanding of the impact of childhood molestation was critical in conceptualizing Laurel's distress and developing a treatment plan to address her avoidance, low self-esteem, and mistrust of others. Using everyday situations, the counselor frequently confronted Laurel's destructive coping behaviors while validating her motivation and exploring alternatives that could be practiced.

Interventions

Recommended intervention strategies incorporate feminist and trauma therapy as applied to sexual victimization (e.g., Brown, 2003; Herman, 1992; Walker, 1994). Feminist models externalize the trauma, viewing sexual victimization within the context of sexism and other forms of oppression, and emphasize shared power in the therapy relationship. Herman (1992) characterizes psychological trauma as disempowerment and disconnection from others, and views the recovery process as occurring in a healing relationship that empowers the survivor and creates new connections. The goals of "survivor therapy" (Walker, 1994) are to ensure safety; restore a sense of control; move toward interdependence on others; acknowledge sociopolitical, cultural, and economic contexts; provide respect and empathy for the victim; and develop new coping strategies. For Koss and Harvey (1991), recovery is a "victim to survivor process" in which traumatic symptoms are reduced, effect is no longer overwhelming, reconnection with others occurs, meaning is assigned, and self-blame is replaced by self-esteem. Sue and Sue (2003) espouse integration of multicultural factors to address significant contextual variables. Reviewing all these models, there is considerable overlap and consistency with clear implications for counseling.

Bearing witness to victims' stories of abuse can be difficult for counselors, who should strive to empathize with the pain and helplessness without getting trapped in it. Counselors need to balance clients' emotional processing and disclosure with containment and control, so that clients are not overwhelmed.

Working together with the client helps determine the optimal pace and depth of exploration. Specific techniques found to be helpful with sexual victimization, such as eye movement desensitization reprocessing (Shapiro, 2001), narrative therapy, and art therapy, may be integrated into the counseling process but require specialized training. Attention to the somatic aspects of trauma (Brown, 2003) may include recommendations for exercise and relaxation techniques, consideration of antidepressant or anti-anxiety medications, and testing for pregnancy and sexually transmitted diseases, including HIV/AIDS. Bibliotherapy may be useful to provide information on the process of recovery and coping skills, such as the cognitively based self-help guide, *The Rape Recovery Handbook* (Matsakis, 2003).

Group counseling can be effective as a primary intervention or an adjunct to individual therapy. Typically, specific groups are recommended, although mixed-abuse groups can be successful (Walker, 1994). Various group theoretical orientations can be used, including insight-oriented, relational, feminist, and cognitive-behavioral approaches. Benefits of group treatment include reduced isolation, explicit support, validation, confirmation of experience, reduced self-blame and enhanced self-esteem, egalitarian mode of care, opportunities for safe attachment, shared grief, and assignment of meaning (Koss & Harvey, 1991). Group participation can facilitate social skill redevelopment, educate regarding victimization, and allow for exploration of the traumatic event's impact. Selection criteria, assessment of client readiness, treatment goals, format, process, duration, and structure are other important considerations. Guidelines include clearly delineating expectations, creating group norms, sharing time and focus as equally as possible among participants, and facilitating a sense of safety, respect, and trust. Participants often report that they are able to extend compassion and kindness to other members that they are not yet able to bestow on themselves.

Rape and Sexual Assault

Sexual assault, sometimes referred to as rape or sexual battery, can be considered an extreme form of sexual harassment. When defining sexual assault, state laws now typically include forced oral, anal, or vaginal penetration by the penis or digital or manual penetration. Most state laws consider same-gender assault and marital rape as forms of sexual assault. Definitions have broadened to acknowledge that consent cannot be given when victims are incapacitated and that many victims do not use physical resistance in order to survive the assault. Counselors are encouraged to learn their state laws and the university protocols that apply to assaults on and off campus.

Although the frequency of stranger rape, where the victim does not know the attacker, is lower than other types, it is the most feared by women, who typically regard it as life-threatening. Police involvement, evidence collection, and prosecution are more likely than in other types of sexual assault. While pressing charges is empowering for some victims, it also extends the time that they must deal with the assault. The following case illustrates the feelings of shame and blame that stranger rape induces, the often painful aftermath, and the distress caused when victims can't recall the event due to intoxication or the sedative effects of "date rape" drugs.

Amy, a 19-year-old white female, was referred to the counseling center by a student affairs official following a sexual battery by a man who dragged her to an apartment rooftop. Police reports indicated that she fought against her attacker, making enough noise that police were called. Amy was found with her clothes ripped off; the assailant had fled and was later apprehended. Upon awakening at the hospital, Amy had no recollection of what had happened. She had been drinking heavily that night, but "no more than usual," and wondered if drugs had been slipped into her drink. She was angry and felt as if she was the one "on trial" and "under the microscope," while her assailant was released on bond and able to return home. She told only her roommates and parents about the assault because of her confusion about her role in it. Troubled and ashamed, Amy isolated herself, avoiding a planned holiday with friends. Her father, generally supportive, took her out to buy new, "less revealing" clothes. Her mother, by contrast, blamed her for having been drinking. Amy wanted to put it all behind her, but had trouble concentrating on studies. Involvement with prosecutors in preparation for the trial, 5 months away, made it hard to move forward and regain a sense of control.

With the counselor's encouragement, Amy agreed to very short term counseling, which focused on validation, support, and engaging her in the counseling process. Amy decided to terminate after three sessions, stating that she was "handling things well." Amy's determined self-reliance was born out of her responsibilities as a child due to her mother's mental illness. The counselor explored and supported Amy's decision, framing it as a reasonable option that also reflected her reluctance to depend on others. The counselor explained that more distress could emerge in the future and that Amy could return to counseling as needed. In addition, Amy was provided with psychoeducational materials on sexual assault recovery. Amy was appreciative of the counseling and indicated a willingness to seek help again if necessary.

Acquaintance (or date) rape is far more prevalent than stranger rape. Because of the relationship with the perpetrator, recovery is often complicated. The victim rarely identifies the act as sexual assault and often experiences guilt and self-blame, especially if there was drinking or drug use, she at all went along with the perpetrator's advances, or they had a prior consensual sexual relationship. Indeed, the majority of assaults involve alcohol use, typically where both victim and perpetrator have been drinking (Abbey, 2002). It is important that counselors understand their own attitudes and beliefs regarding acquaintance rape, especially in the context of a victim who demonstrates high-risk behaviors. Even if a person had been drinking or taking other risks, a rape victim is still a victim.

Sometimes victims refuse professional help due to minimization or denial. In these cases, as long as safety is assured, counselors should meet clients "where they are," provide psychoeducational information that normalizes their response, and offer future counseling and other support services when needed. The following case is typical of students who come in at the behest of others, are reluctant to explore the event or acknowledge its impact, and simply wish to return to their usual level of functioning.

LaVerne, an 18-year-old African-American, first-generation college student, was referred by a family friend after she confided that she had been sexually assaulted by an acquaintance during a visit home. Unable to talk with her family about the event, she was determined to remain in school; however, she had difficulty concentrating, her grades suffered, and she was ashamed and self-blaming, thinking she should be strong enough to "get over it." Short-term counseling helped LaVerne acknowledge that something of consequence was impacting her functioning. The counselor normalized her response and supported her desire to carry on, while discussing alternatives that would protect her academic standing and scholarships. In the final session, the counselor communicated the following: "I know you think this incident should not have affected your studies as much as it did. You are used to doing well and being in control. Now you feel like you have let everyone down. . . . I hope that counseling has helped you to see that many people have reactions just like yours, and you are not to blame. You showed courage in coming in for help and I respect your desire to do your best and try to complete the term. If later you find that this decision does not work, please know that you can come back to the Counseling Center for assistance in obtaining a retroactive withdrawal. The university understands that experiences like yours can be very disruptive. You are also welcome to come back to discuss any issues of concern as you make your way through college."

The next case illustrates working with an acquaintance rape victim whose problems are complicated by an abusive relationship history and difficult family of origin. The counselor's interventions were strengths based—focusing on establishment of trust, reempowerment, self-acceptance, development of boundaries, and establishment of personal connections.

Pam, a 19-year-old white female in her second year, experienced a vicious sexual assault within a dating relationship. Twenty-four hours after the assault, Pam required hospital transport to treat extensive vaginal/uterine injuries. She rejected offers for follow-up treatment at that time, but at her friends' insistence later presented to the counseling center. She reported intrusive recollections, disruptions of her studies and social activities, feelings of being violated and betrayed, self-blame for "being stupid," and hostile feelings toward men.

To establish a safe environment and help restore Pam's feelings of control, the counselor encouraged Pam to choose the sessions' content, while noting that telling the story of the rape would eventually be part of her recovery. For a long time, Pam avoided discussing it, focusing instead on difficulties with school and family. The counselor provided validation, confronted her negative, self-defeating behaviors, and supported her reempowerment through setting boundaries with her mother. Counseling also examined Pam's history of being stalked and her aggression toward men. When Pam described how she liked scratching and slapping a male friend, the counselor explored Pam's feelings of power and being in control. Pam acknowledged these feelings, stating, "I know it sounds sick. Mostly, I don't feel I have control." The counselor nonjudgmentally validated her desire to feel in control, and then said, "I wonder in what other ways you can be in control without abusing someone."

In the 10th session, the counselor invited her to talk about the rape, suggesting that Pam's recent acting out was an indicator that containment was becoming harder. Pam then recounted the story of the rape. She said that she'd felt negated and physically overpowered, yet doubted that this mattered because of prior consensual sexual acts with the assailant. The counselor helped her see the difference between those earlier experiences and the nonconsensual violence that transpired on that night. As Pam made the distinction between behaviors for which she was responsible and assaults, where she lacked control, her self-blame abated. In the 12th session, just before she left for the summer, Pam identified changes in the way she perceived the assault, reported that her symptoms had decreased, and said she had moved on in her life and felt "stitched" (Resnick, 2001).

Child Sexual Abuse and Repeated Victimizations

Child sexual abuse typically involves a child victim and a perpetrator known to the victim, usually a family member, caretaker, or neighbor. The impact of the abuse depends on the age of the victim and the perpetrator, behavior, type of contact, and perception of the abuse. Like other kinds of sexual victimization, it is best to consider child sexual abuse along a continuum rather than as a dichotomous, yes-or-no phenomenon. In general, though, child abuse is devastating. Children who experience sexual violence are most vulnerable to repeat victimization and negative life outcomes for years afterward, including mental, reproductive, and sexual health problems; studies show that 12–17% of girls and 5–8% of boys suffer these consequences (Doll, Koenig, & Purcell, 2004).

Walker (2004) cautions that the reactions of repeatedly victimized people should not be pathologized, although we might be tempted to do so because they frequently display poor judgment or self-destructive behaviors. Those who have been repeatedly victimized perceive life differently from those in the majority culture, often experiencing their world as hurtful rather than caring and their family as unsafe rather than secure. Lynn, Pintar, Fite, Ecklund, and Stafford (2004) suggest that they may deal with this discrepancy between their own and the mainstream worldview by making choices that reduce the dissonance—repeatedly putting themselves in vulnerable situations to fit their expectations of an unsafe world. Using this framework, their behaviors can be understood as dysfunctionally functional rather than pathological (Lynn et al., 2004, p. 173). To break the pattern of repeated victimizations, counselors need to help clients recognize traumas, find new and constructive ways of coping, separate from dangerous relationships, and avoid high-risk behaviors. Some clients may find additional healing in reaching out to other victims or engaging in activism against sexual assault.

The following case illustrates heightened vulnerability, dissociation from feelings, and use of numbing to handle anxiety, all associated with revictimization.

Tara returned to school after dropping out following a hospitalization for a suicide attempt. Her presenting problem in counseling was severe bulimia, which had begun in high school. Though she had a history of sexual abuse, she stated it was no longer an issue. She disclosed that in the preceding term she thought she'd been raped by a male friend; she stated that she had been drunk at the time and was uncertain about what had happened, except that she had contracted a sexually transmitted disease. Questions about the onset of bulimia in high school also revealed that at the time, she had been secretly having sex with a coach. Sessions later, Tara further disclosed that at age 6, after her father's death, she had been sexually molested for 2 years by a trusted member of the clergy. Thus, while she initially discounted the significance of sexual abuse, it was clearly a main source of her current concerns. Gradually she was able to see the impact of her past on her present distress.

Progress was not linear. When dealing with especially disturbing emotions, Tara's bulimia tended to worsen and she engaged in high-risk behaviors. Most difficult for the counselor was observing Tara's involvement with a predatory man, which had begun as an exciting involvement with a "forbidden" partner but soon turned into abuse. As the relationship became more dangerous, the counselor explored various ways that Tara might end it and create safety for herself. Reluctantly, Tara decided to take some action and obtained a restraining order. The counselor reviewed the relationship with Tara and confronted her lack of awareness of danger signs as it evolved. Using narrative techniques, the counselor discussed alternative actions that would better protect her in the future.

A breakthrough occurred in a session using Gestalt art techniques. Tara obliterated her drawing with forceful black marks and began to cry, recalling the "hairy hands" of the man who had violated her as a child and describing the seduction in detail. As the profound betrayal finally came to the fore, Tara felt some relief, and she was able to love both the abused child she had been and her adult self. By termination, Tara had stopped bulimic behaviors and begun having healthier relationships. The counselor later learned that after graduation she had applied for graduate school in counseling because of her desire to help others.

Bass and Davis (1988), writing for victims of child sexual abuse, advise that the healing process begins by taking stock, recognizing the damage, and honoring what the victim had to do to survive. Healing steps include accepting that the abuse happened; breaking the silence; understanding that it wasn't one's own fault; identifying the child within; trusting oneself; grieving; and anger. Sometimes there is a difficult stage where remembering is easily triggered and can be overwhelming. Resolution may include disclosures and confrontations, forgiveness, and spirituality. It entails developing self-esteem and personal power, experiencing feelings, and reconnecting with one's body and with intimacy and sex. Resolution also requires that victim/survivors understand the impact of the abuse on their interactions with romantic partners, families of origin, friends, and their own children. Follow-up readings (e.g. by Davis [1990, 1991]) are also helpful for counselors, clients, and those close to clients.

It is important to utilize grounding and containment strategies along with relaxation techniques so that clients can create emotional distance from the abuse when reprocessing it. Containment, a key clinical concept for regulating regression, dissociation, and/or retraumatization, provides safety for victims by creating a "holding space" for unprocessed memories so they can be identified, explored, and expressed. Visual, physical, or cognitive grounding strategies, such as deep breathing, help clients who dissociate or have intrusive memories.

Often victims of child sexual abuse tell no one, keeping their secret out of shame, fear, or the wish to protect others. The therapist may be the first person they disclose it to, and this revelation must be authentically heard and not lost or minimized, as counselors are entrusted recipients. The following case exemplifies how sexual victimization is sometimes hidden even from the victim.

Jana, a quiet and withdrawn first-year student of Jamaican descent, presented with depression, anxiety, inability to concentrate, and vague concern about going to visit her extended family in Jamaica over the holiday break. The counselor was uncertain about the influence of cultural differences and tried to sensitively explore these issues, specifically her feelings about working with a white counselor and about the idea of seeking counseling. When asked about her history and whether she had ever felt this depressed before, she mentioned bedwetting when she was 6, which caused her shame and made her parents angry. She did not have many other childhood memories, but those she had were mostly sad.

This was where matters stood until the sixth session, when Jana stated she heard some music that brought back memories of molestation by a cousin. He had been 15 and she 5 or 6—around the time of the bedwetting. Not only did the molestation plausibly trigger the bedwetting, but it added to the isolation and shame the bedwetting caused. Jana hadn't told anyone about these incidents before, or even recalled them. She now realized that she was fearful about seeing her cousin on the upcoming trip. Her recollections were vivid and the session was extended beyond the usual time frame to enable her to tell her story.

Giving voice to her experience was a breakthrough for Jana and provided needed catharsis. Telling her story validated the reality of what she experienced and helped her gain control over what was previously unprocessed. The counselor's role was to serve as a witness and support and provide validation, but not to lead or prompt.

There has been controversy over the accuracy of recovered memories of abuse. Pope and Brown (1996) provide an in-depth discussion of clinical considerations when working with clients who report recovered memories, and suggest that this work requires specific competencies and knowledge.

Sexual Harassment

Sexual harassment (SH) is a form of gender-based abuse and a violation of Title VII of the Civil Rights Act and of Title IX of the Education Amendment. The legal definition of SH refers to unwelcome sexual advances, requests for sexual favors, and other verbal or physical conduct of a sexual nature where there is a *quid pro quo*—i.e., acceptance or rejection of the harasser's advances affects one's employment or academic status. In a *hostile work environment,* the harasser's conduct substantially interferes with the victim's work or academic performance. Harassing behaviors include repeated unwanted sexual remarks, suggestive looks, deliberate touching, pressure for dates or sexual favors, and actual or attempted rape or sexual assault.

Unwanted sexual attention, sexual coercion, and harassment based on one's gender are the most common types of harassment. As with other forms of sexual victimization, typically women are victims and men are perpetrators, although there are exceptions where men are victims and same-gender harassment occurs. Female students who may be at higher risk on campuses include students in smaller colleges or small departments, women of color, women and men in nontraditional fields, and students who are economically disadvantaged (Rabinowitz, 1996). The American Psychological Association's website on myths and realities of SH describes types of harassment and psychological, physiological, and career-related consequences (American Psychological Association, n.d.).

Although sexual harassment is widespread in academia and the workplace, most victims don't take direct action when harassed, even though when asked hypothetically respondents say that they should and would act assertively (Koss et al., 1994). Very few victims confront their harasser, and even fewer make formal reports. They fear they will be blamed, will not be believed and will be retaliated against, the reporting process will make it worse, nothing will be done, or they will get the harasser in trouble. Magley (2002) reconceptualizes this seeming inaction as a form of coping, observing that those who indicated that they "did nothing" reported using numerous tactics to manage their experiences, such as avoiding or ignoring the offender. Victims may use internal (e.g., endure, deny, detach) and/or external (avoid, appease, assert, report) coping means to manage cognitions and emotions. Counselors must confront any bias that assertive responses (reporting or confronting) are good and disengaging responses are weak and inadequate. To be most helpful to clients, counselors should also be familiar with campus sexual harassment polices and procedures.

SH victims often find themselves harassed by persons who exert some power over them socially, academically, or on the job; such as faculty or administrators harassing students or supervisors harassing employees. However, peer harassment is also common, as when staff harass coworkers or students harass fellow students. Harassment can even occur when the harasser appears to have less power than the victim, which is labeled *contra-power harassment*. This last situation is particularly confusing for victims, who often do not recognize what is happening and blame themselves for being inadequate. In these cases, ascribed power (e.g., gender) and informal power (e.g., anonymous harassment) can be used by the offender.

Polly, a 27-year-old white female returning to school for an advanced degree after working successfully in the high-tech sector, came to the counseling center frustrated with her academic program and thinking of dropping out. She felt ostracized by her predominantly male workgroup peers and was the butt of frequent verbal insults and taunts. Her work performance suffered, making her even more vulnerable. Incensed that no one was intervening, she voiced her feelings but was told to "get a sense of humor." The head of the lab indicated that he was not aware of any problems and offered Polly a workgroup change—but this meant altering her research focus without addressing the hostile environment.

Counseling focused on validating Polly's experience, supporting her remaining in school, and developing an action plan using the formal complaint process. The counselor also used role-playing, assertiveness training, and goal setting to prepare her for the complaint process, which was drawn out and painful because she confronted feelings of humiliation and rejection; however, Polly felt reempowered when her complaint resulted in departmental changes.

An alternative to using the formal complaint process is for the victim to write a letter to the harasser, which objectively describes the offensive behavior, includes the victim's feelings, and calls for the behavior to stop. Mailed to the harasser with return receipt requested, it puts the harasser on notice that the behavior is unwelcome. If the behavior continues, the letter is part of the evidence in a formal complaint process. Additionally, the office of the campus ombudsperson is typically trained to deal with complaints of sexual harassment and can be provided as a resource to clients.

Lali, a biological sciences graduate student of Indian descent, was distressed over personal comments made by the professor directing her research. He asked about her dating and sexual relationships and related tales of his troubled marriage and experiences with other women. When planning a trip to a conference where they were presenting a joint paper, he informed her they would have to share a room due to limited funds. Lali's cultural values of deference and respect for professors left her confused and uncertain about what to do. Very short term counseling confirmed that her discomfort was understandable and that the professor's actions were inappropriate. In reviewing her options, Lali decided to write a letter. She reported later that the harassing behaviors stopped. An otherwise high functioning individual, Lali was able to continue in her program, albeit with a more distant relationship with her professor.

Stalking

Stalking is a crime involving pursuing an individual in a threatening and potentially dangerous way; state laws vary on legal definitions (Meloy, 1998). More broadly defined, college students experience stalking as unwanted, repeated attention or harassment that creates fear in a reasonable person. Fisher et al. (2000) found that 13% of college females experienced being stalked; 80% knew their stalkers (often a boyfriend, ex-boyfriend, or classmate); the stalking lasted about 60 days (occurring several times per week); 17% of the victims reported the stalking to police; and 90% confided in a friend, family member, or roommate.

Examples of stalking include being followed, watched, phoned, written, or e-mailed in ways that seem obsessive or make the victim fear for her safety. Counselors may be surprised to learn that in many jurisdictions police are unable to intervene unless the stalker has met the legal definition for threatened harm. Students are often frustrated and angered that police cannot "do something," since they experience intrusion and fear. At the same time, actions that victims can take—changing phone numbers or e-mail accounts, altering their usual behavior to avoid the stalker, or filing a student conduct complaint—may feel burdensome. Since stalking can end in violent outcomes or even death, the behavior needs to be taken seriously, and the impact on the victim should not be minimized. A Cornell University website (Haugaard, Seri, & March, 2004) is an excellent resource for counselors and students.

Angelica was a 20-year-old Latina in her third year. After she decided to break up with Ric, her boyfriend of several months, because he had become increasingly controlling, Angelica was surprised to receive phone calls from him afterward insisting that they get back together. The more she tried to dissuade him, the more he pressured her. He began sitting on the balcony across from her apartment every night, staring for hours, using the excuse that he was visiting with friends. Angelica left to attend a summer program in another state, but to her dismay Ric tracked her down and visited unannounced. She tearfully called her parents, who notified campus police, and she spoke with him briefly, telling him to leave, which he did only when she said the police were coming. When Angelica returned to college in the fall, Ric again started to sit vigil across from her apartment.

At this point, Angelica sought counseling, focusing on stress management and ways to handle Ric. Since Ric had not threatened harm, a restraining order was not possible, and she was reluctant to use the student conduct code. Helpful interventions were validation and developing new coping strategies such as journaling, positive self-statements, and relaxation exercises. Encouraged in counseling to give meaning to her experience, she decided to get involved in campus outreach related to the promotion of healthy relationships in college students. As an otherwise high functioning student who had the support of friends and family, Angelica was able to move forward and reclaim her power. However, the vulnerability, helplessness, and fear she felt for many months were now a part of her reality.

Intimate Partner Violence

Intimate partner violence (IPV), also known as domestic or relationship violence, refers to hurtful or unwanted physical, sexual, and/or verbal abuse inflicted by one partner or the other in a dating, partnered, or married relationship. Women experience IPV at a rate three to six times that of males (Tjaden & Thoennes, 2000). IPV can damage students' physical and emotional safety (and can be fatal), reduce trust in the campus community, and interrupt students' academic progress. Silverman, Raj, Mucci, and Hathaway (2001) found that approximately 1 in 10 female students reported being physically abused by a date, approximately 1 in 25 reported being sexually assaulted by a date, and approximately 1 in 20 reported being both sexually and physically assaulted by dating partners.

IPV is used by the offender to gain power and control over the other person, who is left with a sense of isolation and powerlessness. It tends to occur in a cyclical fashion (typically the violence stops for periods) and to escalate in frequency and severity over time. Factors associated with vulnerability to partner abuse include traditional sex-role beliefs, low self-esteem, a history of experiencing or witnessing violence in one's family of origin, and the seriousness of the relationship (Arriaga & Oskamp, 1999). The risk of violence was associated with substance use, unhealthy weight control behaviors, sexually risky behaviors, pregnancy, and suicidality (Silverman et al., 2001).

An assessment of clients' abuse history should cover a number of areas: a description of the most recent incident, frequency and severity of the violence, the mechanism of injury or abuse, the presence of firearms, escalating patterns of violence, and legal actions (Kaslow, 2004). Assessments should also determine clients' coping strategies, social support, and access to needed resources. Kaslow notes that many clients terminate after a crisis passes, so it is important to create as much movement and provide as much information as possible in the initial sessions. It is imperative to help clients understand the cycle of violence (Walker, 1994), address safety concerns, and create a safety plan. The client should be encouraged and empowered to look at options and make choices. If the therapeutic relationship extends beyond the first few sessions, counseling can address deeper self-esteem issues, increase stress-management skills, and further encourage resiliency and social support development. Counselors should be aware that there is an increased risk of offender violence when a victim attempts to leave or obtain a restraining order.

Couples counseling remains controversial when there is partner violence, but may be requested when the victim wishes to return to the relationship. Sometimes sequential treatment is needed, with the victim and the perpetrator receiving separate individual or group counseling prior to the couples intervention, which occurs only if the violence has ended. Goals include examining the dysfunctional and coercive interactions between partners, establishing nonviolent means of conflict resolution, and establishing a more equalitarian style of relating (Kaslow, 2004). The following case highlights important considerations when working with couples.

Lea and Sherri, a lesbian, African-American couple, both 21 years old, were living together for 8 months prior to counseling. The more Sherri pressured Lea for greater intimacy in the relationship, the more remote Lea became. One night, Sherri shouted at Lea and ended up shoving her. Lea was incensed and wanted to break up but was convinced to try counseling first. The couple agreed that resorting to violence was wrong and expressed their commitment to finding alternatives. In counseling, it emerged that Sherri had an abuse history, lacked social support, and was estranged from her family, who rejected her as a lesbian. Lea, in contrast, had a supportive family and many friends. Discovering these factors helped them understand their different needs in the relationship; Sherri understood why she wanted more. Both of them realized that being female, women of color, and lesbians (often termed "triple jeopardy") placed them in a disadvantaged position, which put pressure on the relationship to meet their intimacy, relational, and social needs. Counseling also focused on improving their communication skills, setting boundaries, and building on their mutual caring. Sherri worked on distinguishing assertive versus aggressive communication, and Lea worked on being a better listener and hearing Sherri's concerns and fears. They also explored the dynamics of power in their relationship, recognizing that Sherri's greater dependence on the relationship created a power imbalance.

Sexual Victimization of Men

Less than 5% of reported sexual assault victims are male (Abbey, 2002). However, these cases are underreported by victims because of the social stigma, fear of not being believed, and lack of knowledge about where to report or get help. Using a broad definition of sexual victimization, Struckman-Johnson and Struckman-Johnson (1994) found that one third of male university students had experienced at least one coercive episode since the age of 16; 12% of these incidents involved physical restraint, physical intimidation, harm, or threat of harm. Because a majority of male victimization is perpetrated by other men (Abbey, 2002), the sequelae of sexual trauma for victims can include sexual identity confusion and concern about whether others will question their sexual orientation (King & Woollett, 1997).

Though interventions for working with male victims tend to be based on clinical experience with female victims, there are specific professional and self-help books aimed at working with males (e.g., Lew, 2004). In some ways, male victims respond differently from female victims. For males, the stigma and shame accompanying the trauma are particularly difficult given the myth that males should be able to protect themselves. Unlike women, who generally show tearfulness, withdrawal, and fear after an assault, men may react with increased aggression and hostility; destructive and illegal behaviors; abuse of alcohol and other substances; sexually aggressive acting out; and minimization of the impact of the assault (Mezey & King, 2000).

Anthony was an 18-year-old Hispanic male who came to counseling because of difficulty achieving erections with his girlfriend. He said that after a date a year ago with a woman friend, he'd let her stay in his room because her roommates were away for the weekend and she did not feel safe staying alone. In the middle of the night, he awoke to find her kissing him and placing her hand down his pants to masturbate him. When he resisted her efforts to put his penis in her mouth, she became angry and made degrading comments about his sexuality, and they did not speak again. Now, whenever he was in a sexual situation with his current girlfriend, he had intrusive thoughts of this event. The counselor helped Anthony realize that he had been the victim of sexual assault by dispelling myths and stereotypes that men cannot be sexually victimized by women. Counseling focused on decreasing Anthony's shame, self-blame, and embarrassment and increasing his sense of control, positive self-statements, and ability to express anger and resentment.

Gay, Lesbian, Bisexual, and Transgender Issues

Gay, lesbian, bisexual, and transgender (GLBT) victims confront the same issues as all other victims of sexual violence. However, their experiences are compounded by the oppression and hostility encountered by sexual minorities. They frequently report being afraid to reveal their sexual orientation or their relationship with the perpetrator to police officers, medical providers, or student affairs professionals. Factors that further disempower GLBT victims include the fear of being "outed," the wish to protect same-gender relationships from further discrimination, gender myths that women do not batter and that men are equals in a fight, and societal homophobia.

For gay men, assaults tend to be physically violent and have a high likelihood of causing severe physical injuries. Gay men are often targeted because of their sexual orientation; rape is more likely to be perpetrated by heterosexual men (Groth & Burgess, 1980). For lesbian women, vaginal penetration during an assault can be particularly painful if they have not had prior intercourse; additionally, lesbian victims must contend with the stereotype that women "become" lesbians as a result of sexual victimization by men. Loulan (1987) found that 38% of lesbians had experienced sexual abuse by the age of 18, so statistically there is a strong possibility for one or both lesbian partners to have some history of victimization. Sexual victimization is a particular concern for transgendered individuals, who are often stalked, harassed, and assaulted because of their transgendered status, as vividly portrayed in the movie *Boys Don't Cry*. For that matter, physical and sexual violence are often perpetrated on anyone who expresses or shows visible cross-gender behavior. The complexity of issues facing GLBT victims of sexual victimization requires open, caring, and affirming therapy.

Paul, a 22-year-old gay-identified graduate student, began to date his teaching assistant, Rob, who was 6 years older. Over time, Rob grew increasingly jealous of Paul's younger friends. One night, Paul and Rob began fighting about attention Paul had paid to a male friend. Rob slapped Paul several times, pushed him into bed, held him down, and anally penetrated him, all the while verbally abusing him. When Paul later came to the counseling center, the counselor helped him understand the power Rob exerted and the impact of the physical and verbal abuse he experienced. The counselor dispelled the myth that sexual assault cannot occur in relationships where there has been prior sexual contact, and also helped Paul process his reluctance to report the assault due to fears of a homophobic response from the university and of outing his partner.

Counseling Offenders

In a national survey, college men acknowledged carrying out forced intercourse at a rate of 5–15% and sexual aggression at a rate of 15–25%; 84% of those whose behavior met the legal definition of rape did not consider their actions to be illegal (Koss et al., 1987). Most perpetrators can be regarded as "hidden" offenders (Koss, Leonard, Beezley, & Oros, 1985), because few sexual assaults are reported to campus authorities or identified as assaults by the victim or perpetrator. Perpetrators' attitudes, beliefs, and socialization experiences determine the context in which they sexually assault or when they believe that sexual assault is justifiable (Berkowitz, 1992).

Most offenders do not present to counseling voluntarily and do not voluntarily continue beyond what is required of them by legal or disciplinary bodies. For as long as they are in counseling, it's important to explore their use of alcohol or other drugs (often co-occurring) and motivation for change. Perpetrators may use victim blaming as a way to cope with and avoid feelings of shame and guilt. Therapeutic goals include taking responsibility for their actions, disclosing their history of perpetrating violence, and recognizing the impact of the violence on themselves, victims, and others.

For those offenders who engage in counseling beyond the initial sessions, further therapy can help them express and experience genuine empathy, understand and challenge traditional male gender roles, become open to a wider range of emotional self-expression, and increase awareness of their own and others' physical, spiritual, emotional, and sexual boundaries. Additional interventions include increasing healthy responsiveness to physical and emotional cues, substituting negative thoughts with positive self-talk, and creating positive support systems that validate their change process.

Jose, a 22-year-old international graduate student from a privileged, upper-class South American family, was advised by the university police department and his attorney to go to the counseling center after he was charged with sexually assaulting his friend, Lisa. During the intake session, Jose spent a great deal of time recounting specific details of the event, which he did not define as an assault. He stated that Lisa did not say yes but did not say no, that she willfully came to his apartment and kissed him. When Jose tried to have sex with her, Lisa pulled away slightly and told him that she had a boyfriend, but he persisted. He regarded the sex as consensual, but the next day Lisa called and told him he raped her. He stated that he saw counseling as an "opportunity to come and talk about philosophical beliefs and relationship issues."

This case challenged the counselor to build rapport in order to eventually confront Jose's minimization, defensiveness, and denial of the assault. Perpetrators like Jose can have considerable resistance to seeing themselves clearly and honestly. If they falsely attribute their behavior to others, particularly the victims, they will not deal with issues of control and anger that potentially lead to additional violence. Counselors should confront the discrepancy between offenders' reality and external reality, pointing out legal or social consequences of their behavior. Additionally, psychoeducation about victims' recovery process and revictimization may push perpetrators toward increased responsibility for their behaviors.

It is important for counselors to examine their own beliefs about offenders' behavior, capacity for change, violence, socialization, relationships, and conflict. On one hand, counselors must clearly convey that there are no situations in which sexual victimization is justifiable and that sexual assault, SH, stalking, and IPV are wrongful acts of power and control. Yet in order to work effectively with offenders, counselors must also retain empathy and avoid being judgmental.

Some practitioners believe that counseling with perpetrators must be voluntary rather than mandated by the university or legal system. Others accept mandated initial assessments, but require ongoing counseling to be voluntary. Still others argue that treatment should be provided even if it's not voluntary, believing that practitioners have an obligation to both the perpetrator and potential future victims to try to help the perpetrator. "The perspective that advocates precluding mandatory treatment of undesirable clients simply ensures that there will always be victims and consequently always be clients for those who will treat only victims" (Pollard, 1994, p. 53).

Final Considerations

Collaboration among various campus and community groups is vital to managing and treating victims and offenders. A coordinated, comprehensive, culturally competent, and strengths-based campus response should include crisis responders and residence life personnel, the counseling center, the health center, victim advocates, academic and student affairs, student groups, law enforcement, legal and judicial systems, shelters, and other community resources.

While many clients seen in counseling centers will not be involved in formal charges, Pope and Brown (1996) caution that any clinical case is potentially a forensic case; record-keeping guidelines from professional organizations such as the American Psychological Association (Committee on Professional Practice and Standards, 1993) can facilitate preparation of case notes that can withstand legal scrutiny. Counseling records should be accurate and concise, avoiding specificity of detail that could later be used to impeach testimony. Safety plans should be well documented, and interventions should be informed by current scientific data and standards of practice.

The legal and medical definitions regarding sexual victimization do not always match up to behavioral definitions and psychological experiences. Counselors should be aware of these potential discrepancies; clients may have been raped, battered, or harassed without labeling it as such or without "the system" recognizing it, whether due to insufficient evidence or failure to meet legal criteria. Regardless of the law, counselors can validate clients' experience by labeling events as traumatic and victimizing.

Therapeutic interventions combine crisis intervention and trauma theory with feminist and multiculturally competent approaches, and may integrate other counseling theories as well. Therapy may be very brief or long-term, depending on the type of event and the victim's response. Those with complicated histories, multiple victimization, and comorbid conditions usually require lengthier interventions. Demonstrating nonjudgmental respect and empathy toward clients, facilitating their regaining control, emphasizing their resiliency, and incorporating their developmental phase are crucial. Interventions can facilitate or impede recovery, depending on their sensitivity and timeliness. As counselors, our knowledge, attitudes, and skills must reflect an understanding of the sociocultural context regarding sexual victimization and how it affects our own and clients' worldviews.

Victimization and traumatic events leave scars but do not have to disempower victims forever. Victims can become survivors—reempowered, reconnected, and potentially strengthened by their experiences. As Brown (2003, p. 143) notes, "Recovery from trauma does not mean we go back to who we were before the trauma—trauma changes us. Our view of the world, ourselves, and the meanings that we give to life will always take into account the reality of the trauma. . . . We regain our sense of hope and efficacy grounded . . . in knowledge that we can heal from traumatic experiences."

References

Abbey, A. (2002). Alcohol-related sexual assault: A common problem among college students. *Journal of Studies on Alcohol, 63*(Suppl.), S118–S129.

American Psychological Association. (n.d.). *Sexual harassment: Myths and realities.* Retrieved June 23, 2005, from http://all.net/games/sex/harass.html

American Psychiatric Association. (2000). *Diagnostic and statistical manual of mental disorders* (4th ed., text revision). Washington, DC: Author.

Arriaga, X. B., & Oskamp, S. (1999). The nature, correlates and consequences of violence in intimate relationships. In X. B. Arriaga & S. Oskamp (Eds.), *Violence in intimate relationships.* Thousand Oaks, CA: Sage Publications, Inc.

Bass, E., & Davis, L. (1988). *The courage to heal: A guide for women survivors of child sexual abuse.* New York: Harper & Row.

Berkowitz, A. D. (1992). College men as perpetrators of acquaintance rape and sexual assault: A review of recent research. *Journal of American College Health, 40,* 175–181.

Brown, L. S. (2003). Women and trauma. In L. Slater, J. H. Daniel, & A. E. Banks (Eds.), *The complete guide to mental health for women* (pp. 134–135). Boston: Beacon Press.

Burgess, A. W., & Holmstrom, L. L. (1974). Rape trauma syndrome. *American Journal of Psychiatry, 131,* 981–986.

Committee on Professional Practice and Standards. (1993). Record keeping guidelines. *American Psychologist, 48,* 984–986.

Davis, L. (1990). *The courage to heal workbook: For women and men survivors of child sexual abuse.* New York: Harper & Row.

Davis, L. (1991). *Allies in healing: When the person you love was sexually abused as a child.* New York: Harper Collins.

Doll, L. S., Koenig, L. J., & Purcell, D. W. (2004). Child sexual abuse and adult sexual risk: Where are we now? In L. J. Koenig, L. S. Doll, A. O'Leary, & W. Pequegnat (Eds.), *From child sexual abuse to adult sexual risk* (pp. 3–10). Washington, DC: American Psychological Association.

Fisher, B. S., Cullen, F. T., & Turner, M. G. (2000). *The sexual victimization of college women* (NCJ 182369). Washington, DC: U.S. Department of Justice.

Groth, A. N., & Burgess, A. W. (1980). Male rape: Offenders and victims. *American Journal of Psychiatry, 137,* 806–810.

Haugaard, J., Seri, L., & March, A. (2004). *Stalking.* Retrieved April 20, 2006, from http://www.humec.cornell.edu/stalking

Herman, J. L. (1992). *Trauma and recovery.* New York: Basic Books.

Kaslow, N. J. (2004, May). *Therapeutic interventions with survivors of intimate partner violence (IPV).* Paper presented at the annual sexual battery conference of the Gainesville (FL) Commission on the Status of Women, Inc.

King, M. B., & Woollett, E. (1997). Sexually assaulted males: 115 men consulting a counseling service. *Archives of Sexual Behavior, 26,* 579–588.

Koss, M. P., Gidycz, C. A., & Wisniewski, N. (1987). The scope of rape: Incidence and prevalence of sexual aggression and victimization in a national sample of higher-education students. *Journal of Consulting and Clinical Psychology, 55,* 162–170.

Koss, M. P., Goodman, L. A., Browne, A., Fitzgerald, L. F., Keita, G. P., & Russo, N. F. (1994). *No safe haven: Male violence against women at home, at work, and in the community.* Washington, DC: American Psychological Association.

Koss, M. P., & Harvey, M. R. (1991). *The rape victim* (2nd ed.). Newbury Park, CA: Sage Publications.

Koss, M. P., Leonard, K. E., & Beezley, D. A., & Oros, C. (1985). Nonstranger sexual aggression: A discriminant analysis of the psychological characteristics of undetected offenders. *Sex Roles, 12,* 981–992.

Lew, M. (2004). *Victims no longer: The classic guide for men recovering from sexual child abuse* (2nd ed.). New York: HarperCollins.

Loulan, J. (1987). *Lesbian passion: Loving ourselves and each other.* San Francisco: Spinsters/Auntlute.

Lynn, S. J., Pintar, J., Fite, R., Ecklund, K., & Stafford, J. (2004). Toward a social-narrative model of revictimization. In L. J. Koenig, L. S. Doll, A. O'Leary, & W. Pequegnat (Eds.), *From child sexual abuse to adult sexual risk* (pp. 159–180). Washington, DC: American Psychological Association.

Magley, V. J. (2002). Coping with sexual harassment: Reconceptualizing women's resistance. *Journal of Personality and Social Psychology, 83,* 930–946.

Matsakis, A. (2003). *The rape recovery handbook.* Oakland, CA: New Harbinger Publications.

Meloy, J. R. (1998). *The psychology of stalking: Clinical and forensic perspectives.* San Diego, CA: Academic Press.

Mezey, G. C., & King, M. B. (Eds.). (2000). *Male victims of sexual assault.* Oxford: Oxford University Press.

Nelson, M. L. (1996). Separation versus connection, the gender controversy: Implications for counseling women. *Journal of Counseling and Development, 74,* 339–344.

Pipes, R. B., & LeBov-Keeler, K. (1997). Psychological abuse among college women in exclusive heterosexual dating relationships. *Sex Roles: A Journal of Research, 36,* 585–604.

Pollard, J. W. (1994). Treatment for perpetrators of rape and other violence. In A. D. Berkowitz (Ed.), *Men and rape: Theory, research, and prevention programs in higher education* (pp. 51–66). San Francisco: Jossey-Bass.

Pope, K. S., & Brown, L. S. (1996). *Recovered memories of abuse.* Washington, DC: American Psychological Association.

Rabinowitz, V. C. (1996). Coping with sexual harassment. In M. A. Paludi (Ed.), *Sexual harassment on college campuses: Abusing the ivory power* (pp. 199–214). Albany: State University of New York Press.

Resnick, J. L. (2001). From hate to healing: Sexual assault recovery. *Journal of College Student Psychotherapy, 16,* 43–63.

Shapiro, F. (2001). *Eye movement desensitization and reprocessing: Basic principles, protocols, and procedures* (2nd ed.). New York: Guilford Press.

Silverman, J. G., Raj, A., Mucci, L. A., & Hathaway, J. E. (2001). Dating violence against adolescent girls and associated substance use, unhealthy weight control, sexual risk behavior, pregnancy, and suicidality. *Journal of the American Medical Association, 286,* 572–579.

Struckman-Johnson, C., & Struckman-Johnson, D. (1994). Men pressured and forced into sexual experience. *Archives of Sexual Behavior, 329,* 93–114.

Sue, D. W., & Sue, D. (2003). *Counseling the culturally diverse* (4th ed.). New York: John Wiley Sons.

Sutherland, S., & Scherl, D. J. (1970). Patterns of response among victims of rape. *American Journal of Orthopsychiatry, 28,* 527–529.

Tjaden, P., & Thoennes, N. (2000). *Extent, nature, and consequences of intimate partner violence: Findings from the National Violence Against Women Survey.* Washington, DC: U.S. Department of Justice.

Walker, L. E. A. (1994). *Abused women and survivor therapy.* Washington, DC: American Psychological Association.

Walker, M. (2004). How relationships heal. In M. Walker & W. B. Rosen (Eds.), *How connections heal* (pp. 3–21). New York: Guilford Press.

14

Eating Disorders

JULIA SHEEHY AND MARY COMMERFORD

The treatment of eating disorders continues to be a major challenge for college counseling centers. Getting people into treatment is often difficult due to denial of illness, fears of giving it up, and shame about the behaviors. Therapists struggle with how to help, given the brief, time-limited treatment models of most college services. Finally, managing the severely ill, those very low-weight students who are barely medically stable, places enormous demands on staff—both therapists and administrators, who struggle with the question of when to ask students to withdraw.

This chapter reviews the most recent efforts at engaging these challenges. We discuss definitions, prevalence rate, and etiology of eating problems, considerations for assessment and treatment planning, popular treatments for each disorder, as well as psychopharmacology, groups, nutritional counseling, and medical monitoring. Challenges of working with this population are discussed in the transference/countertransference section. Suggestions for managing high-risk clients, community considerations, and outreach complete our overview.

Definitions

Eating disorders are defined in the *Diagnostic and Statistical Manual*, fourth edition (DSM-IV), as "severe disturbances in eating behaviors" (American Psychiatric Association, 1994, p. 539). Anorexia nervosa (AN), bulimia nervosa (BN), and binge eating disorder (BED) (still a proposed new diagnostic category) are the major disorders. A residual category of *eating disorder, not otherwise specified* (ED-nos) describes disordered eating that does not meet criteria for the other disorders. The criteria for each disorder are listed below. However, in practice, it is becoming increasingly difficult to distinguish between the groups. For example, many students present with all the symptoms of AN, except that their weight mysteriously doesn't drop, or their menses continue despite very low weights. Attempting to define clear categories continues to be a struggle in the mental health community, and there may be changes in the next DSM.

AN (restricting or binge-eating/purging type) is marked by the refusal to maintain normal body weight (<85% of expected weight), intense fear of gaining weight, body image distortion, and amenorrhea for at least 3 months. The restricting subtype is characterized by the absence of bingeing or purging, while the binge-eating/purging subtype includes those behaviors.

BN (purging or nonpurging type) is defined by recurrent episodes of bingeing; recurrent and inappropriate compensatory behavior to prevent weight gain, e.g., vomiting, fasting, use of laxatives, diet pills, diuretics, enemas (purging subtype); or excessive exercise (nonpurging subtype). To warrant the diagnosis, these bingeing and compensatory behaviors must occur at least twice weekly for 3 months, with self-evaluation overly influenced by body shape and weight.

BED refers to recurrent episodes of bingeing which produces marked distress. The bingeing episodes occur at least twice weekly for 6 months with no inappropriate compensatory behaviors.

ED-nos refers to any problems that nearly meet criteria for the above disorders. It also describes the chewing and spitting out, but not swallowing, of large amounts of food (American Psychiatric Association, 1994).

Prevalence

It is extremely difficult to estimate prevalence of eating disorders due to the large numbers of sufferers who never seek help. Studies suggest that 1–2% of women meet criteria for AN, 3% meet DSM-IV criteria for BN (Mintz & Betz, 1988), and 2–5% meet DSM-IV criteria for BED (Telch & Stice, 1998). However, one study reports that 61% of college women have some form of disordered eating, like chronic dieting, bingeing or purging alone, or subthreshold bulimia, while only 33% reported normal eating habits (Mintz & Betz, 1988).

Early sociocultural models of eating disorders suggested that ethnic minority groups would show fewer eating problems than whites. However, although research results are mixed, there is evidence that the prevalence of eating disorders among ethnic minority groups is reaching parity with whites (Mulholland & Mintz, 2001; Shaw, Ramirez, Trost, Randall, & Stice, 2004).

Eating disorders are on the rise among men too, particularly gay men (Herzog, Newman, & Warshaw, 1991). General estimates indicate that men comprise 10% of eating disorder cases (American Psychiatric Association, 1994). However, in BED, the female to male ratio is closer to 2.5:1 (Spitzer et al., 1992).

Athletics, particularly sports that emphasize a trim body, like gymnastics, figure skating, running, body building, and wrestling, can promote eating disorders. Female athletes often present with the "athletic triad"—amenorrhea, disordered eating, and osteoporosis (Johnson et al., 2004; Johnson, Powers, & Dick, 1999).

Etiology

Eating disorders arise in the context of multiple factors: personality, familial, interpersonal, sociocultural, and biological (Striegel-Moore & Smolak, 2001;

Tylka & Subich, 2004). Personality factors include lack of self-awareness, which makes it difficult for students to recognize their own needs and feelings. People prone to eating disorders are more likely to accept standards of worth and beauty presented by society and the media (Frank & Thomas, 2003). Many struggle with entrenched feelings of incompetence and unworthiness. They are relentlessly self-critical, turning angry feelings inward against the self.

Family factors include depressed, obsessional, or phobic parents. Patterns of overprotectiveness, enmeshment, and lack of conflict resolution can set the stage for eating difficulties (Friedlander & Siegel, 1990). Families often have excessive interests in food, weight, and shape. Parents may not recognize or respond to emotional cues and needs. In general, people with eating disorders do not feel nourished by their relationships. They respond mostly to others' needs, forgetting or ignoring their own.

As for sociocultural influences, the image of women presented in magazines, television, and film pressure women to be thin. This emphasis on their bodies leads women to treat themselves as objects to be evaluated on the basis of appearance (Fredrickson & Roberts, 1997).

Eating disorders can run in families. Studies of twins suggest genetic involvement, since monozygotic twins have a higher incidence than dizygotic twins. Neurobiological studies show serotonin levels related to eating disorders (Jacobi, Hayward, deZwann, Kraemer, & Agras, 2004).

Histories of trauma, particularly sexual abuse, have been related to anorexia and bulimia, but not BED. Trauma histories are roughly as prevalent in eating disordered clients as in persons diagnosed with other psychiatric disorders (Jacobi et al., 2004).

Assessment and Treatment Planning

Intake Interview

Since students may not identify eating problems when they initially present at the counseling service, all intake interviews should include a question or two about possible eating issues: "Our society today is so diet conscious. Do you ever go on diets, or worry about your weight?" Most women in our culture would answer yes. Watch how they respond. If they seem vague or evasive, ask for a sample of a typical day's intake, from the time of getting up to going to bed. Are all food groups included? Do they eat junk food? If not, continue to question about foods not eaten and reasons why. Reasons like food allergies, lactose intolerance, or vegetarianism can often mask eating disorder issues.

If the student identifies concerns about eating or food as part of the presenting problem, assessment should become more straightforward. Inquiry should include weight history; medical concerns; restricting, bingeing, or purging behaviors and their precipitants; and preoccupation with food and body image. Some key questions concern highest and lowest weights (as adults); menstrual frequency; exercise patterns; physical problems like dizziness, constipation, and diarrhea; nature and frequency of thoughts about food; and degree of distress about body size and shape. A sample of a typical day's food intake will give you an idea of what foods are avoided (usually fats and/or carbs). This can also elicit food rules like eating nothing after 6 p.m., vomiting foods with fat, etc. Reviewing many purging options may uncover behaviors not mentioned (vomiting; use of laxatives, diuretics, diet pills; frequency/type of exercise).

Establishing Treatment Goals

Denial and insight are crucial variables in setting treatment goals. Follow-up is critical to ensure medical safety. Once you have first established that clients are medically stable, it is safe to ignore the food issues. You can sometimes engage clients in considering underlying emotional aspects of the problem— improving their relationships to provide better emotional nourishment, or learning new strategies for managing anger and hurt. With this group, setting goals to address food issues is pointless.

When students acknowledge a problem but don't want to change (they feel their eating problem works for them), you can highlight the costs of the eating disordered behaviors—noting how many foods they used to enjoy are now forbidden, how food restriction limits their social life, how the amount of time obsessing about food or weight takes away from other pursuits, and how they risk their physical health. Students may be open to nutritional counseling, to find "safe" foods that they can add to ensure adequate nutrition.

When students reach the point of recognizing the problem and its costs, they are ready to address the symptoms. Cognitive-behavioral therapy (CBT) can be used for weight restoration and return to normal eating. Stress inoculation is important—warning clients that they'll probably feel worse before feeling better. Clinicians can use a surgical analogy: "Immediately after surgery, you feel worse than before you went in, but in time you feel better. Similarly, changing your eating behaviors will increase your anxiety—but it will diminish with time."

Treatment

The Team Approach

Eating disorders are multidimensional syndromes that often require treatment from multiple disciplines: psychology, medicine, nutrition, and psychiatry. Practitioners need to communicate regularly with one another to pool their assessments and impressions of clients and to make united decisions about type and duration of treatment. Operating as a team also helps to counteract the splitting and denial that characterize students with these disorders.

Practice guidelines for the treatment of eating disorders were generated and revised by a task force of the American Psychiatric Association (1993, 2000). The guidelines were based on extensive interviews with clinicians and reviews of the scientific literature. They reflect the field's collective expertise on eating disorders and include level-of-care recommendations based on physiological and psychiatric status. Treatment strategies should be informed by these guidelines.

By virtue of requiring multidisciplinary care, eating disorders present an exacting challenge to college health centers, which often must treat students with limited resources. College health centers must identify and monitor students with eating disorders, introduce them to psychotherapy, and arrange ongoing care for them off-campus.

Individual Treatment for Anorexia Nervosa

Psychotherapy alone has little effect on anorectics who are markedly malnourished. The negativistic mindset and depressed and irritable emotional state of a starved person render exploratory work nearly useless. On the contrary, nutritional rehabilitation, often in a hospital setting, is required for severely underweight anorectics. Such rehabilitation helps to mitigate symptoms of obsessiveness, rigidity, and depression, and in so doing, enhances receptivity to psychotherapeutic interventions. On-campus nutritionists can do nutritional remediation with students who are both motivated and medically safe.

Patients with anorexia are able to benefit from psychotherapy once they have initiated weight gain and are no longer medically compromised (American Psychiatric Association, 2000). Many clinicians who specialize in psychotherapy with anorectics use concepts of both interpersonal theorists, most notably those of Bruch and Crisp, and cognitive-behavioral techniques.

Bruch (1978) believed that anorexia emerged from dysfunction in the mother–child dyad. Specifically, she believed that the deficits in self-awareness and competence that characterize anorexia are the outcome of maternal misattunement and failure to promote autonomy. Sufficient maternal perceptiveness of children's internal states is necessary, she argued, for children to come to know their own impulses, feelings, and bodily sensations. Such self-knowledge, which she termed "introceptive awareness," is what guides children to act effectively in the world. Maternal affirmation of child-initiated actions is also necessary for children to develop a sense of agency. In contrast, chronic maternal misattunement and discouragement of independent strivings leave children confused about their internal experiences and ill-equipped to meet their own needs.

According to Bruch, the clinician's role is to remedy anorectics' deficits by fostering introceptive awareness and encouraging expression and autonomous action. For example, one clinician sensed hurt and anger from a student who repeatedly fell into protracted silences in sessions and said only, "I'm blank." The clinician shared her hunches and urged the student to tend to and voice what she felt at these times. Gradually, the student began to know and practice conveying what for many years she had not allowed herself to experience.

Crisp (1980) saw anorexia as a defense against an avoided family problem, such as sexual abuse or a strained marital relationship. According to his view, puberty, with its attendant biological urges and separations, threatens to accentuate the unresolved problem and destabilize the family. The anorectic halts maturation to rein in her impulses and to maintain the existing, albeit fragile, family structure. Treatment involves helping the anorectic tolerate the anxiety and interpersonal consequences of moving away from the stasis of self-starvation toward psychobiological growth.

CBT aims to enlist the anorectic as an active collaborator in treatment, since accurate self-report data are essential to this approach. Motivation must therefore be assessed and usually strengthened through an analysis of the drawbacks of continuing with the disorder. Weight- and food-related distortions can then be addressed through monitoring of symptoms and psychoeducation about chronic undereating and the futility of dieting behaviors. Patients are also urged to experiment with making the behavioral changes they fear, such as normalizing eating patterns and weight. Later stages of CBT include examining the multiple functions of symptoms and challenging internalized cultural values (Garner, Vitousek, & Pike, 1997).

Most college counseling centers are able to offer only short-term psychotherapy. Because the average duration of anorexia is 7 years and rates of full recovery are modest, what can be accomplished in college settings is limited. Nevertheless, introducing ways of thinking about and ameliorating their symptoms can help ready students for ongoing treatment. For example, students may be encouraged to attend closely to their internal experiences, including sensations of hunger and fullness, and to use those experiences to guide behavior. Students may be asked to consider the possibility that their disorder is connected to a larger family problem. This may open up inquiry about family vulnerabilities and patterns of avoidance to be pursued in ongoing treatment. Self-monitoring and behavioral experimentation, even on a short-term basis, can also help clarify diagnoses and chip away at students' denial. Whatever the approach, therapists who convey interest in students' internal workings and initiate behavior change offer anorectic students much-needed responsiveness and hope.

Individual Treatment for Bulimia Nervosa

Considerable evidence supports the effectiveness of CBT for bulimia and indicates good maintenance of symptom reduction at 6-month and 1-year follow-ups (Wilson, Fairburn, & Agras, 1997). Although interpersonal therapy has also produced good results, improvement occurs more slowly, and fewer outcome studies have been conducted (American Psychiatric Association, 2000).

A CBT manual (Fairburn, 1985; Fairburn, Marcus, & Wilson, 1993) based on Christopher Fairburn's formulation of the disorder is widely used, strictly applied in research studies and more loosely followed in clinical settings. This approach aims to correct the inaccurate cognitions and destructive behaviors that perpetuate the disorder.

According to Fairburn, unrealistic pursuit of an ideal body is at the root of bulimia. Females with low self-esteem assume this pursuit in an attempt to boost feelings of self-worth. They restrict their intake in the hopes of approaching an ideal, but in actuality prime themselves both psychologically and physiologically to lose control by overeating. Although purging is used to compensate for bingeing, it actually perpetuates bingeing by alleviating anxiety about weight gain and by confusing signals of fullness, both of which ordinarily regulate intake. Bingeing and purging further damage self-esteem and, in so doing, worsen the vulnerability that gives rise to and perpetuates the disorder.

Treatment begins with an explanation of the model and an overview of general treatment strategies. Common misconceptions held by most bulimics about the weight-regulating effects of laxatives and vomiting are dispelled, and the detriments of over- and undereating are detailed. Self-monitoring is introduced by having clients record everything they eat, times of eating, associated thoughts and feelings, and antecedents to bingeing and purging. Clients are also asked to weigh themselves only once a week and to begin implementing a normal eating pattern.

Weekly weigh-ins are a powerful tool in addressing bulimia. If you have a bathroom for the exclusive use of the counseling center, you can place a scale there for students to weigh themselves before their sessions. If clients have eaten feared foods, like a piece of cake or a cookie, and are positive that their weight has ballooned, getting on the scale and discovering that this has not happened will astonish them. And if their weight has in fact increased, the therapist can work with them immediately on possible reasons—water retention, menstrual bloating, etc., cognitively challenging them to identify other possible explanations besides the piece of cake. The scale brings their weight fears and false beliefs immediately into the consulting room.

CBT makes clients anxious. They are eating foods they normally avoid, eating and digesting foods they usually purge, and feeling unnerved by sensations of fullness and fears of immediate weight gain. They are urged to abide the discomfort. Doing so allows them to test out their weight fears and discover that their anxiety doesn't spiral endlessly but reliably wanes with time.

Self-monitoring reveals the triggers to starving, bingeing, and purging. Common triggers include flare-ups of low self-esteem and strong emotion. Once these triggers are identified, adaptive means of coping can be generated, such as regulating emotion by journaling or taking a walk instead of resorting to bulimic symptoms. For example, one student discovered through self-monitoring that she often binged and purged in the evenings, when she became flooded with the feelings she had put "on hold" all day. Journaling throughout the day helped her to label and discharge emotions periodically, and so avoid an overwhelming buildup of feeling. Self-monitoring also helps to reveal the many food- and weight-related cognitive distortions that characterize bulimia—for example, that eating a forbidden food will inevitably lead to bingeing and a noticeable change in appearance. Clients are asked to be aware of distorted thoughts and to immediately counter them with realistic ones.

The final phase of treatment reviews progress and remaining vulnerabilities. Depending on what has worked well, strategies are put into place to maintain recovery and prevent relapse.

The course of treatment depicted in the Fairburn manual spans 19 sessions. Although most college counseling centers cannot provide that many sessions, an abbreviated version may be helpful for those whose motivation is high and symptom severity low. For students with higher levels of pathology, an introduction to the model and some experience with behavior change may strengthen their motivation and willingness to continue with treatment off-campus.

Fairburn (1995) has provided a self-help manual which explains the self-maintaining cycle of restricting/bingeing/purging and offers strategies to break out of the cycle and to establish normal eating. The book familiarizes the reader with CBT principles and can be used alone or in conjunction with individual and group therapy. It is recommended for students with either bulimia or BED.

Individual Treatment for Binge Eating Disorder

Cognitive-behavioral and interpersonal approaches used with bulimia have been adapted for BED. Dialectical behavior therapy, originally designed for borderline personality disorder, has also been utilized. All three approaches have been shown to be reasonably successful at reducing short-term bingeing but are relatively ineffective at producing long-term weight loss (Wonderlich, de Zwaan, Mitchell, Peterson, & Crow, 2003).

Interpersonal therapy (Fairburn, 1997) for BED aims to modify the underlying relational difficulties, assessing the interpersonal context out of which the eating pathology emerged, along with clients' current relationships. Triggers to binges are also identified. After this assessment phase, little focus is given to eating disorder symptoms per se.

Interpersonal difficulties usually fall into one of four categories: unresolved grief, role disputes, relational transitions, or interpersonal deficits. After the most pressing problem area is targeted, clients are asked to take the lead in sessions by generating ways to improve their relational difficulties. Clinicians' role is to offer feedback and encouragement. Treatment concludes with a review of progress and relational areas requiring further work. For example, interpersonal therapy with one student revealed that her eating problem took hold after the sudden death of her father. Instead of grieving her own loss, she felt obliged to comfort and counsel her mother, who had slipped into a debilitating and isolating depression. Treatment focused on helping the student go through the mourning process and on changing her long-standing tendency to negate her own needs in the service of caring for others.

Dialectical behavior therapy, which was created by Marsha Linehan (1993), targets impulsive behaviors by enhancing emotion-regulation skills. According to this theory, individuals who regularly engage in impulsive and destructive behaviors are unable to mediate the physiological arousal that accompanies affect. When faced with strong emotion, they are prone to feeling overwhelmed and inept and to engage in maladaptive behaviors such as bingeing. However, these behaviors further diminish self-esteem and reinforce fear of emotion, thereby increasing the likelihood of the behaviors. Treatment begins with an explanation of the model and an introduction to *behavioral chain analysis*, i.e., thoroughly examining the thoughts, feelings, body sensations, and events that lead to impulsive behaviors. Clients are asked to keep a diary detailing maladaptive behaviors, their emotional precipitants, and attempts to cope using skills acquired in treatment. These skills include core mindfulness (being aware of and abiding one's internal experiences without judging them), emotion regulation (labeling emotions, using them as sources of information, and, when possible, changing circumstances that give rise to intense emotions), and distress tolerance (managing unavoidable distress with strategies such as distraction, self-soothing, and weighing the pros and cons of tolerating the distress versus bingeing). Treatment concludes by planning ways to prevent relapses.

BED is more amenable to self-help and group approaches than is either anorexia or bulimia (Wonderlich et al., 2003), making it the most conducive to treatment in college counseling centers.

Psychiatric Treatment

Anorexia

Although medication is frequently used in the treatment of anorexia, there is little evidence to support its efficacy in acute stages of the illness. Antipsychotics, lithium, various antidepressants, and appetite stimulants have all produced disappointing results (Zhu & Walsh, 2002). Although there are promising case reports on the use of the antipsychotic olanzapine (Jensen & Mejihede, 2000; La Via, Gray, & Kaye, 2000), to date there have been no scientific studies published on its effectiveness. Studies also suggest that fluoxetine helps to prevent relapse among patients who have attained a healthy weight (Peterson & Mitchell, 1999).

Bulimia

A substantial number of studies have found that the various antidepressants are equally effective in the treatment of bulimia. Fluoxetine, studied the most extensively, is known to reduce anxiety and depression as well as purging and bingeing. Few studies, however, have demonstrated its long-term effectiveness.

CBT has been found to be superior to medication alone. Although medication enhances the effectiveness of CBT, it is unclear by how much. Existing research suggests that antidepressants may augment psychotherapy for some bulimic individuals but should not be the sole intervention (Zhu & Walsh, 2002).

Binge Eating Disorder

Research on the pharmacological treatment of BED is preliminary. Although antidepressants, appetite suppressants, and anticonvulsants have all shown promise, the selective serotonin reuptake inhibitors (SSRIs) have been studied the most and cause the fewest side effects. If used, higher-end doses given for 6 to 12 months are recommended (Carter et al., 2003).

As with bulimia, CBT has been found to be superior to medication alone in the treatment of BED (Devlin, 2002; Ricca et al., 2001). Whether antidepressants enhance the effects of CBT has not yet been empirically established (Wonderlich et. al, 2003).

Group Therapy

Numerous studies support the efficacy of group therapy for individuals with eating disorders (e.g., Garner, Fairburn, & Davis, 1997; Rosenvinge, 1990). Various group therapies—psychodynamic, cognitive-behavioral, psychoeducational, topic-focused, and self-help—have all been shown to be effective. Nonspecific factors, such as a sense of belonging and interpersonal feedback, are considered to be more important than the orientation used. Groups are capable of diminishing eating disordered patients' common fantasies of uniqueness and feelings of alienation.

General guidelines include screening out patients with low motivation, comorbid psychiatric disorders, or extreme shyness, and preparing clients by making expectations explicit. Groups that emphasize the interpersonal process should be kept small, whereas didactic groups can accommodate more clients (Polivy & Federoff, 1997). Harper-Giuffre and MacKenzie (1992) provide an excellent guide.

Opinions differ as to whether eating disorder groups should be homogeneous with regard to type of disorder and symptom severity, and specifically whether homogeneous groups minimize or maximize competition and emulation. When mixed eating disorder groups work well, members recognize the suffering and isolation common to all eating disorders and encourage one another to strive toward health.

Nutritional Counseling

Nutritionists help clients stabilize eating patterns by addressing dietary deficiencies and excesses and correcting food- and weight-related distortions with education about the body's functioning and nutritional requirements. Clients are helped to eat a variety of healthful foods and, when necessary, to restore their weight to a normal level. Special attention is paid to restrictive eating, which produces many of the symptoms associated with anorexia and perpetuates the binge/purge cycle by producing overwhelming urges to eat. Nutritionists often use meal plans, which help counter entrenched tendencies to under- or overeat.

Medical Monitoring

Eating disorders carry numerous serious health risks and can be fatal. Anorexia is the most potentially fatal of all the psychiatric disorders, with a mortality rate as high as 20% among the most severely ill, most commonly resulting from cardiac arrest or suicide (American Psychiatric Association, 2000). Mortality resulting from bulimia is much less common, although the disorder can cause a host of medical complications (Mitchell, Pomeroy, & Adson, 1997). Obesity, which is sometimes but not always associated with BED, also causes physical concerns, including shortened life expectancy.

Eating disorders require thorough medical assessment and often ongoing medical monitoring. Individuals with anorexia or bulimia need to be monitored for electrolyte imbalances, heart irregularities, low blood pressure, anemia, and osteoporosis. Anorectics need to have their weight monitored closely. Individuals with BED who are significantly overweight need to be assessed for high blood pressure, high cholesterol, and diabetes (Zerbie, 1993).

Medical practitioners are often the first to diagnose eating disorders when taking a history of weight and eating or performing a physical exam. Medical practitioners also set weight parameters when necessary and make critical decisions about when students are too physically ill for outpatient treatment.

Transference and Countertransference

Students with eating disorders bring deep uncertainties and strong yearnings to their treatment relationships: They both fear domination and long for soothing and empathy (Zerbie, 1998). They also bring high levels of aggression, as reflected in the destructiveness and persistence of their symptoms. In psychodynamic terms, strong transference and countertransference reactions are to be expected and, many believe, are necessary for change to occur.

Transference

The Value of Symptoms   Patients often highly value anorectic symptoms. Feelings of mastery and distinction, derived from the ability to fast, counteract feelings of worthlessness. As one student said, "Whenever I walk into a room, I immediately determine who is the skinniest. When it's me, I feel great. When it's not, I feel so insecure I can barely talk." Obsessions with food and weight, though tormenting, can be easier to contend with than the complexities and threats of interpersonal relationships. Patients' experience is also fairly predictable, which appeals to those who are otherwise easily overwhelmed. Their thoughts and routines are repetitive, and their emotional range is narrow. Although individuals with bulimia and BED tend to be more ashamed than anorectics, they do value the regulatory function of their symptoms. These individuals are prone to extremes in impulse and mood, wavering between states of boredom and intensity. Bingeing and purging temporarily replace boredom, numbness, or stress with stimulation and focus, and moderate the edges of intense experiences by relieving bodily tension (Goodsitt, 1983).

The psychological payoff of symptoms often makes for power struggles in the therapeutic relationship; clients fear clinicians want to take away what gives them self-definition and regulation. The challenge for clinicians is to acknowledge the purpose served by the symptoms while simultaneously helping clients find identity and modulation in ways that do not damage the body and diminish vitality.

Ambivalence   Eating disorder symptoms help students manage distress by providing distraction and illusory feelings of control. Yet they also isolate students into an existence of obsessive and ritualistic self-involvement. Sufferers are thus strongly and ambivalently attached to their symptoms. They feel both devoted to and tormented by them.

Letting go of symptoms entails disengaging from an internal relationship with them that has served protective psychological functions and that has come to determine moods, thoughts, and actions. Doing so involves internal upheaval and giving up the reinforcing aspects of the disorders.

Ambivalence about getting better often manifests in treatment as artificial compliance, dishonesty, or attacks against clinicians. To pull clients out of their symptoms, clinicians need to offer a treatment relationship that is compelling and hopeful enough to compete with clients' attachments to their disorders (Davis, 1991). When students begin to feel nourished by their therapist's empathy and acceptance, they can disengage from their symptoms.

Rage   Eating disorders are associated with high levels of anger and anger suppression (Waller et al., 2003). Individuals with eating disorders are often perfectionists who believe that their anger is unacceptable (Siegel, Brisman, & Weinshel, 1988). In conflict about an emotion they have in abundance, they turn to the body for help. Fasting blunts interpersonal responsiveness and, in so doing, contains anger. Bingeing and purging dull feeling and lower arousal.

In the treatment with eating disordered individuals, anger is often cloaked. These clients tend to be outwardly compliant and pleasing, while subverting attempts at progress (Goldner, Birmingham, & Smye, 1997). The clinician's challenge is to halt the acting out of anger through eating disorder symptoms and to invite direct expressions of anger into the therapy. Open expressions of negative transference signal progress in treatment.

Countertransference

Feeling Ineffective   The refractory nature of eating disorders often leaves clinicians doubting their best efforts and training. It is helpful to remember that feelings of inadequacy are at the core of eating disorders (Bruch, 1962). Moreover, individuals with eating disorders are uncomfortable with their feelings and are adept at obscuring them.

It behooves clinicians who feel ineffectual to consider what clients are playing out with them. Clinicians who find themselves beset with feelings of ineffectiveness may be resonating with their clients' experience. Clients may also be sabotaging therapeutic interventions to avoid feeling controlled (Zerbie, 1998).

Rage   Based on past experiences, individuals with eating disorders have come to believe that their anger, if expressed directly, will provoke retaliation or abandonment. To preserve attachments, they have rerouted anger into their bodies through eating disorder symptoms. Aggression toward others does seep out, but often unwittingly and obliquely.

When therapists allow expression of clients' hostility in the therapy relationship, they help redirect clients' anger away from themselves and their bodies. But being the target of clients' aggressive feelings is difficult, especially if the anger is built up and unmodulated. Clinicians may find themselves counterattacking by disengaging, being silently punishing, or offering critical interpretations. The therapeutic challenge is to receive and contain clients' anger without shutting down or retaliating. This is not to say that clinicians need to masochistically absorb clients' hostility; rather, the role of the clinician is to help clients own and, ultimately, modulate and constructively communicate anger. Clinicians who are able to do so send clients the corrective message that all aspects of them, including rage, are knowable and tolerable (Zerbie, 1998).

For example, one client snapped at her therapist for being "too analytical" whenever the therapist asked questions designed to tap into feelings. The therapist felt belittled and slipped into quiet passivity. When the therapist was able to avow and use her own anger to inform inquiries about and resonate with the student's rage, the treatment gained momentum. She said to the client, "I can imagine you might feel threatened and defensive when I ask you pointed questions, given how intolerant and shaming your parents were of your feelings, especially your vulnerable ones. You protect yourself by letting me know to back off, like when you tell me I'm too analytical."

Fear   Eating disorders are stubborn illnesses with high rates of recidivism and grave medical risks. Many of those afflicted with the disorders, moreover, are attached to their symptoms and in denial about their severity.

Clinicians must bear and process anxiety for their eating disorder clients, who are deficient at both gauging and regulating their own emotion. Often, therapists find themselves worried and preoccupied about students who appear calm and unconcerned even as they participate in dangerous behaviors. Fear needs to be fed back to clients in doses they can tolerate and use. Too much fear triggers panic and urgency, while too little colludes with denial. A therapist might say, for example, "The treatment team is concerned about your recent drop in weight. You have several weeks to demonstrate to yourself and to us that you're healthy enough to be at college at this time. Specifically, this means you'll need to adhere to your meal plan and regain the weight that you lost. If you can't, we'll have to heed your symptoms and recognize that you need more help and support than you can get while being a full-time student." Being clear and objective about the required changes helps relieve the therapist and shifts the anxiety and the need for change back onto the student.

Working as part of a treatment team ensures that the fears and responsibilities that accompany this work are shared. Continual supervision also lets clinicians discharge and distill overwhelming anxieties.

Managing At-Risk Clients

Who Stays and Who Goes?

The Rehabilitation Act of 1973 and the Americans with Disabilities Act of 1990 prohibit colleges and universities from discriminating against individuals with physical or mental disabilities. By law, students with eating disorders have the right to attend institutions of higher education. Academic institutions can, however, request and even require students to withdraw if they pose a danger to themselves or others, or if they disrupt the learning environment.

Generally, schools allow students with eating disorders to remain enrolled if they are not at imminent risk for life-threatening medical problems and if they demonstrate awareness of their illness by participating faithfully in treatment. A few college health centers, however, have established physiological requirements for all enrolled students. These include a minimum body mass index (an assessment of body fat based on height and weight) and minimum vital signs (pulse, blood pressure, and temperature). These medical markers are rough estimates of health that point to severity of eating pathology.

Setting Up a Contract

Some students with eating disorders fall just short of requiring medical leave. They hover just above a weight that would necessitate intensive care, or they miss several exams in a semester due to bingeing and purging. The severity of their symptoms calls out for close monitoring and heightened concern, but not immediate withdrawal from school.

For such students, contracts that stipulate agreed-upon terms for maintained enrollment are useful. Stipulations might include a minimum weight and vital signs, participation in specified modes of treatment, progress updates communicated by treatment providers to a school administrator, and goals to be met by semester's end. Allowances for variation can be built in. Because many students will maintain their weight at the bottom of the prescribed range, it's easy for them to slip. Adding to the contract that should they slip they have 1 week to get back in range provides a compassionate cushion for natural weight fluctuations and occasional decreases in intake. Allowing students to help create and sign contracts enlists them in their monitoring and care and ensures consensus about the conditions under which medical leave would automatically take place.

Involuntary Leaves

Medical leaves are preferably taken voluntarily. However, since eating disorders are often associated with denial, mandated leaves are sometimes necessary. Typically, treatment teams issue involuntary leave recommendations to school deans, who ultimately carry out involuntary action against students. At some schools, students have the right to appeal leave decisions. Involuntary leave edicts should always include treatment recommendations for the leave period and conditions for return. For example, a highly symptomatic bulimic student who was enjoined to take a leave was urged to enter a residential treatment program where she would receive structured and intensive care. When her electrolyte balances and vital signs had been at healthy levels for at least 3 months (outside of a treatment program), and her treatment providers could attest to her psychological readiness, she was allowed to return. For severely underweight anorectic students, setting a minimum weight required to return can provide incentive to fight the disorder and regain the weight. Many students are able to relinquish their anorexia only for something they want more—like returning to college.

Although students may threaten to pursue legal action when forced to take leave, most colleges and universities prefer to err on the side of caution when it comes to protecting the integrity of the learning environment and the safety of students.

Community Considerations

Contagion Effects

When eating disordered students cluster, competition and contagion of pathology can ensue. Eating disorder websites, which depict the disorders as chosen lifestyles and provide a forum for encouraging symptoms, are egregious examples. Competition and contagion are also common on inpatient units and in outpatient programs for eating disorders, and can occur at colleges as well, particularly in sororities and certain female athletic teams. Subtle encouragement to engage in eating disordered behaviors can be expressed implicitly, e.g., with approving or disapproving looks, or explicitly, as in the sharing of dangerous weight-loss techniques. Sadly, many eating disordered students learned the behaviors from their roommates or friends.

Roommate Issues

Living with someone who regularly starves, binges, or purges can be very stressful. Emotional reactions range from panic to resentment, and concrete conflicts range from hoarded food that goes rotten to messy bathrooms. Roommates may be tempted to silently accommodate the eating disordered student or to ostracize her. Some roommates become the "food police," watching and interrogating the student about her intake.

Working with roommates about normal emotional reactions is important. Many friends say things like, "I can't be angry with him, he can't help it," when in fact they're furious, feeling put-upon and impotent.

It's often helpful and sometimes necessary for students with an eating disordered roommate to establish ground rules, for example that foods should be replaced and bathrooms should be cleaned immediately (Siegel et al., 1988). If rules are repeatedly broken, a residential staff person can be brought in to assess the difficulty and to determine whether the living situation is workable.

Outreach

Prevention   Given contagion effects, efforts at outreach and prevention run the risk of turning into "how to" sessions. Programs must be designed cautiously, highlighting the damaging effects of the illness rather than dramatizing the symptoms.

Although it is the most common approach to outreach, psychoeducation is not effective in preventing eating pathology. The most effective interventions target established risk factors like the thin-is-ideal internalization or body dissatisfaction. The most effective prevention programming targets at-risk groups, uses an interactive (as opposed to didactic) format, and consists of multiple rather than single sessions (Stice & Shaw, 2004).

Certain academic departments are more likely to have at-risk students. These include the performing arts (particularly dance and acting), broadcast journalism, nutrition, and psychology, as well as highly competitive graduate programs like law and medicine. In addition to programs that address these students, it helps to educate the faculty to recognize warning signs and refer to the counseling service.

Getting students to attend eating disorder programs is a challenge. The "eating disorder" label is tantamount to a "Keep Away" sign. Much more effective is publicizing programs related to "nutritional health," in which some eating disorder information is included. Students flock to any program they think might offer weight loss tips. Covert prevention is the name of the game.

Another approach is to make the focus be "how to help a friend." Given the high incidence of eating disordered behavior on college campuses, many vulnerable students also have friends who are struggling. This can become a "teach what you need to learn" intervention.

Eating Disorders Awareness Week, in February, is generally a time for outreach on college campuses. Relatively inexpensive programs like College-Response and EDAP (Eating Disorders Awareness Program) sell kits with advertisements, screening tools, and informational brochures.

Training Student Groups

An essential aspect of outreach is training student groups like resident assistants (RAs) and health educators. RAs, in particular, are often on the front lines in recognizing and responding to problems. Our training program reviews the definitions of eating disorders and warning signs of possible eating problems, clarifies gray areas like how to tell when irregular eating or exercise becomes a problem, and offers a list of factors to consider when deciding how to respond.

We define the formal eating disorders from the DSM-IV and discuss disordered eating. Behavior becomes problematic, we explain, when there is no flexibility in eating or in exercise rules or patterns. For example, one student realized he had a problem when he couldn't eat a piece of his own birthday cake. When someone has the flu and worries all day because she can't work out, that's an indicator that "normal" behaviors have become compulsive.

Warning signs of possible eating difficulties are discussed in terms of food, body, and social behaviors. We indicate that some of these behaviors are common and may have nothing to do with an eating disorder, although they may mask problems and are good markers for further investigation.

We also teach that food-related behaviors that involve the elimination of a whole food group, like being vegetarian or vegan, or claims of lactose intolerance or food allergies may signal problems. Another warning sign is frequent use of appetite suppressors like gum, hard or gummy candies, diet sodas, coffee, or cigarettes. Also worrisome are students who express fears or false beliefs about food—for example, that one dessert can make you fat—or who never eat in public.

A further point we make is that body obsessions can indicate a problem. People who are overly preoccupied with their bodies or parts of their bodies may be struggling with an eating disorder. They can spend hours getting dressed to find an outfit in which they don't "look fat." Another indicator is compulsive exercise—for example, going to the gym when they're sick, or running in a blizzard. Social behaviors that may predict eating problems include avoiding plans involving meals or canceling at the last minute (they ate "bad food" that day and it shows). Sudden abstinence from alcohol because of the "empty calories" warrants further questioning. Obviously, always going to the bathroom after meals can also indicate eating problems.

Once a student at risk has been identified through outreach, a number of factors should be considered in deciding how to approach the student:

- Is there evidence of health problems? Does she feel dizzy, faint, or weak? If there are many indicators of ill health, a physical evaluation may be mandated.
- How disturbed are the behaviors? A student leaving vomit in jars around her suite may require a more urgent response than someone whose purges are hidden.
- How much insight does he have? Interventions with someone who denies everything will be different than with someone who can talk about his struggles.
- What, if anything, has been tried already? The first intervention, if not a dire situation, is usually gentle and inviting—expressing concern or recommending student support services like counseling or health service. However, if the person has been approached many times but continues to demonstrate problems, more directive approaches may be indicated.
- What is the effect of this person's behavior on the community? People who are upsetting their roommate, suitemates, or the whole floor necessitate stronger intervention than others who suffer privately. Their behavior may invoke disciplinary action from the residential life authority, as well as a referral to the health or counseling service.

Treating eating disorders continues to be one of the greatest challenges for a counseling service. We ask students in treatment to take risks, be flexible, and try new things. As therapists, we must be willing to do the same to continue our progress in managing these devastating illnesses.

References

American Psychiatric Association. (1993). Practice guidelines for eating disorders. *American Journal of Psychiatry, 150,* 212–228.

American Psychiatric Association. (1994). *Diagnostic and Statistical Manual of Mental Disorders* (4th ed.). Washington DC: American Psychiatric Association.

American Psychiatric Association. (2000). Practice guidelines for eating disorders (revised). *American Journal of Psychiatry, 157*(Suppl. 1), S1–S39.

Bruch, H. (1962). Perceptual and conceptual disturbances in anorexia nervosa. *Psychosomatic Medicine, 24,* 187–194.

Bruch, H. (1978). *The golden cage: The enigma of anorexia nervosa.* Cambridge, MA: Harvard University Press.

Carter, W. P., Hudson, J. I., Lalonde, J. K., Pindyck, L., McElroy, S. L., & Pope, H. G. (2003). Pharmacologic treatment of binge eating disorder. *International Journal of Eating Disorders, 34*(Suppl.), 575–588.

Crisp, A. (1980). *Anorexia nervosa: Let me be.* London: Academic Press.

Davis, W. N. (1991). Reflections of boundaries in the psychotherapeutic relationship. In C. Johnson (Ed.), *Psychodynamic treatment of anorexia and bulimia* (pp. 68–85). New York: Guilford Press.

Devlin M. J. (2002). Psychotherapy and medication for binge eating disorder. Paper presented at the Academy for Eating Disorders 2002 International Conference on Eating Disorders and Clinical Teaching Day. Boston, April 25–28.

Fairburn, C. G. (1985). Cognitive-behavioral approach to the management of bulimia. *Psychological Medicine, 141,* 631–633.

Fairburn, C. G. (1995). *Overcoming binge eating.* Guilford Press: New York.

Fairburn, C. G. (1997). Interpersonal psychotherapy for bulimia nervosa. In D. M. Garner & P. E. Garfinkel (Eds.), *Handbook of treatment for eating disorders* (pp. 278–294). New York: Guilford Press.

Fairburn, C. G., Marcus, M. D., & Wilson, G. W. (1993). Cognitive-behavioral therapy for binge eating and bulimia nervosa. In C. G. Fairburn & G. T. Wilson (Eds.), *Binge eating: Nature, assessment, and treatment* (pp. 361–404). New York: Guilford Press.

Frank, J. B., & Thomas, C. D. (2003). Externalized self-perceptions, self-silencing and the prediction of eating pathology. *Canadian Journal of Behavioural Science, 35,* 219–228.

Fredrickson, B. L., & Roberts, T. A. (1997). Objectification theory: Toward understanding women's lived experiences and mental health risks. *Psychology of Women, 21,* 173–206.

Friedlander, M. L., & Siegel, S. M. (1990). Separation-individuation difficulties and cognitive-behavioral indicators of eating disorders among college women. *Journal of Counseling Psychology, 37,* 74–78.

Garner, D. M., Fairburn, C. G., & Davis, R. (1997). Cognitive-behavioral treatment of bulimia nervosa: A critical appraisal. *Behavior Modification, 11,* 398–431.

Garner, D. M., Vitousek, K. M., & Pike, K. M. (1997). Cognitive-behavioral treatment for anorexia nervosa. In D. M. Garner & P. E. Garfinkel (Eds.), *Handbook of treatment for eating disorders* (pp. 94–144). New York: Guilford Press.

Goldner, E. M., Birmingham, C. L., & Smye, V. (1997). Addressing treatment refusal in anorexia nervosa: Clinical, ethical, and legal considerations. In D. M. Garner & P. E. Garfinkel (Eds.), *Handbook of treatment for eating disorders* (pp. 450–461). New York: Guilford Press.

Goodsitt, A. (1983). Self-regulatory disturbances in eating disorders. *International Journal of Eating Disorders, 2,* 51–60.

Harper-Giuffre, H., & MacKenzie, K. R. (1992). *Group psychotherapy for eating disorders.* Washington DC: American Psychiatric Press.

Herzog, D. B., Newman, K. L., & Warshaw, M. (1991). Body image dissatisfaction in homosexual and heterosexual males. *Journal of Nervous and Mental Disease, 179,* 356–359.

Jacobi, C., Hayward, C., deZwann, M., Kraemer, H. C., & Agras, W. S. (2004). Coming to terms with risk factors for eating disorders: Application of risk terminology and suggestions for a general taxonomy. *Psychological Bulletin, 130,* 19–65.

Jensen, V. S., & Mejihede, A. (2000). Anorexia nervosa: Treatment with olanzapine. *British Journal of Psychiatry, 177,* 87.

Johnson, C., Crosby, R., Engel S., Mitchell, J., Powers, P., Whittrock, D., & Wonderlich, S. (2004). Gender, ethnicity, self-esteem, and disordered eating among college athletes. *Eating Behaviors, 5,* 147–156.

Johnson, C., Powers, P., & Dick, R. (1999). Athletes and eating disorders: The National Collegiate Athletic Association study. *International Journal of Eating Disorders, 26,* 179–188.

La Via, M. C., Gray, N., & Kaye, W. H. (2000). Case reports of olanzapine treatment of anorexia nervosa. *International Journal of Eating Disorders, 27,* 363.

Linehan, M. M. (1993). *Cognitive behavioral therapy of borderline personality disorder.* New York: Guilford Press.

Mintz, L. B., & Betz, N. E. (1988). Prevalence and correlates of eating disordered behaviors among undergraduate women. *Journal of Counseling Psychology, 35,* 463–471.

Mitchell, J. E., Pomeroy, C., & Adson, D. E. (1997). Managing medical complications. In D. M. Garner & P. E. Garfinkel (Eds.), *Handbook of treatment for eating disorders* (pp. 383–393). New York: Guilford Press.

Mulholland, A. M., & Mintz, L. B. (2001). Prevalence of eating disorders among African-American women. *Journal of Counseling Psychology, 48,* 111–116.

Peterson, C. B., & Mitchell, J. E. (1999). Psychosocial and pharmacological treatment of eating disorders: A review of research findings. *Journal of Clinical Psychology, 55,* 685–697.

Polivy, J., & Federoff, I. (1997). Group psychotherapy. In D. M. Garner & P. E. Garfinkel (Eds.), *Handbook of treatment for eating disorders* (pp. 462–475). New York: Guilford Press.

Ricca, V., Mannucci, E., Mezzani, B., Moretti, S., Di Bernardo, M., Bertelli, M., et al. (2001). Fluoxetine and fluvoxamine combined with individual cognitive-behavioral therapy in binge eating disorder: A one-year follow-up study. *Psychotherapy and Psychosomatics, 70,* 298–306.

Rosenvinge, J. H. (1990). Group therapy for anorexic and bulimic patients. *Acta Psychiatrica Scandinavica, 82*(Suppl. 361), 38–43.

Shaw, H., Ramirez, L., Trost, A., Randall, P., & Stice, E. (2004). Body image and eating disturbances across ethnic groups: More similarities than differences. *Psychology of Addicted Behaviors, 18,* 12–18.

Siegel, M., Brisman, J., & Weinshel, M. (1988). *Surviving an eating disorder.* New York: HarperCollins.

Spitzer, R. L., Devlin, M., Walsh, B. T., Hasin, D., Wing, R., Marcus, M., et al. (1992). Binge-eating disorder: A multi-site field trial of the diagnostic criteria. *International Journal of Eating Disorders, 11,* 191–203.

Striegel-Moore, R. H., & Smolak, L. (2001). *Eating disorders: Innovative directions for research and practice.* Washington, DC: American Psychological Association.

Stice, E., & Shaw, H. (2004). Eating disorder prevention programs: A meta-analytic review. *Psychological Bulletin, 130,* 206–227.

Telch, C. F., & Stice, E. (1998). Psychiatric comorbidity in women with binge eating disorder: Prevalence rates from a non-treatment-seeking sample. *Journal of Counseling and Clinical Psychology, 66,* 768–776.

Tylka, T. L., & Subich, L. M. (2004). Examining a multidimensional model of eating disorder symptomatology among college women. *Journal of Counseling Psychology, 51,* 314–328.

Waller, G., Babbs, M., Milligan, R., Meyer, C., Ohanian, V., & Leung, N. (2003). Anger and core beliefs in the eating disorders. *International Journal of Eating Disorders, 34,* 118–124.

Wilson, G. T., Fairburn, C. G., & Agras, W. S. (1997). Cognitive-behavioral therapy for bulimia nervosa. In D. M. Garner & P. E. Garfinkel (Eds.), *Handbook of treatment for eating disorders.* New York: Guilford Press.

Wonderlich, S. A., de Zwaan, M., Mitchell, J. E., Peterson, C., & Crow, S. (2003). Psychological and dietary treatments of binge eating disorder: Conceptual implications. *International Journal of Eating Disorders 34*(Suppl.), S598–S573.

Zerbie, K. J. (1993). *The body betrayed: A deeper understanding of women, eating disorders, and treatment.* Carlsbad, CA: Gurze Books.

Zerbie, K. J. (1998). Knowable secrets: Transference and countertransference manifestations in eating disorder patients. In W. Vandereycken & P. J. V. Beumont (Eds.), *Treating eating disorders: Ethical, legal and personal issues.* New York: NYU Press.

Zhu, A. J., & Walsh, B. T. (2002). Pharmacologic treatment of eating disorders. *Canadian Journal of Psychiatry, 47,* 227–234.

15
Personality Disorders

ILENE C. ROSENSTEIN

Perhaps the most difficult issue for mental health practitioners on college campuses is dealing with students with personality disorders. The reasons are many: Often students do not view their behaviors as problematic, have poor insight and judgment, and tend to externalize their concerns. In addition, these students often do not establish therapeutic alliances quickly, and they often have comorbid conditions, making it difficult to treat them, especially in the short-term model typical for many college counseling centers. Even if students do not initiate contact with the counseling service, others in the campus community may be worried or bothered by their behavior and often turn to the college counseling staff for guidance. This type of consultation puts a specific pressure on the counseling center.

This chapter will first review general features of personality disorders and then describe the nature of each cluster and associated disorders as defined by the *Diagnostic and Statistical Manual* (DSM-IV-TR) (American Psychiatric Association, 2000), suggesting possible interventions along with specific therapeutic challenges.

Defining Features of Personality Disorders

Personality disorders differ from other mental disorders in that they are traits and features of personality and not a transient state of being. Recognizing this difference, the American Psychiatric Association (1980) created a separate axis for personality disorders distinct from other mental disorders in the DSM third edition. Whether personality disorders actually are distinct from Axis 1 disorders is still questioned, but such a separation remains (Livesley, 2001).

Currently, the DSM-IV-TR definition of a personality disorder is "an enduring pattern of inner experience and behavior that deviates markedly from the expectations of the individual's culture, is pervasive and inflexible, has an onset in adolescence or early adulthood, is stable over time, and leads to distress and impairment" (American Psychiatric Association, 2000). In practice, diagnosing can be complicated, with many college counselors also being ambivalent about labeling students due to the stigma and seriousness of personality disorder diagnoses.

Personality disorders may first emerge and be recognized when students are in college. Thus, it may be difficult to establish the "enduring pattern" criterion. What one might see, however, is the beginning of a set pattern in which dysfunctional behaviors or experiences persist across environments. Frequently, students will say that they expected things to change when they came to college, only to continue to have the same pattern of life experiences.

With college students, it is usually best to focus on dysfunctional patterns of behavior and experiences. The clinician may have to look for such mal-adaptive responses as extremely inaccurate perceptions and interpretations of the self, others, and events; inappropriate and/or extreme rage, intensity, and lability of emotional response; and very poor interpersonal functioning and impulse control (Livesley, 2001). In supervision of clinicians, I have often used the term "wired wrong" for students with personality disorders; how the student responds is not what you would expect from the typical college student.

Cultural context is a particularly important consideration in a multicultural setting such as a college. Students with personality disorders respond significantly differently from what one would expect in their culture.

An Asian first-year graduate student was brought to the counseling center by his American girlfriend. He dramatically had shaved his beautiful long hair after a fight with her, stating that he could not see or speak with her for one month because he had been "rough with her." He felt shame for "trying to force" himself on her and needed to make public his feelings. This was something quite acceptable and consistent with his culture. Further, he was able to understand how his behavior looked odd and upsetting to his girlfriend and others. Not being rigid, he decided to speak to the girlfriend about his reaction so she would have a better understanding. In his case no diagnosis of a personality disorder was given, because his behavior made sense in a cultural context.

In another case, a young white American college undergraduate went to the train station and had sexual contact with random strangers every time she felt rejected—for example, by a boyfriend, friend, professor, or residential advisor. This student felt no fear in having unprotected sexual contact, reported feeling in "total control," and laughed at others' concern for her. Hers was not a culturally common or acceptable response. In fact, this self-defeating behavior often led to more rejection by those for whom she truly cared. This student had little insight into how her behavior affected others. In addition, her emotional responses were off, ranging from overreaction to an absence of emotions, and she was unable to sustain meaningful relationships. Her decision to have sex with strangers was impulsive, lacking any consideration about the possible consequences. In short, her case did warrant a diagnosis of personality disorder.

The level of distress and impairment is revealing. Kernberg (1984) refers to personality disorders as "constellations of abnormal or pathological characteristic traits of sufficient intensity to imply significant disturbance in intrapsychic and/or interpersonal functioning" (p. 77). These personality traits are viewed as personality disorders when they are not just maladaptive and inflexible but also significantly impair social and occupational functioning or cause tremendous subjective distress (Maxmen & Ward, 1995). Whereas students with neurotic conditions may react inappropriately to the situation at hand, students with personality disorders respond so inappropriately time and time again that they have difficulty progressing academically, vocationally, or socially. Lacking adequate social skills, the ability to form solid relationships, and a clear sense of self, they have difficulty achieving the developmental tasks of college.

The prevalence of personality disorders in a college counseling population has been little studied. The average percentage of clients diagnosed at one Midwestern college counseling center was 7.23 for the years 1996 until 2001 (Benton, Robertson, Tseng, Newton, & Benton, 2003). Lewinsohn, Rohde, Seeley, and Klein (1997) found only a 3.3% rate of prevalence of personality disorders in young adults. Ranges for prevalence of at least one personality disorder in clinical settings were 10% to 35.9%, with borderline personality disorder the most frequently diagnosed personality disorder at 12% and substance use disorders the most common comorbid Axis I diagnosis (Koeningberg, Kaplan, Gilmore, & Cooper, 1985; Torgersen, Kringlen, & Cramer, 2001; Weissman, 1993). Nearly 75% of all patients diagnosed with a personality disorder also present with an Axis I disorder (Dolan-Sewell, Krueger, & Shea, 2001).

There are various models, including biopsychosocial systems, to explain the etiology of personality disorders. Frequently discussed developmental factors include genetic predisposition, disturbed attachment experiences, exposure to trauma, temperament issues, family psychopathology, and, to some degree, sociocultural and political forces such as socioeconomic levels and gender (Magnavita, 2004).

In summary, personality disorders manifest in adolescence but often are first diagnosed in young adults. Their maladaptive behaviors include an inability to reach personal goals or successfully complete the developmental tasks of college. Students with a personality disorder often justify and rationalize dysfunctional behaviors and long-standing patterns. Since they do not see any reason to change, their maladaptive behaviors continue, resulting in disturbances in the emotional, social, academic, and career domains of their lives.

Specific Personality Disorders

Although there are various classification systems of personality disorders (Magnavita, 2004), the DSM-IV-TR (American Psychiatric Association, 2000) criteria will be utilized in this chapter, because they are most used by clinicians.

The DSM describes three clusters of personality disorders and 10 specific diagnoses, including *personality disorder nonspecified*. While the three clusters appear quite different in description and characteristics, there are similarities within each cluster.

Cluster A

Cluster A includes paranoid, schizoid, and schizotypal personality disorders, which are characterized by odd and eccentric behavior, odd patterns of affect and cognitions, and interpersonal isolation. Some researchers see a possible symptomatic and genetic relationship to schizophrenia (Livesley, 1995; Magnavita, 2004; Parnas, Licht, & Bovet, 2005). Thus, Cluster A disorders most frequently co-occur with psychotic disorders such as schizophrenia or psychotic symptoms such as delusions. Cluster A personality disorders may represent clinical variation of more severe psychotic disorders (Dolan-Sewell et al., 2001).

Braff (2005) found that Cluster A diagnoses account for only 4.1% of all cluster diagnoses. People with these disorders often do not seek treatment, and when they do, associated symptoms of depression, loneliness, or anxiety may prompt the help-seeking behavior (Parnas et al., 2005; Klein, 1995). There is a paucity of research on the prevalence of these diagnoses in the general college population. When students with these disorders come for treatment, it typically is at the insistence of faculty, administrators, residential staff, or parents. There are times when the behaviors of these students are so bizarre or preventive of academic and career progress that a medical leave of absence with a mandate to get therapy may be in order, which may be one way these students engage in treatment.

Paranoid Personality Disorder   Paranoid personality disorder (PPD) has three main features: (1) a pervasive, long-standing, and unwarranted suspiciousness and mistrust of people, (2) hypersensitivity when interacting with others, seeing their motivation as malevolent, and (3) emotional detachment (Maxmen and Ward, 1995).

Robert, a second-year doctoral student, was referred to the counseling services by numerous administrators and faculty. He stated that he was clearly the brightest student, but faculty members were threatened by his intellectual superiority. He also noted that no one was willing to chair his dissertation committee and fellow classmates were spreading "vicious" rumors. He spent most of his time alone, thinking about how to "outsmart everyone at their game." Like many students with PPD, Robert viewed himself as without fault and a victim of others' maliciousness.

Although there are no psychotherapy outcome studies for PPD (Crits-Christoph & Barber, 2004), case reports suggest success for cognitive therapy

(Livesley, 1995). Williams (1988), in a detailed case study of a college student with PPD and depression, found that brief cognitive therapy utilizing cognitive restructuring and progressive muscle relaxation showed promise.

Utilizing cognitive therapy, therapists can modify PPD's core belief that others are out to hurt the sufferer by increasing the client's ability to handle problems effectively. Beck, Freeman, Davis, and associates (2004) suggest that increasing sense of self-efficacy and confidence diminishes individuals' need for extreme vigilance and defensiveness. First the clinician must obtain a clear understanding and mutual agreement with the student about current goals. If the student underestimates his or her ability to handle a situation and overestimates the perceived threat, the goal is to give the student a more realistic appraisal of self. If the student cannot handle the problem, coping skills need to be taught (Beck et al., 2004).

In the case of Robert, it was important to validate his desire to get a degree and problem-solve how not to alienate others, so that his goals could be achieved. Social skills training—such as role playing and behavioral rehearsal—and assertiveness communication training were employed. The therapist also helped Robert tolerate his anxiety and depression about perceived failures and losses in his life, normalized his feelings, and empathically helped him integrate his black-and-white thinking and all-bad/all-good object representations, offering possible alternative interpretations for the behavior of others.

A key task of treatment is to minimize distrust of the therapist and therapy, which can take months (Maxmen & Ward, 1995). The therapist needs to help these students understand that feelings of vulnerability do not mean that they are being attacked (Benjamin, 1996). The trick is to be patient and empathetic but not overly focused on emotions or directly confrontational about semidelusional material, since students with PPD tend to feel too vulnerable.

Grossman (2004) found no published data to support the use of medication for PPD, although it is reasonable to consider use of an atypical antipsychotic medication if the paranoia is viewed as a psychotic symptom. Sperry (2003) mentioned that pimozide might be helpful for clients who show hypersensitivity and fluoxetine has been effective in reducing suspiciousness. Full disclosure about the medications and side effects is crucial in order to build and maintain a trusting environment.

Schizoid Personality Disorder   Schizoid personality disorder (SdPD) is seen as an ego-syntonic introversion, with the sufferer having little interest in others, no close friends except first-degree relatives, and no pleasure in anything except for a few activities (Parnas et al., 2005). SdPD is characterized as "a pervasive pattern of detachment from social relationships and a restricted range of expression of emotions in interpersonal settings" (American Psychiatric Association, 2000, p. 694). Harry Guntrip (1969) described nine fundamental characteristics of SdPD: introversion, withdrawnness, narcissism, self-suffi-ciency, sense of superiority, loss of affect, loneliness, depersonalization, and regression.

Individuals with SdPD seldom seek help until their thirties or forties (Stone, 2001), when the possibility of a relationship grows more tenuous and loneli-ness likely (Klein, 1995). When they do come for treatment, the usual reason is acute stress or a shift in life circumstances (Klaus, Bernstein, & Siever, 1995). With SdPD students, distortions in reality do not necessarily occur, but the lack of interest in others can make the therapeutic process difficult.

Angela was an exceptionally beautiful first-year student. She was brought to the counseling service by her parents, who noticed at Thanksgiving that she had lost quite a bit of weight. The parents were also troubled that Angela was still not making friends, a pattern since childhood. Angela said that she preferred spending time by herself on her computer. She matter-of-factly explained to the counselor that she lost the weight because she found the college dining halls very loud and the people who tried to talk with her annoying. She preferred microwaving a cup of soup in her single dorm room.

With SdPD students like Angela, the transition to college creates a crisis in that they are forced to develop new routines and confront new interpersonal relations. The goal of treatment is to reduce their social isolation, increase their experience of pleasure, and assist their adjustment during this transition. From the outset, the rationale for treatment should be outlined, along with the possible advantages, disadvantages, and concrete gains (Freeman, Pretzer, Fleming, & Simon, 1990). Since therapists often feel frustrated and defeated by these clients and may give up on them (Millon, Davis, Millon, Escovar, & Meagher, 2000), it is important to have realistic goals and not expect too much. In Angela's case, social skills training and gradual social exposure were helpful. She was able to find another student to share meals with and as a result gained some weight, and also became more assertive in expressing what she wanted.

Although there is no outcome research evaluating treatment approaches (Crits-Christoph & Barber, 2004; Klaus et al., 1995), Pretzer (2004) cited uncontrolled clinical reports supporting the effectiveness of cognitive-behav-ioral treatment for people with SdPD. In some cases, individuals might require the use of psychotropic medication to activate their flat mood/temperament (Millon & Grossman, 2004), but there are few studies (Grossman, 2004).

Schizotypal Personality Disorder Schizotypal personality disorder (SPD) is characterized by "a pervasive pattern of social and interpersonal deficits marked by acute discomfort with, and reduced capacity for, close relationships as well as by cognitive or perceptual distortions and eccentricities of behavior"

(American Psychiatric Association, 2000, p. 697). People with SPD are seen by others as eccentric or weird, are extremely anxious around people, and prefer to remain alone. They may hold odd beliefs and have difficulty expressing themselves emotionally or intellectually. Given this presentation, most researchers now view SPD as a part of a continuum with schizophrenia (Kernberg, 1984; Livesley, 2003; Millon et al., 2000; Siever, Bernstein, & Silverman, 1995). Additionally, some studies have found that these individuals often are diagnosed with major depressive order and/or borderline personality disorder (Klaus et al., 1995; Maxmen & Ward, 1995).

Because SPD often first occurs in childhood and adolescence, associated with underachievement in school, social isolation, poor peer relationships, eccentricity, and peculiar thoughts and language (American Psychiatric Association, 2000), it is unclear how many individuals actually make it to college. Persons with SPD may go for treatment more than those with the other Cluster A disorders because they often experience social anxiety (Stone, 2001).

Stanley came to treatment because he felt anxious, suspicious, and tense around other students and professors. He was 34 years old, living at home with his parents and taking a couple of classes at the university. When asked about a dish towel he wore around his neck, Stanley said it protected him from other students' germs.

Like other people with SPD, Stanley presented with magical thinking, ideas of reference, suspiciousness, poor reality testing, and overall odd behavior—difficulties that make it hard to succeed at college. Therapy with these individuals tends to be difficult due to their problems communicating and the thought disorder and paranoia that block the forming of a therapeutic relationship. Therefore, communication should be "simple, straightforward, shorn of psychological jargon, and require a minimum of inference" (Millon et al., 2000, p. 367).

Treatment goals in short-term work should be connected to presenting concerns, focusing on current sources of anxiety. For example, since Stanley felt severe anxiety in class and around other people, the therapist used social skills training and, from a cognitive perspective, helped him to objectively "investigate" the data to prove or disprove his beliefs, in this case that contact with others made him sick. Common goals of treatment for these students are to focus on reality testing, provide structure in their everyday lives, and enhance understanding of interpersonal relationships and boundary issues.

But to accomplish all the necessary gains, a referral for long-term treatment is necessary, since it takes a long time to establish a therapeutic relationship. Treatment with a psychiatrist can also be very beneficial. Fluoxetine and lithium help with aggression, and neuroleptic treatment has been linked to improvement in clients with moderate to severe symptoms; however, students often are reluctant to take neuroleptic medication (Coccaro, 2001; Markovitz, 2001), partly because of side effects, such as sedation. Moleman, van Dam, and Dings (1999) state that poorly controlled studies make it difficult to draw conclusions about the use of antipsychotic drugs, but in one study roughly half the subjects on low doses of haloperidol moderately improved, especially with regard to ideas of reference, social isolation, and odd communication. Stanley, who showed many odd behaviors, responded well to neuroleptic medication.

Group therapy is often not recommended, since clients with SPD typically cannot tolerate the intense level of social interaction. If the student is not too unusual or paranoid, however, a very basic social skills group may be recommended, but only after individual treatment reduces the student's social anxiety.

Workshops can help staff and faculty deal with these students who are often perceived to be "weird." The facilitator stresses the importance of simple, concrete, and supportive communications and the provision of structure in the student's life.

Cluster B

Cluster B is characterized by erratic, overemotional, and dramatic presentations (American Psychiatric Association, 2000). Magnavita (1997) terms this cluster the "mixed-results" group, because there is significant diversity of symptoms and rates of improvement. This cluster—the antisocial, borderline, histrionic, and narcissistic personality disorders—involves craving of stimulation but difficulties getting needs met appropriately and delaying gratification. All these personality disorders are familiar to college counseling centers.

Individuals with Cluster B diagnoses have a high co-occurrence of Axis I disorders, especially substance abuse and dependence (Dolan-Sewell et al., 2001), and mood, anxiety, and eating disorders (Oldham et al., 1995; Tryer, Gunderson, Lyons, & Tohen, 1997). At a university counseling center, students with Cluster B disorders often self-refer due to their Axis I concerns (e.g., eating disorder, depression), or they may be referred by judicial officers or residential living staff due to substance use or violations of academic or residential codes of conduct.

Antisocial Personality Disorder Antisocial personality disorder (ASPD) is characterized by "a pervasive pattern of disregard for, and violation of, the rights of others that begins in childhood or early adolescence and continues into adulthood" (American Psychiatric Association, 2000, p. 701). Individuals with ASPD exploit, deceive, dominate, and bully others and derive pleasure as victimizers, showing no true expression of remorse or guilt (Maxmen & Ward, 1995).

Sam, a junior studying business, was referred to the counseling service by his school dean. Sam repeatedly requested that faculty credit work he had not done. Thanks to his personable and charming style, faculty members would in fact often change his grade, give him extended time on exams or papers, or bypass a course requirement. But prior to the referral, he "blew up" at and threatened an advisor who didn't give Sam his way, refusing to let him register for classes if he did not finish three incompletes. Lying to his parents about why he hadn't gotten grades that semester, Sam stated that the school "messed up" his grades. His father called the business school dean, suspecting that his son was, as usual, trying to pull the wool over the his eyes. When confronted by the dean about his lying and inappropriate aggressive behavior, Sam agreed to treatment, presumably because he was under profound stress and was out of options.

Maxmen and Ward (1995) state that no treatments have been found helpful with ASPD, because symptoms are ego-syntonic and these persons often see themselves as smarter than and superior to their therapists. Not only don't they take therapy seriously, they potentially can become threatening to therapists; in dangerous cases, treatment simply cannot continue. However, with antisocial individuals who also have major depression, cognitive therapy and supportive-expressive psychotherapy are found to be effective (Pretzer, 2004).

Cognitive therapy with ASPD students focuses on specific problem situations, utilizing problem solving and behavioral, impulse, and anger management strategies (Sperry, 2003). Instead of trying to get ASPD-diagnosed clients to admit to problems, Beck et al. (2004) suggest having them compare the DSM criteria for ASPD with their own histories. The therapist should explain that this is a serious disorder that has negative long-term consequences. If substance-use disorders are diagnosed, as they often are (Dolan-Sewell et al., 2001), this issue often needs to be addressed first, since substance abuse overrides feelings of remorse (B. R. Meier, personal communication, July 16, 2005).

Though there are few drug studies, a variety of medications like lithium and antipsychotic medications may be helpful in decreasing the aggressive impulses associated with ASPD (Grossman, 2004; Markovitz, 2001; Sperry, 2003). However, students typically do not see the need to take these medications.

Working with these students' significant others can be helpful, perhaps more so than individual therapy. (To preserve confidentiality, the clinician should be someone other than the patient's therapist.) In the case of Sam, a clinician addressed the school's and Sam's parents' concerns and helped them establish and enforce clear boundaries and expectations. This helped decrease the control Sam wielded over the family and the advising office and exposed Sam to the direct consequences of his antisocial behavior. The counselor/consultant helped the school adhere to policies and regulations, including disciplinary actions.

Borderline Personality Disorder   Borderline personality disorder (BPD) is unlike the other personality disorders in that it shows individual and cultural variations and may improve with age, even without treatment. Typical characteristics of BPD include impulsivity; unstable and intense interpersonal relations; poorly regulated emotions, including pronounced feelings of rage, emptiness, and boredom; poor anxiety tolerance; identity disturbance; self-destructive behavior, including suicide attempts, parasuicidal behaviors, sexual acting out, and substance abuse; and possible transitory psychosis (Kernberg, 1984; Linehan, 1993; Stone, 2005).

BPD is the most frequently diagnosed personality disorder (Koeningberg et al., 1985; Maxmen & Ward, 1995), and certainly is the most common at college counseling centers. Clinicians may question the appropriateness of treating BPD on campus on the grounds that these students take too much of the center's resources, often needing scheduled phone contacts in addition to weekly sessions to contain their acting-out behavior. Each college center needs to determine the level of care it can provide to such students. If the center's policy is not to do ongoing, long-term work, therapists should make careful referrals to off-campus providers and fully explain the clinic's policies. Otherwise, these students will feel abandoned and may start acting-out/suicidal/parasuicidal behaviors. If long-term treatment is possible at the counseling service, supervision and consultations with colleagues are essential to contain countertransference issues and burnout.

Sharon came to treatment at the insistence of her department chair. A master's art student, she was bright, talented, and beautiful. One late night at the art studio, she was sexually forward with her department chair, who rejected her advances. Afterward, she felt so empty and alone that she took a knife and made shallow cuts on both her arms. That next night Sharon appeared at the chair's home, crying to his wife about being rejected "after having a special relationship." When the chair clearly stated that he had no such special feelings, Sharon again felt betrayed, threatened to charge him with sexual harassment, and threw a planter at his head. The chair responded by requiring Sharon to get professional help or else face disciplinary procedures.

Sharon fit the BPD diagnosis with her self-destructive behavior, angry disruptions in her interpersonal relationships, impulsivity, and chronic feelings of emptiness and abandonment. Her prognosis was good, however, as it often can be for college students. Stone (2005) associates the following factors with treatment success: high intelligence, self-discipline, artistic talent, attractiveness, and, in cases of substance abuse, the ability to commit to a 12-step recovery program like Alcoholic Anonymous. These are the very characteristics that many BPD college students possess.

Students with BPD usually should be assigned to an experienced, senior clinician. Very close supervision is needed if the therapist is a trainee or new professional, since students with BPD can sense professional insecurity and may then prematurely leave treatment or feel more out of control and increase their acting out. All this causes tremendous strain on the counseling center staff in the form of increased time needed for supervision and crisis intervention.

If the student is being prescribed medication, and the center has enough resources, the primary therapist probably should be a psychiatrist or psychiatric nurse. The student then has less opportunity to split clinicians (viewing one as all-good and another as all-bad) and is more likely to take the medication properly, and the effectiveness of the pharmacotherapy can be efficiently monitored. According to Markovitz (2001), because BPD is frequently accompanied by symptoms like anxiety, depression, psychosis, impulsivity, hostility, and mood lability, medications like lithium, anticonvulsants, neuroleptics, and antidepressants can be helpful, the particular medication chosen depending on the specific targeted symptoms.

Clients with BPD who call the center's on-call crisis counselor should be asked if they have a primary college therapist and, if so, informed that this professional will follow up at the next scheduled meeting or sooner if necessary. Such coordination of care meets the needs of these students, who are prone to risky behavior.

Dialectical behavior therapy (DBT) and supportive psychodynamic approaches help with suicidal activity, but their long-term benefits are still unclear (Crits-Christoph & Barber, 2004; Stone, 2005). As with any other client, ensuring the student's safety and decreasing self-harm should be the first step in treatment. Over 70% of patients with BPD have a history of suicide attempts, and approximately 5–10% actually commit suicide (Livesley, 2003). The current and future risk level for suicide should be carefully determined, whether through clinical interview techniques or actual suicide assessment inventories such as the Suicide Probability Scale (Cull & Gill, 1982).

Linehan (1993), in discussing DBT, presents a comprehensive list of factors to assess the imminent and long-term risk for suicide or parasuicide. The therapist should understand in detail what methods the student would use and the availability of such methods, and convince the client to remove the lethal means—but not get into a power struggle if the student is not prepared to comply. Therapists should clearly state the desire that students not harm themselves, and emphasize that therapy does work and that the student's quality of life can improve.

The question of when to hospitalize these students hinges on level of risk. Reasons for a brief hospitalization include significant risk for suicide or a serious suicide attempt (which may be induced by a strain in the therapeutic relationship), the combination of suicidal thoughts and psychoses, and the need for medications to be stabilized under close monitoring of professionals (Linehan, 1993).

There are times when considerable risk does *not* warrant hospitalizing the student. If so, having someone closely watch the student may provide protection and decrease feelings of isolation. On the other hand, other students and housing staff have individual and institutional limits. Because they feel overwhelmed and afraid, sometimes administrators, family members, roommates, and residential staff put pressure on counselors to hospitalize a borderline student. Patience is needed. Frequent hospitalizations are not the answer. It is useful to talk to both the client and other concerned individuals about the process of treatment, when the therapist should be called, and when the student should be taken to the hospital. A referral to partial hospitalization programs in the community is often a good alternative to inpatient stays, giving students necessary structure and intense treatment.

Once life-threatening behaviors have been addressed, the other goals of treatment are as follows: decreasing behaviors that threaten the process of therapy; fixing problems so that there can be a reasonable quality of life; stabilizing coping skills; resolving posttraumatic stress; and achieving self-validation and self-respect (Linehan, 1993). These can be achieved by the application of problem-solving skills, such as identifying target behaviors; generating, evaluating, and implementing alternative behavior solutions; and using validating strategies that support the "correctness" of students' emotions.

Similar strategies are employed by interpersonal and psychodynamic theorists. Helping the student find a kind, accepting inner voice is essential. The therapist models and mirrors such acceptance and acknowledges the wishes or desires of the client. In the case of Sharon, her wish to be special and known was valid and did not warrant shame or embarrassment. However, she had to find healthier behavioral alternatives to achieve her wish.

The psychodynamic literature emphasizes that therapists must maintain the proper professional distance and closeness, giving support without rescuing clients; encouraging independence without creating feelings of abandonment (Maxmen & Ward, 1995). This requires the awareness of countertransference feelings and "staying put"—neither withdrawing nor becoming aggressive when the going gets tough. The idea is that students will give up their self-destructive behavior when they are able to separate their sense of self from internalized abusive attachment figures (Benjamin, 2004). Therapists' task is to validate students' inner goodness and help them understand their self-destructive behavior in the context of past and present relations, as well as in the therapeutic relationship. According to Kernberg (1984), the practice of differentiating self from nonself and confronting students' tendency to fluctuate between idealization and devaluation helps them develop an observing ego, and so decreases problematic behaviors and thoughts.

Cognitive therapy focuses on students' dichotomous thinking or maladaptive schemas. Students with BPD see the world as a scary place where others abandon or reject them (Sperry, 2003). They often jump to conclusions without proper data. Developing "shades of gray" in their view of themselves and others leads to more realistic perceptions, better reality testing, and stable relationships.

Short-term work with BPD students can focus on specific relational or situational problems. Through the therapeutic process, Sharon was able to see that the chair did respect and admire her work. Her ability to trust that he did not reject her, even after she acted out, was critical to the success of treatment. She learned to contain her rage by verbalizing her feelings rather than acting them out.

Histrionic Personality Disorder Histrionic personality disorder (HPD) is characterized by excessive emotionality and attention-seeking behavior (American Psychiatric Association, 2000). Individuals with HPD are lively, overdramatic, demanding, dependent, and overreactive, always looking for reassurance. They also have been characterized as shallow, egocentric, and manipulative (Maxmen & Ward, 1995). Millon et al. (2000) describe them as viewing "the world through their own imprecise and overemotional lens," whereby they "tend to make broad overgeneralizations . . . [and] fail to develop a well-formed sense of identity[,] . . . never identifying goals and putting together a life plan" (p. 268).

These dysfunctional behaviors are particularly problematic at college. Histrionic students feel incapable of making the many decisions that college life demands or committing to fields of study, career paths, or social relations. The college years can also be a time of sexual awakening and experimentation. Individuals with HPD tend to be sexually unaggressive and have a negative attitude about sex, yet, at the same time, are preoccupied with sex and often experience sexual dysfunction (Stone, 2005).

There is little agreement about prevalence, but the range of HPD seems to be about 10–15% in clinical settings, with the majority of individuals being female (Maj, Akiskal, Mezzich, & Okasha, 2005), though in young adults equal numbers of males and females are diagnosed (Nestadt et al., 1999). The prevalence of HPD at college counseling centers is unclear and often confusing because comorbid diagnoses may be present.

Kimberly was a junior brought to the counseling service by her roommates, who were getting tired of her dramatic and inconsistent behavior. Kimberly told them that she was extremely depressed and questioned the point in living, yet immediately became the life of the party, all giggles and full of stories about herself when the boys across the hall invited people to watch a movie. Kimberly admitted that she liked male attention and acknowledged her flirtatious behaviors. She was quite noticeable in the counseling service waiting area, conspicuously applying makeup and wearing a halter top in the middle of winter. In her session Kimberly dramatically talked about herself, producing only a vague and difficult-to-follow history with unremarkable symptoms or problems, and often tried to get her young male therapist to smile or laugh.

The therapist needed to be careful not to be seduced by Kimberly's flirtatiousness or wish to be liked. The goal of treatment with these students is to develop mature coping skills. To do this, they must first learn to focus attention and come up with goals that give immediate gratification. In her case, the focus was on improving Kimberly's relations with her roommates and peers. The therapist helped her recognize her anxiety when she was not the center of attention and gave her listening skills to use during these anxious moments.

Maxmen and Ward (1995) suggest that the treatments of choice for HPD include psychoanalytical approaches and supportive, problem-solving, or cognitive therapy. However, there have been no controlled or uncontrolled studies of treatment modalities (Crits-Christoph & Barber, 2004). Short-term psychodynamic treatments such as those of Davanloo (1980) and Mann (1973) might focus on how past dysfunctional relationships may be re-occurring in current relationships, including the therapeutic relationship. Cognitive therapy can be used to counter the simplistic, global generalizations that students with HPD often make. Having the student identify with detail and clarification what she truly likes and dislikes helps her develop a clearer identity. Assertiveness workshops have also been useful for some students who have trouble asking for what they want in a direct manner. If the student is unable to cope at college, taking a medical leave from school might be in order. In these cases, day treatment programs that utilize both unstructured, insight-oriented groups as well as structured, skill-oriented groups have been reported as effective (Livesley, 2003).

Narcissistic Personality Disorder   Narcissistic personality disorder (NPD) is characterized by a "pervasive pattern of grandiosity, need for admiration, and lack of empathy that begins in early adulthood" (American Psychiatric Association, 2000, p. 714). Often viewed as the most obnoxious of the personality disorders, NPD individuals not only are arrogant but also have disdain for others and expect to be catered to (Millon et al., 2000). Typically the primary diagnosis of NPD has a prevalence in a clinical setting of only from 2% to 16% and of less than 1% to 5% in the general population; however, NPD accounts for up to 21% of clients receiving personality disorder diagnoses (Gunderson, Ronningstam, & Smith, 1995).

Often narcissistic disturbances occur in the late teen years and early twenties, presumably due to developmental challenges at this time. Self-absorption at this developmental point is not unusual, but these individuals have a pathological level of self-importance, with dramatic variations from strong feelings of entitlement and rage to shame and envy. They lack sustained commitment to others and often exploit others to serve their own self-esteem (Ronningstam,

2005). These persons often come to treatment in the midst of a career crisis or following an ultimatum from a significant other.

Bart is a very attractive, intelligent third-year medical student from a successful family of physicians. Within the first 10 minutes, he informs the therapist that his parents are "best friends" with the president of the university and that a bust of his grandfather sits in the medical school library. He asks the therapist about her degree and laughs when she reports that she is a licensed psychologist: "What, med school too hard for you?" He identifies medical school as easy for him, notes his very high IQ, says that while other students need to do clinical rotations it's a waste of time for him, and says that the medical school should be thankful he chose to train there. The dean of the medical school, he reports, is "an idiot" for recommending that Bart come to counseling because of poor relationships with faculty and students. He does admit that he can be boastful and arrogant but insists that he has reason to be.

Kohut (1977) conceptualizes narcissism as a developmental arrest requiring the therapist to provide accurate empathy and appropriate mirroring, which helps the student move beyond the needs of the grandiose self. Typically students with NPD require long-term treatment, but getting them to accept this is difficult. Linking the NPD student with an outside provider identified as an expert appeals to their narcissism and may make the transition easier.

Aims of treatment with Bart were to decrease his sense of entitlement and increase his awareness of his impact on others. Another focus was to increase his awareness of life's inevitable disappointments and his responses to them. Bart may have been unconsciously wounded that he was not accepted in the medical school where his family members were prominent. From a cognitive perspective, it was important to challenge Bart's perception that his family was disappointed in him and to alter his affective reaction to this disappointment. By reviewing his life goals and aspirations, Bart recognized that doing well at this medical school would help him reach his career dream.

Cluster C

Cluster C entails pervasive anxiety and fear. This cluster is the most ambiguous of the three because it overlaps with Axis I diagnoses, especially anxiety, mood, eating, and somatoform disorders (Dolan-Sewell et al., 2001). The "central features of timidity, persistent tension, proneness to anxiety, dependence, lack of confidence, and the constant expectation of distress and disaster in these personality disorders are similar features of anxiety disorders" (Tyrer, 2005, p. 351). Magnavita (1997) views Cluster C as characterized by difficulty experiencing and expressing anger, with much self-blame and lack of assertiveness. Because these individuals are aware of their suffering, they may be the most treatable among the personality disorders. Left untreated, however, these disorders can cause significant impairments.

Cluster C consists of avoidant personality disorder (APD), dependent personality disorder (DPD), and obsessive-compulsive personality disorder (OCPD). Students with these disorders tend to initiate treatment due to struggles with mood, anxiety, and adjustment. The developmental challenges of separating from home, developing new relationships, and handling novel situations can be overwhelming for them and exacerbate internal turmoil.

Avoidant Personality Disorder Avoidant personality disorder (APD) is characterized by "the pervasive pattern of social inhibition, feelings of inadequacy, and hypersensitivity to negative evaluation" (American Psychiatric Association, 2000, p. 718). In addition, these individuals often have low self-esteem and social phobia and tend to enter relationships only when unconditional acceptance is guaranteed (Maxmen and Ward, 1995).

Jennifer, a graduating senior, comes in for treatment because of an inability to go on job interviews. Extremely anxious around other people, she lives at home—unusual for most students at her university—and hates to leave the house even to go to the store. She has never dated and doubts anyone would be interested in her, although she wants to get married one day. She has one friend from elementary school whom she rarely sees. She feels criticized and often misunderstood by her large family. Despite being an A student, she still views herself as having no skills, and says that she never can be good enough in her own or others' eyes. She does not want to go on job interviews and be "examined under a microscope."

To help such students, Benjamin (1996) states that "accurate empathy and uncritical support" are necessary to establish a good therapeutic relationship. The counselor should carefully and consistently ask for feedback to see if the student feels criticized. Beck et al. (2004) suggest asking students at the end of the session if they made any assumptions about how the therapist felt about them. Using a proper pace and having the client report if the clinician is pushing too hard also builds the therapeutic alliance (Millon et al., 2000). Sometimes these clients feel criticized by the counselor's overt or covert push "to change." It also can be helpful to explore clients' ambivalence about their ability to cope with the various developmental tasks of college. While it's essential to help these students recognize their positive traits, this can be difficult, since they are afraid of being seen as arrogant.

Jennifer attended a three-session workshop teaching concrete steps to finding a job. Sometimes such specific knowledge can reduce baseline anxiety and increase confidence. Also effective are psychoeducational workshops, to normalize the student's feelings and reduce overgeneralizations. Due to her isolation, Jennifer hadn't realized that many other seniors were also confused about their career direction and skills. Also helpful can be role playing and behavioral rehearsal in sessions, self-image work, assertiveness training, utilization of relaxation techniques, and systematic desensitization using a hierarchy of anxiety-provoking situations.

Group-based adjunct treatments can focus on graded exposure, social skills, or intimacy social skills, depending on the interpersonal difficulties the client experiences (Crits-Christoph & Barber, 2004). Ongoing therapy groups are appropriate provided the group members are friendly, gentle, and reassuring. Selective serotonin reuptake inhibitors (SSRIs) and monoamine oxidase inhibitors (MAOIs) have been used to treat the social phobia that most APD clients experience (Grossman, 2004; Maxmen & Ward, 1995).

At a college counseling center, the focus is usually on symptom relief or targeted behavioral change. Changes in the organization of the student's overall personality typically require longer-term work, beyond the resources of most college centers. Care must be taken in referral to an off-campus provider so that the student does not feel anxious or rejected.

Dependent Personality Disorder   According to the DSM-IV-TR (American Psychiatric Association, 2000, p. 721), dependent personality disorder (DPD), one of the most prevalent disorders reported in mental health settings, is characterized by "a pervasive and excessive need to be taken care of that leads to submissive and clinging behaviors and fears of separation." With these college students, parents may decide what college to attend, what major to pursue, and even what courses to select. But these students feel unprepared not only to make these decisions, but also to decide where and with whom to eat and how to spend their time. Lacking any confidence in their decision-making skills, these students look to others to take care of them and make their decisions.

Jodi, a sophomore who looks younger than her stated age, has come to the counseling center feeling devastated because her boyfriend, Tom, has broken up with her. They met at orientation last year and did everything together. She tried to please Tom by becoming involved in his hobbies and interests, and always had him review her academic work and approve of her decisions. When he broke up with her, Tom said that Jodi was too needy and suffocating and should go for help. Jodi wanted to go home but her parents were opposed to the idea. Feeling stuck and unsure, she predictably asks the therapist what she should do.

One temptation when working with these students is to take control, give advice, and become the authority in response to the underlying message of

"Help me, and I will do exactly what you say. I will please you" (Millon et al., 2000, p. 231). Although therapy can helpfully become a safe haven for these students, they also need to become more independent, maintain healthy relationships without being submissive, and ultimately not depend on therapy. The therapist must overtly state these goals in the beginning of treatment and explore the student's fears of abandonment.

Another temptation is to respond to their fear of rejection and abandonment with reassuring statements. Far better is to explore these fears and their connection to significant interpersonal relations (Birtchnell & Borgherini, 1999). Having the student understand healthy dependence or the concept of interdependence also can be useful.

Procedures about emergencies and extra contacts such as advice-seeking phone calls or e-mails should be discussed early in treatment. More frequent appointments may be necessary if the student presents too many crises. Since many counseling centers cannot provide more than one weekly session, someone like Jodi might need to be referred to an off-campus provider, taking care, of course, to make a smooth transition.

Although no controlled outcome studies exist (Crits-Christoph & Barber, 2004), an interpersonal approach seems appropriate due to these students' attachment and dependency issues. This approach helps students to understand their interactive patterns, including underlying reinforcements, and then to decide if change is desired; the therapist provides support and a feeling of safety so that clients can manage their anxiety. One approach utilizes a time limit, making clear the exact number of sessions at the outset, so students can form a quick therapeutic alliance, concentrate on a circumscribed focus, and not regress or act out (Luborsky, 1984).

If a student with DPD has only mild to moderate impairment, an ongoing interpersonal therapy group might be indicated. With severe cases, assertiveness training, decision-making training, or a supportive problem-solving or social skills group might be helpful. Group therapy as an adjunct to individual treatment helps students recognize that there are many people who can be relied upon for support. Involvement in an ongoing group also may decrease the chance of relapse following the termination of individual therapy. There are no pharmacological treatment studies for DPD per se, but medication can be used if panic attacks emerge (Grossman, 2004).

Obsessive-Compulsive Personality Disorder Obsessive-compulsive personality disorder (OCPD) has the essential feature of "a preoccupation with orderliness, perfectionism, and mental and interpersonal control, at the expense of flexibility, openness, and efficiency" (American Psychiatric Association, 2000, p. 725). Although students often talk about being "anal," and an academic environment does reinforce a moderate amount of compulsivity, OCPD students' need for order, preciseness, and details are extreme and interfere significantly with interpersonal and career goals. These students believe that they know best, details are crucial, and people should strive for perfection.

Ralph is "driving everyone crazy" on the required work team of his MBA program. He spends the entire time going over irrelevant details and reviewing "to do lists" he's created for the other members. If the others do not complete assignments in the way he expects, he takes an inordinate amount of time insisting on his way. Concerned that they're not accomplishing their goals, Ralph's teammates requested his removal from the team. Ralph also admits to having similar troubles with his roommate, who no longer wants to live with him.

Individuals with OCPD dislike ambiguity, but ambiguity is what students like Ralph face given the many novel situations in academic programs. By clinging to rules, he tries to ease the anxiety of the unknown. Fearful of making a mistake or failing, he has become overly detailed, analyzing and reanalyzing everything. The goals of treatment therefore are to reduce his anxiety and to help him see the big picture and recognize the emotional nuances of the group situation.

Individuals with OCPD often respond to cognitive-behavioral interventions, which appeal to their sense of structure (Millon et al., 2000). A hierarchy of goals should be established, starting with the least anxiety producing, to instill a sense of accomplishment. Also helpful is identifying ways to reduce anxiety. Ralph picked exercise and mindful meditation, known to decrease ruminative worry in individuals with OCPD; another option would be progressive relaxation, especially for students who need more structure. As Benjamin (1996) emphasizes, therapy can be viewed as a scientific investigation, and so can appeal to students with OCPD because of its analytical and logical nature. The therapist may have to remind the student that blaming people is not as helpful as understanding what the student wants from others and how best to achieve rewarding relationships. Since OCPD students can become detail oriented and tangential, it is important to direct their focus to feelings rather than facts. A therapy group might be helpful as well, but again the therapist may need to intervene if the student becomes tangential, gets into power struggles, or feels overwhelmed by affect.

Crits-Christoph and Barber (2004) recommend interpersonal therapy or psychodynamic individual therapy approaches, giving clients a measure of control and autonomy. The goal of treatment is for students to replace impossible expectations of self and others with realistic expectations. Typically the treatment is long term, although short-term supportive-expressive therapy shows some promise (Sperry, 2003). No controlled pharmacological studies have been reported, but there is some research support for the use of the SSRIs citalopram and paroxetine to increase cooperative and affiliative behaviors.

Summary

Personality disorders typically emerge in adolescence and young adulthood, where the severity of distress and intensity of impairment can greatly impede ability to function at college. These students can, in many cases, be treated effectively at college counseling centers, though typically they initially come in not to work on their self-defeating traits but to find symptomatic relief. Depending on the type of personality disorder, students may respond well to cognitive behavioral techniques, social skills groups, psychodynamic groups, long-term psychotherapy, and/or medications. In many cases, day treatment programs are an appropriate referral option, and in severe cases medical leaves of absence may be appropriate. Considering the difficulties that personality disordered students present, college clinicians also often must provide consultations with faculty, administrators, and other students to contain campus alarm and punitive interaction and also reinforce the importance of setting appropriate behavioral limits. As for the difficulties for clinicians, ongoing peer consultations and supervision are recommended in working with these challenging and complicated, but rarely boring, clients.

References

American Psychiatric Association. (1980). *Diagnostic and statistical manual of mental disorders* (3rd ed.). Washington, DC: Author.

American Psychiatric Association. (2000). *Diagnostic and statistical manual of mental disorders* (4th ed., text revision). Washington, DC: Author.

Beck, A. T., Freeman, A., Davis, D. D., and associates. (2004). *Cognitive therapy of personality disorders* (2nd ed.). New York: Guilford Press.

Benjamin, L. S. (1996). *Interpersonal diagnosis and treatment of personality disorders* (2nd ed.). New York: Guilford Press.

Benjamin, L. S. (2004). Interpersonal reconstructive therapy (IRT) for individuals with personality disorders. In J. Magnavita (Ed.), *Handbook of personality disorders*. Hoboken, NJ: John Wiley & Sons.

Benton, S. A., Robertson, J. M., Tseng, W.-C., Newton, F. B., & Benton, S. L. (2003). Changes in counseling center client problems across 13 years. *Professional Psychology: Research and Practice, 34,* 66–72.

Birtchnell, J. & Borgherini, G. (1999). A new interpersonal theory and the treatment of dependent personality disorder. In J. Derksen, C. Maffei, & H. Groen (Eds.), *Treatment of personality disorders* (pp. 269–288). New York: Kluwer Academic/Plenum Publishers.

Braff, D. L. (2005). Cluster A personality disorders: Conundrums and new directions. In M. Maj, H. S. Akiskal, J. E. Mezzich, & A. Okasha (Eds.), *Personality disorders*. West Sussex, England: John Wiley & Sons.

Coccaro, E. (2001). Biological and treatment correlates. In W. J. Livesley (Ed.), *Handbook of personality disorders: Theory, research, and treatment* (pp. 124–135). New York: Guilford Press.

Crits-Christoph, P., & Barber, J. P. (2004). Empirical research on the treatment of personality disorders. In J. J. Magnavita (Ed.), *Handbook of personality disorders*. Hoboken, NJ: Wiley.

Cull, J. G., & Gill, W. S. (1982) *Suicide probability scale.* Los Angeles: Western Psychological Services.

Davanloo, H. (Ed.). (1980). *Short-term dynamic psychotherapy.* New York: Jason Aronson.

Dolan-Sewell, R. T., Krueger, R. F., & Shea M. T. (2001). Co-occurrence with syndrome disorders. In W. J. Livesley (Ed.), *Handbook of personality disorders: Theory, research, and treatment* (pp. 84–104). New York: Guilford Press.

Freeman, A., Pretzer, J., Fleming, B., & Simon, K. (1990). *Clinical applications of cognitive therapy.* New York: Plenum.

Grossman, R. (2004) Pharmacotherapy of personality disorders. In J. J. Magnavita (Ed.), *Handbook of personality disorders: Theory and practice* (pp. 331–355). Hoboken, NJ: Wiley.

Gunderson, J. G., Ronningstam, E., & Smith, L. E. (1995). Narcissistic personality disorder. In W. J. Livesley (Ed.), *The DSM-IV Personality Disorders* (pp. 201–212). New York: Guilford Press.

Guntrip, H. (1969). *Schizoid phenomena, object relations and the self.* New York: International Universities Press.

Kernberg, O. (1984). *Severe personality disorders: Psychotherapeutic strategies.* New Haven, CT: Yale University Press.

Klaus, O., Bernstein, D. P., & Siever, L. J. (1995). Schizoid personality disorder. In W. J. Livesley (Ed.), *The DSM-IV personality disorders* (pp. 58–70). New York: Guilford.

Klein, R. (1995). Description. In J. F. Masterson & R. Klein (Eds.), *Disorders of the self: New therapeutic horizons, the Masterson approach* (pp. 13–32). New York: Brunner/Mazel.

Koeningberg, H. W., Kaplan, R. D., Gilmore, M. M., & Cooper, A. M. (1985). The relationship between syndrome and personality disorders in DSM-III: Experience with 2,642 patients. *American Journal of Psychiatry, 142,* 207–212.

Kohut, H. (1977). *The restoration of the self.* New York: International Universities Press.

Lewinsohn, P., Rohde, P., Seeley, J., & Klein, D. (1997). Axis II psychopathology as a function of Axis I disorders in childhood and adolescence. *Journal of the American Academy of Child and Adolescent Psychiatry, 36,* 1752–1759.

Linehan, M. M. (1993). *Cognitive-behavioral treatment of borderline personality disorder.* New York: Guilford Press.

Livesley, W. J. (Ed.). (1995). *The DSM-IV personality disorders.* New York: Guilford Press.

Livesley, W. J. (Ed.). (2001). *Handbook of personality disorders: Theory, research, and treatment.* New York: Guilford.

Livesley, W. J. (2003). *Practical management of personality disorder.* New York: Guilford.

Luborsky, L. (1984). *Principles of psychoanalytic psychotherapy: A manual for supportive-expressive treatment.* New York: Basic Books.

Magnavita, J. (1997). *Restructuring personality disorders.* New York: Guilford.

Magnavita, J. (2004). Classification, prevalence, and etiology of personality disorders: Related issues and controversy. In J. Magnavita (Ed.), *Handbook of personality disorders.* Hoboken, NJ: John Wiley & Sons.

Maj, M., Akiskal, H. S., Mezzich, J. E., & Okasha, A. (Eds.). (2005). *Personality disorders.* West Sussex, England: John Wiley & Sons.

Mann, J. (1973). *Time limited psychotherapy.* Cambridge, MA: Harvard University Press.

Markovitz, P. (2001). Pharmacotherapy. In W. J. Livesley (Ed.), *Handbook of personality disorders: Theory, research, and treatment* (pp. 475–496). New York: Guilford Press.

Maxmen, J. S., & Ward, N. G. (1995). *Essential psychopathology and its treatment.* New York: W. W. Norton & Company.

Millon, T., Davis, R., Millon, C., Escovar, L., & Meagher, S. (2000). *Personality disorders in modern life.* New York: John Wiley & Sons.

Millon, T., & Grossman, S. D. (2004). Psychopathologic assessment can usefully inform therapy: A view from the study of personality. In J. Magnavita (Ed.), *Handbook of personality disorders.* Hoboken, NJ: John Wiley & Sons.

Moleman, P., van Dam, K., & Dings, V. (1999). Psychopharmacological treatment of personality disorders: A review. In J. Derksen, C. Maffei, & H. Groen (Eds.), *Treatment of personality disorders* (pp. 207–228). New York: Kluwer Academic/Plenum Publishers.

Nestadt, G., Romanoski, A. J., Chahal, R., Merchant, A., Folstein, M. F., Gruenberg, E. M., et al. (1999). An epidemiological study of histrionic personality disorder. *Psychological Medicine, 20,* 413–422.

Oldham, K. M., Skodol, A. E., Kellerman, H. D., Hyler, S. E., Doidge, N., Rosnick, L., & Gallaher, P. E. (1995). Comorbidity of Axis I and Axis II disorders. *American Journal of Psychiatry, 152,* 571–578.

302 • Ilene C. Rosenstein

Parnas, J., Licht, D., & Bovet, P. (2005). Cluster A personality disorders: A review. In M. Maj, H. S. Akiskal, J. E. Mezzich, & A. Okasha (Eds.), *Personality disorders* (pp. 1–74). West Sussex, England: John Wiley & Sons.

Pretzer, J. (2004). Cognitive therapy of personality disorders. In J. Magnavita (Ed.), *Handbook of personality disorders*. Hoboken, NJ: John Wiley & Sons.

Ronningstam, E. (2005). Narcissistic personality disorder: A review. In M. Maj, H. S. Akiskal, J. E. Mezzich, & A. Okasha (Eds.), *Personality disorders* (pp. 277–327). West Sussex, England: John Wiley & Sons.

Siever, L. J., Bernstein, D. P., & Silverman, J. M. (1995). Schizotypal personality disorder. In W. J. Livesley (Ed.), *The DSM-IV personality disorders* (pp. 71–90). New York: Guilford Press.

Sperry, L. (2003). *Handbook of diagnosis and treatment of DSM–IV-TR personality disorders.* New York: Brunner-Routledge.

Stone, M. H. (2001). Natural history and long-term outcome. In W. J. Livesley (Ed.), *Handbook of personality disorders: Theory, research, and treatment* (pp. 259–273). New York: Guilford Press.

Stone, M. H. (2005). Borderline and histrionic personality disorder: A review. In M. Maj, H. S. Akiskal, J. E. Mezzich, & A. Okasha (Eds.), *Personality disorders* (pp. 201–231). West Sussex, England: John Wiley & Sons.

Torgersen, S., Kringlen, E., & Cramer, V. (2001). The prevalence of personality disorders in a community sample. *Archive of General Psychiatry, 58,* 590–596.

Tyrer, P. (2005). The anxious cluster of personality disorders: A review. In M. Maj, H. S. Akiskal, J. E. Mezzich, & A. Okasha (Eds.), *Personality disorders* (pp. 349–375). West Sussex, England: John Wiley & Sons.

Tyrer, P., Gunderson, J., Lyons, M., & Tohen, M. (1997). Special feature: Extent of comorbidity between mental state and personality disorders. *Journal of Personality Disorders, 11,* 242–259.

Weissman, M. M. (1993). The epidemiology of personality disorders: A 1990 update. *Journal of Personality Disorders* (Suppl. 7), 44–62.

Williams, J. (1988). Cognitive intervention for a paranoid personality disorder. *Psychotherapy, 25,* 570–575.

16
Suicide and Suicidal Behaviors

MORTON M. SILVERMAN

There is no more painful disruption to the structure of campus life than that caused by a student suicide. A suicide brings to a halt the daily patterns of teaching, research, and scholarship that define college life, and calls into question a campus's safety, security, and stability (Silverman, 2005a).

Greater awareness of the rate of suicidal behaviors and completed suicide, as well as the relationship of suicidal behaviors to precipitating stressors and depressive symptoms, may well elevate the importance of focusing on campus outreach and treatment programs (Kitzrow, 2003). But despite the self-evident significance of this leading cause of death for the college-aged student, suicide on campuses remains a very poorly understood phenomenon, shrouded by inconsistent findings derived from noncomparable studies. Further, while the general literature on young adults' suicidal behaviors (ideation, threats, gestures, attempts, and completions) is large and diverse, any serious attempt to synthesize the findings is marred by major inconsistencies in definitions, methodologies, and reporting techniques (Maris, Berman, Maltsberger, & Yufit, 1992; O'Carroll et al., 1996; Silverman, 1993).

College students (predominantly 17–23 years old) and graduate students (mainly 24–34 years old) remain a particularly neglected population in terms of accurate epidemiological health surveys (Patrick, Grace, & Lovato, 1992). One reason is because they fall into age groups that straddle the conventional reporting categories (15–19, 20–24, 25–29, and so forth) used to identify behavioral health risk factors. As a result, the early survey studies of Schwartz and Reifler (1980, 1988) were unable to answer many of the epidemiological questions associated with completed suicide, leaving unaddressed the identification of modifiable risk factors (Silverman, 1993).

And while the literature is now growing on these risk factors (psychological, biological, genetic, sociocultural, and environmental), public attention has focused mainly on the rates of completed suicides (Silverman, 1993; Silverman, Meyer, Sloane, Raffel, & Pratt, 1997). The inquiries generated by campus officials and professionals always begin with concerns about "how many" and "how often." To understand suicide we obviously must dig deeper and explore the underlying risk factors.

Epidemiology

Suicide Rates

In 2000, there were approximately 2,775 four-year colleges and 2,000 community or junior colleges in the United States, enrolling approximately 15 million students (U.S. Department of Education, 2002). One fourth of all persons aged 18–24 in the United States are either full- or part-time college students—an age group with a high suicide rate. Plainly, the suicide problem on campus is an important societal issue.

The Big Ten Student Suicide Study was undertaken from 1980 to 1990 to determine the suicide rates on university campuses in the collegiate athletic conference known as the Big Ten, centered in the upper Midwest (Silverman et al., 1997). The most comprehensive attempt to report on the incidence of suicides in undergraduate and graduate school populations by age, gender, and race, it collected demographic and correlational data on 261 suicides of registered students at 12 Midwestern campuses. It found that the overall college student suicide rate of 7.5/100,000 was one half of the computed national suicide rate (15.0/100,000) for a matched sample by age, gender, and race.

The study found that students' suicide risk rises with age. Male and female students least at risk were in the 17–19 range. The 20- to 24-year-olds had suicide rates in proportion with their numbers. Finally, students 25 and over (whether undergraduates or graduate students) had a significantly higher risk than younger students. In general, graduate students had higher rates of suicides than undergraduates.

Women had rates roughly half those of men throughout their undergraduate years, but graduate women had rates not significantly different from their male counterparts (9.1/100,000 vs. 11.6/100,000). According to this study, the female student suicide rate is below the national rates during the first 2 years of college life, about equal during the junior and senior years, and above the national rates during the graduate school years. In other words, there is a continuous trend toward suicide as female students grow older. There is also an increase in rates for older male students, but the increase is far less dramatic.

Suicidal Ideation

The American College Health Association (ACHA) conducted the Spring 2000 National College Health Assessment (NCHA), which, along with other health indicators, measured depression, suicidal ideation, and suicide attempts among 15,977 college students on 28 campuses (ACHA, 2001). Its findings were comparable to the National College Health Risk Behavior Survey (NCHRBS) conducted by the Centers for Disease Control and Prevention (CDC) in 1995: 9.5% had seriously considered suicide within the past school year (Kisch, Leino, & Silverman, 2005). They repeated the study in 2004 and found that 10.1% had seriously considered suicide at least once during the past school year (Silverman, 2005b).

Meanwhile, the National Comorbidity Study found that in the general population aged 18–54, the lifetime prevalence of ideation was 13.5% (Kessler, Borges, & Walters, 1999). This rather startling number might make it appear that suicidal ideation is "normative" and not necessarily indicative of more serious underlying psychological or emotional disturbance, and one might be tempted to dismiss ideation as a true harbinger of future problems, inasmuch as only approximately 1.3% of deaths in the general U.S. population are due to suicide. I would strongly caution against such reassuring conclusions, however, since the majority of individuals who engage in self-destructive behaviors report prior suicidal ideation, and suicidal ideation may be a precursor to future suicidal planning and attempts (Kessler et al., 1999).

Suicide Attempts

The 2004 ACHA survey found that 1.4% of college students surveyed had attempted suicide within the past school year—a remarkably similar rate to that found by the CDC in 1995 (CDC, 1997; Brener, Hassan, & Barrios, 1999). Among those who reported a suicide attempt, 0.4% reported doing so on three or more occasions. Others have found that prevalence ranges from 3–5% over the previous year (Duane, Stewart, & Bridgeland, 2003) to 10% over a lifetime (Meehan, Lamb, Saltzman, & O'Carroll, 1992).

Risk and Protective Factors

Risk Factors

Although true one-to-one causation is difficult to establish, certain risk factors, alone or in combination, are associated with increased risk for suicidal behaviors and completed suicides. Due to the overlap in age between adolescents and college students, the risk factors for adolescents also generally apply to college students. Recently a major report on treating and preventing adolescent mental health disorders listed the following factors associated with suicidal behavior (Hendin et al., 2005):

Psychopathology
- Depression
- Drug and alcohol abuse
- Aggressive-impulsive behavior
- Hopelessness
- Pessimism
- Conduct disorder (male)
- Panic disorder (female)

Family and genetic
- Family history of suicidal behavior
- Parental psychopathology

Environment
- Firearm availability
- Diminished family cohesion
- Lack of parental support
- Parent–child conflict
- Negative life-events
- Child sex abuse
- Suicide contagion

Biology
- High 5-HT (5-hydroxytryptamine = serotonin) receptor expression in prefrontal cortex and hippocampus
- Serotonergic dysfunction

Previous suicidal behavior
- Suicide attempts

Sexual orientation
- Same-sex sexual orientation

Warning Signs

Many risk factors are historical or immutable, and hence not targets of intervention, such as age, gender, race/ethnicity, and family history of psychiatric illness. Therefore attention has focused on elucidating warning signs of acute risk (Rudd, 2003; Rudd et al., in press). Verbal warning signs are as follows: "I'm thinking of ending it all," "I wish I were dead," "Life is no longer worth living," "I just want to go to sleep forever," and "My family will be better off without me." Behavioral warning signs among at-risk students include writing or talking about death and dying, seeking means to kill themselves, increased use and abuse of alcohol or other drugs, withdrawing from friends and academics, deterioration of physical appearance or hygiene, putting affairs in order, and stopping the use of prescribed medications. Psychiatric warning signs include exacerbation of psychiatric symptoms such as hallucinations and delusions, increased agitation and anxiety, aggressiveness, unrest and instability, anhedonia, panic attacks, and impulsivity.

Protective Factors

Protective factors are believed to enhance resilience and counterbalance risk factors (U.S. DHHS, 2001). Promoting healthy behaviors and protecting students from health risks are some of the preventive interventions available to college students (Silverman et al., 1997).

College campuses provide student support services, including easy and low-cost access to physical and mental health services, and a supportive peer and mentor environment. The wide range of student supports includes coaches, professors, residential advisors and staff, career and placement experts, university health service professionals, campus ministries, clinical therapists, student activities professionals, and other administrators whose careers are devoted to nurturing healthy minds and healthy bodies. A lower in the overall suicide rate among college students compared to the general population may also be due to the general campus prohibitions on the availability and use of firearms, the careful monitoring and control for the abuse of alcohol, the stated prohibition on the possession and use of illicit drugs, and students' realization that attaining a college degree can advance their career, enhance skills and knowledge, and promote personal growth and development.

Assessment

While we cannot predict future behavior with certainty, clinicians can make a reasonable judgment regarding the degree of present danger. A thorough assessment of all aspects of suicidality—ideation, behavioral rehearsals of lethal actions, prior attempts, and past and current intentions—will inquire into risk factors, warning signs, and protective factors. These can be embedded in a more complete biopsychosocial investigation. In doing so, it is useful to cover as many of the following content areas as possible:

- Reasons for living and reasons for dying: "What would have to happen to make you want to kill yourself?" "List all those things that are keeping you alive."
- Sense of hope and future orientation: "Do you think things will get better?"
- Likelihood of past circumstances repeating themselves in the future: "What is the same or different about this episode compared with prior episodes?"
- Insight into current and/or chronic problems: "How do you understand what is happening to you?"
- Current and past use of alcohol and other drugs, including prescription and over-the-counter medications (since these, of course, can impair reality testing, information processing, and judgment): "What role does alcohol play in your management of your problems?" "How does alcohol make things better or worse?"
- Imminent versus chronic risk for self-destructive thoughts and behaviors: "Are these thoughts and/or feelings overwhelming or frightening to you, or are they familiar?"
- Presence of a support network: "How important are your friends/ family/teammates?" "To whom are you closest?" "To whom can you confide?" "What role does spirituality and/or religion play in your life?" "Who can you count on in an emergency?"
- Prior exposure to suicidal behavior (family, friends, etc.): "Do you know anyone who has died by suicide or made a suicide attempt?"

- Development of social skills (e.g., peer pressure resistance) and cognitive skills (e.g., problem solving): "How well do you negotiate what you need from others?" "Are you able to say no when you don't want to go along with what others are doing?" "What kinds of situations and relationships are difficult for you to manage?"
- History of impulsivity and aggression: "Have you gotten into trouble with the law?" "Are you prone to make snap judgments or fly off the handle without much warning?"
- Sleep patterns and sleep hygiene: "Have you noticed any difficulties with falling asleep, staying asleep, or waking up earlier in the morning than you intend?"
- Instrumental, psychological, and interpersonal messages contained in suicidal behaviors, including acting-out behaviors: "What did you hope would happen after the last attempt?" "Did this current attempt give you any relief from your distress?" "What would be the best outcome from this current episode?"

Suicidal patients may be reluctant to explore their suicidality without first feeling assured that the clinician is well versed and comfortable with the topic. Such assurance can be conveyed by discussing the topic in a calm and nonjudgmental manner, knowing the range of self-injurious and self-destructive behaviors, and understanding the motives behind suicidal behaviors. Demonstrating comfort with the subject of suicide helps build trust and a therapeutic alliance, which are critical to the treatment outcome.

It is not unusual for clients to deny suicidal thoughts when asked outright, due to the ongoing stigma associated with suicide and the fear of unknown consequences when admitting to suicidal ideation ("They might send me to the hospital or kick me out of school"). Therefore, if there's any indication at all of suicidal material, the clinician must go beyond the initial "no" response, and explore further.

One way to gently introduce the topic is by inquiring into the client's general state of well-being and then proceeding to issues of ideation, intent, and planning as noted above. A potential sequence might start as follows: "How bad have you been feeling?" "Does it seem as though things will change for the better?" Depending upon the responses, the clinician might then advance: "Do you see much point in going on?" "Have you been feeling like a burden to others?" "Do you wish you were dead?" "What does suicide mean to you?" "Have you thought about a particular way to end your life?" "Do you have access to a method to do this?" "Have you tried this out?" "Have you imagined or engaged in 'rehearsals' for a planned suicide?" "Does anything make these feelings get better or worse?" "How likely do you think you would be to harm yourself?" "Under what set of circumstances?" (Davidson, 1999; Goldman, Silverman, & Alpert, 1998).

If the student does acknowledge some suicidal content, it's vitally important to understand the context, the "who, what, when, where, why, and how" of the circumstances that engendered it. For example: "Where were you when the thought occurred?" "Who was present?" "What happened?" "When did it start?" "How long did it last?" "Why do you think it occurred when it did?" "How did you deal with it?" "Did you act on it?" "Would you act on it next time?" (Barrios, Everett, Simon, & Brener, 2000). The answers will allow the clinician to answer the ultimate questions of "Why now?" and "Is it likely to happen again?"

Finally, in assessing lethality, the clinician should weigh the character of any ideation (Was it serious? Pervasive? Fleeting? Disturbing? Distressing? Comforting? Relieving? Familiar? Logical? Paranoid?) and its possible progression (Did it go from a thought to a wish, desire, or intent? Did it go from a thought to a plan?) (Silverman, 2005). If there was an actual attempt, the clinician additionally needs to consider the following: Was the attempt intended to end a life? Was it instrumental in nature (a behavior to accomplish some specific end rather than self-destruction or death)? Did it appear to be a "cry for help"? Did the student plan to be rescued? Did the attempt involve lethal methods? Did the student use coping behaviors learned from others? Does the student have accurate knowledge of lethal means—amounts, dosages, accessibility, time frames, etc.? Is there a pattern to the behavior? How does the student feel now? (Berman, Shepherd, & Silverman, 2003; Silverman, 2005a).

All of the above can then be interpreted in context along with the quality of the therapeutic interaction (e.g., degree of cooperation, presence of anger, demeanor); conduct of the interview (eye contact, verbal interchange, ability to track the sequence of questions, level of distress/anxiety); and physical attributes (attention to personal grooming, how the student sits in a chair) (Silverman, 2005a).

Crisis Intervention

With regard to suicidality there is one primary goal of crisis intervention: to keep the patient safe until the crisis has resolved. Therefore, extraordinary means of maintaining safety and stability, including voluntary or even involuntary hospitalization, are sometimes necessary. Crisis intervention with suicidal students typically includes these protective measures: (a) restricting access to means of death; (b) decreasing the patient's interpersonal isolation; (c) decreasing agitation, anxiety, sleep loss; (d) structuring the treatment (e.g., increasing the number of sessions, providing increased accessibility via phone contacts); (e) working on problem-solving skills; (f) creating future linkages; (g) negotiating the maintenance of safety and the development of a contingency plan; and (h) use of hospitalization in cases of clear and imminent suicide risk (Berman, Jobes, & Silverman, 2006; Cimbolic & Jobes, 1990; Jobes & Berman, 1993).

Often an acute suicidal crisis emerges from a synergy of intrapersonal, environmental, social, and situational variables. Because young adults may respond to life crises with suicidal behaviors, clinicians must be prepared to assess possible and imminent self-harm behavior while concurrently protecting against that possibility. Often these twin tasks must be accomplished under conditions of incongruent expectations and goals between clinician and patient. Suicidal people tend to defy the professional's expectation that fostering and maintaining a positive approach to life is a shared aim of patient and clinician (Hoff, 1984). Indeed, the assessment, treatment, and general management of acute suicidal crises, even though these crises are not uncommon, are among the most difficult mental health emergencies faced by any mental health professional (Kleespies, 1998; Roberts, 1991).

It is well established that suicidal impulses and behaviors are, for the most part, transient and situation specific. Suicide intent is state dependent and tends to wax and wane. Empirical research indicates that most people who kill themselves give some form of prior warning and often desire an outcome other than the termination of their biological existence (Shneidman, 1993). The crisis clinician is thus in a pivotal, and potentially lifesaving, position. The accuracy of risk assessment and appropriateness of interventions can literally mean life or death.

Hospitalization

Given the stigma, managed care constraints, significantly reduced numbers of available inpatient beds, and other issues, hospitalizations are not the answer for every suicidal student. Indeed, the need for hospitalization, management while hospitalized, and postdischarge planning are all tinged with medical-legal implications and liability issues for clinicians, other counseling center staff, and the college administration.

When do you hospitalize a college student? First, a thorough clinical assessment must be made based on all the facts—epidemiological factors, risk and protective factors, prior history of self-destructive behaviors, psychiatric diagnosis, and current status. The clinician needs to assess the benefits of a hospitalization—safety, security, stability, possible removal from a toxic environment, and the opportunity to reassess diagnosis, therapeutic protocols and medications. The assessment must also review the negative consequences—removal from a possible supportive living situation, potential regression, loss of time in the classroom. If on balance the decision is made to hospitalize, it should be shared with and explained to the student. The next decision concerns whether the admission should be voluntary or involuntary. At this point the clinician must discuss with the student issues of confidentiality, especially regarding notification of "need to know" college administrators, friends, roommates, and parents (or significant others).

John, a pre-law senior, received disappointingly low LSAT scores in the mail. That evening he got quite drunk; feeling despondent and hopeless, he tried to jump out of his eighth-floor apartment window and had to be restrained by his roommate. Brought by the campus police to be evaluated by the on-call clinician, he now vociferously denied being suicidal and strenuously argued that he couldn't go to the hospital because it would jeopardize his chances of going to law school. The clinician weighed the costs and benefits of hospitalization. He preferred not to send John to the hospital against his will, and John's assurances that his suicidal urges had passed raised the possibility that he could be safely monitored and treated on an outpatient basis. On the other hand, the impulsiveness and seriousness of his near attempt coupled with use of alcohol had placed him in great danger, and it was quite likely that John really hadn't abandoned his suicidal wishes but was simply denying them to avoid going to the hospital. On balance, the clinician decided it would be irresponsible to gamble with John's safety and so admitted him involuntarily for further observation and stabilization.

Other Treatment Strategies

A number of studies are emerging which elucidate the psychology of suicide and suicidal behaviors, particularly the hopelessness, absence of future thinking, lack of problem-solving skills, tendency toward impulsivity, and presence of psychological pain (Berman et al., 2006). These larger conceptual constructs are not necessarily diagnosis specific (Henriques, Beck, & Brown, 2003; Jobes, 2003a; Salkovskis, 2001) and they suggest new directions in clinical practice (Jobes, 2003b). In fact, there is a growing consensus that many acute suicidal risk factors cut across diagnostic categories: psychic anxiety, panic attacks, global insomnia, depressive turmoil, recent onset of alcohol abuse, and agitation (Busch, Fawcett, & Jacobs, 2003).

At the core of virtually every suicidal struggle is an intense need for escape and relief from psychological pain. Suicidal states also typically involve a fundamental struggle related to the presence or absence, and perception, of certain key relationships. Jobes believes that many suicidal students need "asylum," which often can be found in a well-formed and carefully monitored *outpatient* therapeutic alliance rather than an inpatient setting (Jobes, 2003a). Clearly, however, there are different kinds of suicidal young adults; a one-size treatment does not fit all (Rogers & Soyka, 2004). Suicidal students often need a full range of interventions—psychotherapy, medication, engagement of peers, and spiritual and existential experiences.

Evidence-based research consistently shows that a combination of psychotherapy and medication is more efficacious than either approach by itself (TADS Team, 2004). Most suicidal students can benefit directly from psychotherapy that helps them problem-solve, cope, and develop a thicker and more resilient "psychological skin."

Despite considerable disagreement as to their appropriateness, scientific foundation, and clinical utility, practice guidelines continue to emerge (Rudd et al., 1999). Recently, guidelines from the American Academy of Child and Adolescent Psychiatry (Shaffer & Pfeffer, 2001) and the American Psychiatric Association (2003), though disclaiming to be authoritative, have become "must reading" for those actively engaged in working with adolescent and young adult suicidal patients.

The following case illustrates the suicidal person's wish to escape from psychological pain, the pivotal role played by a disruption in key relationships, and how therapy and medication in combination can provide relief and help the person surmount the suicidal crisis.

Steve told his therapist that he just couldn't shake feeling "down" following the recent news that his parents were divorcing, and intimated that he might have been responsible for their breaking up. Over the next week he reported that he was feeling increased hopelessness about what would happen to his younger sister, pessimism that he would ever be able to go home again, and decreased motivation for studying, since his parents probably wouldn't be able to send him to college in the future. He reported other depressive symptoms as well: decreased ability to follow class discussions, crying over "stupid stuff," and loss of interest in socializing with friends. When he told his therapist that he just wanted to go hide somewhere and never be seen again, the therapist thoroughly assessed his suicidal potential and discovered that Steve was harboring strong urges to take his life by an overdose of pills.

Fortunately, Steve had a trusting, positive relationship with his therapist and was able to credibly agree to a safety plan, stating emphatically that if he felt an immediate urge to commit suicide he would promptly call either the therapist or the campus's emergency phone number. Steve agreed to twice-weekly therapy sessions for the next few weeks and also to a psychiatric consultation in order to be evaluated for antidepressant medication. Therapy focused on providing support during this difficult time and gently helping Steve question his pessimistic assumptions about his parents' divorce. Perhaps it wasn't true that his sister's fate was sealed or that he couldn't go home again or must drop out of school. Thanks to the combination of therapy and medication, the suicidal crisis and his depressive symptoms subsided and he was able to resume his course of studies.

Empirical Treatment Literature

Much of the limited suicide treatment literature is not specific to the late adolescent and young adult suicidal patient. Indeed, in general there has been a lack of research in the treatment of suicidality (Hawton et al., 1998; Linehan, 1997; Rudd, 2000). Linehan (1997) scrutinized all investigations that included randomized clinical trials (RCTs) of psychosocial and behavioral interventions for suicidal behaviors in adults and adolescents. Remarkably, only 20 studies were found that randomly assigned individuals to experimental treatment groups, treatment-as-usual groups, and control groups. Four of these studies showed a significant effect for psychosocial interventions, and one showed a significant effect for pharmacotherapy. In addition, focused behavioral interventions appeared to hold promise for reducing suicide attempts and nonsuicidal self-injurious behaviors.

Major Treatment Approaches

My purpose here is not to provide an extensive review of major treatment approaches for working with suicidal young adults. An emerging literature that addresses treatment of late adolescent and young adult suicidal individuals now exists (Berman et al., 2006; Ellis & Newman, 1996; Leenaars, 2004; Linehan, 1993a, 1993b; Quinnett, 2000; Rudd, Joiner, & Rajab, 2001; Spirito & Overholser, 2003; Zimmerman & Asnis, 1995), including the pros and cons of conducting therapy over the Internet (Hsiung, 2002). Furthermore, there are general writings on the standard of care in the assessment, treatment, and management of suicidal individuals (Bongar, 1992, 2002; Bongar et al., 1998; Gutheil, 1992; Simon, 1992, 2004). Here I will simply highlight some key points of various treatment approaches for suicidal college students.

Psychodynamic Psychotherapy

Beyond theoretical and clinical discussions, there is unfortunately no direct empirical support for the efficacy of psychodynamic treatment of suicidal adolescents or young adults. While there is little dispute that psychodynamic theories have much to offer both clinically and conceptually, some caution about psychodynamic psychotherapy's usefulness is in order until supportive data emerge. Psychodynamic treatments for suicidal college students tend to emphasize the impact of family relationships on personality development and relationships, the development of the self, and the central healing role of the clinical relationship (Berman et al., 2006).

Cognitive-Behavioral Therapy

Cognitive-behavioral therapy (CBT) has been shown to be an effective intervention for depressive symptoms (Beck, Rush, Shaw, & Emery, 1978, 1979; Clarke, Rohde, Lewinsohn, Hops, & Seeley, 1999). Cognitive therapy postulates three primary areas of maladaptive thinking: (a) the "cognitive triad": the idiosyncratic and negative view of self, experience, and future; (b) "schemas," stable patterns of molding data or events into cognitions; and (c) "systematic errors" in thinking that establish and maintain a depressed mood, and the hopelessness that Beck believes is "at the core of the suicidal wishes" (Beck et al., 1978, p. 151).

Beck and his associates (Henriques et al., 2003) have recently developed a specific 10-session cognitive therapy intervention for adolescent and young adult suicide attempters. A novel element is that the treatment can be applied to all individuals exhibiting suicidal behavior regardless of psychiatric diagnosis. A central premise is the notion that suicidal behavior, though dangerous, is understandable given the patient's frame of reference.

Rudd et al. (2001) have written a treatment guide that presents a theoretical (CBT) model of suicidality, incorporates a system of clinical assessment, and explains how to deal with crisis intervention and symptom management through skill building and the development of enduring adaptive modes.

As an example of applying CBT, Gena, a sophomore who suffered from chronic minor depression and suicidal thoughts, revealed upon being questioned by her therapist her beliefs that "I am a bad person and don't deserve to live" and "I know that I'm unlovable, so why would anyone care if I was alive or dead?" Having these familiar but usually subterranean beliefs brought to life was an important step for Gena. She had never told anyone about them before and hadn't really stopped to examine them—they were simply always there, like a wall painting she'd long since stopped noticing. The therapist then helped her to break down these negative cognitions into their component parts, addressing the logical inconsistencies and challenging the truncated thinking patterns. How did Gena know she was a bad person? On what basis had she decided she didn't deserve to live? Was it really true that nobody—not her family or friends or her boyfriend—cared if she was dead or alive? Invited to examine her cognitions in this way, Gena started to question them and noticed after several weeks that they seemed to come up less often in her thinking. Not surprisingly, she also reported that her suicidal thoughts became less ubiquitous and pressing.

Dialectical Behavior Therapy

Dialectical behavior therapy (DBT) (Linehan, 1993a, 1993b) is an evidence-based outpatient psychotherapy for chronically "parasuicidal" adults diagnosed with borderline personality disorder. *Parasuicide* is defined as acute, deliberate nonfatal self-injury or harm that includes suicide attempts and nonsuicidal self-injurious behaviors (Linehan, 1993a). Suicidal behaviors are considered to be maladaptive solutions to painful negative emotions engaged in because of their affect-regulating qualities and the help they elicit from others.

DBT treatment focuses on validation and empowerment. The therapist aims to help patients modulate their emotional reactions, reduce the associated extreme behaviors, and accept their own reactions. Problem solving is a core component of skills training, supplemented by a range of ancillary treatments, supportive group sessions, and telephone consultations. Emphasis is placed on the therapeutic relationship, though more in the style of cognitive than psychodynamic psychotherapy. Other core DBT skills include mindfulness training, interpersonal effectiveness skills, and techniques to deal with psychological distress.

Interpersonal Psychotherapy

The focus of interpersonal therapy (IPT) is the link between depressive symptoms and current interpersonal problems. The emphasis is on the person's immediate personal context and life events, his or her reactions to them, and how these factors relate to symptom formation (Mufson, Moreau, Weissman, & Klerman, 1993). IPT may be a useful treatment for addressing students' use of suicidal behavior as a method of communicating anger or distress, or resolving conflict.

Collaborative Assessment and Management of Suicidality

This approach is a novel clinical protocol designed to quickly identify and effectively engage suicidal outpatients in their own clinical care (Jobes, 2000, 2003b; Jobes & Drozd, 2004). The approach taken by collaborative assessment and management of suicidality (CAMS) emphasizes a thorough and *collaborative* assessment of suicidality at every session and a problem-solving approach to treatment planning. In effect, the clinician and suicidal patient coauthor a treatment plan that constructs viable ways of coping and living. The heart of CAMS is a strong therapeutic alliance, where both parties work together to develop a shared phenomenological understanding of the patient's suicidality.

From this perspective, clinicians approach suicidality in an empathic, matter-of-fact and nonjudgmental fashion, appreciating the viability and attraction of suicide as a coping option. The aim is to understand what it means for the patient to be suicidal, and with that shared knowledge to determine how to clinically manage the risk (Jobes, Wong, Conrad, Drozd, & Beal-Walden, 2005).

Psychopharmacology: General Considerations

Medications and medication management may be helpful with certain diagnostic conditions and related symptoms associated with suicidality (Maris,

Berman, & Silverman, 2000). In these cases, symptom reduction is necessary for cognitive, behavioral, or verbal modes of clinical intervention to succeed.

One of the most exciting advances in understanding the genetic and biological bases for suicidal behavior is John Mann's stress-diathesis model (Mann, 1998; Mann, Waternaux, Haas, & Malone, 1999). Based on neurobiological research about the role of neurotransmitters (e.g., serotonin, dopamine, norepinephrine) in modulating brain function, this model proposes that a vulnerability to suicidality (diathesis) may exist independently of stressors (risk factors) that are correlated with suicidal behavior, such as mood disorders, anxiety disorder, and substance abuse disorders.

Decreased brain serotonin function (as measured by CSF 5-HIAA [cerebrospinal fluid 5-hydroxyindoleacetic acid]) has been found in suicidal patients, independent of psychiatric disorders. Hopelessness, low self-esteem, social isolation, and inadequate control of aggressive impulses may be core symptoms of such individuals (Ahrens & Linden, 1996). Of note, persons who exhibit aggressive and impulsive behavior toward others are also more prone to impulsive and aggressive behaviors toward themselves (Verkes & Cowen, 2000).

Medications for Depressive Disorders

Of all the medications for the treatment of psychiatric disorders and dysfunctions related to suicidality, I will focus solely on antidepressants, because studies consistently find that affective disorders are the most common diagnoses related to suicide.

There are well over 20 antidepressants currently available, only a few of which are selective serotonin reuptake inhibitors (SSRIs). Some studies suggest that the use of antidepressants has lowered suicide rates in clinical populations (Isacsson, Holmgren, Druid, & Bergman, 1997), although these studies need to be prospectively replicated and carefully controlled. Global statements about causal mechanisms cannot be made, because truly rigorous studies have not been undertaken that compare and contrast all the available medications with specific target symptoms. Meanwhile, currently there is controversy as to whether certain classes of antidepressants can be associated with the worsening, or even the emergence, of suicidal ideation or behavior in the early weeks of treatment, particularly in children and adolescents (Mann & Kapur, 1991).

However, there are reasons to believe that SSRIs might reduce suicidality and suicidal ideation because of their potential to reduce irritability, affective response to stress, hypersensitivity, depression, and anxiety (Isacsson et al., 1997; Leon et al., 1999). SSRIs remain the preferred psychopharmacological treatment for young adult depression, with the caution that suicidal patients on SSRIs must be watched for any increase in agitation or suicidality, especially in the early phase of treatment (Montgomery, 1997).

When medications are prescribed to suicidal individuals, careful monitoring of dosage levels is essential. It's important to prevent patients from hoarding pills or having inappropriate access to them. While medications may be essential in stabilizing and treating the suicidal young adult, all administration must be carefully monitored for any unexpected change of mood, increase in agitation or emergency state, or unwanted side effects, so that dosages can be regulated (American Psychiatric Association, 2003; Shaffer & Pfeffer, 2001).

When the primary therapist works with a prescribing physician, it is essential that interactive lines of communication remain open. The nonmedical therapist should be familiar with the common dosages, properties, therapeutic effects, and side effects of prescribed medications. Moreover, the therapist should inquire about, and report to the psychopharmacologist, significant changes in the patient's behavior, significant events threatening the behavioral response, and any observed responses to medication (lack of compliance, side effects, etc.).

Practice Recommendations

Working with suicidal patients is often difficult and psychologically draining. More often than not the clinician is working at two levels at once. Suicidal patients almost always have an underlying psychological or psychiatric disorder which finds expression in suicidal behavior. Hence the clinician must treat the underlying emotional, cognitive, or perceptual dysfunction. At the same time, the clinician must monitor and address self-destructive thoughts and behaviors while working with a patient who may not share the goal of getting better, or even remaining alive. It's important to acknowledge and monitor one's countertransference when working with acutely or chronically suicidal patients (Maltsberger & Buie, 1974). It's also important to assess if one possesses the skills and temperament to work with these individuals. If not, one should sensitively arrange for a suicidal student to be followed by a more suitable clinician. At the very least, clinicians working with suicidal cases should regularly seek consultation, supervision and support from other clinicians. There is no place for complacency when working with self-destructive patients.

Another issue is the false reassurance provided by suicide or safety "contracts." Although I can support the value of such contracts on occasion, their effectiveness is possible only within the context of a strong therapeutic relationship and overall safety plan, including such key components as a crisis intervention plan (Berman et al., 2006). In the absence of a good therapeutic relationship and overall safety plan, a suicide contract is of limited usefulness or is worthless and may even be potentially damaging in legal cases.

Rudd et al.'s (1999) review of the treatment literature provides a useful set of practice recommendations that make intuitive and clinical sense. For example, the clinician should provide information pertaining to the limits of confidentiality in relation to clear and imminent suicide risk, and offer a detailed review of available treatment options. The clinician should routinely monitor, assess, and document a patient's initial and ongoing suicide risk, and document interventions for maintaining outpatient safety until suicidality has clinically resolved.

It is important to ensure the appropriate standard of care to students seeking psychological help (Bongar, 2002; Bongar et al., 1998). Key to the appropriate care of at-risk students is full documentation, frequent consultation with clinical and administrative peers, and adherence to established college policies and protocols—for example, regarding parental notification or required evaluations for returning to a residence hall following a hospitalization.

Parental Notification

Probably no topic in college student mental health has received as much national attention as parental notification when a student is deemed to be at risk for suicide. These complicated occasions when parental notification becomes a consideration raise questions about how comprehensive the missions of institutions of higher education are, to what extent campuses are harbingers of more general societal problems, and to what degree campuses are expected to function *in loco parentis* (Silverman, 1993). The final word on how college counseling centers and college student administrators should respond to the potential suicidal risk of a student will be debated as a number of high-profile student suicide cases will likely reach the courtroom in the upcoming years.

Until the courts may clarify this issue, there are no universally agreed upon criteria for when to contact parents in the case of suicidal students. Three sensible rules of thumb, however, are whether the student's ability to function academically is compromised, whether the suicidal behavior is disruptive to the overall welfare and stability of the campus community, and whether the student's life is truly and imminently at risk. If these conditions hold, particularly the final one, the need to communicate with parents should override concerns about students' right to privacy and confidentiality.

Future Directions

The Jed Foundation

The mission of the Jed Foundation (www.jedfoundation.com), founded by the parents of a college student who died by suicide, is to improve mental health and prevent suicides on college campuses. In 2001, the National Mental Health Association (NMHA) and the Jed Foundation published a monograph that recommends strategies that might enhance intervention and ultimately reduce the rate of suicide, suicide attempts, and related behaviors among college students (NMHA & Jed Foundation, 2002). As of this writing, the

Jed Foundation is also developing a template of suggested practices for colleges and universities in assessing and dealing with suicidal students and notifying parents where appropriate.

The foundation developed Ulifeline, a website (www.ulifeline.org) that allows students to anonymously complete a validated self-screening instrument. This instrument provides feedback and refers students who report risk characteristics to their school counseling or health centers. College counseling centers can link their websites to this and other screening tools to encourage students to self-assess and self-refer.

American Foundation for Suicide Prevention

The American Foundation for Suicide Prevention (AFSP) (www.afsp.org) has developed a Web-based depression screening instrument in which an experienced clinician reviews responses and sends a personalized, confidential assessment to the student's self-assigned user name on the website. Students whose responses suggest significant psychological difficulties are urged to meet with the clinician for an evaluation.

In addition, AFSP has developed a 27-minute film (along with a facilitator's guide), *The Truth About Suicide: Real Stories of Depression in College*. The film's primary goal is to present a realistic and recognizable picture of depression in college-aged students, encourage those suffering from depression and other emotional disorders to seek treatment, and encourage those who recognize the signs of mental disorders in a friend, roommate, or classmate to help them seek treatment.

Screening for Mental Health / CollegeResponse Program

Screening for Mental Health (www.mentalhealthscreening.org), which is best known for its National Screening Days and its Signs of Suicide Program (SOS) for secondary school students, has developed a College*Response* Program which promotes prevention, early detection and treatment of prevalent, underdiagnosed and treatable mental health disorders and alcohol problems. Through online and in-person screening tools, College*Response* provides confidential and effective programs for depression, bipolar disorder, anxiety, posttraumatic stress disorder, eating disorders, and alcohol problems. The components include a one-day in-person event, year-round online screening, health center screenings, and an SOS Suicide Prevention Program.

The University of Illinois Approach

In 1984, the University of Illinois established a policy mandating any student who threatened or attempted suicide to attend four sessions of professional assessment with a social worker or psychologist at the counseling center. Failure to comply ran the risk of the student's being withdrawn from the university. The first appointment was to occur within a week of the incident or release from the hospital. Despite criticism about mandating treatment on a college campus, the University of Illinois has documented that in the 18 years of the program's existence, 1,531 students have gone through the program without a subsequent suicide, and the overall suicide rate on the university's campus has decreased by 55%. This approach is now being replicated at other campuses nationwide.

Final Thoughts

When treating suicidal college students, one overriding theme is that failures in relatedness are central to the etiology of suicidal problems, but in turn relationships may prove to be pivotal to successful clinical outcomes. Thus, from beginning to end, treatment demands attention to linkage, attachment, and relatedness, and its potential success often depends on these themes (Jobes et al., 2005). Such linkage is the idea behind the concept of "buddy care," which was part of the successful U.S. Air Force suicide prevention program. Care and support provided by peers can be offered while waiting for professional care and in fact may obviate the need for professional involvement altogether (Knox, Litts, Talcott, Feig, & Caine, 2003). Naturally, in the college setting, linkages with other students as well as counseling center personnel, residence life staff, and deans are important and may in fact be lifesaving.

A second theme is that students' suicidal behavior must be understood from a developmental perspective. The clinician must sensitively take into account the particular circumstances of the student and the related developmental challenges that students face at this point in their lives. College mental health personnel are ideally suited to do this.

References

ACHA [American College Health Association]. (2001). *National College Health Assessment: Aggregate report spring 2000.* Baltimore: American College Health Association.

Ahrens, B., & Linden, M. (1996). Is there a suicidality syndrome independent of specific major psychiatric disorder? Results of a split-half multiple regression analysis. *Acta Psychiatrica Scandinavia, 94,* 79–86.

American Psychiatric Association. (2003). Practice guideline for the assessment and treatment of patients with suicidal behaviors. *American Journal of Psychiatry, 160*(Suppl.), 1–60.

Barrios, L. C., Everett, S. A., Simon, T. R., & Brener, N. D. (2000). Suicidal ideation among U.S. college students: Associations with other injury risk behaviors. *Journal of the American College Health Association, 48,* 229–233.

Beck, A. T., Rush, A. J., Shaw, B. F., & Emery, G. (1978). *Cognitive therapy of depression.* New York: Guilford Publications

Beck, A. T., Rush, A. J., Shaw, B. F., & Emery, G. (1979). *Cognitive therapy of depression: A treatment manual.* New York: Guilford Press.

Berman, A. L., Shepherd, G., & Silverman, M. M. (2003). The LSARS-II: Lethality of suicide attempt rating scale—updated. *Suicide and Life-Threatening Behavior, 33,* 261–276.

Berman, A. L., Jobes, D. A., & Silverman, M. M. (2006). *Adolescent suicide: Assessment and intervention* (2nd ed.). Washington, DC: American Psychological Association.

Bongar, B. (Ed.). (1992). *Suicide: Guidelines for assessment, management and treatment.* New York: Oxford University Press, Inc.

Bongar, B. (2002). *The suicidal patient: Clinical and legal standards of care* (2nd ed.). Washington, DC: American Psychological Association.

Bongar, B., Berman, A. L., Maris, R. W., Silverman, M. M., Harris, E. A., & Packman, W. L. (Eds.). (1998). *Risk management with suicidal patients.* New York: Guilford Press.

Brener, N. D., Hassan, S., & Barrios, L. (1999). Suicidal ideation among college students in the United States. *Journal of Consulting and Clinical Psychology, 67,* 1004–1008.

Busch, K. A., Fawcett, J., & Jacobs, D. G. (2003). Clinical correlates of inpatient suicide. *Journal of Clinical Psychiatry, 64,* 14–19.

CDC [Centers for Disease Control and Prevention]. (1997). CDC surveillance summaries, November 14, 1997. *Morbidity and Mortality Weekly Report, 46* (No. SS-6).

Cimbolic, P., & Jobes, D. A. (Eds.). (1990). *Youth suicide: Assessment, intervention, and issues.* Springfield, IL: Charles C. Thomas.

Clarke, G. N., Rohde, P., Lewinsohn, P. M., Hops, H., & Seeley, J. R. (1999). Cognitive-behavioral treatment of adolescent depression: Efficacy of acute group treatment and booster sessions. *Journal of the American Academy of Child & Adolescent Psychiatry, 38,* 272–279.

Davidson L. (1999). Discharge decision making with recently suicidal patients. *Directions in psychiatry, 19,* 19–26. New York: Hatherleigh Company, Ltd.

Duane, E. A., Stewart, C. S., & Bridgeland, W. M. (2003). College student suicidality and family issues. *College Student Journal, 37,* 135–144.

Ellis, T. E., & Newman, C. F. (1996). *Choosing to live: How to defeat suicide through cognitive therapy.* Oakland, CA: New Harbinger Publications, Inc.

Goldman L. S., Silverman, M. M., & Alpert, E. (1998). Violence and aggression. In L. S. Goldman, T. N. Wise, & D. S. Brody (Eds.), *Psychiatry for primary care physicians* (pp. 155–180). Chicago: American Medical Association.

Gutheil, T. G. (1992). Suicide and suit: Liability after self-destruction. In D. G. Jacobs (Ed.), *Suicide and clinical practice* (pp. 147–168). Washington, DC: American Psychiatric Press, Inc.

Hawton, K., Arensman, E., Townsend, E., Bremner, S., Feldman, E., Goldney, R., et al. (1998). Deliberate self harm: Systematic review of efficacy of psychosocial and pharmacological treatments in preventing repetition. *British Medical Journal, 31,* 441–447.

Hendin, H., Brent, D. A., Cornelius, J. R., Coyne-Beasley, T., Greenberg, T., Gould, M., et al. (2005). Youth suicide. In D. L. Evans, E. B. Foa, R. E. Gur, H. Hendin, C. P. O'Brien, M. E. P. Seligman, et al. (Eds.), *Treating and preventing adolescent mental health disorders.* New York: Oxford University Press.

Henriques, G., Beck, A. T., & Brown, G. K. (2003). Cognitive therapy for adolescent and young adult suicide attempters. *American Behavioral Scientist, 46,* 1258–1268.

Hoff, L. A. (1984). *People in crisis: Understanding and helping.* Menlo Park, CA: Addison-Wesley Publishing.

Hsiung, R. C. (Ed.). (2002). *E-therapy: Case studies, guiding principles, and the clinical potential of the Internet.* New York: W. W. Norton & Company.

Isacsson, G., Holmgren, P., Druid, H., & Bergman, U. (1997). The utilization of antidepressants: A key issue in the prevention of suicide. An analysis of 5281 suicides in Sweden during the period 1992–1994. *Acta Psychiatrica Scandinavia, 96,* 94–100.

Jobes, D. A. (2000). Collaborating to prevent suicide: A clinical-research perspective. *Suicide and Life-Threatening Behavior, 25,* 437–449.

Jobes, D. A. (2003a). Understanding suicide in the 21st century. *Preventing Suicide: The National Journal, 2,* 2–4.

Jobes, D. A. (2003b). *Manual for the Collaborative Assessment and Management of Suicidality–Revised* (CAMS-R). Unpublished manuscript.

Jobes, D. A., & Berman, A. L. (1993). Suicide and malpractice liability: Assessing and revising policies, procedures, and practice in outpatient settings. *Professional Psychology: Research and Practice, 24,* 91–99.

Jobes, D. A., & Drozd, J. F. (2004). The CAMS approach to working with suicidal patients. *Journal of Contemporary Psychotherapy, 34,* 73–86.

Jobes, D. A., Wong, S. A., Conrad, A., Drozd, J. F., & Beal-Walden, T. (2005). The collaborative assessment and management of suicidality vs. treatment as usual: A retrospective study with suicidal outpatients. *Suicide and Life-Threatening Behavior, 36.*

Kessler R. C., Borges, G., & Walters, E. E. (1999). Prevalence of and risk factors for lifetime suicide attempts in the national comorbidity survey. *Archives of General Psychiatry, 56,* 617–626.

Kisch, J., Leino, E. V., & Silverman, M. M. (2005). Aspects of suicidal behavior, depression, and treatment in college students: Results from the Spring 2000 National College Health Assessment. *Suicide and Life-Threatening Behavior, 35,* 3–13.

Kitzrow, M. A. (2003). The mental health needs of today's college students: Challenges and recommendations. *NASPA Journal, 41,* 165–179.

Kleespies, P. M. (Ed.). (1998). *Emergencies in mental health practice: Evaluation and management* (pp. 413–425). New York: Guilford Press.

Knox, K. L., Litts, D. A., Talcott, G. W., Feig, J. C., & Caine, E. (2003). Risk of suicide and related adverse outcomes after exposure to a suicide prevention programme in the US Air Force: Cohort study. *British Medical Journal, 327,* 1376–1378.

Leenaars, A. A. (2004). Psychotherapy with suicidal people: A person-centered approach. Hoboken, NJ: John Wiley & Sons, Ltd.

Leon, A. C., Keller, M. B., Warshaw, M. G., Mueller, T. I., Solomon, D. A., Coryell, W., & Endicott, J. (1999). Prospective study of fluoxetine treatment and suicidal behavior in affectively ill subjects. *American Journal of Psychiatry, 156,* 195–201.

Linehan, M. M. (1993a). *Cognitive behavioral therapy of borderline personality disorder.* New York: Guilford Publications.

Linehan, M. M. (1993b). *Skills training manual for treating borderline personality disorder.* New York: Guilford Publications.

Linehan, M. M. (1997). Behavioral treatments of suicidal behaviors. In D. M. Stoff and J. J. Mann (Eds.), *The neurobiology of suicidal behavior* (pp. 302–328). New York: Annals of the New York Academy of Sciences.

Maltsberger J. T., & Buie, E. H. (1974). Countertransference hate in the treatment of suicidal patients. *Archives of General Psychiatry, 30,* 625–633.

Mann, J. J. (1998). The neurobiology of suicide. *Nature Medicine, 4,* 25–30.

Mann, J. J., & Kapur, S. (1991). The emergence of suicidal ideation and behavior during antidepressant pharmacotherapy. *Archives of General Psychiatry, 48,* 1027–1033.

Mann, J. J., Waternaux, C., Haas, G. L., & Malone, K. M. (1999). Toward a clinical model of suicidal behavior in psychiatric patients. *American Journal of Psychiatry, 156,* 181–189.

Maris, R. W., Berman, A. L., Maltsberger, J. T., & Yufit, R. (Eds.). (1992). *Assessment and prediction of suicide.* New York: Guilford Press.

Maris, R. W., Berman, A. L., & Silverman, M. M. (2000). *Comprehensive textbook of suicidology.* New York: Guilford Publications, Inc.

Meehan, P. J., Lamb, J. A., Saltzman, L. E., & O'Carroll, P. W.(1992). Attempted suicide among young adults: Progress toward a meaningful estimate of prevalence. *American Journal of Psychiatry, 149,* 41–44.

Montgomery, S. A. (1997). Suicide and antidepressants. *Annals of the New York Academy of Sciences, 836,* 329–338.

Mufson, L., Moreau, D., Weissman, M. M., & Klerman, G. L. (1993). *Interpersonal psychotherapy for depressed adolescents.* New York: Guilford Publications.

NMHA [National Mental Health Association] & Jed Foundation. (2002). *Safeguarding your students against suicide: Expanding the safety network.* Alexandria, VA: Author.

O'Carroll, P. W., Berman, A. L., Maris, R. W., Moscicki, E. K., Tanney, B. L., & Silverman, M. M. (1996). Beyond the tower of Babel: A nomenclature for suicidology. *Suicide and Life-Threatening Behavior, 26,* 237–252.

Patrick, K., Grace, T. W., & Lovato, C. Y. (1992). Health issues for college students. In G. S. Omenn, J. E. Fielding, & L. B. Love (Eds.), *Annual review of public health: 1992* (Vol. 13, 253–268). Palo Alto, CA: Annual Reviews.

Quinnett, P. G. (2000). *Counseling suicidal people: A therapy of hope.* Spokane, WA: QPR Institute, Inc.

Roberts, A. (Ed.). (1991). *Contemporary perspectives on crisis intervention and prevention.* Englewood Cliffs, NJ: Prentice-Hall.

Rogers, J. R., & Soyka, K. M. (2004). "One size fits all": An existential-constructivist perspective on the crisis intervention approach with suicidal individuals. *Journal of Contemporary Psychotherapy, 34,* 7–22.

Rudd, M. D. (2000). Integrating science into the practice of clinical suicidology: A review of the psychotherapy literature and a research agenda for the future. In R. W. Maris, S. S. Canetto, J. McIntosh, & M. M. Silverman (Eds.), *Review of suicidology 2000* (pp. 47–67). New York: Guilford Press.

Rudd, M. D. (2003). Warning signs for suicide. *Suicide and Life-Threatening Behavior, 33,* 99–100.

Rudd, M. D., Berman, A. L., Joiner, T., Nock, M. K., Silverman M. M., Mandrusiak, M., et al. (in press). Warning signs for suicide: Theory, research and clinical application. *Suicide and Life-Threatening Behavior.*

Rudd, M. D., Joiner, T. E., Jr., Jobes, D. A., & King, C. A. (1999). The outpatient treatment of suicidality: An integration of science and recognition of its limitations. *Professional Psychology: Research and Practice, 30,* 437–446.

Rudd, M. D., Joiner, T. E., Jr., & Rajab, M. H. (2001). *Treating suicidal behavior: An effective time-limited approach.* New York: Guilford Press.

Salkovskis, P. M. (2001). Psychological treatment of suicidal patients. In D. Wasserman (Ed.), *Suicide, an unnecessary death* (pp. 161–172), London: Martin Duritz.

Schwartz, A. J., & Reifler, C. B. (1980). Suicide among American college and university students from 1970–71 through 1975–76. *Journal of the American College Health Association, 28,* 205–209.

Schwartz, A. J., & Reifler, C. B. (1988). College student suicide in the United States: Incidence data and prospects for demonstrating the efficacy of preventive programs. *Journal of the American College Health Association, 37,* 53–59.

Shaffer, D., & Pfeffer, C. (2001). Practice parameter for the assessment and treatment of children and adolescents with suicidal behavior. *Journal of the American Academy of Child and Adolescent Psychiatry, 40*(Suppl.), 24S–51S.

Shneidman, E. S. (1993). *Suicide as psychache: A clinical approach to self-destructive behavior.* Northvale, NJ: Aronson.

Silverman, M. M. (1993). Campus student suicide rates: Fact or artifact? *Suicide and Life-Threatening Behavior, 23,* 329–342.

Silverman, M. M. (2005). Helping college students cope with suicidal impulses. In R. I. Yufit and D. Lester (Eds.), *Assessment, treatment, and prevention of suicidal behavior* (pp. 379–429). Hoboken, NJ: John Wiley & Sons, Inc.

Silverman, M. M., Meyer, P. M., Sloane F., Raffel, M., & Pratt, D. M. (1997). The Big Ten student suicide study: A 10-year study of suicides on Midwestern university campuses. *Suicide and Life-Threatening Behavior, 27,* 285–303.

Silverman, M. M. (2005b). The Big 10 Universities Student Suicide Study ... and Beyond. SAMHSA Suicide Prevention Grantee Orientation Meeting, December 13, 2005, Washington, D.C. Available at http://www.sprc.org/grantees/pdf/SP_Campus_silverman.pdf

Simon, R. I. (1992). Clinical risk management of suicidal patients: Assessing the unpredictable. In R. I. Simon (Ed.), *Review of clinical psychiatry and the law, 3,* (pp. 3–66). Washington, DC: American Psychiatric Press, Inc.

Simon, R. I. (2004). *Assessing and managing suicide risk: Guidelines for clinically based risk management.* Washington, DC: American Psychiatric Press, Inc.

Spirito, A., & Overholser, J. C. (Eds.). (2003). *Evaluating and treating adolescent suicide attempters: From research to practice.* New York: Academic Press.

TADS Team. (2004). Fluoxetine, cognitive-behavioral therapy, and their combination for adolescents with depression. Treatment for Adolescents with Depression Study (TADS) Randomized Controlled Trial. *Journal of the American Medical Association, 292,* 807–820.

U.S. Department of Education. (2002). *Digest of educational statistics: Postsecondary education.* Washington, DC: National Center for Education Statistics. http://nces.ed.gov

U.S. DHHS [Department of Health and Human Services]. (2001). *National strategy for suicide prevention: Goals and objectives for action.* Rockville, MD: U.S. Public Health Service (Document no. SMA 3517). http://www.mentalhealth.samhsa.gov/suicideprevention

Verkes, R. J., & Cowen, P. J. (2000). Pharmacotherapy of suicidal ideation and behavior. In K. Hawton and K. van Heeringen (Eds.), *The international handbook of suicide and attempted suicide* (pp. 487–502). New York: John Wiley & Sons, Inc.

Zimmerman, J. K., & Asnis, G. M. (Eds.). (1995). *Treatment approaches with suicidal adolescents.* New York: John Wiley & Sons.

Contributors

Linda Berg-Cross, Ph.D., is a professor of psychology at Howard University. She is the author of two textbooks, *Basic Concepts in Family Therapy* and *Couples Therapy*, as well as numerous articles on diversity and psychotherapy.

Mary Commerford, Ph.D., is director of the Furman Counseling Center at Barnard College. She previously served as coordinator of the Eating Disorder Treatment Team at New York University, and served on the faculty at Cornell University Medical College, where she was involved in the treatment and research of eating disorders. She has authored several articles in the *International Journal of Eating Disorders* and in *Eating Disorders: Treatment and Prevention*. She maintains a private practice in Manhattan.

Martha Dennis Christiansen, Ph.D., is interim associate vice president of student affairs and director of the Counseling and Consultation Service at Arizona State University. She is also on the affiliated faculty at Arizona State in the Division of Psychology in Education. Previously, she served as director of the Counseling Center at the College of William and Mary and as president of the Association of Counseling Center Training Agencies. She also served as training director at the University of Iowa's counseling center.

Kenneth M. Cohen, Ph.D., specializes in gay, lesbian, and bisexual (GLB) issues at Cornell University's office of Counseling and Psychological Services and is a lecturer in feminist, gender, and sexuality studies. Cohen has authored or coauthored numerous articles about GLB development and mental health, focusing on the biological origins of homoeroticism. He coedited *The Lives of Lesbians, Gays, and Bisexuals: Children to Adults*.

Stewart Cooper, Ph.D., ABPP, is director of Counseling Services and professor of psychology at Valparaiso University. He has published articles, book chapters, and monographs on prevention, psychometric analysis, substance abuse, dual-career issues, organizational consultation, and sex therapy. He is coauthor of *Counseling and Mental Health Services on Campus: A Handbook of Contemporary Practices* and *Case Book of Brief Psychotherapy with College Students*, and editor of *Evidence-Based Psychotherapy Practice with College Students*.

Charles P. Ducey, Ph.D., teaches at the Harvard Graduate School of Education and Harvard Extension School. He served as director of the Bureau of Study Counsel at Harvard University and of Psychological Services at Cambridge

Hospital, where he established its clinical psychology internship training program. He has published works on academic underachievement, psycho-therapeutic influence of suggestion, psychological processing of trauma, and transcultural psychoanalyses of child and adolescent development, literature, and mythology.

Richard J. Eichler, Ph.D., is director of Columbia University's Counsel-ing and Psychological Services. He is on the teaching and supervising faculty of the Child and Adolescent Psychotherapy Training Program at the William Alanson White Institute, and has taught courses in human devel-opment, psychodynamic psychotherapy, and developmental psychopathology at Columbia. He is a consultant to the College Mental Health section of the Group for the Advancement of Psychiatry.

Lynn Gerstein, MSW, serves as coordinator for alcohol and other drug programs at Cornell University and previously held a similar position at Ithaca College. She also previously served as the executive director of the Alcoholism Council of Tompkins County (NY). Over the past 25 years, she has worked in all aspects of substance abuse treatment, intervention, and prevention, includ-ing development of employee assistance and student assistance programs.

Paul A. Grayson, Ph.D., is director of the Counseling and Behavioral Health Service at New York University and clinical assistant professor of psychiatry at New York University Medical School. Previously he served as director of counseling at SUNY-Purchase and associate director of the Office of Student Mental Health at Wesleyan University. He has published many articles about college mental health and was the coeditor of *College Psychotherapy* and of two editions of *Beating the College Blues*.

David S. Hargrove, Ph.D., is professor of psychology at the University of Mississippi. He was chairperson of the Department of Psychology at the University of Mississippi for 12 years, and previously served as director of the clinical psychology training program at the University of Nebraska. He has also served as president of the Mississippi Board of Psychology and the Mississippi Psychological Association, and currently serves as vice chairper-son of the Mississippi State Department of Mental Health.

Natalie Arce Indelicato, Ph.D., is a visiting clinical assistant professor at the University of Florida Counseling Center. Indelicato has coauthored a chapter on feminist therapy for a compendium on theories of counseling and psycho-therapy and has published on topics such as depression in college women and the impact of men's disclosure of their HIV status.

Deborah K. Lewis, M.Ed., serves as the Alcohol Project coordinator at Cornell University. She has spoken frequently on the role of harm reduction to address high-risk college student drinking. Prior to working at Cornell, Lewis oversaw a New Jersey state-funded HIV prevention program and served on the board of the Chai Project, a harm reduction program in New Brunswick, NJ.

Elizabeth Malone is a doctoral student in clinical psychology at the University of Mississippi, specializing in family psychology and family therapy, and has published on applying family systems theory to the work of Jane Austen.

Robert May, Ph.D., is director emeritus at the Counseling and Mental Health Service at Amherst College, having previously served as director of training and for 30 years as director. He is the author of *Sex and Fantasy: Patterns of Male and Female Development,* editor and primary contributor to *Psychoanalytic Psychotherapy in a College Context,* and author of several dozen papers in the areas of psychodynamic psychotherapy and college mental health practice.

Susan H. McDaniel, Ph.D., is professor of psychiatry and family medicine, director of family programs at the Wynne Center for Family Research in Psychiatry, and associate chair of family medicine at the University of Rochester School of Medicine and Dentistry. She has authored or coauthored numerous journal articles and 12 books, including *Primary Care Psychology, Family-Oriented Primary Care,* and *Individuals, Families and the New Era of Genetics.*

Robert McGrath, Psy.D., ABPP, is director of counseling and consultation services at the University of Wisconsin–Madison, clinical professor in the Department of Counseling Psychology, and coordinator of Health Enhancement Services, which offers stress management programming.

Philip W. Meilman, Ph.D., is the director of the Counseling and Psychiatric Service at Georgetown and clinical professor of psychiatry at Georgetown University. He previously served as director of counseling at Cornell University and at the College of William and Mary. He has published extensively in the areas of collegiate alcohol use and college mental health issues. He coedited two editions of the self-help book *Beating the College Blues.*

Victoria Pak, M.A., is a doctoral candidate in clinical psychology at Howard University. Her research and clinical interests include ethnic minority issues and cultural differences.

Jacquelyn Liss Resnick, Ph.D., is director and professor at the University of Florida counseling center and an affiliate professor in the departments of psychology and counselor education. Resnick has written and presented extensively on issues related to counseling women, including sexual assault/ abuse/harassment and eating disorders. Resnick is past-president of the Association for University and College Counseling Centers and of the International Association of Counseling Services, Inc.

Ilene C. Rosenstein, Ph.D., is director of counseling and psychological services at the University of Pennsylvania. She has over 25 years of experience working in college counseling, in addition to several years working in community mental health.

Victor Schwartz, M.D., is director of the Counseling Center at Yeshiva University. Previously he served as medical director and chief psychiatrist at the counseling services at New York University. He is a member of the American Psychiatric Association Presidential Task Force on College Mental Health.

Julia Sheehy, Ph.D., is associate director at Barnard College's Rosemary Furman Counseling Center, where she coordinates the eating disorders treatment team and directs the training program. She has authored articles that have appeared in *Eating Disorders: The Journal of Treatment and Prevention*. Before coming to Barnard, Julia worked at the Renfrew Center and at the Eating Disorders Resource Center.

Morton M. Silverman, M.D., is the senior advisor to and formerly the director of the National Suicide Prevention Technical Resource Center. From 1987 to 2002, he was an associate professor of psychiatry, associate dean of students, and director of the Student Counseling and Resource Service at the University of Chicago, where he currently serves as a clinical associate professor of psychiatry. Published extensively in the fields of college student mental health, disease prevention, health promotion, alcohol and other drug abuse, and standards of care, he is also the coeditor or coauthor of five books on suicidology, including the *Comprehensive Textbook of Suicidology* and *Adolescent Suicide: Assessment and Intervention*. He is the 2005 recipient of the Louis I. Dublin Award from the American Association of Suicidology.

Leighton C. Whitaker, Ph.D., is editor of the *Journal of College Student Psychotherapy*. He has served as associate professor, University of Colorado Medical School, professor and director of the University of Massachusetts Mental Health Services, director of Swarthmore's College Psychological Services, and mental health consultant to the U.S. Department of Labor's Job Corps. He has published numerous articles, book chapters, and books on clinical and social issues, including *Schizophrenic Disorders* and *Understanding and Preventing Violence*.

Index